THE BUSINESS OF REFLECTION

The Business of Reflection
Hawthorne in His Notebooks

EDITED BY
Robert Milder and Randall Fuller

THE OHIO STATE UNIVERSITY PRESS
COLUMBUS

Copyright © 2009 by The Ohio State University.
All rights reserved.

Library of Congress Cataloging-in-Publication Data
Hawthorne, Nathaniel, 1804–1864.
The business of reflection : Hawthorne in his notebooks / edited by Robert Milder and Randall Fuller.
  p. cm.
Includes bibliographical references and index.
ISBN 978-0-8142-0476-4 (cloth : alk. paper)—ISBN 978-0-8142-5170-6 (pbk. : alk. paper)—ISBN 978-0-8142-9185-6 (CD-ROM) 1. Hawthorne, Nathaniel, 1804–1864—Diaries. 2. Hawthorne, Nathaniel, 1804–1864—Notebooks, sketchbooks, etc. 3. Authors, American—19th century—Diaries. 4. Hawthorne, Nathaniel, 1804–1864—Travel. I. Milder, Robert. II. Fuller, Randall, 1963– III. Hawthorne, Nathaniel, 1804–1864. Passages from the American note-books of Nathaniel Hawthorne. IV. Hawthorne, Nathaniel, 1804–1864. Passages from the English note-books of Nathaniel Hawthorne. V. Hawthorne, Nathaniel, 1804–1864. Passages from the French and Italian note-books of Nathaniel Hawthorne. VI. Title.
PS1881.A33 2009
818.'303—dc22
[B]
                    2008043240

This book is available in the following editions:
Cloth (ISBN 978-0-8142-0476-4)
Paper (ISBN 978-0-8142-5170-6)
CD-ROM (ISBN 978-0-8142-9185-6)

Cover design by Jenny Poff
Text design by Juliet Williams
Typeset in Adobe Caslon Pro
Printed by Thomson-Shore, Inc.

∞ The paper used in this publication meets the minimum requirements of the American National Standard for Information Sciences—Permanence of Paper for Printed Library Materials. ANSI Z39.48-1992.
9 8 7 6 5 4 3 2 1

CONTENTS

Acknowledgments / vii
Abbreviations / ix

Introduction / 1

PART I
The American Notebooks / 27

PART II
The English Notebooks / 125

PART III
The French and Italian Notebooks / 179

Notes / 237
Selected Bibliography / 263
Index / 265

ACKNOWLEDGMENTS

The editors would like to thank The Ohio State University Press for making available materials from the Centenary Edition of Hawthorne's notebooks. Thanks are given, in particular, to Senior Editor Sandra Crooms for her encouragement and advice. We would also like to thank David Walsh and his staff in the Washington University Department of English, without whose technical expertise this project would not have been feasible.

The project was jointly developed by the editors. Robert Milder wrote sections i, ii, and iv of the introduction; Randall Fuller, section iii. The notes were written primarily by Fuller, originally or with adaptations from the Centenary Edition. The notes to the French and Italian notebooks also incorporate the scholarly research of Matthew W. DeVoll.

ABBREVIATIONS

All references to Hawthorne's published writings and notebooks, except for the Lost Notebook, are to *The Centenary Edition of the Works of Nathaniel Hawthorne*, 23 vols., ed. William Charvat et al. (Columbus: The Ohio State University Press, 1962–80). Individual volumes are abbreviated as follows and cited parenthetically in the text.

CE I	*The Scarlet Letter*
CE II	*The House of the Seven Gables*
CE III	*The Blithedale Romance and Fanshawe*
CE IV	*The Marble Faun*
CE V	*Our Old Home*
CE VIII	*The American Notebooks*
CE IX	*Twice-Told Tales*
CE X	*Mosses from an Old Manse*
CE XI	*The Snow Image and Uncollected Tales*
CE XII	*The American Claimant Manuscripts*
CE XIV	*The French and Italian Notebooks*
CE XV	*The Letters, 1813–1843*
CE XVI	*The Letters, 1843–1853*
CE XVII	*The Letters, 1853–1856*
CE XVIII	*The Letters, 1857–1864*
CE XXI	*The English Notebooks, 1853–1856*
CE XXII	*The English Notebooks, 1856–1860*

ABBREVIATIONS

Other abbreviations include the following:

NH	Nathaniel Hawthorne
SH	Sophia Hawthorne
JH	Julian Hawthorne
TTT	*Twice-Told Tales*
SL	*The Scarlet Letter*
HSG	*The House of the Seven Gables*
BR	*The Blithedale Romance*
MF	*The Marble Faun*
OOH	*Our Old Home*
AN	*The American Notebooks*
EN	*The English Notebooks*
FIN	*The French and Italian Notebooks*
WB/TT	*A Wonder Book for Girls and Boys/Tanglewood Tales*
HLN	*Hawthorne's Lost Notebook 1835–1841,* Transcript and Preface by Barbara S. Mouffe, Introduction by Hyatt H. Waggoner (University Park: Pennsylvania State University Press, 1978)
NHHW	Julian Hawthorne, *Nathaniel Hawthorne and His Wife*, 2 vols. (Boston: J. R. Osgood, 1884)

INTRODUCTION

(i) Hawthorne in His Notebooks

Writers keep journals for different purposes, and for different purposes at various times in their careers. Emerson spoke of his journal as a "'Savings Bank' where he could deposit his daily 'fractions' and hope to see them grow into 'integers,'"[1] as they often did as he moved from journal to lecture to published essay. Emerson writes about books and ideas, he comments on people, and he trains his eye on what he perceives to be signs of the times; only intermittently, after his youthful self-preoccupation, does he take stock of himself beyond questions of vocation. Thoreau writes of his daily walks and his quarrels with society, but he is also absorbed with his spiritual development and his prickly personal relationship with the world; his journal is a calendar of nature's microseasons and of his own.

Hawthorne's notebooks (so his wife Sophia titled them in her editions after his death) resemble neither of these, nor do they fully resemble one another. Commenting on Hawthorne's "Lost Notebook" of 1835–41, Hyatt Waggoner characterizes its author as "very clearly not a 'thinker,' not concerned with the current of thought in his day or with conceptual, philosophic, or theological problems of any sort"; his interest is "in the 'real world' outside himself, in the workings of the human psyche under stress, the 'deeper psychology,' and in curious facts, especially if they suggested what he once called 'the moral picturesque.'"[2] The earlier American notebooks are divided between descriptive accounts of daily reality (travels included) and brief notations for stories and sketches, the realist and the allegorist existing side by side in ways that almost defy literary and psychological understanding. The surprising thing, given Hawthorne's fictional themes of sin and guilt, is his apparent *normality* in the descriptive sections of the notebooks; he is open, inquisitive, ready to take people as he finds them, sociable, and even mildly flirtatious (when away from Salem), with few hints of the obscure guilts of the early tales or of their quasi-theological contextualization of human frailty. The Henry James who objected that "Hawthorne was not a realist" was quick to add that "he had a high sense of reality—his Note-Books superabundantly testify to it."[3] They do. Their writer seems secular, tolerant, oriented to the present and immediate, and, though solitary before his marriage, rarely introspective. Hawthorne's travel notebooks, especially, show him moving easily in the world, consorting with all classes of people and observing them with a shrewdness that belies contemporary critic E. P. Whipple's otherwise keen remark that Hawthorne's "eye is more certain in detecting remote spiritual laws and their relations, than in the sure grasp of individual character."[4]

The Manse notebook, begun in July 1842 shortly after his marriage to Sophia Peabody and the couple's removal to Emerson's Concord, is Hawthorne's idyll. Reborn himself (so he feels), Hawthorne imbibes much of the morning atmosphere of transcendentalism, if little of its philosophical and social radicalism. It is the happiest period of his adult life, clouded only by the urgencies of making money, and the journal is genial, quietly humorous, and appreciative of life's bounty in what seemed, illusorily he knew, a perpetual New England summer. With the birth of daughter Una in 1844 and son Julian in 1846, the reality principle entered from another side. The notebooks show Hawthorne an attentive and loving father, though uneasy about Una's mercurial temper; yet having wished for family life and joined fictively in its cultural consecration, Hawthorne seems also to have found himself prematurely burdened by it. Fatherhood "ought not to come too early in a man's life—not till he has fully enjoyed his youth," he told George Hillard shortly after the birth of Una (CE XVI: 22–23). The gentle joyousness that shines through the first year of the Manse notebook represents a high-water mark of Hawthorne's emotional life; it would not be forgotten. Within the stout, sober, formally dressed personage of later photographs lay the embers, never fully extinguished, of the adventuring newlywed who felt his life of the senses curtailed too soon after it began.

The English and the French and Italian notebooks are the work of a riper and more capacious man—not yet a man of the world so much as a man *coming into* the world and fronting a complexity of culture and history at once exhilarating and overwhelming. Though rarely "about" Hawthorne, the later notebooks disclose him everywhere as he observes, judges, and reflects with the conservatism of a mind struggling to retain its core values and suppositions in a world immensely larger and more attractive and repellent than he has known.

England seemed comfortably familiar to Hawthorne, as it would have to almost any literary American; the English countryside especially delighted him. Nothing could have prepared him, however, for the appalling squalor and degradation of the Liverpool slums with their suggestion not only of material conditions beyond imaginable remedy (Melville had similarly despaired about lower-class Liverpool in *Redburn*) but also of a quasi-hereditary brutishness of body and soul that seemed an inherent casualty of the British class system. Even among the upper middle classes, a certain coarseness struck Hawthorne as the defining quality of national life. Always uneasy about humanity's "animal nature," Hawthorne felt himself more "surrounded by materialisms, and hemmed in with the grossness of this earthly life, than anywhere else" in his experience (CE XXII: 433). The bluff, commonsensical beef-and-ale Englishman, John Bull, won his grudging affection and, within limits, his respect. Jane Bull was another matter. Except perhaps for his comments on Margaret Fuller in Rome, Hawthorne's characterization of English women ("They are gross, gross, gross. Who would not shrink from such a mother! Who would not abhor such a wife!" [CE XXI: 133]) is the harshest pronouncement in his notebooks. Hawthorne was always fastidious about feminine appearance—he fretted about the on-again, off-again beauty of young Una—but women were also the locus of spirituality for him, and the sight of a nation of beefy dowagers was more than an affront to his aesthetic sense; it was a mockery of his deep, if sometimes tenuous, belief in the reality of the soul.

Hawthorne's descriptions of England are chiefly of city and country, tourist sites, and occasional social calls or formal occasions; they are rarely cultural or philosophical, nor do they bear fruit in published writing, the essayistic *Our Old Home* (1863) excepted. Although Hawthorne enjoyed England and even sporadically imagined settling there, it cannot be said to have deeply stimulated his imagination or his emotions. Even his literary pilgrimages to Shakespeare's birthplace and grave, to Samuel Johnson's Lichfield and Uttoxeter, and to Sir Walter Scott's Abbotsford failed to move him profoundly, leaving him, as he said of Abbotsford, "angry and dissatisfied with myself for not feeling something which I did not and could not feel" (CE XXII: 26), and half regretting he had come. It is as if the literary enthusiasms of youthful days were best left alone, in the hermetic world of memory. Art galleries also depressed him. "Doubtless, this is my fault—my own deficiency"—he wrote of his indifference to Turner, "but I cannot help it; not, at least, without sophisticating myself by the effort" (CE XXII: 347).

The Continent virtually forced Hawthorne to sophisticate himself, and much to his surprise he found himself enjoying it, though in the matter of French cookery he was not certain whether he ought to enjoy it. In the sublimity of their architecture and art, France and, even more, Italy were a revelation; so, too, were the filth and "nastiness" that frequently displayed themselves beside it. James's portrait of a "youthful-elderly mind, contending so late in the day with new opportunities for learning old things, and, on the whole, profiting by them so freely and gracefully"[5] is only half of the truth, at most. If Hawthorne anticipates Lambert Strether in James's *The Ambassadors,* progressively yielding to the charm of Europe, he also resembles Strether's provincial friend Waymarsh, gnashing his teeth at European slackness, dirt, and corruption. Indeed, the running tension between "Strether" and "Waymarsh"—the reawakened sensualist and aesthete in Hawthorne and the unbending moralist and Victorian paterfamilias—might be said to define much of the European notebooks. Rome, in particular, came to symbolize for Hawthorne not only the double aspect of Europe, grand and appalling, but also, in some sense, the bewildering extremities of human experience. Hawthorne hated and loved Rome, alternately or at once. The slower life of Florence and Siena was more beckoning yet fraught with the dangers exemplified by the life of expatriate sculptor Hiram Powers, who had lost touch with one country without rooting himself in another. Hawthorne wanted to stay in Italy forever and he could not wait to get home. Leaving the galleries of the Uffizi one day, he wondered, "What shall we do in America!" (CE XIV: 428).

For readers acquainted with Hawthorne only through his fiction, the style and manner of the journals (notes for stories excepted) will seem most like the limpid prose of "The Custom House" and "The Old Manse." As his son Julian remarked, "the impression produced by his notebooks is oddly different from that of the romances—a difference comparable in kind and degree to that between the voice in ordinary speech and in singing."[6] "Ordinary speech," yes, but not without considerable art and deliberation. Centenary editor Thomas Woodson observes that Hawthorne's "notebooks and letters both show frequent signs of copying from earlier versions.... By all accounts not a ready conversationalist, Hawthorne often mistrusted spontaneity in writing as well" (CE XV: 7). Notebook entries were revised, expanded, embellished, and subtilized through qualifiers and added nuance (CE VIII: 682). The fine-grained fluency of their prose was a wrought, not casual, achievement, despite the fact that the notebooks were probably never intended for public view. Critics of Thoreau have sometimes argued that his greatest literary production was his journal. Hawthorne's notebooks will never displace *The Scarlet Letter* or a handful of his best tales, but the comparison is futile because the notebooks are writings of a different kind with interests and excellences of their own. If "Ethan Brand" testifies to what James called "the deeper psychology,"[7] the Berkshire journal that was its outward source shows Hawthorne with a realist's eye for telling surfaces of character and with a prose as elegant as, if less formal than, that of the stylized tale.

Like Hawthorne's autobiographical prefaces, the notebooks encourage readers to feel that they "know" Hawthorne. Certainly they know him better, and on more sides, but there are reticences even in the notebooks. "People who write about themselves and their feelings, as Byron did, may be said to serve up their own hearts, spiced, and with brain-sauce out of their own heads, as a repast for the public" (CE VIII: 253), Hawthorne remarked in July 1844, a comment whose elaboration in "The Old Manse"—"nor am I, nor have ever been, one of those supremely hospitable people, who serve up their own hearts delicately fried, with brain-sauce, as a tidbit for their beloved public" (CE X: 33)—applies in principle to the notebooks as well. Still, if seldom revelatory of "the inmost ME" (CE I: 4)—according to his wife, Hawthorne "hid from himself even more cunningly than he hid himself from others"[8]—the notebooks can be surprisingly irreverent and nihilistic. Things that could not be said, or said only glancingly, in the public writing are broached in the private. Most instructive are those slight amendments by which a subversive idea in the notebooks is transformed into a conventional one in the fiction. Even after her prudent omissions and alterations, Sophia Hawthorne felt obliged to preface her edition of *Passages from the English Note-Books* (1870) with the disclaimer that "throughout his journals it will be seen that Hawthorne is *entertaining*, and not *asserting*, opinions and ideas. He questions, doubts, and reflects with his pen, and, as it were, instructs himself"—his *"conclusions,"* so far as he came to any, lying in his published work (CE XII: 739). There is truth to Sophia's words beyond her genteel guardianship of her husband's posthumous reputation. Hawthorne was a man of moods, self-doubting at times, susceptible to weather, prone to irritability as he aged, uneasy about sensual enjoyment even as he was drawn to it, and yet capable of what Melville called "short, quick probings at the very axis of reality"[9] that punctured, temporarily at least, his most urgent moral and spiritual beliefs. Nothing that Hawthorne writes in the notebooks can be lifted from context and taken as final, but neither can anything, however discordant with postures in the fiction, be lightly dismissed.

Aside from their inherent literary and biographical interest, the notebooks have implications for criticism. Some of these are local and particular: the dating of an idea for a story or romance; the origin of a descriptive passage that appears in the fiction. But the notebooks also raise important questions about the kind of writer Hawthorne was. For example, against Michael J. Colacurcio's contention that Hawthorne was a "moral historian" whose finest early tales aim "to recover the affective quality of human lives lived under conditions or assumptions different from those which prevailed in his own later and moral liberal age,"[10] it might be observed that the extant notebooks of the 1830s contain only infrequent and usually slight entries on the New England past. Hawthorne's ideas for tales and sketches are recorded atemporally in abstract moral terms (e.g., "The story of a man, cold and hard-hearted, and acknowledging no brotherhood with mankind" [CE VIII: 13]), not, as Colacurcio says of the fiction, in the context of crises "referable back to some actuality" and "stand[ing] for the limits of perception or experience at a certain critical moment in the historical past."[11] On the larger matter of Hawthorne's literary mode, the notebooks call into question the claim, advanced publicly by Hawthorne himself and often taken as a truism, that allegory was his natural literary bent. After describing an 1837 tavern scene in which a rustic simpleton comes looking for his prostitute-wife and is met with laughter and scorn, Hawthorne reflects, "On the whole there was a moral picturesqueness in the contrasts of this scene—a man moved as deeply as his nature would admit, in the midst of hardened, gibing spectators, heartless towards him. It is worth thinking over and studying out" (CE VIII: 59). If Hawthorne would never write such a tale in such a literary manner, it was not for want of ability; the scene is brilliantly rendered, with a humanity wholly devoid of sentimentality: Hawthorne as Chekhov. The notebooks are filled with vignettes of this sort, nearly all of them fictively unused.

Taken together, the notebooks are not simply a context for Hawthorne's fiction; they are a supplement to it that enriches and deepens one's apprehension of the artist and the man, much as the publication of Virginia Woolf's five-volume diary did with the author of *Mrs. Dalloway* and *To the Lighthouse*. Woolf had seemed to many brittle, ethereal, and out of touch with the "real world." So may Hawthorne, whether in his dark, sin-obsessed writings or in his sunnier, sentimental ones—so much so that a recent collection of bicentennial essays pointedly titled itself *Hawthorne and the Real*.[12] The notebooks show a more robust and many-sided humanity, not always admirable—Hawthorne can be fastidious, impatient, moody, severe—but precisely for that reason closer to the complete personality than the deftly managed literary persona Hawthorne tendered the public in its stead. In the sketch "Monsieur du Miroir," Hawthorne confesses that "there is nobody, in the whole circle of my acquaintance, whom I have more attentively studied, yet of whom I have less real knowledge, beneath the surface which it pleases him to present" (CE X: 159). Like Monsieur du Miroir, Hawthorne does not reveal himself in acts of self-reflection, but we may catch aspects of him as he turns his mind outward and reflects upon the world. To perceive, for Hawthorne, was characteristically to weigh, to interpret, to evaluate, and to seek to understand. "Reflection" was his "business" (CE X: 171). To read Hawthorne in his notebooks is to reflect with him and on him. It is to meet him afresh, often with surprise, nearly always with pleasure, and with a sense that the published writings may never look quite the same again.

(ii) The American Notebooks

Hawthorne's American notebooks, totaling about two hundred thousand words, begin in 1835 and end in 1853 with Hawthorne's departure for England as newly appointed consul at Liverpool. In need of money after Hawthorne's death in 1864, and with the encouragement and advice of his publisher, James T. Fields, Sophia Hawthorne edited a selection of the notebooks for the *Atlantic Monthly* in twelve installments (1866), and two years later she published *Passages from the American Note-Books of Nathaniel Hawthorne.* Sophia edited freely, omitting and reordering passages, erasing, inking over, and sometimes scissoring out lines in the manuscripts, and changing words for reasons of elegance or, more often, of propriety. "Her central aim," editor Claude M. Simpson comments, "was to be a worthy surrogate to her husband" (CE VIII: 686). Practically, this meant not only excluding what she believed Hawthorne would not have wanted the public to read—often rightly: "her cautious changing of private attitudes to public ones is consistent . . . with [Hawthorne's] use of the notebook in *The Marble Faun*" (CE XIV: 925)—but also retouching him according to how she wished him to appear to family, public, and posterity. Allusions to smoking and drinking were toned down or excluded, as were sexual passages of nearly every kind. Significantly, as Simpson notes, "her hand is equally conspicuous in the notebooks from which she did not print" (CE VIII: 690), as if she were expurgating Hawthorne to preserve an ideal image for herself and her children as well as to memorialize him for the world. Five of the seven American notebooks from which Sophia worked survived and were restored as far as was technically possible by Randall Stewart in 1931. Volume VIII of the Centenary Edition (1972) builds upon and extends Stewart's scholarship, but in the absence of the two lost notebooks it was forced to rely on Sophia's renderings with their alterations, rearrangements, and uncertain chronology.

INTRODUCTION

In 1976 one of the lost notebooks—forty-three leaves in small handwriting, covering the period 1835–41—was discovered in a family heirloom by Barbara S. Mouffe, who transcribed the manuscript, had it authenticated, and took it to Hawthorne scholar Hyatt H. Waggoner; the notebook was published by Pennsylvania State University Press in 1978, with an introduction by Waggoner. Of the seventy-one passages of varying length not contained in the Centenary Edition, the most dramatic is a very brief one. "In this dismal chamber FAME was won" (CE VIII: 20), the Centenary text has Hawthorne writing of his Salem room in 1836. "In this dismal *and squalid* chamber, fame was won," the Lost Notebook reads[13]—"squalid," according to Waggoner, retaining its historical connotation of "impure, morally polluted, morally shameful,"[14] and reinforcing the notion of sexual transgression (if only fantasized) sounded elsewhere in Hawthorne's early work. In another passage from the Lost Notebook, mostly excised by Sophia, Hawthorne admires working-class girls as they parade about on an island resort near Boston, "their petticoats being few and thin, and short withal, showing a good deal of leg in a stocking, and the entire shape of both legs, with the mist of a flimsy gown floating about it."[15] Hawthorne's sexual voyeurism is of a piece with the physical and psychological voyeurism in his writing from "Sights from a Steeple" onward, yet on the whole, judging from the notebooks, Waggoner has reason to claim that the younger Hawthorne "had a normal interest" in sex and "could write about it without either prurience or euphemism."[16] To put it more precisely, sexual guilt belongs to Hawthorne's tales and sketches; his journal entries are healthily appreciative of women and sexuality, save when they touch on the matter of unchastity in a respectable woman. Listening to an acquaintance tell the story of a girl's tearful confession to him of a single premarital lapse, Hawthorne enters into the feelings of the girl and her would-be suitor. The artist in him senses that "much might be made of such a scene"; the moralist is appalled that his acquaintance can speak "as if one deviation from chastity might not be an altogether insuperable objection to making a girl his wife!!" (CE VIII: 146).

The above anecdote is from Hawthorne's travel notebook of the summer of 1838, when he spent nearly two months exploring the Berkshires in western Massachusetts and filling what amounts to more than seventy pages of printed text. The Berkshire journal is one of the notebooks' masterpieces, not simply or primarily for the passages of local color that would nourish "Ethan Brand." If anything, the notebook's account of "Remarkable characters" (CE VIII: 90) is more engaging, because more keenly observant, realistic, subtle, and humane, than that of the story, whose defining interest is in the timeless, placeless notion of the Unpardonable Sin. As he travels

· 8 ·

through the towns, villages, and wild, romantic scenery of a half-civilized America, Hawthorne encounters a colorful array of stage passengers, peddlers, doctors, lawyers, itinerant preachers, and tavern haunters—Chaucerian figures rendered with a Chaucerian gusto far removed from the characterization, style, and sensibility usually associated with "Hawthorne." The travel journal of the preceding summer describes an extended visit to his friend Horatio Bridge in Maine and includes, among other sketches, a portrait of a "sturdy blacksmith" who seemed to Hawthorne "more like a man—more indescribably human" than anyone he had ever met (CE VIII: 95), and a fascinating cameo of his college classmate, then-Congressman Jonathan Cilley, a lesser Aaron Burr, crafty-sincere, who would soon be killed in a duel. So far as Hawthorne's fiction is concerned, the style and picaresque content of the travel journals represent a road not taken, yet they belong as much to Hawthorne the man, and to Hawthorne the writer, as "The May-Pole of Merry Mount" or "The Minister's Black Veil."[17]

Apropos of the division in Hawthorne between realist and allegorist, it should be noted that "two-thirds of all dated entries" in the American notebooks "were written during the four months between July and October" (CE VIII: 681). "Early in his career," biographer James R. Mellow observes, Hawthorne "discovered that the summer was an unfavorable time for writing,"[18] and conversely that the New England winter was an unfavorable time for living and enjoying. Except during his first rush of creativity in the years around 1830 and again as he worked on *The Scarlet Letter*, writing came hard for Hawthorne, who several times expressed the thought that he would never write again and who seems to have greeted spring as an occasion to put aside his work. "In the spring and summer time," he wrote in "Buds and Bird-Voices" (1843), "all somber thoughts should follow the winter northward, with the somber and thoughtful crows" (CE X: 148–49). So they did, so far as the bulk of the American notebooks are concerned. Hawthorne journalized in the summer as he traveled or simply lazed; he wrote for publication in the fall and winter, though he might conceive a tale or sketch in other months. This bifurcation of life was more than a compositional habit with Hawthorne; it was the symptom and symbol of a division of sensibility not uncommon among New Englanders. As Henry Adams would put it, "Winter was always the effort to live; summer was tropical license": "two hostile lives" that bred in New Englanders a chronically self-divided moral nature.[19]

A more familiar Hawthorne appears in the notebook jottings of idea and theme that sometimes germinated and flowered in published works. Because the extant notebooks begin with 1835, there are no entries for tales such as "Young Goodman Brown," "My Kinsman, Major Molineux," and

"Roger Malvin's Burial," but many of the notes do anticipate works to be written, not necessarily in the immediate future: "A snake, taken into a man's stomach and nourished there from fifteen years to thirty-five, tormenting him most horribly. A type of envy or some other evil passion" ([CE VIII: 22] "Egotism; or The Bosom-Serpent"); "To make one's own reflection in a mirror the subject of a story" ([CE VIII: 15] "Monsieur du Miroir"); "The race of mankind to be swept away, leaving all their cities and works. Then another human pair to be placed in the world, with native intelligence like Adam and Eve, but knowing nothing of their predecessors or of their own nature and destiny" ([CE VIII: 21] "The New Adam and Eve"); and so on. Simpson assigns such idea-centered fictions to the genre Northrop Frye calls the "anatomy" (CE VIII: 679),[20] a form of intellectual prose that would become an important vehicle for Hawthorne in the Manse period as he turned away from historical settings, but whose abstraction, the notebooks indicate, was characteristic of his imagination even in the mid-1830s when he was writing dramatic tales.

Among the most intriguing of the hints for stories are those pertaining to *The Scarlet Letter* (e.g., "The life of a woman, who, by the old colony law, was condemned always to wear the letter A, sewed on her garment, in token of her having committed adultery"; "To symbolize moral or spiritual disease by disease of the body;—thus, when a person committed any sin, it might cause a sore to appear on the body"; "To trace out the influence of a frightful and disgraceful crime, in debasing and destroying a character naturally high and noble"; "A story of the effects of revenge, in diabolizing him who indulges in it"; "Pearl—the English of Margaret—a pretty name for a girl in a story" (CE VIII: 254, 222, 227, 278, 242). By what process these isolated themes came together and were alchemized into *The Scarlet Letter* we can never know. The notebooks rarely touch upon the creative process, and only with the Berkshire journal and "Ethan Brand" are we able to observe, if not the process itself, then at least its beginnings and achieved result.

Hawthorne did not keep an ongoing journal during his residence at the Utopian community Brook Farm in 1841, but he did describe the progress of a glorious New England autumn near the farm, the frail seamstress who would become the outward model for Priscilla in *The Blithedale Romance*, and the horrific late-night search for a young woman who had drowned herself in a river, the source for Coverdale's and Hollingsworth's midnight search for Zenobia. The real Utopia in Hawthorne's life was his first year at the Old Manse, chronicled at length in the notebook he kept jointly with Sophia (her contribution was published by Patricia Dunlavy Valenti in the 1996 volume of *Studies in the American Renaissance*). Valenti sees "an antiphonal quality" in the couple's entries; "one spouse calls, the other answers."[21] Passages in Hawthorne's notebook sometimes do assume added point when set against Sophia's, and in judging Hawthorne's attitudes of the time (toward "ideality," for example) it is important to keep Sophia in mind not simply as a reader but as a muse, a tacit censor (there were things Hawthorne would not write for her eyes), and a resident priestess of sunshine and spiritualized domesticity.

The defining circumstance of the Manse notebook is the happy convergence of honeymoon, season, historical moment (the reformist 1840s), and geographical site (Concord), which makes the notebook, more than *The Blithedale Romance*, Hawthorne's most sympathetic contribution to the literature of renewal characteristic of the American Renaissance. Hawthorne meets Emerson, Thoreau, Margaret Fuller, Ellery Channing; he buys Thoreau's boat and learns to manage it with tolerable skill; he hoes beans, fishes for dinner in the Concord River, and reads the transcendentalist journal, *The Dial*, if only after dinner as a soporific. When Emerson comes by with the local minister, Barzillai Frost (the "spectral" preacher of the Divinity School Address), Hawthorne reacts much as Emerson did: "We certainly do need a new revelation—a new system—for there seems to be no life in the old one" (CE VIII: 352) A notebook entry recording a long afternoon in Concord's Sleepy Hollow is Hawthorne's *Walden:* he listens to the sounds of the day, broken by the "long shriek, harsh, above all other harshness," of a locomotive (CE VIII: 248); he observes the small particulars of nature; he watches a colony of ants and briefly intrudes into their world as a willful god; he feels the infinitude of things to observe, reflect upon, and express. On another occasion he visits Walden itself and, along with the crystalline purity of the water, notes the shanties of the Irish railroad-builders around it, which somehow do not seem to profane "the repose and sanctity" of the woods (CE VIII: 396). Through everything, he feels the attraction of "a true relation with nature" and wishes he "could run wild" in it (CE VIII: 358). The Manse notebook covers fifteen months. Its outward matter would be distilled for Hawthorne's 1846 preface "The Old Manse"; the tenor of being it memorializes would remain for him a touchstone of life at its most felicitous.

Obliged to leave the Old Manse in 1845, Hawthorne returned to Salem, where political influence secured him the post of Surveyor of Customs in the local custom house. Hawthorne would use the sinecure poorly, writing little during his three-year tenure. Notebook entries are also sparse, but they resume, intensely, during the summer of 1849 as the family gathers around the deathbed of Hawthorne's mother and Hawthorne appears simultaneously, at midlife, as besieged father and grieving son. Within weeks of his mother's death he would begin *The Scarlet Letter*, and the following May

(1850) the family would leave Salem for a cottage in Lenox, Massachusetts, where daughter Rose would be born, where Hawthorne would write *The House of the Seven Gables,* and where in August 1850 he would begin a friendship with Herman Melville, himself about to settle in neighboring Pittsfield.

Unlike Melville's extraordinary letters to Hawthorne, Hawthorne's to Melville have not survived, and Hawthorne, though liking Melville uncommonly well and admiring his work (he had favorably reviewed *Typee* in 1846 for the *Salem Advertiser*), is reticent about him in journal passages. The most engaging section of the later American notebooks is the seriocomic "Twenty Days with Julian & Little Bunny, By Papa," written when Hawthorne was left to fend with his son and their housekeeper in the Lenox cottage, Sophia having gone to visit her sister, Mary Mann, with Una and the infant Rose. Hawthorne is an astute observer of the character of both his older children: Julian is humorous, easy-going, sturdy; Una, clearly the more brilliant, is disturbing and complex, "her life, at present, . . . a tempestuous day, with blinks of sunshine gushing between the rifts of cloud" (CE VIII: 411). In Sophia's absence, Hawthorne and Melville solidified their friendship, exchanging visits and talking freely about "time and eternity, things of this world and of the next, and books, and publishers, and all possible and impossible matters," a conversation scarcely imaginable with any other acquaintance of Hawthorne's, before or after. Hawthorne left the Berkshires in November 1851, and his relationship with Melville, or Melville's with him, grew more wary and distant. After Lenox, except for the record of an 1852 visit to the Isles of Shoals off New Hampshire, the notebooks trail off. James T. Fields had helped make Hawthorne a "personage," and finding himself, belatedly, with an audience, Hawthorne turned his energies to supplying it with published prose.

(iii) The English Notebooks

When Hawthorne sailed with his family on July 6, 1853, for England, he was arguably a different person from the one indirectly chronicled in the American notebooks. Entering his fiftieth year and widely recognized at home and abroad as the foremost writer of fiction in America, he was on the cusp of becoming more financially secure than at any other time in his life. The English notebooks reflect this new amplitude: at nearly four hundred thousand words (covering five and a half years of residence in Great Britain) they represent the most lengthy and sustained journalizing of his career as well as their author's expanding sense of a world, social and historical, previously encountered in books alone.

Making these widened horizons possible was an appointment to the U.S. Consul at Liverpool by Hawthorne's college friend and incoming president Franklin Pierce. A reward for the laudatory campaign biography written in 1852, the job proved vexing to Hawthorne, who at one point diligently produced a 107-page document in reply to a list of queries about maritime practices by the U.S. Secretary of State William L. Marcy. Plagued by importunate Americans seeking passage home or introductions to British aristocracy, asked to adjudicate conflicts that arose within the notoriously cruel American merchant marines, and besieged by dinner invitations in his dual capacity as consul and literary lion, Hawthorne soon conceded the need to postpone plans to write the romance he hoped to base on his English experiences. "The pleasantest incident of the day," he candidly confessed, occurred with the appearance of "the account books, containing the receipts and expenditures of the preceding day," accompanied by "a little rouleau of the Queen's coin, wrapt in a piece of paper" (CE XXI: 3).

The consulship's "net emoluments" (CE XVII: 204), as he described the generous commissions to his friend Horatio Bridge, nevertheless afforded the opportunity for the Hawthorne family to travel extensively.[22] The notebooks chronicle in meticulous and voluminous detail numerous sojourns to Scotland, Wales, and various points of interest throughout England, trips consisting largely of obligatory visits to cathedrals, museums, and literary shrines, including those of Shakespeare, Johnson, Scott, Burns, Wordsworth, Southey, and others. Comparing the England he saw to the England he had long imagined, Hawthorne was frequently disappointed. Shakespeare's gravestone was "the commonest looking slab of all, just such a flagstone as a sidewalk of the street might be paved with" (CE XXI: 201); about Johnson's hometown, he was, "to say the truth,... heartily tired of it" (CE XXI: 228–29). While the intricacies of Gothic architecture elicited some of his most appreciative descriptions, he was almost invariably bored and unmoved by the nation's art treasures. In a valiant effort to please Sophia and, at the same time, to prepare for an art-filled tour of Italy, he visited the vast Manchester Art Exhibit on a daily basis, to little avail.

Hawthorne was more pleased by the ordered hedgerows, the undulating landscape, and the time-stained cemeteries of the English countryside. The flash of unexpected detail—bags of salt "swinging and vibrating in the air" (CE XXI: 4) over the Liverpool docks; Tennyson studying paintings "through a pair of spectacles which he held in his hand, and then standing a minute before those that interested him, with his hands folded behind his back" (CE XXII: 352)—appears on practically every page of the notebooks, revealing a novelistic observer delighting in the height of his powers. The same is true with the descriptions of people he encountered. In *Our Old*

Home, he described the duty of the consul to "consist in building up for himself a recognized position in the society where he resides so that his local influence might be felt in behalf of his own country" (CE V: 37). To this end he attended numerous boat christenings and civic banquets: wine-flushed events in which he often was called to deliver speeches that seldom find their way into the journals. In their place are carefully wrought—and often acerbic—portraits of the English upper classes, glimpses of aristocratic society that combine insight with prejudice, revelatory detail with provincial attitude, as in his anti-Semitic reaction to London's lord mayor or his more general repulsion to fleshly English women. Hawthorne is more tolerant of those less constrained by social convention and protocol. His assessment of Melville—who visited Hawthorne in November 1856, on his way to the Holy Land following the disappointments of *Pierre* and *The Confidence Man*—remains the most penetrating and perspicacious we have. Acting as a tour guide for two days, Hawthorne directs his guest to sit down "in a hollow among the sand hills (sheltering ourselves from the high, cool wind)" in order to smoke cigars and discuss "Providence and futurity, and everything that lies beyond human ken" (CE XXII: 163). His encounter with the Shakespearean conspiracy theorist, Delia Bacon—surely one of the strangest episodes in his biography—is similarly buoyed by a mixture of cool analysis and empathy. An Ahabian figure consumed by the notion that Shakespeare's plays were written by a secret cabal of intellectuals, Bacon acquired a surprisingly devoted advocate in Hawthorne, who saw her book through publication even as he discerned in her precarious reason "a system growing up in a person's mind without the volition—contrary to the volition—and substituting itself in place of everything that originally grew there" (CE XXII: 92).

Equally sympathetic are his descriptions of working people, such as the servant at Scott's estate who unwittingly sat Hawthorne in the great novelist's chair so that "you may catch some inspiration!" (CE XXII: 24) as well as the poor of Liverpool and London with whom he was everywhere besieged. Thomas Woodson notes that by the time Hawthorne had arrived in England, he must "have become aware that his lack of realism was out of tune with current fiction" (CE XVII: 6–7). Indeed, writing to his editor James T. Fields in 1860 just before leaving England for Concord, he unfavorably compared his recently completed *Marble Faun* to the novels of Trollope, which, he continued, "precisely suit my taste; [they are] solid and substantial, written on the strength of beef and through the inspiration of ale, and just as real as if some giant had hewn a great lump out of the earth and put it under a glass case" (CE XVIII: 229). To a large extent, the English notebooks may be seen as Hawthorne's experiment in realism, confirming the prediction by Mary Russell Mitford, an English admirer and writer, who noted that "A consulship in a bustling town will give him the cheerful reality, the healthy air of every-day life, which is his only want" (CE XXI: 713). Hawthorne's long walks through Liverpool and London constantly yield descriptions of the poor, "filthy in clothes and person, ragged, pale, often afflicted with humors; women, nursing their babies at dirty bosoms; men haggard, drunken, care-worn, hopeless, but with a kind of patience" (CE XXI: 18). Observing an impoverished mother with her infant, Hawthorne adopts the perspective of Dickens, whom he wished to meet, though never did, during his time in England: "I heard [her] laughing and priding herself on the pretty ways of her dirty infant—just as a Christian mother might in a nursery or drawing room." He then adds: "I must study this street-life more, and think of it more deeply" (CE XXI: 25).

Yet unlike his experience in Rome—where he set and wrote his fourth and final romance, *The Marble Faun*—Hawthorne found it impossible to incorporate into fiction the English experiences he so meticulously recorded in his journals. Beginning as early as 1853, he imagined himself writing a romance on the theme of an American claimant returning to the mother country to receive his legacy. The idea gained additional heft and impetus after his visit to Smithell's Hall, where he first learned of the legend of a bloody footstep in the flagstone of the hallway. But his plans were soon thwarted, in part by the duties of the consulship, in part by the intensity and frequency of his travels, in part by his difficulty in etherealizing the real he so persistently encountered in the literature and life of England. In *The Scarlet Letter* he had described the romance as an imagined space designed to mediate the fraught exchange between the real and ideal, between existing actuality and the ideas or concepts for which they might stand.[23] England seemed to eclipse that imagined space; "It is human life," he wrote, in an uneasy blend of appreciation and claustrophobia, "it is this material world; it is a grim and heavy reality. I have never had the same sense of being surrounded by materialism, and hemmed in with the grossness of this earthly life, anywhere else" (CE XXII: 433). Not until January 1855 would he mention his fiction again, this time to assert that it will be "all the better for ripening slowly" (CE XVII: 304). The multiple drafts and false starts of the romance, collected in the Centenary Edition as *The American Claimant*, contain notations of creative blockage and despair that are among the most heartrending in American letters: "Still there is something wanting to make an action for the story," he interjects after working on his ever-growing manuscript. "There is still a want of something, which I can by no means get at, nor describe what it is.... Oh, Heavens! I have not the least notion how to get on. I never was in such a sad predicament before" (CE XII: 286).

Creatively balked, Hawthorne increasingly devoted himself to journalizing, his letters home testifying to pride in their orotund completeness. "I think my Journals (which are getting to be voluminous) would already enable me to give you a book" (CE XVII: 370), he wrote his publisher, William D. Ticknor, half a year after confessing his slowness in drafting a romance. Nine months later, he again wrote, "I keep a journal of all my travels and adventures, and I could easily make up a couple of nice volumes for you; but, unluckily, they would be too good and true to bear publication. It would bring a terrible hornet's nest about my ear" (CE XVII: 493). Presumably referring to his unflattering depictions of the English aristocracy, Hawthorne could not know at the time that the publication of *Our Old Home* would in fact bring about a hornet's nest, but for reasons unimaginable in the mid-1850s. Many of the notebooks' most memorable set pieces—the encounters with Bacon and the debauched clergyman, the visit to Lichfield and Uttoxeter, the speechifying at civic banquets—would be extracted and reworked for *Our Old Home* when Hawthorne returned to Concord in 1860. But the America he found was as different and changed as himself: bitterly divided, nervous with impending war. From 1861 to 1863, Hawthorne would transform his English notebooks into a collection of essays published first in the *Atlantic* and then collected in his final book. When he decided to dedicate the book to Pierce—who had made his travels to England possible in the first place but who was now vilified by Republicans and abolitionists for his appeasement of the South—he created an uproar. Fields beseeched Hawthorne to reconsider, claiming the dedication would affect sales. The author was adamant: "I find that it would be a piece of poltroonery in me to withdraw either the dedication or the dedicatory letter" (CE XVIII: 586). When *Our Old Home* was published, many of Hawthorne's New England readers simply overlooked the dedicatory note (or cut it out) before plunging into the pellucid prose for which its author was famous.

Passages from the English Note-books was published in 1870 by Fields, Osgood & Co. following the appearance of one installment in the *Atlantic* about Hawthorne's visit to Wordsworth's house. As with the American notebooks, Sophia excised passages with scissors and pen, especially those referring to tobacco, alcohol, and sexual or bodily functions. This time, however, she worked in consultation with Francis Bennoch, the London merchant and patron of the arts who had introduced Hawthorne to London society and made available his summer home, Blackheath, to the family. The book was well received in the United States; Bronson Alcott (who had been among those who excised the dedication to *Our Old Home*) admiringly noted about Hawthorne's portrait of England, "Few of his contemporaries have observed with finer eyes than did our American Romancer. His facts are better facts than most historians, since he dealt with life and living things as only poets can."[24]

Not surprisingly, England had a somewhat different perspective. Hawthorne's consistent Americanism and especially his shuddering remarks about English women led the *Athenaeum* to find Hawthorne's "most kindly spirit ... somewhat soured by that miserable feeling of jealousy towards England which seems so common" in America.[25] Horace Bright—Hawthorne's other close English friend—believed Sophia had been misguided by Bennoch into including Hawthorne's impolitic descriptions. To have censored those descriptions may have improved the reception of the notebooks in England, but it would have also been to remove the pungent earthiness Hawthorne saw and recorded even at the expense of his ability to write a romance. It would be to excise what for Hawthorne was, however briefly, the romance of the real. Writing from Dickens's London in December, he would, in a tone unlike that to be found anywhere else in his writings, rhapsodize over "the dingy brick edifices heaving themselves up, and shutting out all but a strip of sullen cloud that serves London for a sky;—in short, a general impression of grime and sordidness, and, at this season, always a fog scattered along the vista of streets, sometimes so densely as almost to spiritualize the materialism and make the scene resemble the other world of worldly people, gross even to ghostliness" (CE XXII: 433).

(iv) The French and Italian Notebooks

Culturally and intellectually as well as descriptively, the French and Italian notebooks (somewhat less than two hundred thousand words) are the richest that Hawthorne kept. They are also, in sheer mass, among the most fictively productive. "Nine-tenths of the chapters [in *The Marble Faun*] include material directly from the notebooks" (CE XIV: 920); even this only barely suggests the influence of Italy on Hawthorne's imagination. Not since his residence in Concord had Hawthorne been so challenged by notions of life radically different from his own. Concord was exhilarating for him because his private feeling of renewal coincided with the spirit of time and place; for all its differences, Concord was also provincial and familiar, and the Old Manse, as the Hawthornes made themselves comfortable in it, became a haven of stability that allowed Hawthorne to test the winds of change without feeling himself blown about by them. As Brenda Wineapple remarked,

"Hawthorne was a fastidious man who depended on regulation—regular living, regular loving, rituals of predictable routine—as if to contain or curb his own sense of the underside of things, that stuff of terror and despair and dissolution (or so he thought)."[26] Italy disoriented and overwhelmed Hawthorne, awakening both the aesthete's sense of beauty and pleasure and the aesthete's nervous irritability, and troubling the moralist and the historian with incursions of chaos that could not be contained within Protestant New World ideas of virtue and historical design. The English title of *The Marble Faun—Transformation—*applies to its author as well.

It cannot be said that Hawthorne responded to the Continent with fresh enthusiasm, as Sophia did. Even apart from the logistics of steering a family of five (plus governess) through the complications of foreign travel and residence, Hawthorne seems to have approached France and Italy much as he approached museums, with a combination of trepidation, awe, and weary resignation to spousal and cultural duty. Yet as with museums, he found himself coming increasingly to enjoy Europe and to appreciate the refinements of taste and sensibility that were gradually "making their way into [his] mind," "very sturdy Goth" though he continued to be (CE XIV: 166). If "Hawthorne felt out of his element in Europe" (CE XIV: 910), as Thomas Woodson remarks, he was nonetheless broadened, deepened, and unsettled enough by it to feel that America was no longer his element, either. "I wish I were more patriotic," he wrote Ticknor in April 1858, "but to confess the truth, I had rather be a sojourner in any other country than return to my own. The United States are fit for many excellent purposes, but they are certainly not fit to live in" (CE XVIII: 140).

The notebooks open with Hawthorne's arrival in Paris on January 6, 1858; they conclude with his leaving Havre for England eighteen months later. The vast majority of entries occur between January 1858, when Hawthorne arrived in Rome, and October 1858, when fourteen-year-old Una contracted malaria. Her illness continued intermittently through the spring of 1859; at times she seemed near death. In a pocket diary (printed in the Centenary Edition of *The French and Italian Notebooks*), Hawthorne recorded the vicissitudes of her condition, which took a severe toll on both parents and effectively suspended the expeditions to galleries, churches, and historical sites, as well as the social calls, that formed the staple of Hawthorne's journalizing. Bowdoin classmate and former president Franklin Pierce, visiting Rome at the time, proved a godsend to Hawthorne during this trying period, and Hawthorne's grateful tribute to him ("Well; I have found in him, here in Rome, the whole of my early friend, and even better than I used to know him" [CE XIV: 519]) is one of the most deeply felt celebrations of friendship in his notebooks. His farewell tribute to Rome the following month is more ambivalent: "I seem to know it better than my birth place, and to have known it longer; and though I have been very miserable here, and languid with the effects of the atmosphere, and disgusted with a thousand things in daily life, still I cannot say I hate it—perhaps might fairly own a love for it. But (life being too short for such questionable and troublesome enjoyments) I desire never to set eyes on it again" (CE XIV: 524).

Sophia Hawthorne's *Passages from the French and Italian Note-Books* was excerpted in the magazine *Good Words* from January through November 1871 and published that same November by James R. Osgood and Company, Sophia having quarreled with James T. Fields over royalties. Julian Hawthorne later printed additional passages in *Nathaniel Hawthorne and His Wife* (1884), which included a devastatingly censorious one on Margaret Fuller,[27] and in *Hawthorne and His Circle* (1903). Woodson observes that although Sophia by this time "had become an experienced copyist and editor," no longer inking or scissoring out offending passages, she had no qualms about refining Hawthorne's diction or muting graphic, indecorous, or heterodox words and ideas to suit propriety; the result was a "less colorful and realistic account than her husband wrote" (CE XIV: 924–25). In 1941, then–doctoral student Norman Holmes Pearson transcribed the manuscripts, with extended commentary. The Centenary Edition of 1980 drew upon Pearson's work but performed its own transcription, with commentary, under the direction of Thomas Woodson.

Hawthorne's visit to France was brief—a scant two weeks—but it strikes the note of his response to the Continent generally. The life of the senses made its initial appeal to Hawthorne by way of French cookery, which he enjoyed warily at first before concluding that it might be a good thing for a man "to afford himself a little discipline in this line" (CE XIV: 26). A few days in Paris were enough to make the Hawthornes fledgling gourmets, who could dismiss an indifferent meal with the aplomb of connoisseurs. The "splendor of Paris," its "unwearying magnificence and beauty," took Hawthorne "altogether by surprise" (CE XIV: 13, 14), as did the architectural grandeur of the Louvre, whose halls impressed him more than its paintings. Yet as would happen recurrently in France and Italy, Hawthorne's receptive power wore thin, novelty yielded to familiarity, the life of the city felt alien and unhomelike to him, its uncleanness was offensive, and after a week he confessed that he was "quite tired of Paris, and never longed for a home so much" (CE XIV: 34).

Italy was Paris writ large, its heights higher (Hawthorne was dazzled by the beauty and opulence of the Italian churches), its depths deeper (he was appalled by the filth and decay of its urban life). Rome in January was bone-chillingly cold, and Hawthorne never fully overcame, or wanted to overcome, the "first freshness of [his] discomfort" in the city (CE XIV: 54). As it was for Anglo-American tourists generally, Rome for Hawthorne was a layered city: ancient Rome, Catholic High Renaissance Rome, and contemporary Rome, an island under papal rule (supported by French troops) in a still-disunited Italy.

Ancient Rome confounded Hawthorne's sense of time and history. In America, the House of the Seven Gables was old; in Rome, St. Peter's and the Palazzo Barbarini were comparatively new alongside the ruins of classical Rome, which, unlike English ruins, the dry climate preserved as agelessly and unendearingly white. Culturally, although Hawthorne could see traces of familiar humanity in the busts of the Roman emperors in the Capitol Museum, he felt himself and all Christendom "morally unlike, and disconnected with [the Romans], and not belonging to the same train of thought" (CE XIV: 167). Nor could he accustom himself to the juxtaposition of epochs and to the intermingling of the sublime and the paltry (or worse) that assaulted him everywhere in Rome: washerwomen hanging out clothes in the Forum; monuments used as public privies; the temple of Minerva occupied by a bakeshop; the Coliseum patrolled by French soldiers, with a Christian shrine at its center and youths gaily running footraces around it. To one who prided himself on his deep historical sense, Rome seemed to proclaim that he knew nothing about history at all. Rome encapsulated 2,500 years of Western moral, intellectual, and spiritual life, and Hawthorne the provincial American felt tasked, at age fifty-four, with comprehending its meaning. Of all Roman monuments, the Pantheon pleased him most, partly because it managed to bridge pagan, Renaissance, and modern—a Roman temple converted into a Christian church and surrounded by the lively confusion of a neighborhood market—but chiefly because its open dome symbolized to him a connection to heaven and the eternal that bypassed the conundrums of historical being.

The museums of Rome and Florence also challenged Hawthorne. Sculpture had limited appeal for him, but he did admire and revisit the four classical statues reverenced by contemporary taste—the *Apollo Belvedere*, the *Venus de Medici*, the *Dying Gladiator* (as it was then known), and the *Laocöon*—though his response to them varied according to his mood and degree of receptive empathy—that "free and generous surrender of myself, which ... is essential to the proper estimate of anything excellent" (CE XIV: 110–11). One other statue also caught his attention: the Faun of Praxiteles, which suggested to him a "story, with all sorts of fun and pathos in it, [that] might be contrived on the idea of their species having become intermingled with the human race" (CE XIV: 178). He came to know expatriate American sculptors such as William Wetmore Story (whose Cleopatra would become Kenyon's in *The Marble Faun*), Hiram Powers, Harriet Hosmer, and young Salemite Louisa Lander, who befriended the family and undertook to model a bust of Hawthorne. But he objected strongly to the sculptors' use of nudity in their works, aesthetically because it seemed an absurd anachronism with modern subjects (Washington nude or in a toga?), morally because it offended and embarrassed him, especially when viewed in mixed company. The life of art and the senses halted abruptly for Hawthorne whenever it verged on the sexual, even in cold marble.

Painting was the art that fascinated and exasperated Hawthorne and to which he devoted numerous passages in the notebooks. Sophia was an indefatigable museumgoer, dragging Hawthorne with her. In England paintings had bored him, but in Italy he conscientiously undertook to make himself conversant with and, if possible, appreciative of Renaissance art. Despite what he called the "external weariness and sense of thousand-fold sameness to be overcome"—"the terrible lack of variety in [the painters'] subjects" (CE XIV: 111)—he did come to make distinctions. He lacked enthusiasm for Fra Angelico, the ethereal painter so beloved by Sophia; he disliked the accomplished but soulless Andrea del Sarto; he was transfixed by Guido Reni, supposed painter of a supposed portrait of Beatrice Cenci and of Michael triumphing over Lucifer (both paintings would figure prominently in *The Marble Faun*); and he loathingly admired, or admiringly loathed, Titian, painter of a "naked and lustful" Venus and of a Magdalene with "golden hair clustering round her naked body," which he could hardly avert his eyes and mind from: "This Magdelene [*sic*] is very coarse and sensual, with only an impudent assumption of penitence and religious sentiment, scarcely so deep as the eyelids; but it is a splendid picture, nevertheless, with those naked, lifelike arms, and the hands that press the rich locks about her, and so carefully let those two voluptuous breasts be seen. She a penitent! She would shake off all pretence to it, as easily as she would shake aside that clustering hair and offer her nude front to the next comer. Titian must have been a very good-for-nothing old man" (CE XIV: 334).

The question that Hawthorne is silently revolving through many of his entries on art is the relationship between the spiritual and the physical. The Hawthorne of the early notebooks seldom concerns himself with matters of religion, certainly not with salvation through Christ. The later Hawthorne does, apropos of painting at least. This may have been an effect of osmosis—what gallery haunter can avoid thinking about Christ?—but it may also have been an aging man's longing, if not for deliverance from sin, then at least for reassurance of eternal life. The need to find spirit confirmed in and through art sheds light on Hawthorne's perplexity and horror at those

Italian masters who could depict a Virgin Mary but "were just as ready, or more so, to paint a lewd and naked woman, and call her Venus" (CE XIV: 111). Raphael, considered "the greatest painter of all time, indisputably,"[28] epitomized the problem. *The Transfiguration* was a masterpiece, but Raphael was also taken to be the artist of *La Fornarina* (a reputed portrait of his mistress, a baker's daughter), "a brunette, with a deep, bright glow in her face, naked below the navel and well pleased to be so for the sake of your admiration—ready for any extent of nudity, for love or money,—the brazen trollope that she is" (CE XIV: 93). As with Titian, Hawthorne vents indignation even as his prose lingers graphically on the details of the woman's body. Hawthorne never outgrew the voyeurism of his youth; he simply outgrew its comparatively good-natured innocence and came to clothe it in Victorian prudery even in the privacy of his notebook.

Whenever the gallery collection enabled it, Hawthorne was always pleased to pass from the Italian masters to the Dutch and Flemish—"men of flesh and blood, with warm fists, and human hearts," who "address[ed] themselves" to "human sympathies" rather than to the "formed intellectual taste" of a church-endowed genre (CE XIV: 112). This is nothing new: Hawthorne had always admired the Dutch realists, who seemed to him analogous to realists in fiction, his own form (the romance) being closer to Italianate rarefaction. The ideal was to combine the two: to spiritualize matter or, as Christ did and his Italian depicters tried to do, to materialize spirit. Viewing *The Transfiguration*, Hawthorne wished that Raphael had painted it in the style of Gerard Duow while "at the same time preserving [the] breadth and grandeur of [his] design" (CE XIV: 317). Hawthorne wants spirituality in art and he wants, simultaneously, the "petty miracles" of "a Dutch fly settling on a peach, or a humble-bee burying himself in a flower" (CE XIV: 317, 318).

The work of art that came nearest to achieving such a union was the *Venus de Medici*, which seemed to Hawthorne at once real and ideal—a type of essential womanhood, and modest enough to be slightly alarmed that someone might be looking at her nude. "Type" as Hawthorne imagines it here, however, does not imply the transcendent so much as the transpersonal: an *arche*type. The Venus is the work of a naturalistic imagination, and any "spirituality" to be found in it must be superadded by a Pygmalion-like spectator. As he pored over the artworks in Italian galleries, such superadding struck Hawthorne as nearly always the requirement for a spiritual art. However much the artist idealized his subject, he could not reach heaven except by losing touch with earth (like Fra Angelico), and if he were faithful to earth—to the human condition, as we know it in time—he could not sweep aside the clouds of suffering and evil that obscured heaven. Recalling a portrait of the despairing Christ on the cross by Giovanni Sodoma,

Hawthorne feels that it achieves the most an honest art is able to achieve: "Sodoma almost seems to have reconciled the impossibilities of combining an Omnipresent Divinity with a suffering and outraged humanity" (CE XIV: 492). (When he adapted the passage for *The Marble Faun,* Hawthorne recast Sodoma's noble failure as a miraculous success.) Even the journal's "almost" is qualified by Hawthorne's consciousness of idealizing: "But this is one of those cases in which the spectator's imagination completes what the artist merely hints at" (ibid.).

On a different level, the problem of the spiritual and the material was replicated for Hawthorne in the institution of the Catholic Church. His first introduction to Italian Catholicism came through the churches in Genoa, which "dazzled" him with their magnificence and caused him to feel "what a splendid religion it was that reared" them (CE XIV: 48, 49). With its artwork, gilding, and polished marble, St. Peter's impressed him even more, accustomed as he was to the dim vastness of English cathedrals. The Catholic priesthood tapped common Anglo-American prejudices in Hawthorne, as did stories or superstitions about Vatican politics, past and present. Apart from the aesthetic, his attraction to Catholicism centered on its intimacy and spiritual tact. He appreciated the cool, dark side chapels that allowed solitary worshippers a haven for quiet communion, so different from the harsh communal daylight of Protestant worship; and he "wonder[ed] at the exuberance with which [the Catholic Church] responds to the demands of human infirmity" (CE XIV: 91), especially in the sacrament—or was it the psychotherapy?—of confession. Observing a man leaving a confessional, Hawthorne reflected that if "he had been a protestant, I think he would have shut all that up within his heart, and let it burn there till it seared him" (CE XIV: 60). One thinks immediately of Dimmesdale and of whether the moral and psychological themes, not to mention the plot, of *The Scarlet Letter* would have been possible in a Catholic community. A "son of the Puritans," as he would soon call Hilda in *The Marble Faun* a "daughter," Hawthorne had no sympathy with Catholic doctrine, but he marveled at the Church's usefulness for "human occasions" (CE XIV: 59) and at the richness of its sacramental and ornamental life, which made Protestantism seem by contrast a stark, impoverished creed of negation.

Though chronically shy and averse to social gatherings, Hawthorne may have socialized more in Italy than anywhere else, save perhaps in Concord at the Old Manse. Thanks to Sophia, at any rate, he worked at being more companionable. Expatriate American artists, and occasionally English men and women such as the Brownings and sculptor John Gibson, make extended cameo appearances in the notebooks; like most other Anglo-Americans, Hawthorne never entered Italian society or seems to have wanted to. His portraits of sculptors William Wetmore Story (later a friend—and biographical subject—of Henry James) and Hiram Powers are shrewd and judicious, if sometimes deflating; Hawthorne the gossip is always lively reading. Two other sketches are notable, both for their own sake and because they form an instructive moral diptych. The first is of Louisa Lander, the piquant young sculptress who molded a bust of Hawthorne and whose freedom and independence—living alone far from home, she "go[es] fearlessly about these mysterious streets, by night as well as by day, with no household ties, no rule or law but that within her; yet acting with quietness and simplicity, and keeping, after all, within a homely line of right" (CE XIV: 78)—served as a model for the outward situation of Hilda. There the resemblance ends. Lander became a close friend of the Hawthorne family until whispers had it that she had posed in the nude, and perhaps more, at which point Hawthorne assumed the role of guardian of family values and cut her coldly.[29] The other portrait is of a dead woman, Margaret Fuller, and also turns upon sexual rumor. Agitated by sculptor Joseph Mozier's account of Fuller's Roman liaison with Giovanni Ossoli, an intellectual inferior whom she may have married only after their child was born (if at all, according to some), Hawthorne launches into what James R. Mellow aptly calls "the sharpest and most critical judgment he ever made on the human clay":[30]

> It was such an awful joke, that she should have resolved—in all sincerity, no doubt—to make herself the greatest, wisest, best woman of the age; and, to that end, she set to work on her strong, heavy, unpliable, and, in many respects, defective and evil nature, and adorned it with a mosaic of admirable qualities, such as she chose to possess; putting in here a splendid talent, and there a moral excellence, and polishing each separate piece, and the whole together, till it seemed to shine afar and dazzle all who saw it. She took credit to herself for having been her own Redeemer, if not her own Creator; and, indeed, she was far more a work of art than any of Mr. Mozier's statues. But she was not working on inanimate substance, like marble or clay; there was something within her that she could not possibly come at, to re-create and refine it; and, by and by, this rude old potency bestirred itself, and undid all her labor in the twinkling of an eye. On the whole, I do not know but I like her the better for it;—the better, because she proved herself a very woman, after all, and fell as the weakest of her sisters might. (CE XIV: 156–57)

Sexual jealousy and a triumphant antifeminism may account for much of Hawthorne's vehemence toward Fuller, yet, tone apart, the passage is in keeping with Hawthorne's severity toward sexual transgression throughout his published and private writings. Louisa Lander and Margaret Fuller occupy a place beside the once-seduced girl of the Berkshire journal whom no respectable man could think of marrying, and of course with Hawthorne's Fuller-tinged dark heroines—Hester Prynne, Zenobia of *The Blithedale Romance,* and Miriam of *The Marble Faun*—whom Hawthorne admires and may even love but feels obliged to exorcise and punish.

Hawthorne's first three romances draw intermittently upon notebook materials; *The Marble Faun* is saturated with them and unimaginable without them. Critics have sometimes objected that Hawthorne's long descriptions of places, works of art, and events such as the Roman carnival or the unearthing of a Venus in the countryside give the romance a guidebook aspect that impedes its development of plot and theme. The book *is* slower reading than Hawthorne's other romances. The remarkable thing is how aptly Hawthorne uses notebook materials for symbolic purposes, even with a minimum of fictive transformation; it is as if life arranged itself symbolically for Hawthorne on first perception or in the initial act of notebook composition. The faun may be *too* apt—one tires of Hawthorne's overinsistence—but the portrait of Beatrice Cenci that so fascinated him is made to pertain to both Miriam and Hilda, as is the Guidi Reni painting of Michael subduing Lucifer, which the women regard in opposite but characteristic ways. The most dominant symbol in *The Marble Faun* is Rome itself, and beyond its containing theme of the growth of the soul—a near-constant in Hawthorne's work from the beginning—the romance gives expression to the *un*containable phenomenon of a city that had come to represent to Hawthorne nothing less than "the world."

The Marble Faun ends with Kenyon, Hawthorne's sometime alter ego, turning from the bewilderments of Rome and asking the righteous Hilda to guide him home. Physically, "home" is America; metaphysically, it is the structures of belief of a New England village. In Italy Hawthorne had been wooed to a life of beauty and the senses, to the contemplation of a history immeasurably longer, deeper, and more ambiguous than his Salem family's, and to a vertiginous pleasure in edging away from established belief toward chasms of uncertainty. After a residence in England in 1859–60, Hawthorne, too, returned home. Whether he ever returned "home" is another matter.

(v) Editorial Principles

The editors have attempted in the following selections to present a full and rounded self-portrait of Hawthorne—both of his process of thinking and,

INTRODUCTION

so far as the entries gesture outward, of his historical context. To preserve a sense of life and thought unfolding (ragged as all human unfolding is), we have rearranged the Centenary texts by chronology alone rather than by chronology within separate notebooks. We have sought to be as sparing of ellipses as possible, especially with selections from the American notebooks; with the English and French and Italian notebooks, the length and the discursiveness of entries make editing unavoidable.

The text of the selections reproduces that in the four volumes of notebooks in the Centenary Edition. Ellipsis marks have been used to indicate omitted material within or at the beginning or end of a sentence or paragraph but not to indicate omissions at the end of a dated entry, between discrete sections of an entry, or between its inscribed date and the selected material. The irregularities of format in recording dates are Hawthorne's, as are the occasionally erratic spellings. In accordance with the practice of the Centenary Edition, square brackets have been used to mark undeciphered inked-out passages, and pointed brackets excisions from manuscript. Empty brackets of either sort indicate that one or two words are affected; ellipsis dots within brackets signify three or more words. Letters or words inside square brackets are conjectural. *Italicized text refers to material that appears in Hawthorne's Lost Notebook but not in the Centenary Edition.* Explanatory notes are marked by numerals, numbered consecutively for the American, the English, and the French and Italian notebooks; the notes themselves appear in the Notes section at the end of the book.

PART I

The American Notebooks

[Thursday], June 18th, [1835].

A walk in North Salem in the decline of yesterday afternoon,—beautiful weather, bright, sunny, with a western or northwestern wind just cool enough, and a slight superfluity of heat. The verdure, both of trees and grass, is now in its prime, the leaves elastic, all life. The grass-fields are plenteously bestrewn with white-weed, large spaces looking as white as a sheet of snow, at a distance, yet with an indescribably warmer tinge than snow,—living white, intermixed with living green. The hills and hollows beyond the Cold Spring copiously shaded, principally with oaks of good growth, and some walnut-trees, with the rich sun brightening in the midst of the open spaces, and mellowing and fading into the shade,—and single trees, with their cool spot of shade in the waste of sun: quite a picture of beauty, gently picturesque. The surface of the land is so varied, with woodland mingled, that the eye cannot reach far away, except now and then in vistas perhaps across the river, showing houses, or a church and surrounding village, in Upper Beverly. In one of the sunny bits of pasture, walled irregularly in with oak-shade, I saw a gray mare feeding, and, as I drew near, a colt sprang up from amid the grass,—a very small colt. He looked me in the face, and I tried to startle him, so as to make him gallop; but he stretched his long legs, one after another, walked quietly to his mother, and began to suck,—just wetting his lips, not being very hungry. Then he rubbed his head, alternately, with each hind leg. He was a graceful little beast.

I bathed in the cove, overhung with maples and walnuts, the water cool and thrilling. At a distance it sparkled bright and blue in the breeze and sun. There were jelly-fish swimming about, and several left to melt away on the shore. On the shore, sprouting amongst the sand and gravel, I found samphire, growing somewhat like asparagus. It is an excellent salad at this season, salt, yet with an herb-like vivacity, and very tender. I strolled slowly through the pastures, watching my long shadow making grave, fantastic gestures in the sun. It is a pretty sight to see the sunshine brightening the entrance of a road which shortly becomes deeply overshadowed by trees on both sides. At the Cold Spring, three little girls, from six to nine, were seated on the stones in which the fountain is set, and paddling in the water. It was a pretty picture, and would have been prettier, if they had shown bare little legs, instead of pantalets. Very large trees overhung them, and the sun was so nearly gone down that a pleasant gloom made the spot sombre, in contrast with these light and laughing little figures. On perceiving me, they rose up, tittering among themselves. It seemed that there was a sort of playful malice in those who first saw me; for they allowed the other to keep on paddling, without warning her of my approach. I passed along, and heard them come chattering behind.[1]

[Monday], September 7th, 1835.

A sketch to be given of a modern reformer,—a type of the extreme doctrines on the subject of slaves, cold water, and other such topics. He goes about the streets haranguing most eloquently, and is on the point of making many converts, when his labors are suddenly interrupted by the appearance of the keeper of a mad-house, whence he has escaped. Much may be made of this idea.[2]

The world is so sad and solemn, that things meant in jest are liable, by an overpowering influence, to become dreadful earnest,—gayly dressed fantasies turning to ghostly and black-clad images of themselves.

To represent the process by which sober truth gradually strips off all the beautiful draperies with which imagination has enveloped a beloved object, till from an angel she turns out to be a merely ordinary woman. This to be done without caricature, perhaps with a quiet humor interfused, but the prevailing impression to be a sad one. The story might consist of the various alterations in the feelings of the absent lover, caused by successive events that display the true character of his mistress; and the catastrophe should take place at their meeting, when he finds himself equally disappointed in her person; or the whole spirit of the thing may here be reproduced.

Last evening, from the opposite shore of the North River, a view of the town mirrored in the water, which was as smooth as glass, with no perceptible tide or agitation, except a trifling swell and reflux on the sand, although the shadow of the moon danced in it. The picture of the town perfect in the water,—towers of churches, houses, with here and there a light gleaming near the shore above, and more faintly glimmering under water,—all perfect, but somewhat more hazy and indistinct than the reality. There were many clouds flitting about the sky; and the picture of each could be traced in the water,—the ghost of what was itself unsubstantial. The rattling of wheels heard long and far through the town. Voices of people talking on the other side of the river, the tones being so distinguishable in all their variations that it seemed as if what was there said might be understood; but it was not so.

The story of a man, cold and hard-hearted, and acknowledging no brotherhood with mankind. At his death they might try to dig him a grave, but, at a little space beneath the ground, strike upon a rock, as if the earth refused to receive the unnatural son into her bosom. Then they would put him into an old sepulchre, where the coffins and corpses were all turned to dust, and so he would be alone. Then the body would petrify; and he having died in some characteristic act and expression, he would seem, through endless ages of death, to repel society as in life, and no one would be buried in that tomb forever. ["The Man of Adamant"]

In an old house, a mysterious knocking might be heard on the wall, where had formerly been a doorway, now bricked up.

[Saturday], October 17th, [1835].

To make one's own reflection in a mirror the subject of a story. ["Monsieur du Miroir"]

Some common quality or circumstance that should bring together people the most unlike in all other respects, and make a brotherhood and sisterhood of them,—the rich and the proud finding themselves in the same category with the mean and the despised.

[Sunday], October 25th, 1835.

Sentiments in a foreign language, which merely convey the sentiment, without retaining to the reader any graces of style or harmony of sound, have somewhat of the charm of thoughts in one's own mind that have not yet been put into words. No possible words that we might adapt to them could realize the unshaped beauty that they appear to possess. This is the reason that translations are never satisfactory,—and less so, I should think, to one who cannot than to one who can pronounce the language.

A person to be writing a tale, and to find that it shapes itself against his intentions; that the characters act otherwise than he thought; that unforeseen events occur; and a catastrophe comes which he strives in vain to avert. It might shadow forth his own fate,—he having made himself one of the personages.

[Tuesday], October 25th, 1836.

In this dismal *and squalid* chamber FAME was won. (Salem, Union Street.)[3]

A Thanksgiving dinner. All the miserable on earth are to be invited,— as the drunkard, the bereaved parent, the ruined merchant, the broken-hearted lover, the poor widow, the old man and woman who have outlived their generation, the disappointed author, the wounded, sick, and broken soldier, the diseased person, the infidel, the man with an evil conscience, little orphan children, or children of neglectful parents, shall be admitted to the table, and many others. The giver of the feast goes out to deliver his invitations. Some of the guests he meets in the streets, some he knocks for at the doors of their houses. The description must be rapid. But who must be the giver of the feast, and what his claims to preside? A man who has never found out what he is fit for, who has unsettled aims or objects in life, and whose mind gnaws him, making him the sufferer of many kinds of misery. He should meet some pious, old, sorrowful person, with more outward calamities than any other, and invite him with a reflection that piety would make all that miserable company truly thankful. ["The Christmas Banquet"]

We sometimes congratulate ourselves at the moment of waking from a troubled dream: it may be so the moment after death.

The race of mankind to be swept away, leaving all their cities and works. Then another human pair to be placed in the world, with native intelligence like Adam and Eve, but knowing nothing of their predecessors or of their own nature and destiny. They, perhaps, to be described as working out this knowledge by their sympathy with what they saw, and by their own feelings. ["The New Adam and Eve"]

A snake, taken into a man's stomach and nourished there from fifteen years to thirty-five, tormenting him most horribly. A type of envy or some other evil passion. ["Egotism; or The Bosom Serpent"]

A lament for life's wasted sunshine.

A new classification of society to be instituted. Instead of rich and poor, high and low, they are to be classed,—First, by their sorrows: for instance, whenever there are any, whether in fair mansion or hovel, who are mourning the loss of relations and friends, and who wear black, whether the cloth be coarse or superfine, they are to make one class. Secondly, all who have the same maladies, whether they lie under damask canopies or on straw pallets or in the wards of hospitals, they are to form one class. Thirdly, all who are guilty of the same sins, whether the world knows them or not; whether they languish in prison, looking forward to the gallows, or walk honored among men, they also form a class. Then proceed to generalize and classify the whole world together, as none can claim utter exemption from either sorrow, sin, or disease; and if they could, yet Death, like a great parent, comes and sweeps them all through one darksome portal,—all his children. ["The Processions of Life"]

The dying exclamation of the Emperor Augustus, "Has it not been well acted?" An essay on the misery of being always under a mask. A veil may be needful, but never a mask. Instances of people who wear masks in all classes of society, and never take them off even in the most familiar moments, though sometimes they may chance to slip aside.

A recluse, like myself, or a prisoner, to measure time by the progress of sunshine through his chamber.

To show the effect of gratified revenge. As an instance, merely, suppose a woman sues her lover for breach of promise, and gets the money by instalments, through a long series of years. At last, when the miserable victim were utterly trodden down, the triumpher would have become a very devil of evil passions,—they having overgrown his whole nature; so that a far greater evil would have come upon himself than on his victim.[4]

There is *a fund of* evil in every human heart,[5] which may remain latent, perhaps, through the whole of life; but circumstances may rouse it to activity. To imagine such circumstances. A woman, tempted to be false to her husband, apparently through mere whim,—or a young man to feel an instinctive thirst for blood; and to commit murder. This appetite may be traced in the popularity of criminal trials. The appetite might be observed first in a child, and then traced upwards, manifesting itself in crimes suited to every stage of life.

In July–August 1837, Hawthorne paid a visit to his college friend Horatio Bridge in Maine.[6]

[Wednesday], July 5th, 1837.

Here I am settled, since night before last, with Bridge, and living very singularly. He leads a bachelor-life in his paternal mansion, only a small part of which is occupied by a family who do his washing, make the beds, &c. He provides his own breakfast and supper, and occasionally his dinner; though this is oftener, I believe, taken at the hotel or an eating-house, or with some of his relatives. I am his guest, and my presence makes no alteration in his way of life. Our fare, thus far, has consisted of bread, butter, and cheese, crackers, herrings, boiled eggs, coffee, milk, and claret-wine, besides a plentiful variety of liquors, should we desire them. He has another inmate in the person of a queer little Frenchman, who has his breakfast, tea, and lodging here, and finds his dinner elsewhere. Monsieur Schaeffer does not appear to be more than twenty-one years old—a diminutive figure, with eyes askew, and otherwise of ungainly physiognomy; he is ill-dressed also, in a coarse blue coat, thin cotton pantaloons, and unbrushed boots; altogether with as little of French coxcombry as can well be imagined; though with something of the monkey-aspect inseparable from a little Frenchman. He is, nevertheless, an intelligent and well-informed man, apparently of extensive reading in his own language;—a philosopher, Bridge tells me, and an infidel. His insignificant personal appearance stands in the way of his success, and prevents him from receiving the respect which is really due to his talents and acquirements; wherefore he is bitterly dissatisfied with the country and its inhabitants, and often expresses his feelings to Bridge (who has gained his confidence to a certain degree) in very strong terms.

Then here are three characters, each with something out of the common way, living together somewhat like monks. Bridge, our host, combines more high and admirable qualities, of that sort which make up a gentleman, than any other that I have met with. Polished, yet natural, frank, open, and straightforward, yet with a delicate feeling for the sensitiveness of his companions; of excellent temper and warm heart; well-acquainted with the world, with a keen faculty of observation, which he has had many opportunities of exercising [. . .] and never varying from a code of honor and principle, which is really nice and rigid in its way. There is a sort of philosophy developing itself in him, which will not improbably cause him to settle down in this, or some other equally singular course of life. He seems almost to have made up his mind never to be married—which I wonder at; for he has strong affections, and is fond both of women and children.[7]

The little Frenchman impresses me very strongly, too—so lonely as he is here, struggling against the world, with bitter feelings in his breast, and yet talking with the vivacity and gaiety of his nation;—making his home from darkness to daylight, and enjoying here what little domestic comfort and confidence there is for him; and then going about all the live-long day, teaching French to blockheads who sneer at him; and returning at about ten o'clock in the evening (for I was wrong in saying that he supped here—he eats no supper) to his solitary room and bed. Before retiring, he goes to Bridge's bedside, and, if he finds him awake, stands talking French, expressing his dislike of the Americans—"*Je hais—Je hais les Yankees!*"—thus giving vent to the stifled bitterness of the whole day. In the morning, I hear him getting up early—at sunrise or before—humming to himself, scuffling about his chamber with his thick boots, and at last taking his departure for a solitary ramble till breakfast. Then he comes in cheerful and vivacious enough, eats pretty heartily, and is off again, singing a French chanson as he goes down the gravel-walk. The poor fellow has nobody to sympathize with him but Bridge; and thus a singular connection is established between two utterly different characters.

Then here is myself, who am likewise a queer character in my way, and have come here to spend a week or two with my friend of half-a life-time;— the longest space, probably, that we are ever destined to spend together; for fate seems to be preparing changes for both of us. My circumstances, at least, cannot long continue as they are and have been; and Bridge, too, stands betwixt high prosperity and utter ruin.

I think I should soon become strongly attached to our way of life—so independent, and untroubled by the forms and restrictions of society. The house is very pleasantly situated—half a mile distant from where the town begins to be thickly-settled, and on a swell of land, with the road running at a distance of fifty yards, and a grassy tract and gravel walk between. Beyond the road rolls the Kennebec, here two or three hundred yards wide; putting my head out of the window, I can see it flowing steadily along, straightway between wooded banks; but arriving nearly opposite the house, there is a large and level sand-island in the middle of the stream; and just below this island, the current is further interrupted by the works of the Mill Dam, which is perhaps half-finished, yet still in so rude a state, that it looks as much like the ruins of a Dam destroyed by the spring freshets, as like the foundation of a Dam yet to be. Irishmen and Canadians are at work on it, and the echoes of their hammering, and of their voices, come across the river and up to the window.... My position is so far retired from the river and the Mill-Dam, that, though the latter is really rather a busy scene, yet a sort of quiet seems to be diffused over the whole. Two or three times a day, this quiet is broken by the sudden thunder from a quarry, where the workmen are blasting rocks for the Dam;—and a peal of thunder sounds strange in such a green, sunny, and quiet landscape with the blue sky brightening the river.

I have not seen much of the people; there have been, however, several incidents which amused me, though scarcely worth telling. A passionate tavern-keeper, quick as a flash of gunpowder, a nervous man, and showing in his demeanor, it seems, a consciousness of his infirmity of temper. I was a witness to a scuffle of his with a drunken guest; the tavern-keeper, after they were separated, raved like a madman, and in a tone of voice having a queerly pathetic or lamentable sound mingled with its rage, as if he were lifting up his voice to weep. Then he jumped into a chaise which was standing by, whipped up the horse and drove off rapidly; as if to give his rage vent in this way.

On the morning of the fourth of July, two printer's apprentices, lads nearly grown, dressed in jackets and very tight pantaloons of check—tight as their skins; so that they looked like harlequins or circus clowns, yet appeared to think themselves in perfect propriety—a very calm and quiet assurance of the admiration of the town. A common fellow, a carpenter, who, on the strength of political partizanship, asked Bridge's assistance in cutting out great letters from play-bills &c, in order to print Martin Van Buren Forever, on a flag;[8]—but Bridge refused. "Let every man skin his own skunks," says he. Bridge seems to be considerably of a favorite with the lower orders, especially the Irishmen and French Canadians, the latter accosting him in the street to ask his assistance as an interpreter, in making their bargains for work.

I meant to have dined at the Hotel with Bridge to-day; but having returned to the house, leaving him to do some business in the village, I found myself unwilling to move, when the dinner hour approached; and therefore dined very comfortably on bread, cheese and eggs. Some little Canadian children were peeping out between two buildings; they would have talked French, had they been old enough to talk at all.

Nothing of much interest takes place. We live very comfortably in our bachelor-establishment, on a cold shoulder of mutton, with ham, and smoked beef, and boiled eggs; and as to drinkables, we had both claret and brown sherry on the dinner-table to day; but we are neither of us such thirsty souls as we once were. Last evening we had a long literary and philosophical conversation with Mr. Schaeffer. He is rather remarkably well-informed for a man of his age, and seems to have very just notions on ethics &c though damnably perverted as to religion. It is queer to hear philosophy of any sort from such a boyish figure—"we philosophers," he is fond of saying, to distinguish himself and his brethren from the Christians. One of his oddities is, that, while stedfastly maintaining an opinion that he is a very small and slow eater, and that we, in common with other Yankees, eat immensely and at a great rate, he actually eats both faster and longer, and devours, as Bridge avers, more victuals, than both of us together.

Wednesday, July 26th, [1837].

Dined at Barker's yesterday. Before dinner, sitting with several other persons on the stoop of the tavern. There was Bridge—J. A. Chandler, clerk of the court, a dissipated man of middle-age or beyond,—two or three stage-people—and near by a negro, whom they call "the doctor," a crafty-looking fellow, one of whose occupations is that of pimp. In presence of this goodly company, a man of a depressed, neglected air, a soft, simple-looking fellow, with an anxious expression, in a laborer's dress, approached and inquired for Mr. Barker. Mine host being gone to Portland, the stranger was directed to the Barkeeper, who stood at the door. The man asked where he should find one Mary Ann Russel—a question which excited general and hardly suppressed mirth; for the said Mary Ann is one of a knot of whores, who were routed on Sunday evening by Barker and a constable. The man was told that the black fellow could give him all the information he wanted. The black fellow asked "Do you want to use her?" Others of the bystanders, or by-sitters, put various questions as to the nature of the man's business with Mary Ann, and the connection between them. One asked, "Is she your daughter?" "Why, a little nearer than that, I calkilate," said the poor devil. Here the mirth was increased, it being evident that the prostitute was his wife. The man seemed too simple and obtuse to comprehend much of the ridicule of his situation, or to be rendered very miserable of it. Nevertheless, he made some touching points. "A man generally places some little dependence on his wife," said he, "whether she's good or bad." He meant, probably, that he rests some affection on her. He told us that she had behaved well, till committed to jail for striking a child; and I believe he was absent from home at the time, and had not seen her since. And now he was in search of her, intending, doubtless, to do his best to get her out of her troubles, and then to take her back to his bosom. Some advised him not to look after her; others recommended him to pay "the doctor" aforesaid for guiding him to her haunt; which finally the doctor did, in consideration of a treat; and the fellow went off, having heard little but gibes, and not one word of sympathy. I would have given considerable to witness his meeting with his wife. On the whole there was a moral picturesqueness in the contrasts of this scene—a man moved as deeply as his nature would admit, in the midst of hardened, gibing spectators, heartless towards him. It is worth thinking over and studying out. He seemed rather hurt and pricked by the jests thrown at him, yet bore it patiently, and sometimes almost joined in the laugh. He was cowed by his situation; being of an easy, unenergetic nature.

Hints for characters—Nancy, a pretty, black-eyed intelligent servant-girl, living in Captain Harriman's family. She comes daily to make the beds in our part of the house; and exchanges a good morning with me, in a pleasant voice, and with a glance and smile—somewhat shy, because we are not well acquainted, yet capable of being made conversible. She washes once a week, and may be seen standing over her tub, with her handkerchief somewhat displaced from her white bosom, because it is hot. Often, she stands with her bare arms in the water, talking with Mrs. Harriman; or looks through the window, perhaps at Bridge or somebody else crossing the yard—rather thoughtfully, but soon smiling or laughing. Then goeth she for a pail of water. In the afternoon, very probably, she dresses herself in silks, looking not only pretty but ladylike, and strolls round the house, not unconscious that some gentleman may be staring at her from behind our green blinds. After supper, she walks to the village. Morning and evening, she goes a milking—and thus passes her life, cheerfully, usefully, virtuously, with hopes, doubtless, of a husband and children. Mrs. Harriman is a particularly plump, soft-fleshed, fair-complexioned, comely woman enough, with rather a simple countenance—not near so piquant as Nancy's. Her walk has something of the roll or waddle of a fat woman, though it were too much to call her fat. Her breasts swell out round and soft, being abundant with milk for a little she-brat of three or four months old—her first child, though she is not a very young woman. She seems to be a sociable body—probably laughter-loving. Captain Harriman himself has commanded a steam-boat, and has a certain knowledge of life.

Query—in relation to the man's prostitute-wife—how much desire and resolution of doing her duty by her husband can a wife retain, while injuring him in what is deemed the most essential point.

Friday, July 28th, [1837].

Saw my classmate, and formerly intimate associate, Cilley, for the first time since we graduated.[9] He has met with good success in life, and that in spite of circumstance, having struggled upward against bitter opposition, by the force of his own abilities, to be a member of Congress, after having been some time the leader of his party in the state legislature. We met like old friends, and conversed almost as freely as we used to do in College days, twelve years ago and more. He is a singular man, shrewd, crafty, insinuating, with wonderful tact, seizing on each man by his manageable point, and using him for his own purposes, often without the man's suspecting that he is made a tool of; and yet, artificial as his character would seem to be, his conversation, at least to myself, was full of natural feeling, the expression of which can hardly be mistaken; and his revelations with regard to himself had really a great deal of frankness. He spoke of his ambition; of the obstacles which he had encountered; of the means by which he had overcome them, imputing great efficacy to his personal intercourse with people, and study of their characters; then of his course as a member of the legislature and speaker, and of his style of speaking, and its effects; of the dishonorable things which had been imputed to him, and in what manner he had repelled the charges; in short, he would have seemed to have opened himself very freely as to his public life. Then, as to private affairs, he spoke of his marriage, of his wife, his children, and told me with tears in his eyes, of the death of a dear little girl, and how it had affected him, and how impossible it had been for him to believe that she was really to die. A man of the most open nature might well have been more reserved to a friend, after twelve years separation, than Cilly was to me. Nevertheless, he is really a crafty man, concealing like a murder-secret, anything that it is not good for him to have known. He by no means feigns the good feeling that he professes, nor is there anything affected in the frankness of his conversation; and it is this that makes him so very fascinating. There is such a quantity of truth, and kindliness, and warm affections, that a man's heart opens to him in spite of himself; he deceives by truth. And not only is he crafty, but, when occasion demands, bold and fierce as a tiger, determined, and even straightforward and undisguised in his measures—a daring fellow as well as a sly one. Yet, notwithstanding his consummate art, the general estimate of his character seems to be pretty just; hardly anybody, probably, thinks him better than he is, and many think him worse. Nevertheless unless he should fall into some great and overwhelming discovery of rascality, he will always possess influence; though I should hardly think that he could take any prominent part in Congress. As to any rascality, I rather believe that he has thought out for himself a much higher system of morality than any natural integrity would have prompted him to adopt; that he has seen the thorough advantage of morality and honesty; and the sentiment of these qualities has now got into his mind and spirit, and pretty well impregnated them. I believe him to be about as honest, now, as the great run of the world—with something even approaching to high mindedness. His person in some degree accords with his character—thin, and a thin face, sharp features, sallow, a projecting brow, not very high, deep-set eyes; an insinuating smile and look, when he meets you, or is about to address you. I should think he would do away this peculiar expression; for it lets out more of himself than can be detected in any other way, in personal intercourse with him. Upon the whole, I have quite a good liking for him; and mean to go to Thomaston to see him.

Salem, [Tuesday], August 22d, 1837.

The journal of a human heart for a single day in ordinary circumstances. The lights and shadows that flit across it; its internal vicissitudes.

A man tries to be happy in love; he cannot sincerely give his heart, and the affair seems all a dream. In domestic life, the same; in politics, a seeming patriot; but still he is sincere, and all seems like a theatre.

An idle man's pleasures and occupations and thoughts during a day spent by the sea-shore: among them, that of sitting on the top of a cliff, and throwing stones at his own shadow, far below.[10]

[Monday], October 16th, 1837.

A person to be in the possession of something as perfect as mortal man has a right to demand; he tries to make it better, and ruins it entirely. ["The Birth-Mark"]

A person to spend all his life and splendid talents in trying to achieve something naturally impossible,—as to make a conquest over Nature. ["The Birth-Mark"; "The Artist of the Beautiful"]

[Wednesday], December 6th, 1837.

Insincerity in a man's own heart must make all his enjoyments, all that concerns him, unreal; so that his whole life must seem like a merely dramatic representation. And this would be the case, even though he were surrounded by truehearted relatives and friends.[11]

A man living a wicked life in one place, and simultaneously a virtuous and religious one in another.[12]

On being transported to strange scenes, we feel as if all were unreal. This is but the perception of the true unreality of earthly things, made evident by the want of congruity between ourselves and them. By and by we become mutually adapted, and the perception is lost.

Our Indian races having reared no monuments, like the Greeks, Romans, and Egyptians, when they have disappeared from the earth, their history will appear a fable, and they misty phantoms.

The influence of a peculiar mind, in close communion with another, to drive the latter to insanity.[13]

[Friday], June 15th, [1838].

The situation of a man in the midst of a crowd, yet as completely in the power of another, life and all, as if they two were in the deepest solitude.

[Wednesday], July 4th, [1838].

A very hot, bright, sunny day; town much thronged; booths on the Common, selling gingerbread, sugar-plums, and confectionery, spruce beer, lemonade. Spirits forbidden, but probably sold stealthily. On the top of one of the booths a monkey, with a tail two or three feet long. He is fastened by a cord, which, getting tangled with the flag over the booth, he takes hold and tries to free it. He is the object of much attention from the crowd, and played with by the boys, who toss up gingerbread to him, while he nibbles and throws it down again. He reciprocates notice, of some kind or other, with all who notice him. There is a sort of gravity about him. A boy pulls his long tail, whereat he gives a slight squeak, and for the future elevates it as much as possible. Looking at the same booth by and by, I find that the poor monkey has been obliged to betake himself to the top of one of the wooden joists that stick up high above. There are boys, going about with molasses candy, almost melted down in the sun. Shows: A mammoth rat; a collection of pirates, murderers, and the like, in wax. Constables in considerable number, parading about with their staves, sometimes conversing with each other, producing an effect by their presence, without having to interfere actively. One or two old salts, rather the worse for liquor: in general the people are very temperate. At evening the effect of things rather more picturesque; some of the booth-keepers knocking down the temporary structures, and putting the materials in wagons to carry away; other booths lighted up, and the lights gleaming through rents in the sail-cloth tops. The customers are rather riotous, calling loudly and whimsically for what they want; a young fellow and a girl coming arm in arm; two girls approaching the booth, and getting into conversation with the folks thereabout. Perchance a knockdown between two half-sober fellows in the crowd: a knock-down without a heavy blow, the receiver being scarcely able to keep his footing at any rate. Shoutings and hallooings, laughter, oaths,—generally a good-natured tumult; and the constables use no severity, but interfere, if at all, in a friendly sort of way. I talk with one about the way in which the day has passed, and he bears testimony to the orderliness of the crowd, but suspects one booth of selling liquor, and relates one scuffle. There is a talkative and witty seller of gingerbread holding forth to the people from his cart, making himself quite a noted character by his readiness of remark and humor, and disposing of all his wares. Late in the evening, during the fire-works, people are consulting how they are to get home,—many having long miles to walk: a father, with wife and children, saying it will be twelve o'clock before they reach home, the children being already tired to death. The moon beautifully dark-bright, not giving so white a light as sometimes. The girls all look beautiful and fairy-like in it, not exactly distinct, nor yet dim. The different characters of female countenances during the day,—mirthful and mischievous, slyly humorous, stupid, looking genteel generally, but when they speak often betraying plebeianism by the tones of their voices. Two girls are very tired,—one a pale, thin, languid-looking creature; the other plump, rosy, rather overburdened with her own little body. Gingerbread figures, in the shape of Jim Crow and other popularities.

∽

In the summer of 1838 Hawthorne journeyed to the Berkshires in western Massachusetts, the area in which "Ethan Brand" would later be set.

∽

[Friday], July 27th, 1838.

Left home Monday, 23d inst. To Boston by stage, and took the afternoon cars for Worcester.... Started for Northampton at ½ past nine in the morning. A respectable sort of man and his son on their way to Niagara—grocers, I believe, and calculating how to perform the tour, subtracting as few days as possible from the shops. Somewhat inexperienced travellers, and comparing everything, advantageously or otherwise, with Boston customs—and considering themselves a long way from home, while yet short of a hundred miles. Two ladies, rather good looking. I rode out-side, nearly all day, and was very sociable with the driver and another outside passenger. Towards night, took up an essence-pedler for a short lift; he was returning home, after having been out on a tour two or three weeks, and nearly exhausted his stock. He was not exclusively an essence-pedler, having a large tin box, which had been filled with dry goods, combs, jewellery &c—now mostly sold out. His essences were Aniseed, Cloves, Red Cedar, Wormwood, together with Opodeldoc, and an oil for the hair. These matters are concocted at Ashfield, and the pedlers sent about with vast quantities. Cologne water is amongst the essence's manufactured, though the bottles have foreign labels. The pedlar was good-natured and communicative, and spoke very frankly about his trade, which he seemed to like better than farming, though his experience of it is yet brief. Spoke of the trials of temper to which pedlars are subjected, but said that it was necessary to be forbearing, because the same road must be travelled again and again. The pedlers find satisfaction for all contumelies, in making good bargains out of their customers. He was a pedler in quite a small way, making but a narrow circuit, and carrying no more than an open basket full of essences; but some go out with wagon loads. He himself contemplated a trip westward, in which case he would send on quantities of his wares ahead to different stations. He seemed to enjoy the intercourse and seeing of the world. He pointed out a rough place of the road, where his stock of essences had formerly been broken by a jolt of the stage. What a waste of sweet smells on the desert air. The essence labels stated the efficacy of the stuffs for various complaints of children and grown people. The driver was an acquaintance of the pedler, and so gave him his ride for nothing, though the pedler pretended to wish to force some silver into his hand; and afterwards he got off to water the horses, while the driver was busied with other matters. This driver was a little, dark ragamuffin, apparently of irascible temper—speaking with great disapprobation of his way-bill not being *timed* accurately, but so as to make it appear as if he were longer upon the road than he was. As he spoke, the blood darkened in his cheek, and his eye looked ominous and angry, as if he were enraged with the person to whom he was speaking; yet he had not real grit, for he had never said a word of his grievances to those concerned. "I mean to tell him of it by-and-bye. I wont bear it more than three or four times more," said he. Left Northampton next morning between 1 & 2 o'clock. Three other passengers, whose faces were not visible for some hours; so we went on through unknown space, saying nothing,—glancing forth sometimes, to see the gleam of the lanterns on wayside objects. How very desolate looks a forest, when seen in this way,—as if, should you venture one step within its wild, tangled, many-stemmed, and dark-shadowed verge, you would inevitably be lost forever. Sometimes we passed a house, or rumbled through a village—stopping, perhaps, to arouse some drowsy postmaster, who appeared at the door in shirt and pantaloons, yawning, received the mail, returned it again, and was yawning when last seen. A few words exchanged among the passengers, as they roused themselves from their half-slumbers, or dreamy slumber like abstraction. Meantime, dawn came on, our faces became partially visible, the morning air grew colder, and finally cloudy day came on. We found ourselves riding through quite a romantic country, with hills, or mountains, on all sides, a stream on one side—bordered by a high precipitous bank, up which would have grown pines, only that, losing their foothold, many of them had slipt downward. The road was not the safest in the world, for often the carriage approached within two or three feet of a precipice; but the driver, a merry fellow, lolled on his box, with his feet protruding horizontally, and rattled on at the rate of ten miles an hour. Breakfast between four and five, newly caught trout, salmon, ham, boiled eggs, and other niceties—truly excellent....

Wednesday, 25th. Left Pittsfield about eight o'clock in the Bennington stage, intending to go to Williamstown. Inside passengers, a new married couple, taking a jaunt.—The lady, with a clear, pale complexion, rather pensive cast of countenance, slender, and a genteel figure; the bridegroom, a shopkeeper in New-York; probably; a young man with a stout black beard, black eyebrows which formed one line across his forehead,—he rather seeming like a fellow who has [...] his bride's pale cheeks and languished looks. They were very loving; and while the stage stopt, I watched them quite entranced in each other, both leaning sideways against the back of the coach, and perusing their mutual comeliness, and apparently making complimentary observations on one another's comeliness. The bride appeared the most absorbed and devoted, referring her whole being to him. The gentleman seemed in a most Paradisaical mood, smiling ineffably upon his bride, and when she spoke, responding to her with a sort of benign expression, of matrimonial sweetness, and as it were compassion for the weaker vessel, mingled with great love and pleasant humor, that was dreadful queer. The driver peeped into the coach once, and said that he had his arm round her waist. He took little freedoms with her—tapping her, if I mistake not, with his cane—love pats; and she seemed to see nothing amiss. It would be pleasant to meet them again next summer, and note the change. They kept eating gingerbread all along the road; and dined heartily, notwithstanding. . . .

Along our road, we passed villages, and often factories, the machinery whizzing, and girls looking out of the windows at the stage, with heads averted from their tasks, but still busy. These factories have two, three, or more, boarding houses near them, two stories high, and of double length—often with bean vines &c running up round the doors; and altogether a domestic look. There are several factories in different parts of North-Adams, along the banks of a stream, a wild highland rivulet, which, however, does vast work of a civilized nature. It is strange to see such a rough and untamed stream as it looks to be, so tamed down to the purposes of man, and making cotton's, woollens &c—sawing boards, marbles, and giving employment to so many men and girls; and there is a sort of picturesqueness in finding these factories, supremely artificial establishments, in the midst of such wild scenery. For now the stream will be flowing through a rude forest, with the trees, erect and dark, as when the Indians fished there; and it brawls, and tumbles, and eddies, over its rock-strewn current. Perhaps there is a precipice hundreds of feet high, beside it, down which, by heavy rains or the melting of snows, great pine-trees have slid or tumbled headlong, and lie at the bottom or half-way down; while their brethren seem to be gazing at their falls from the summit, and anticipating a like fate. And taking a turn in the road, behold these factories and their range of boarding-houses, with the girls looking out of the window as aforesaid. And perhaps the wild scenery is all around the very site of the factory, and mingles its impressions strangely with those opposite ones. These observations were made during a walk yesterday. I bathed in a part of the stream that was out of sight, and where its brawling waters were deep enough to cover me, when I lay at length. Parts of the road, along which I walked, lay on the edge of a precipice, falling down straight towards the stream; and in one place, the passage of heavy loads had sunk the road, so that soon, probably, there will be an avalanche, perhaps carrying a stage-coach or heavy wagon down into the bed of the stream. I met occasional wayfarers, sometimes two women in a wagon, decent brown visaged country matrons, sometimes an apparent doctor, of whom there are seven or thereabouts, in North Adams; for though the vicinity is very healthy, yet they have to ride considerable distances among the mountain-towns; and their practice is very laborious. A nod is always exchanged between strangers meeting on the road. This morning an underwitted old man met me on a walk, and held a pretty long conversation, insisting upon shaking hands (to which I was averse, lest his hand should not be clean) and insisting on his right to do so, as being a "friend of mankind." He was an old gray, bald-headed, wrinkled-visaged figure, decently dressed, with cowhide shoes, a coat on one arm, and an umbrella on the other; and said that he was going to see a widow in the neighborhood. Finding that I was not provided with a wife, he recommended a certain "maid" of forty years, who had 300 acres of land. He spoke of his children, who are proprietors of a circus establishment, and have taken a granddaughter to bring up in their way of life;[14] and he gave me a message to tell them, in case we should meet. While this old man is wandering among the hills, his children are the gaze of multitudes. He told me the place where he was born, directing me to it by pointing to a wreath of mist which lay on the side of a mountain ridge, which he termed the "smoke yonder." Speaking of the widow, he said, "My wife has been dead these seven years," and why should not I enjoy myself a little. His manner was full of quirks and quips and eccentricities, waving his umbrella and gesticulating strangely, with a great deal of action. I suppose, to help his natural foolishness, he had been drinking. We parted, he exhorting me not to forget his message to his sons, and I shouting after him a request to be remembered to the widow. Conceive something tragical to be talked about; and much might be made of this interview, in a wild road among the hills; with Graylock at no great distance, looking sombre and angry by reason of the gray, heavy mist upon his head....

[Sunday], July 29th, [1838].

Remarkable characters:—a disagreeable figure, waning from middle-age, clad in a pair of tow homespun pantaloons and very dirty shirt, barefoot, and with one of his feet maimed by an axe; also, an arm amputated two or three inches below the elbow.[15] His beard of a week's growth, grim and grisly, with a general effect of black;—altogether a filthy and disgusting object. Yet he has the signs of having been a handsome man in his idea; though now such a beastly figure that, probably, no living thing but his great dog could touch him without an effort. Coming to the stoop, where several persons were sitting,—"Good morning, gentlemen!" said this wretch. Nobody answered for a time, till at last one said, "I dont know who you speak to:—not me, I'm sure;"—meaning that he did not claim to be a gentleman. "Why, I thought you all speak at once," replied the figure laughing. So he sat himself down on the lower step of the stoop, and began to talk; and the conversation being turned upon his bare feet, by one of the company, he related the story of his losing his toes by the glancing aside of an axe, and with what grim fortitude he bore it. Thence he made a transition to the loss of his arm; and setting his teeth and drawing in his breath, said that the pain was dreadful; but this, too, he seems to have borne like an Indian; and a person testified to his fortitude by saying that he did not suppose that there was any feeling in him, from observing how he bore it. The man spoke of the pain of cutting the muscles, and the particular agony at one moment, while the bone was being sawed asunder; and there was a strange expression of remembered agony, as he shrugged his half limb, and described the matter. Afterwards, in reply to a question of mine whether he still seemed to feel the hand that had been amputated, he answered that he did, always—and baring the stump, he moved the severed muscles, saying "there is the thumb, there the forefinger &c." Then he talked to me about phrenology, of which he seems a firm believer and skilful practitioner, telling how he had hit upon the true characters of many people. There was a great deal of sense and acuteness in his talk, and something of elevation in his expression; perhaps a studied elevation—and a sort of courtesy in his manner; but his sense had something out-of-the way in it; something wild, and ruined, and desperate, in his talk, though I can hardly say what it was. There was something of the gentleman and man of intellect in his deep degradation; and a pleasure in intellectual pursuits, and an acuteness and trained judgment, which bespoke a mind once strong and cultivated. "My study is man," said he. And looking at me "I do not know your name," said he, "but there is something of the hawk-eye about you too." This man was formerly a lawyer in good practice, but taking to drinking, was reduced to this lowest state. Yet not the lowest; for, after the amputation of his arm, being advised by divers persons to throw himself upon the public for support, he told them that, even if he should lose his other arm, he would still be able to support himself and a waiter. Certainly he is a strong minded and iron-constitutioned man; but, looking at the stump of his arm, he said that the pain of the mind was a thousand times greater than the pain of the body—"That hand could make the pen go fast," said he. Among people in general, he does not seem to have any greater consideration in his ruin, for the sake of his former standing in society. He supports himself by making soap; and on account of the offals used in that business, there is probably rather an evil smell in his domicile. Talking about a dead horse, near his house, he said that he could not bear the scent of it. "I should not think you could smell carrion in that house," said a stage-agent. Whereupon the soap-maker dropped his head, with a bitter snort, as it were, of wounded feeling; but immediately said that he took all in good part. There was an old squire of the village, a lawyer probably, whose demeanor was different—with a distance, yet a kindliness; for he remembered the times when they met on equal terms. "You and I," said the squire, alluding to their respective troubles and sicknesses, "would have died long ago, if we had not had the courage to live." The poor devil kept talking to me long after everybody else had left the stoop, giving vent to much practical philosophy and just observation on the ways of men, mingled with rather more assumption of literature and cultivation, than belonged to the present condition of his mind.... And, at last, having said many times that he must go and shave and dress himself—and as his beard had been at least a week growing, it might have seemed almost a week's work to get rid of it—he rose from the stoop, and went his way, a forlorn and miserable thing in the light of the cheerful summer Sabbath morning. Yet he seems to keep his spirits up, and still preserves himself a man among men, asking nothing from them—nor is it clearly perceptible what right they have to scorn him, though he seems to acquiesce, in a sort, in their doing so. And yet he cannot wholly have lost his self-respect; and doubtless there were persons on the stoop more grovelling than himself.

Another character—a blacksmith of fifty or upwards; a corpulent figure, big in the belly, and enormous in the backsides; yet there is such an appearance of strength and robustness in his frame, that his corpulence appears very proper and necessary to him. A pound of flesh could not be spared from his abundance, any more than from the leanest man; and he walks about briskly, without any panting, or symptom of labor and pain in his motion. He has a round jolly face, always mirthful and humorous, and shrewd—and the air of a man well to do, and well-respected, yet not caring much about the opinions of men, because his independence is sufficient to itself. Nobody would take him for other than a man of some importance in the community, though his summer dress is a tow cloth pair of pantaloons, a shirt not of the cleanest, open at the breast, and the sleeves rolled up at the elbows, and a straw hat. There is not such a vast difference between this costume and that of lawyer Haynes, above-mentioned—yet never was there a greater diversity of appearance than between these two men; and a glance at them, would be sufficient to mark the difference. The blacksmith loves his glass, and comes to the tavern for it, whenever it seems good to him, not calling for it slily and shyly, but marching sturdily to the bar, or calling across the room for it to be prepared. He speaks with great bitterness against the new license law, and vows if it be not repealed by fair means, it shall be by violence, and that he will be as ready to cock his rifle for such a cause as for any other. On this subject his talk is really fierce; but as to all other matters he is good-natured, and good-hearted, fond of joke, and shaking his jolly sides with frequent laughter. His conversation has much strong, unlettered sense, imbued with humor, as everybody's talk is, in New-England. He takes a queer position sometimes—queer for his figure, particularly—straddling across a chair, facing the back, with his arms resting thereon, and his chin on them, for the benefit of conversing closely with some one. When he has spent as much time in the barroom, or under the stoop, as he chooses to spare, he gets up at once and goes off with a brisk, vigorous pace. He owns a mill, and seems to be well to do in the world. I know no man who seems more like a man—more indescribably human—than this sturdy blacksmith.

[Monday], July 30th, [1838].

Remarkable character.—A travelling "Surgeon Dentist,"[16] who has taken a room here in the North-Adams House, and stuck up his advertising bills on a pillar of the piazza, and all about the town. He is a tall, slim young man, six feet two, dressed in a country-made coat of light blue (taken, as he tells me, in exchange for dental operations) black pantaloons, and clumsy cow-hide boots. Self-conceit is very strongly expressed in his air; and a doctor once told him that he owed his life to that quality; for, by keeping himself so stiffly upright, he opens his chest, and counteracts a consumptive tendency. He is not only a dentist—which trade he follows temporarily—but a licensed preacher of the Baptist persuasion; and is now on his way to the West, to seek a place of settlement in his spiritual vocation. Whatever education he possesses, he has acquired by his own exertions, since the age of twenty-one—he being now twenty-four. We talk together very freely; and he has given me an account, among other matters, of all his love-affairs, which are rather curious, as illustrative of the life of a smart young country-fellow as relates to the gentle sex. Nothing can exceed the exquisite self-conceit which characterizes these confidences, and which is expressed inimitably in his face, his upturned nose, and mouth—so as to be truly a caricature; and he seems strangely to find as much food for this passion in having been jilted once or twice, as in his conquests. It is curious to notice his revengeful feeling against the false ones, hidden from himself under the guise of religious interest and desire that they may be cured of their follies....

A little boy, named Joe, who haunts about the bar-room and the stoop, about four years old, in a thin shore jacket, and full-breeched trowsers, and bare feet.[17] The men plague him, and put quids of tobacco in his mouth, under pretence of giving him a fig, and he gets enraged, and utters a peculiar sharp, spiteful cry, and strikes at them with a stick, to their great mirth. He is always in trouble, yet will not keep away. They dispatch him with two or three cents, to buy candy, and nuts and raisins. They set him down in a nitch of the door, and tell him to remain there a day and a half; he sits down very demurely, as if he really meant to fulfil his penance;—but, a moment after, behold there is little Joe, capering across the street to join two or three boys who are playing in a wagon. Take this boy as the germ of a tavern-haunter, a country roué, to spend a wild and brutal youth, ten years of his prime in the States-Prison, and his age in the poor-house.

Wednesday, August 15th, 1838.

To commencement at Williams College—five miles distant. At the tavern, students, with ribbons, pink or blue, fluttering from their button holes—these being the badges of rival societies. A considerable gathering of people, chiefly arriving in wagons or buggies—some barouches—very few chaises. The most characteristic part of the scene, was where the pedlers, gingerbread-sellers &c were collected, a few hundred yards from the meeting-house. There was a pedler there from New-York state, who sold his wares by auction; and I could have stood and listened to him all day long. Sometimes he would put up a heterogeny of articles in a lot—as a paper of pins, a lead pencil and a shaving-box—and knock them all down, perhaps, for ninepence. Bunches of lead pencils, steel pens; pound cakes of shaving soap, gilt finger-rings, bracelets, clasps, and other jewelry, cards of pearl buttons, or steel—"there is some steel about them, gentlemen; for my brother stole 'em, and I bore him out in it," bundles of wooden combs, boxes of loco-focos, suspenders, &c, &c &c—in short everything—dipping his hand down into his boxes, with the promise of a wonderful lot, and producing, perhaps, a bottle of opodeldoc and joining it with a lead pencil—and when he had sold several things of the same kind, pretending huge surprise at finding "just one more"—if the lads lingered saying, "I could not afford to steal them for the price; for the remorse of conscience would be worth more"—all the time, keeping an eye upon those who bought, calling for the pay, making change with silver or bills, and deciding on the goodness of banks,—and saying to the boys who climbed upon his cart—"Fall down, roll down, tumble down—only get down"—and everything in the queer humorous recitative, in which he sold his articles. Sometimes he pretended that a person had bid, either by word or wink, and raised a laugh thus. Never losing his self-possession, nor getting out of humor;—when a man asked whether a bill was good "No!! Do you suppose I'd give you good money." When he delivered an article, "You're the lucky man." Setting off his wares with the most extravagant eulogies. The people bought very freely, and seemed also to enjoy the fun. One little boy bought a shaving box—perhaps meaning to speculate upon it. This character could not possibly be overdrawn; and he was really excellent, with his allusion to what was passing, intermingled, doubtless with a good deal that was studied. He was a man between thirty and forty, with a face expressive of other ability, as well as humor.

A good many people were the better or worse for liquor. There was one fellow—named Randall, I think—a round shouldered, bulky, ill-hung devil, with a pale, sallow skin, black-beard, and a sort of grin upon his face, a species of laugh, yet not so much mirthful, as indicating a queer mental and moral twist. He was very riotous in the crowd, elbowing, thrusting, seizing hold of people;—and at last a ring was formed, and a regular wrestling match commenced between him and a farmer-looking man. Randall brandished his legs about in the most ridiculous style, but proved himself a good wrestler, and finally threw his antagonist. He got up with the same grin upon his features—not a grin of simplicity, but intimating knowingness. When more intensity of expression was required, he could put on the most strangely ludicrous and ugly aspect, suiting his gesture and attitude to it, that can be imagined. I should like to see this fellow when he was perfectly sober.

There were a good many blacks among the crowd. I suppose they used to emigrate across the border, while New-York was a slave state. There were enough of them to form a party, though greatly in the minority; and a squabble arising, some of the blacks were knocked down and otherwise maltreated. I saw one old negro, a genuine specimen of the slave-negro, without any of the foppery of the race in our parts; an old fellow with a bag, I suppose of broken victuals, on his shoulders; and his pockets stuffed out at his hips with the like provender—full of grimaces, and ridiculous antics, laughing laughably, yet without affectation—then talking with a strange kind of pathos, about the whippings he used to get, while he was a slave—a queer thing of mere feeling, with some glimmerings of sense. Then there was another gray old negro, but of a different stamp, politic, sage, cautious, yet with boldness enough, talking about the rights of his race, yet so as not to provoke his audience, discoursing of the advantages of living under laws—and the murders that might ensue, in that very assemblage, if there were no laws. In the midst of this deep wisdom, turning off the anger of a half drunken fellow, by a merry retort, a leap in the air, and a negro's laugh. I was amused—there being a drunken negro, ascending the meeting-house steps, and near him three or four well dressed and decent negro wenches—to see the look of scorn, and shame, and sorrow, and painful sympathy, which one of them assumed at this disgrace of her color. On the whole, I find myself rather more of an abolitionist in feeling than in principle....[18]

A drunken man, plaguing people with his senseless talk and impertinence—impelled to perform eccentricities by a devil in him.

A pale little boy, with a bandaged leg, whom his father brought out of the tavern and put into a barouche; there the boy carefully placed shawls, cushions, &c about his leg to support it; his face expressive of pain and care—not transitory, but settled pain, of long and forcedly patient endurance; and this painful look, perhaps, gave his face more intelligence than it might otherwise have had; though it was naturally a sensible face.

Well dressed ladies in the meeting-house, in silks and cambrics—their sunburnt necks, in contiguity with the delicate fabric of their dress, showing the yeoman's daughter.

Country graduates—rough, brown-featured, schoolmaster looking, half-bumpkin, half-scholar, figures in black ill-cut broadcloth;—their manners quite spoilt by what little of the gentleman there was in them.

The landlord of the tavern, keeping his eye on a man whom he suspected of an intention to bolt.

Friday, August 31st, [1838].

A ride, on Tuesday, to Shelburne Falls,—twenty-two miles, or thereabouts, distant.—Started at about eight o'clock in a wagon with Mr. Leach and Mr. Buck. Our road lay over the Green Mountain; the long ridge of which was made awful by a dark, heavy, threatening cloud, apparently rolled and condensed along the whole summit. As we ascended the zig-zag road, we looked behind, at every opening through the forest, and beheld a wide landscape of mountain-swells, and vallies intermixt, and old Gray-lock, and the whole of Saddle-back. Over this wide scene, there was a general gloom; but there was a continual vicissitude of bright sunshine flitting over it; now resting for a brief space on portions of the heights, now flooding the vallies with green brightness, now marking out distinctly each dwelling, and the hotels, and then two small brick churches of the distant village—denoting its prosperity, while all around seemed under adverse fortunes. But we, who stood so elevated above mortal things, and saw so wide and far, could see the sunshine of prosperity departing from one spot and rolling towards another; so that we could not think it much matter which spot were sunny or gloomy at any one moment.

The top of this Green Mountain is a long ridge, marked on the county map as 2160 ft. above the sea; the summit is occupied by a valley, not very deep, but one or two miles wide, composing the town of Florida. Here there are respectable farms, though it is a rough, and must be a bleak place. The first house, after reaching the summit, is a small, homely tavern, kept by P. Witt. We left our horse in the shed; and entering the little unpainted bar-room, we heard a voice, in a strange outlandish accent, explaining a diorama. It was an old man, with a full, gray-bearded countenance; and Mr. Leach exclaimed "Ah here's the old Dutchman again!" And he answered "Yes, Captain, here's the old Dutchman;"—tho' by the way, he is a German, and travels the country with this diorama, in a wagon; and had recently been at South Adams, and was now returning from Saratoga Springs. We looked through the glass orifices of his machine, while he exhibited a succession of the very worst scratchings and daubings that can be imagined—worn out, too, and full of cracks and wrinkles, besmeared with tobacco smoke, and every otherwise dilapidated. There were none in a later fashion than thirty years since, except some figures that had been cut from tailors' show-bills. There were views of cities and edifices in Europe, and ruins,—and of Napoleon's battles and Nelson's sea-fights; in the midst of which would be seen a gigantic, brown, hairy hand—the Hand of Destiny—pointing at the principal points of the conflict, while the old Dutchman explained. He gave considerable dramatic effect to his descriptions, but his accent and intonation cannot be written. He seemed to take an interest and pride in his exhibition; yet when the utter and ludicrous miserability thereof made us laugh, he joined in the joke very readily. When the last picture had been exhibited, he caused a country boor, who stood gaping beside the machine, to put his head within it, and thrust his tongue out. The head becoming gigantic, a singular effect was produced.

The old Dutchman's exhibition over, a great dog—apparently an elderly dog—suddenly made himself the object of notice, evidently in rivalship of the Dutchman. He had seemed to be a good-natured, quiet kind of dog, offering his head to be patted by those kindly disposed towards him. This great, old dog, suddenly and of his own motion, began to run round after his own not very long tail, with the utmost eagerness; and catching hold of it, he growled furiously at it, and still continued to circle round, growling and snarling, with increasing rage, as if one half of his body were at deadly enmity with the other. Faster and faster went he round and roundabout, growling still fiercer, till at last he ceased in a state of utter exhaustion; but no sooner had his exhibition finished, than he became the same mild, quiet, sensible old dog as before; and no one could have suspected him of such nonsense as getting enraged with his own tail. He was first taught this trick by attaching a bell to the end of his tail; but he now commences entirely of his own accord, and I really believe feels vain at the attention he excites.[19]

It was chill and bleak on the mountain-top, and a fire was burning in the bar-room. The old Dutchman bestowed on everybody the title of Captain—perhaps because such a title has a great chance of suiting an American.

Leaving the tavern, we rode a mile or two further to the eastern brow of the mountain, whence we had a view over the tops of a multitude of heights, into the intersecting vallies of which we were to plunge,—and beyond them the blue and indistinctive scene extended, to the east and north, to the distance of at least sixty miles. Beyond the hills, it looked almost as if the blue ocean might be seen. Monadnock was visible, like a blue cloud against the sky. Descending the mountain, we by and bye got a view of the Deerfield river, which makes a bend in its course from about north and south to about east and west, coming out from one defile among the mountains, and flowing through another.... Often it would seem a wonder how our road was to continue, the mountains rose so abruptly on either side, and stood so direct a wall across our onward course; while, looking behind, it would be an equal mystery how we had got thither, through the huge base of the mountain that seemed to have reared itself erect after our passage. But passing onward, a narrow defile would give us egress into a scene where new mountains would still seem to bar us. Our road was much of it level, but scooped out among mountains. The river was a brawling stream, shallow, and roughened by rocks; now we rode on a level with it; now there was a sheer descent down from the roadside upon it, often unguarded by any kind of a fence, except by the trees that contrived to grow on the headlong interval. Between the mountains there were gorges and defiles, that led the imagination away into new scenes of wildness. I have never ridden through such romantic scenery, where there was such variety and boldness of mountain-shapes as this; and though it was a broad sunny day, the mountains diversified the scene with sunshine and shadow, and glory, and gloom.

[Friday], September 7th, [1838].

Mr. Leach and I took a walk by moonlight, last evening, on the road that leads over the mountain. Remote from houses, far up on the hill side, we found a lime kiln burning near the road side; and approaching it, a watcher started from the ground, where he had been lying at his length. There are several of these lime-kilns in this vicinity; they are built circular with stones, like a round tower, eighteen or twenty feet high; having a hillock heaped around a considerable of their circumference, so that the marble may be brought and thrown in by cart loads at the top. At the bottom there is a door-way large enough to admit a man in a stooping posture. Thus an edifice of great solidity is composed, which will endure for centuries, unless needless pains are taken to tear it down. There is one on the hill side close to the village, where in weeds grow at the bottom, and grass, and shrubs too are rooted in the interstices of the stones; and its low doorway has a dungeonlike aspect; and we look down from the top as into a roofless tower. It apparently has not been used for many years; and the lime, and weather-stained fragments of marble are scattered about.

But in the one we saw last night, a hard wood fire was burning merrily beneath the superincumbent marble—the kiln being heaped full; and shortly after we came, the man (a dark, black-bearded, figure in shirt-sleeves) opened the iron door, through the chinks of which the fire was gleaming, and thrust in huge logs of wood, and stirred the immense coals with a long pole; and showed us the glowing lime-stone,—the lower layer of it. The glow of the fire was powerful, at the distance of several yards from the open door. He talked very sociably with us,—being doubtless glad to have two visitors to vary his solitary night-watch; for it would not do for him to get asleep; since the fire should be refreshed as often as every twenty minutes. We ascended the hillock to the top of the kiln; and the marble was red-hot and burning with a bluish lambent flame, quivering up, sometimes, nearly a yard high, and resembling the flame of anthracite coal—only, the marble being in larger fragments, the flame was higher. The kiln was perhaps six or eight feet across. Four hundred bushels of marble were then in a state of combustion. The expense of converting this quantity into lime is about fifty dollars; and it sells for 25cts. per bushel at the kiln. We talked with the man about whether he would run across the top of the intensely burning kiln for a thousand dollars, barefooted; and he said he would for ten;—he said that the lime had been burning 48 hours, and would be finished in 36 more, and cooled sufficiently to handle in 12 more. He liked the business of watching it better by night than day; because the days were often hot; but such a mild and beautiful night as the last was just right. [...] Here a poet might make verses, with moonlight in them—and a gleam of fierce firelight flickering through them. It is a shame to use this brilliantly white, almost transparent marble, in this way. A man said of it, the other day, that into some pieces of it, when polished, one could see a considerable distance; and instanced a certain gravestone.

Mr. Leach told me how a girl, to whom he was once paying attention, with some idea of marrying her, made a confession of having forfeited her chastity. He had heard rumors of her having been indiscreet, with reference to a man who was formerly attentive to her—but had no idea of anything more than a merely pardonable indiscretion, in having trusted herself in long and solitary walks with this man. He began to talk with her on this subject, intending gently to reprehend her; but she became greatly agitated, and fell a weeping bitterly—her thoughts flying immediately to her guilt, and probably thinking that he was aware or suspicious of the full extent of it. She told so much, or betrayed so much, that he besought her to say no more. "That was the only time, Mr. Leach," sobbed she, "that I ever strayed from the path of virtue." Much might be made of such a scene—the lover's astoundment, at discovering so much more than he expected. Mr. Leach spoke to me as if one deviation from chastity might not be an altogether insuperable objection to making a girl his wife!!

[Wednesday], October 24th, [1838].

View from a chamber of the Tremont of the brick edifice opposite, on the other side of Beacon Street.[20] At one of the lower windows, a woman at work; at one above, a lady hemming a ruff or some such lady-like thing. She is pretty, young, and married; for a little boy comes to her knees, and she parts his hair, and caresses him in a motherly way. A note on colored paper is brought her; and she reads it, and puts it in her bosom. At another window, at some depth within the apartment, a gentleman in a dressing-gown, reading, and rocking in an easy-chair, &c, &c, &c. A rainy day, and people passing with umbrellas disconsolately between the spectator and these various scenes of indoor occupation and comfort. With this sketch might be mingled and worked up some story that was going on within the chamber where the spectator was situated.

Character of a man who, in himself and his external circumstances, shall be equally and totally false: his fortune resting on baseless credit,—his patriotism assumed,—his domestic affections, his honor and honesty, all a sham. His own misery in the midst of it,—it making the whole universe, heaven and earth alike, an unsubstantial mockery to him.

Dr. Johnson's penance in Uttoxeter Market. A man who does penance in what might appear to lookers-on the most glorious and triumphal circumstance of his life. Each circumstance of the career of an apparently successful man to be a penance and torture to him on account of some fundamental error in early life.[21]

[Friday], January 4th, 1839.

The strange sensation of a person who feels himself an object of deep interest, and close observation, and various construction of all his actions, by another person.[22]

The semblance of a human face to be formed on the side of a mountain, or in the fracture of a small stone, by a *lusus naturae*. The face is an object of curiosity for years or centuries, and by and by a boy is born, whose features gradually assume the aspect of that portrait. At some critical juncture, the resemblance is found to be perfect. A prophecy may be connected. ["The Great Stone Face"]

A person to be the death of his beloved in trying to raise her to more than mortal perfection; yet this should be a comfort to him for having aimed so highly and holily. ["The Birth-Mark"]

1840.

To make a story out of a scarecrow, giving it odd attributes. From different points of view, it should appear to change,—now an old man, now an old woman,—a gunner, a farmer, or the Old Nick. ["Feathertop"]

To represent a man as spending life and the intensest labor in the accomplishment of some mechanical trifle,—as in making a miniature coach to be drawn by fleas, or a dinner-service to be put into a cherry-stone. ["The Artist of the Beautiful"]

A bonfire to be made of the gallows and of all symbols of evil. ["Earth's Holocaust"]

~

The following descriptive entries were written during Hawthorne's residence at Brook Farm.

~

[Sunday], September 26th, 1841.

A walk in the forenoon, along the edge of the meadow towards Cow Island.[23] . . .

Within the verge of the meadow, mostly near the firm shore of pasture ground, I found several grape vines, hung with abundance of large purple grapes.[24] The vines had caught hold of maples and alders, and climbed to the top, curling round about and interwreathing their twisted folds in so intimate a manner, that it was not easy to tell the parasite from the supporting tree or shrub. Sometimes the same vine had enveloped several shrubs, and caused a strange tangled confusion, converting all these poor plants to the purposes of its own support, and hindering them growing to their own benefit and convenience. The broad vine-leaves, some of them yellow or yellowish-tinged, were seen apparently growing on the same stems with the silver maple leaves, and those of the other shrubs, thus married against their will by this conjugal twine; and the purple clusters of grapes hung down from above and in the midst, so that a man might gather grapes, if not of thorns, yet of as alien bushes.[25] One vine had ascended almost to the tip-top of a large white pine tree, spreading its leaves and hanging its purple clusters among all its boughs—still climbing and clambering, as if it would not be content till it crowned the very summit of the tree with a wreath of its own foliage and a cluster of grapes. I mounted high into the tree, and ate grapes there, while the vine wreathed still higher into the depths of the tree, above my head. The grapes were sour, being not yet fully ripe; some of them, however, were sweet and pleasant. The vine embraces the trees like a serpent.

Saturday, October 9th, [1841].

Still dismal weather. Our household, being composed in great measure of children and young people, is generally a cheerful one enough, even in gloomy weather. For a week past, we have been especially gladdened with a little sempstress from Boston, about seventeen years old, but of such a petite figure that, at first view, one would take her to be hardly in her teens.[26] She is very vivacious and smart, laughing, singing, and talking, all the time—talking sensibly, but still taking the view of matters that a city girl naturally would. If she were larger than she is, and of less pleasing aspect, I think she might be intolerable; but being so small, and with a white skin, healthy as a wild flower, she is really very agreeable; and to look at her face is like being shone upon by a ray of the sun. She never walks, but bounds and dances along; and this motion, in her small person, does not give the idea of violence. It is like a bird, hopping from twig to twig, and chirping merrily all the time. Sometimes she is a little vulgar; but even that works well enough into her character, and accords with it. On continued observation and acquaintance, you discover that she is not a little girl, but really a little woman, with all the prerogatives and liabilities of a woman. This gives a new aspect to her character; while her girlish impression still continues, and is strangely combined with the sense that this frolicksome little maiden has the material for that sober character, a wife. She romps with the boys, runs races with them in the yard, and up and down the stairs, and is heard scolding laughingly at their rough play. She asks William Allen to put her "on top of that horse;" whereupon he puts his large brown hands about her waist, and, swinging her to-and-fro, places her on horseback. By the bye, William threatened to rivet two horse shoes round her neck, for having clambered, with the other girls and boys, upon a load of hay; whereby the said load lost its balance, and slided off the cart. She strings the seed-berries of roses together, making a scarlet necklace of them, which she wears about her neck. She gathers everlasting flowers, to wear in her hair or bonnet, arranging them with the skill of a dress-maker. In the evening, she sits singing by the hour together, with the musical part of the establishment—often breaking into laughter, whereto she is incited by the tricks of the boys. The last thing you hear of her, she is tripping up stairs, to bed, talking lightsomely or singing; and you meet her in the morning, the very image of lightsome morn itself, smiling briskly at you, so that one takes her for a promise of cheerfulness through the day. Be it said, among all the rest, there is a perfect maiden modesty in her deportment; though

I doubt whether the boys, in their rompings with her, do not feel that she has past out of her childhood.

This lightsome little maid has left us this morning; and the last thing I saw of her was her vivacious face, peeping through the curtain of the carryall, and nodding a brisk farewell to the family, who were shouting their adieus at the door. With her other merits, she is an excellent daughter, and, I believe, supports her mother by the labor of her hands. It would be difficult to conceive, beforehand, how much can be added to the enjoyment of a household by mere sunniness of temper and smartness of disposition; for her intellect is very ordinary, and she never says anything worth hearing, or even laughing at, in itself. But she herself is an expression, well worth studying.

Monday, October 18th, [1841].

There has been a succession of Autumnal days, cold and bright in the forenoon, and gray, sullen, and chill, towards night. The woods have now assumed a soberer tint than they wore at my last date. Many of the shrubs, which looked brightest a little while ago, are now wholly bare of leaves. The oaks have mostly a russet brown tint; although some of them are still green, as are likewise other scattered trees in the woods. The bright yellow and the rich scarlet are no more to be seen. None of the trees, scarcely, will now bear a close examination; for then they look ragged, wilted, and of faded, frost-bitten hue; but at a distance, and in the mass, and enlivened by sunshine, the woods have still somewhat of the variegated splendor which distinguished them a week ago. It is wonderful what a difference the sunshine makes; it is like varnish, bringing out the hidden veins in a piece of rich wood. In the cold gray atmosphere, such as most of our afternoons are now, the landscape lies dark-brown and unvaried, in a much deeper shadow than if it were clothed in green. But perchance a gleam of sunshine falls on a certain spot of distant shrubbery or woodland; and we see it brighten forth, with varied hues, standing forth prominently from the dark mass around it. The sunshine gradually spreads over the whole landscape; and the whole sombre mass is changed to a variegated picture, the light bringing out many shades of color, and converting its gloom to an almost laughing cheerfulness. At such times, I almost doubt whether the foliage has lost any of its brilliancy; but the gray clouds intercept the sunshine again; and lo! old Autumn, clad in his cloak of russet brown.

Beautiful now, while the general landscape lies in shadow, looks the summit of a distant hill (say a mile off) with the sunshine brightening the trees that cover it. It is noticeable that the outlines of hills, and the whole bulk and mass of them, at the distance of several miles, become stronger, denser, and more substantial, in this autumn atmosphere, and in these autumnal tints, than they were in summer. Then they used to look blue, misty, and dim; now they show their great hump backs more evidently, as if they had drawn nearer to us.

Friday, October 22d, [1841].

A continual succession of unpleasant Novembry days; and Autumn has made rapid progress in the work of decay....

Yet, dreary as the woods are in a bleak, sullen day, there is a very peculiar sense of warmth, and a sort of richness of effect, in the sheltered spots, on the slope of a bank, where bright sunshine falls, and where the brown oaken foliage is gladdened by it, and where green grass is seen among withered leaves. There is then a feeling of shelter and comfort, and consequently a heart-warmth, which cannot be experienced in summer.

[Wednesday], October 27th, [1841].

To symbolize moral or spiritual disease by disease of the body;—thus, when a person committed any sin, it might cause a sore to appear on the body;—this to be wrought out. ["Lady Eleanore's Mantle"][27]

[Sunday], January 23rd, [1842].

An old man in the rail-road station-house at Salem, selling nuts, gingerbread &c. It is his permanent place of business, which I have seen him occupy for many months past. He is clad in old frock coat, or surtout, of Scotch snuff-color, and gray pantaloons—both conveying the impression of being flimsy with much wear. His face, thin, withered, furrowed, looks frost-bitten;—it seems as if he was in a very cold atmosphere, externally, and had not inward vital warmth enough to keep himself comfortable. A patient, long-suffering, quiet, hopeless, shivering, aspect; yet not as a man desperate, but only without hope. His whole life, probably, offers no spots of brightness; and so he takes his present poverty and discomfort as a matter of course;—he thinks the definition of life is to be poor, cold, and uncomfortable.

Before the old man are two baskets, capable of containing his whole stock in trade—baskets to be carried on the arm; but which, throughout the day, are placed upon the floor; and across them is laid a board, on which is arranged a plate of cakes and gingerbread, some apples, and a box containing red and white candy, and gibraltar rocks, neatly done up in white paper. There is also a half peck measure of cracked walnuts, and several little tin half-pint and gill-measures, already filled with these nuts, ready for purchasers.

The old man sits on a settee, at one end of the station-room;—he has a nervous aspect; and though very far from having any violent motion, and though the impression he makes is as if he were sitting quite still, yet you find, on observation, that he is always making some little movement. He looks anxiously at his plate of cakes or heaps of apples, and arranges them somewhat differently, as if a great deal depended on their being placed exactly so and so. Then he looks out of the window a moment; then shivers, quietly, and folds his arms, as if to draw himself closer within himself, and thus keep a little warmth in his heart. Then he turns round again to his display of cakes, apples, and candy (all this time keeping his seat; for he very seldom rises) and finds some new arrangement to make. At times, by an indescribable, not striking, but perfectly quiet movement to his features, the expression of frost bitten, patient despondency becomes very touching. It seems if, just at that moment, he himself had some suspicion that he is a very miserable old fellow;—but not very miserable neither; for he is too much subdued to feel anything acutely.

Some of the passengers awaiting the departure of the cars approach, and look curiously at his stock in trade. Others, striding to-and-fro across the room, glance into his baskets at every turn; and the old man evidently feels as if there is a possibility of their purchasing; although innumerable disappointments forbid him to be too sanguine. He speaks to none—makes no sign of offering his merchantables to purchasers; yet he is not deterred by any pride; for I have seen him do it formerly; but he has probably learned that his custom would not be increased by it. Whenever any approaches, with an evident design of purchasing, the old man looks up with a patient eye, ready to make change; but if he be disappointed, and the customer turns away, still he does not seem to be cast down, or made more despondent than before. He shivers, perhaps, folds his lean arms round his lean figure, and waits as patiently as before. Sometimes a boy comes hastily up, places a cent or two on the board, and takes up a cake or a stick of candy—without any word passing as to the price; that being perfectly known to both parties. The old man never speaks when it can be avoided; not from any sullenness, but from want of energy, from his subdued tone of mind—and because there is none of the cheerfulness and briskness in him, that make people talkers. Sometimes he is greeted by apparently an old acquaintance, a man, perhaps, well to do in the world, who speaks cheerily and with a smile;—and then, with the thought, I suppose, that he is doing a deed of charity to the old man, the acquaintance buys some apples and cakes. The old man presumes not on any past acquaintance; he receives all remarks deferentially and quietly, makes little answer, and shrinks within himself again. After making a purchase, he always takes care to produce another cake, apple, or stick of candy from his basket, to supply the place of that which has been taken from the board; and probably it requires two or three different attempts, before the articles can be re-arranged to his satisfaction. After selling a measure of nuts, he refills the measure. If he have received a piece of silver, he examines it closely after the purchaser has retired, tries to bend it with his fingers, and at length puts it into his waistcoat pocket, with seemingly a gentle sigh. This sigh, not physically perceptible, and not expressive of any great grief, seems to conclude most of his movements. It is the symbol of the chillness and torpid melancholy of his old age, making itself sensible when his repose is slightly disturbed.

I do not think that the old man's half-frozen aspect is so much owing to real physical cold, as because his inward nature is half-frozen by the chillness of his circumstances. Close by a great blazing fire, he would not look comfortable. His atmosphere morally is an extremely chill one. He is not a specimen of the "needy man, who has seen better days"; for, though he doubtless has seen better days in his youth, yet they probably were not so bright as to make his present depressed circumstances anything out of course. He was a mechanic, I suppose, or small trader, and rubbed on narrowly, all his youth and manhood, between passably to do and poverty. A meek, subdued being, he had not the strength to win any more than a bare living from the world,—probably he has not felt himself entitled to more. He considers it not unnatural that he should be selling apples and cakes in his old age; and therefore does not quarrel with fate or Providence, on that account. Perhaps, indeed, he has lost a son, to whom his feeble nature had looked for support—in that case, there be an acuter sense of happiness. But his quietness is what strikes me.

Another pedler of cakes and candy frequents the station house, of a very different description. It is a boy, about ten years old—a very smart and well-dressed boy. He does not sit down, like the old man, but moves briskly about, asking in a pert voice, yet with somewhat of a well-bred tone and pronunciation, "Any cake, Sir?—any candy?" The contrast produces an unfavorable feeling (at least in my mind) to-wards the pert, brisk boy; and so I am a customer of the old man.

After all this description, I have not expressed the aspect and character of the old man, in anything like a satisfactory manner. It requires a very delicate pencil to depict a portrait which has so much of negative in it—where every touch must be kept down, or else you destroy the subdued tone, which is most essential to the character. I will only add, that he is rather a small man, with gray hair, and gray stubble beard. There is nothing venerable about him, but he is altogether decent and respectable. You pity him without scruple. Now imagine this old man, so subdued, so hopeless, so without a stake in the world—and yet not positively miserable—this old man, wearing out dismal day after dismal day, over his little stock of apples and candy—imagine him sitting in the Station house, in the very midst of the bustle and movement of the world, where all our go-ahead stream of populations rushes and roars along beside him. Travellers from afar, traders going up to Boston business, young men on a jaunt—all sorts of various people sweep by him; and there he remains, nervous, chill, patient.

I should like, if I could, to follow him home, and see his domestic life—all that I know of him, thus far, being merely his outward image, as shown to the world. ["The Old Apple Dealer"]

To trace out the influence of a frightful and disgraceful crime, in debasing and destroying a character naturally high and noble—the guilty person being alone conscious of the crime.[28]

A man, virtuous in his general conduct, but committing habitually some monstrous crime—as murder—and doing this without the sense of guilt, but with a peaceful conscience. Habit, probably, has reconciled him to it; but something (for instance, discovery) occurs to make him sensible of his enormity. His horrors then.

A man to swallow a small snake—and it to be a symbol of a cherished sin. ["Egotism; or The Bosom Serpent"]

[Wednesday], June 1st, 1842.

A physician for the cure of moral diseases.

Men's accidents are God's purposes. S.A.H.[29]

A moral philosopher to buy a slave, or otherwise get possession of a human being, and to use him for the sake of experiment, by trying the operation of a certain vice on him.[30]

When the reformation of the world is complete, a fire shall be made of the gallows; and the Hangman shall come and sit down by it, in solitude and despair. To him shall come the Last Thief, the Last Prostitute, the Last Drunkard, and other representatives of past crime and vice; and they shall hold a dismal merry-making, quaffing the contents of the Drunkard's last Brandy Bottle. ["Earth's Holocaust"]

The human Heart to be allegorized as a cavern; at the entrance there is sunshine, and flowers growing about it. You step within, but a short distance, and begin to find yourself surrounded with a terrible gloom, and monsters of divers kinds; it seems like Hell itself. You are bewildered, and wander long without hope. At last a light strikes upon you. You press towards it yon, and find yourself in a region that seems, in some sort, to reproduce the flowers and sunny beauty of the entrance, but all perfect. These are the depths of the heart, or of human nature, bright and peaceful; the gloom and terror may lie deep; but deeper still is this eternal beauty.

The greater picturesqueness and reality of back-yards, and everything appertaining to the rear of a house; as compared with the front, which is fitted up for the public eye. There is much to be learnt, always, by getting a glimpse at rears. When the direction of a road has been altered, so as to pass the rear of farm-houses, instead of the front, a very noticeable aspect is presented.[31]

The print in blood of a naked foot to be traced through the street of a town.[32]

To write a dream, which shall resemble the real course of a dream, with all its inconsistency, its strange transformations, which are all taken as a matter of course, its eccentricities and aimlessness—with nevertheless a leading idea running through the whole. Up to this old age of the world, no such thing ever has been written.

Pearl—the English of Margaret—a pretty name for a girl in a story.[33]

Great expectation to be entertained in the allegorical Grub-street of the appearance of the great American writer. Or a search warrant to be sent thither to catch a poet. On the former supposition, he shall be discovered under some most unlikely form; or shall be supposed to have lived and died unrecognized. ["A Select Party"]

In moods of heavy despondency, one feels as if it would be delightful to sink down in some quiet spot, and lie there forever, letting the soil gradually accumulate and form a little hillock over us, and the grass and perhaps flowers gather over it. At such times, death is too much of an event to be wished for;—we have not spirits to encounter it; but choose to pass out of existence in this sluggish way.[34]

Hawthorne was married to Sophia Peabody on July 9, 1842. The couple immediately took up residence at the Old Manse in Concord, Massachusetts, a parsonage built by Emerson's grandfather just beside the Concord River bridge that would be the scene of the Revolutionary War battle of 1775. Kept jointly with Sophia—her contribution was published separately in 1996—the Manse notebook primarily covers the Hawthornes' blissful first year in Concord (1842–43). Daughter Una would be born in 1844, son Julian in 1846.

Friday, August 5th, 1842.

A rainy day—a rainy day—and I do verily believe there is no sunshine in this world, except what beams from my wife's eyes. At present, she has laid her strict command on me to take pen in hand; and, to ensure my obedience has banished me to the little ten-foot-square apartment, misnamed my study; but she must not be surprised, if the dismalness of the day, and the dulness of my solitude, should be the prominent characteristics of what I write. And what is there to write about at all? Happiness has no succession of events; because it is a part of eternity; and we have been living in eternity, ever since we came to this old Manse. Like Enoch, we seem to have been translated to the other state of being, without having passed through death.[35] Our spirits must have flitted away, unconsciously, in the deep and quiet rapture of some long embrace; and we can only perceive that we have cast off our mortal part, by the more real and earnest life of our spirits. Externally, our Paradise has very much the aspect of a pleasant old domicile, on earth. The antique house (for it looks antique, though it was created by Providence expressly for our use, and at the precise time when we wanted it) stands behind a noble avenue of Balm of Gilead trees; and when we chance to observe a passing traveller, through the sunshine and the shadow of this long avenue, his figure appears too dim and remote to disturb our sense of blissful seclusion. Few, indeed, are the mortals who venture within our sacred precincts. George Prescott—who has not yet grown earthly enough, I suppose, to be debarred from occasional visits to Paradise—comes daily to bring three pints of milk, from some ambrosial cow;—occasionally, also, he makes an offering of mortal flowers, at the shrine of a certain angelic personage. Mr. Emerson comes sometimes, and has been so far favored as to be feasted (with a gnome, yclept Ellery Channing) on our nectar and ambrosia. Mr. Thorow has twice listened to the music of the spheres, which, for our private convenience, we have packed into a musical box. Elizabeth Hoar (who is much more at home among spirits than among fleshly bodies) came hither a few times, merely to welcome us to the ethereal world; but latterly she has vanished into some other region of infinite space.[36] One rash mortal, on the second Sunday after our arrival, obtruded himself upon us in a gig. There have since been three or four callers, who preposterously think that the courtesies of the lower world are to be responded to by people whose home is in Paradise. [...] I must not forget to mention that the butcher comes twice or thrice a week; and we have so far improved upon the custom of Adam and Eve, that we generally furnish forth our feasts with a portion of some delicate calf or lamb, whose unspotted innocence entitles them to the happiness of becoming our sustenance. Would that my wife would permit me to record the ethereal dainties, that kind Heaven provided for us, on the first day of our arrival! Never, surely, was such food heard of on earth—at least, not by me. Well; the above mentioned persons are nearly all that have intruded into the hallowed shade of our avenue;—except, indeed, a certain sinner who came to bargain for the grass in our orchard, and another who came with a new cistern; for it is one of the drawbacks upon our Paradise, that it contains no water fit either to drink or to bathe in; so that the showers of Heaven have become, in good truth, a godsend. I wonder why Providence does not cause a clear, cold fountain to bubble up at our doorstep;—methinks it would not be unreasonable to pray for such a favor. At present, we are under the ridiculous necessity of sending to the outer world for water. Only imagine Adam trudging out of Paradise with a bucket in each hand, to get water to drink, or for Eve to bathe in! Intolerable! I shall absolutely think myself wronged, unless I find the aforesaid fountain bubbling at our doorstep, the next time I look out. In other respects, Providence has treated us pretty tolerably well; but here I shall expect something further to be done. Also, in the way of future favors, a kitten would be very acceptable. Animals (except, perhaps, a pig) seem never out of place, even in the most paradisaical spheres. And, by the bye, a young colt comes up our avenue, now and then, to crop the seldom trodden herbage; and so do a company of cows, whose sweet breath well repays us for the food which they obtain. There are likewise a few hens, whose quiet cluck is heard pleasantly about the house. A black dog sometimes stands at the farther extremity of the avenue, and looks wistfully towards the house; but when I whistle to him, he puts his tail between his legs, and trots away. Foolish dog!—if he had more faith, he should have bones enough.

Saturday, August 6th, [1842].

Still a dull day, threatening rain, yet without energy of character enough to rain outright. However, yesterday there were showers enough to fill our washing-tubs, which we eagerly set forth to receive the beneficent downpouring. As to the new cistern, it seems to be bewitched; for while the spout pours into it like a cataract, it still remains almost empty. I wonder where Mr. Hosmer got it;—perhaps from Tantalus, under the eaves of whose palace it must formerly have stood; for, like his drinking-cup in Hades, it has the property of filling itself forever, and never being full.

After breakfast, I took my fishing-rod, and went down through our orchard to the river-side; but as three or four boys were already in possession of the best spots along the shore, I did not fish. This river of ours is the most sluggish stream that I ever was acquainted with. I had spent three weeks by its side, and swam across it every day, before I could determine which way its current ran; and then I was compelled to decide the question by the testimony of others—not by my own observation. Owing to this torpor of the stream, it has nowhere a bright pebbly shore, nor is there so much as a narrow strip of glistening sand, in any part of its course; but it slumbers along between broad meadows, or kisses the tangled grass of mowing fields and pastures, or bathes the overhanging boughs of elder bushes, and other water-loving plants. Flags and rushes grow along its shallow margin; the yellow water lily spreads its broad flat leaves upon its surface; and the fragrant white pond-lily occurs in many favored spots, generally selecting a situation just so far from the river's brink, that it cannot be grasped, except at the hazard of plunging in. But thanks be to this beautiful flower for growing at any rate. It is a marvel whence it derives its loveliness and perfume, sprouting as it does from the black mud over which the river sleeps, and from which, likewise, the yellow lily draws its unclean life and noisome perfume. So it is with many people in this world;—the same soil and circumstances may produce the good and beautiful, and the wicked and ugly;—some have the faculty of assimilating to themselves only what is evil, and so they become as noisome as the yellow water-lily. A few assimilate none but good influences; and their emblem is the spotless and fragrant pond-lily, whose very breath is a blessing to all the region roundabout. I possess such a human and heavenly lily, and wear it in my bosom. Heaven grant that I myself may not be symbolized by its yellow companion. Among the productions of the river's margin, I must not forget the pickerel-weed, which grows just on the edge of the water, and shoots up a long stalk, crowned with a blue spire, from among large green leaves. Both the flower and the leaves look well in a vase with pond-lilies, and relieve the unvaried whiteness of the latter; and being all alike children of the waters, they are perfectly in keeping with one another. My wife should have the credit of introducing this improvement into the arrangement of pond-lilies. She has, in perfection, the love and taste for flowers, without which a woman is a monster—and which it would be well for men to possess, if they can.

I bathe once, and often twice a day, in our river; but one dip into the salt-sea would be worth more than a whole week's soaking in such a lifeless tide. I have read of a river somewhere (whether it be in classic regions, or among our western Indians, I know not) which seemed to dissolve and steal away the vigor of those who bathed in it. Perhaps our stream will be found to have this property. Its water, however, is pleasant in its immediate effect, being as soft as milk, and always warmer than the air. Its hue has a slight tinge of gold; and my limbs, when I behold them through its medium, look tawny. I am not aware that the inhabitants of Concord resemble their native river in any of their moral characteristics; their forefathers, certainly, seem to have had the energy and impetus of a mountain torrent, rather than the torpor of this listless stream—as was proved by the blood with which they stained their River of Peace. There are said to be plenty of fish in it; but my most important captures have been a mud-turtle and an enormous eel. The former made his escape to his native element—the latter we ate; and truly he had the taste of the whole river in his flesh, with a very prominent flavor of mud. On the whole, Concord river is no great favorite of mine; but I am glad to have any river at all so near at hand, being just at the bottom of our orchard. Neither is it without a degree and kind of picturesqueness, both in its nearness and in the distance, when a blue gleam from its surface, among the green meadows and woods, seems like an open eye in earth's countenance. Pleasant it is, too, to behold a little flat-bottomed skiff gliding along its quiet bosom, which yields lazily to the stroke of the paddle, and allows the boat to go against its current almost as freely as with it. Pleasant too, to watch an angler, as he strays along the margin, sometimes sheltering himself behind a tuft of bushes, and trailing his line along the water, in hopes to catch a pickerel. But, taking the river for all in all, I can find nothing more fit to compare it with, than one of the half torpid earthworms, which I dig up for the purpose of bait. The worm is sluggish, and so is the river—the river is muddy, and so is the worm—you hardly know whether either of them is alive or dead; but still, in the course of time, they both manage to creep away. The best aspect of our river is when there is a north-west breeze curling its surface, in a bright sunshiny day; it then assumes a vivacity not its own. Moonlight, also, gives it beauty—as it does to all scenery of earth or water.

Sunday, August 7th, [1842].

At sunset, last evening, I ascended the hill-top opposite our house; and looking downward at a long extent of the river, it struck me that I had done it some injustice in my remarks. Perhaps, like other gentle and quiet characters, it will be better appreciated, the longer I am acquainted with it. Certainly, as I beheld it then, it was one of the loveliest features in a scene of great rural beauty. It was visible through a course of two or three miles, sweeping in a semi-circle round the hill on which I stood, and being the central line of a broad vale, on either side. At a distance, it looked like a strip of sky set into the earth, which it so etherealized and idealized that it seemed akin to the upper regions. Nearer the base of the hill, I could discern the shadows of every tree and rock, imaged with a distinctness that made them even more charming than the reality; because, knowing them to be unsubstantial, they assumed the ideality which the soul always craves, in the contemplation of earthly beauty. All the sky, too, and the rich clouds of sunset, were reflected in the peaceful bosom of the river; and surely, if its bosom can give such an adequate reflection of Heaven, it cannot be so gross and impure as I described it yesterday. Or, if so, it shall be a symbol to me, that even a human breast which may appear least spiritual in some aspects, may still have the capability of reflecting an infinite Heaven in its depths, and therefore of enjoying it. It is a comfortable thought, that the smallest and most turbid mud-puddle can contain its own picture of Heaven. Let us remember this, when we feel inclined to deny all spiritual life to some people, in whom, nevertheless, our Father may perhaps see the image of his face. This dull river has a deep religion of its own; so, let us trust, has the dullest human soul, perhaps unconsciously.

The scenery of Concord, as I beheld it from the summit of the hill, has no very marked characteristics, but has a great deal of quiet beauty, in keeping with the river. There are broad and peaceful meadows, which, I think, are among the most satisfying objects in natural scenery; the heart reposes on them, with a feeling that few things else can give, because almost all other objects are abrupt and clearly defined; but a meadow stretches out like a small infinity, yet with a secure homeliness, which we do not find either in an expanse of water or of air. The hills, which border these meadows, are broad swells of land, or long and gradual ridges, some of them densely crowned with wood. The white village of Concord, at a distance on the left, appears to be embosomed among wooded hills. The verdure of the country is much more perfect than is usual at this season of the year, when the autumnal hue has generally made considerable progress over trees and grass. Last evening, after the copious showers of the preceding two days, it was worthy of early June—or, indeed, of a world just created. Had my wife been with me, I should have had a far deeper sense of beauty; for I should have looked through the medium of her spirit.

Along the horizon, there were masses of those deep clouds in which the fancy may see images of all things that ever existed or were dreamed of. Over our old manse (of which I could catch but a glimpse, among its embowering trees) appeared the immensely gigantic figure of a hound, crouching down, with head erect, as if keeping watchful guard, while the master of the mansion was away. May the powers of the upper regions always keep guard over my heart's treasure, whether I am at her side, or afar off! How sweet it was to draw near my own home, after having lived so long homeless in the world; for no man can know what home is, until, as he approaches it, he feels that a wife will meet him at the threshold. With thoughts like these, I descended the hill, and clambered over the stone-wall, and crossed the road, and passed up our avenue; while the quaint old house put on an aspect of welcome.

Monday, August 8th, [1842].

I wish I could give a description of our house; for it really has a character of its own—which is more than can be said of most edifices in these days. It is two stories high, with a third story of attic chambers in the gamble-roof. When I first visited the house, early in June, it looked pretty much as it did during the old clergyman's life-time, showing all the dust and disarray that might be supposed to have gathered about him, in the course of sixty years of occupancy. The rooms, I believe, had never been painted; at all events, the walls and panels, as well as the huge cross-beams, had a venerable and most dismal tinge of brown. The furniture consisted of high-backed, short-legged, rheumatic chairs, small old tables, bedsteads with lofty posts, stately chests of drawers, looking-glasses in antique black frames—all which were probably fashionable in the days of Dr. Ripley's predecessor. It required some energy of imagination to conceive the idea of transforming this musty edifice, where the good old minister had been writing sleepy sermons for more than half a century, into a comfortable modern residence. However, it has been successfully accomplished. The old Doctor's sleeping apartment (which was the front room on the ground floor) we have converted into a parlor; and by the aid of cheerful paint and paper, a gladsome carpet, pictures and engravings, new furniture, *bijouterie,* and a daily supply of flowers, it has become one of the prettiest and pleasantest rooms in the whole world. The shade of our departed host will never haunt it; for its aspect has been changed as completely as the scenery of a theatre. Probably the ghost gave one peep into it, uttered a groan, and vanished forever. The opposite front-room has been metamorphosed into a store-room. Through the house, both in the first and second story, runs a spacious hall or entry, occupying more space than is ever devoted to such a purpose, in modern times. This feature contributes to give the whole house an airy, roomy, and convenient appearance; we can breathe the freer for the sake of this broad passage-way. The front door of the hall looks up the stately avenue, which I have already mentioned; and the opposite door opens into the orchard, through which a path descends to the river-side. In the second story, we have fitted up three rooms, one being our own bed chamber, which I leave my wife to describe, as her taste has adorned it. The opposite room is reserved as a guest-chamber, and contains the most presentable of the old Doctor's ante-revolutionary furniture. After all, the moderns have invented nothing better, as chamber furniture, than those chests of drawers, which stand on four long, slender legs, and rear an absolute tower of mahogany to the cieling, the whole terminating in a fantastically carved summit. Such a venerable structure adorns our guest-chamber. In the rear of the house is the little room which I call my study, and which, in its day, has witnessed the intellectual labors of better students than myself. It contains, with some additions and alterations, the furniture of my bachelor-room in Boston; but it is not difficult to detect the hand and heart of woman in many of its arrangements—for instance, in the happy disposal of the furniture,—in the little vase of flowers on one of the book-cases, and the larger bronze vase of graceful ferns, that surmounts the bureau. In size, the room is just what it ought to be; for I never could compress my thoughts sufficiently to write, in a very spacious room. It has three windows, two of which are shaded by a large and beautiful willow-tree, which sweeps against the overhanging eaves; on this side, we have a view into the orchard, and, beyond, a glimpse of the river. The other window is the one from which Mr. Emerson,[37] the predecessor of Dr. Ripley, beheld the first fight of the Revolution—which he might well do, as the British troops were drawn up within a hundred yards of the house; and on looking forth, just now, I could still perceive the western abutment of the old bridge, the passage of which was contested. The new monument is visible from base to summit.

Notwithstanding all we have done to modernize the old house, we seem scarcely to have disturbed its air of antiquity. It is evident that other wedded pairs have spent their honeymoons here, though none so happily as ourselves—that children have been born here, and people have grown old and died in these rooms and chambers; although, for our behoof, the same apartments have consented to look cheerful once again. Then there are dark closets, and strange nooks and corners, where the ghosts of former occupants might hide themselves in the day time, and stalk forth, when night conceals all our sacrilegious improvements. We have seen no apparitions, as yet; but we hear strange noises, especially in the kitchen; and, last night, my wife, while sitting in the parlor, heard a thumping and pounding, as of somebody at work in my study. Nay, if I mistake not (for I was half asleep when she told me) she heard a sound as of some person crumpling paper in his hand, in our very bedchamber. This must have been old Doctor Ripley, with one of his sermons;—there is a whole chest full of them in the garret; but he need have no apprehensions of our disturbing them. I never saw the old patriarch myself;—which I regret, as I should have been glad to associate his venerable figure, at ninety years of age, with the house in which he dwelt.

Externally, the house presents the same appearance as in the Doctor's day. It had once a coat of white paint; but the storms and sunshine of many years have almost obliterated it, and produced a sober greyish hue, which entirely suits the antique form of the structure. To repaint its venerable face would be a real sacrilege; it would look like old Doctor Ripley in a brown wig. I hardly know why it is that our cheerful and lightsome repairs and improvements, in the interior of the house, seem to be in perfectly good taste, though the heavy old beams, and high panelling of the walls, speak of ages gone by. But so it is;—the cheerful paper-hangings have the air of belonging to the old walls; and such modernisms as astral-lamps, card-vases, gilded Cologne bottles, silver taper-stands, and bronze and alabaster card-vases, do not seem at all impertinent. It is thus that an aged man may keep his heart warm for new things and new friends, and often furnish himself anew with ideas, though it would not be graceful for him to attempt to suit his exterior to the passing fashions of the day.

Tuesday, August 9th, [1842].

Our orchard, in its day, has been a very productive and profitable one; and we were told that, in one year, it returned Dr. Ripley a hundred dollars, besides defraying the expense of repairing the house. It is now long past its prime. Many of the trees are moss-grown, and have dead and rotten branches intermixed among the green and fruitful ones;—and it may well be so; for I suppose some of the trees may have been set out by Mr. Emerson, who died in the first year of the Revolutionary war. Neither will the fruit, probably, bear comparison with the delicate productions of modern pomology. Most of the trees seem to have abundant burthens upon them; but they are homely russet apples, fit only for baking and cooking. Justice Shallow's orchard,[38] with its choice pippins and leather-coats, was doubtless much superior. Nevertheless, it pleases me to think of the good minister, walking in the shadow of these old, fantastically shaped apple-trees, here plucking some of the fruit to taste, there pruning away a too luxuriant branch, and all the while computing how many barrels will be filled, and how large a sum will be added to his stipend, by the sale. And the same trees offer their fruit to me, as freely as they did to him—their old branches, like withered hands and arms, holding out apples of the same flavor as they held out to Dr. Ripley, in his life-time. Thus the trees, as living existences, form a peculiar link between the dead and the living. My fancy has always found something very interesting in an orchard—especially an old orchard. Apple-trees, and all fruit-trees, have a domestic character, which brings them into relationship with man; they have lost, in a great measure, the wild nature of the forest-tree, and have grown humanized, by receiving the care of man, and by contributing to his wants. They have become a part of the family; and their individual characters are as well understood and appreciated as those of the human members. One tree is harsh and crabbed—another mild—one is churlish and illiberal—another exhausts itself with its free-hearted bounties. Even the shapes of apple-trees have great individuality, into such strange postures do they put themselves, and thrust their contorted branches so grotesquely in all directions. And when they have stood around a house for many years, and held converse with successive dynasties of occupants, and gladdened their hearts so often in the fruitful autumn, then it would seem almost sacrilege to cut them down.

Besides the apple trees, there are various other kinds of fruit in close vicinity to the house. When we first arrived, there were several trees of ripe cherries, but so sour that we allowed them to rot upon the branches. Two long rows of currant bushes supplied us abundantly, for nearly four weeks. There is a considerable number of peach-trees, but all of an old date, their branches rotten, gummy, and mossy, and their fruit, I fear, of very inferior quality. They produce most abundantly, however—the peaches being almost as numerous as the leaves; and even the sprouts and suckers, from the roots of the old trees, have fruit upon them. Then there are pear trees of various kinds, and one or two quince trees. On the whole, these fruit trees, and the other items and adjuncts of the place, convey a very agreeable idea of the outward comfort in which our good old Doctor must have spent his life. Everything seems to have fallen to his lot, that could possibly be supposed to render the life of a country clergyman easy and abundant. There is a barn, which probably used to be filled, annually, with his hay and other agricultural products. There are sheds, and a hen-house, and a pigeon-house, and an old stone pig-stye, the open portion of which is overgrown with tall weeds, indicating that no grunter has recently occupied it. If my wife's permission can be obtained, I have serious thoughts of inducting a new incumbent into this part of the parsonage. It is our duty to support a pig, even if we have no design of feasting upon his flesh; and for my own part, I have a great sympathy and interest for the whole race of porkers, and should have much amusement in studying the character of a pig. Perhaps I might try to bring out his moral and intellectual nature, and cultivate his affections. A cat, too, and perhaps a dog, would be desirable additions to our household.

Wednesday, August 10th, [1842].

The natural taste of man for the original Adam's occupation is fast developing itself in me. I find that I am a good deal interested in our garden; although, as it was planted before we came here, I do not feel the same affection for the plants as if the seed had been sown by my own hands. It is something like nursing and educating another person's children. Still, it was a very pleasant moment when I gathered the first mess of string beans, which were the earliest esculents that the garden contributed to our table. And I love to watch the successive developement of each new vegetable, and mark their daily growth, which always affects me with a new surprise. It is as if something were being created under my own inspection, and partly by my own aid. One day, perchance, I look at my bean-vines, and see only the green leaves clambering up the poles; again, tomorrow, I give a second glance, and there are the delicate blossoms; and a third day, on somewhat closer inspection, I discover the delicate young beans, hiding among the depths of the foliage. Then, each morning, I watch the swelling of the pods, and calculate how soon they will be ready to yield their treasures. All this gives a pleasure and an ideality, hitherto unthought of, to the business of providing sustenance for my family. I suppose Adam felt it in Paradise; and of merely and exclusively earthly enjoyments, there are few purer and more harmless to be experienced. Speaking of beans, by the way, they are a classical food, and their culture must have been the occupation of many ancient sages and heroes. Summer squashes are a very pleasant vegetable to be acquainted with—they grow in the forms of urns and vases, some shallow, others of considerable depth, and all with a beautifully scalloped edge. Almost any squash in our garden might be copied by a sculptor, and would look beautifully in marble, or in china-ware; and if I could afford it, I would have exact imitations of the real vegetable as portions of my dining-service. They would be very appropriate dishes for holding garden vegetables. Besides the summer-squashes, we have the crook-necked winter squash, which I always delight to look at, when it turns up its big belly to ripen in the autumnal sun. Except a pumpkin, there is no vegetable production that imparts such an idea of warmth and comfort to the beholder. Our own crop, however, does not promise to be very abundant; for the leaves formed such a superfluous shade over the young blossoms, that most of the latter dropped off without producing the germ of fruit. Yesterday and to-day, I have cut off an immense number of leaves, and thus given the remaining blossoms a chance to profit by the air and sunshine; but the season is too far advanced, I am afraid, for the squashes to attain any considerable bulk, and grow yellow in the sun. We have musk-melons and water melons, which promise to supply us with as many as we can eat. After all, the greatest interest of these vegetables does not seem to consist in their being articles of food;—it is rather that we love to see something born into the world; and when a great squash or melon is produced, it is a large and tangible existence, which the imagination can seize hold of and rejoice in. I love, also, to see my own works contributing to the life and well-being of animate nature,—it is pleasant to have the bees come and suck honey out of my squash-blossoms, though, when they have laden themselves, they fly away to some unknown hive, which will give me back nothing in return for what my garden has contributed. But there is so much more honey in the world; and therefore I am content....

I find that I have not given a very complete account of our garden; although, certainly, it deserves an ample record in this chronicle; since my labors in it are the only present labor of my life....

Saturday, August 13th, [1842].

My life, at this time, is more like that of a boy, externally, than it has been since I was really a boy. It is usually supposed that the cares of life come with matrimony; but I seem to have cast off all care, and live on with as much easy trust in Providence, as Adam could possibly have felt, before he had learned that there was a world beyond his Paradise. My chief anxiety consists in watching the prosperity of my vegetables—in observing how they are affected by the rain or sunshine—in lamenting the blight of one squash, and rejoicing at the luxurious growth of another. It is as if the original relation between Man and Nature were restored in my case, and that I were to look exclusively to her for the support of my Eve and myself—to trust to her for food and clothing, and all things needful, with the full assurance that she would not fail me. The fight with the world—the struggle of a man among men—the agony of the universal effort to wrench the means of life from a host of greedy competitors—all this seems like a dream to me. My business is merely to live and to enjoy; and whatever is essential to life and enjoyment will come as naturally as the dew from Heaven. This is—practically, at least—my faith. And so I awake in the morning with a boyish thoughtlessness as to how the outgoings of the day are to be provided for, and its incomings rendered certain. After breakfast, I go forth into my garden, and gather whatever the bountiful Mother has made fit for our present sustenance; and, of late days, she generally gives me two squashes and a cucumber, and promises me green corn and shell-beans, very soon. Then I pass down through our orchard to the river-side, and ramble along its margin, in search of flowers for my wife. Usually I discern a fragrant white lily here and there along the shore, growing, with sweet prudishness, beyond the grasp of mortal arm. But it does not escape me so. I know what is its fitting destiny, better than the silly flower knows for itself; so I wade in, heedless of wet pantaloons, and seize the shy lily by its slender stem. Thus I make prize of five or six, which are as many as usually blossom within my reach, in a single morning—some of them partially worm-eaten or blighted, like virgins of tainted fame, or with an eating sorrow at the heart; others as fair and perfect as Nature's own idea was, when she first imagined this lovely flower. A perfect pond-lily is the most satisfactory of flowers. Besides the pond-lilies, I gather whatever else of beautiful chances to be growing in the moist soil by the river-side—an amphibious tribe, yet with more richness and grace than the wild flowers of the deep and dry woodlands and hedge-rows.... This important affair being disposed of, I ascend to my study, and generally read, or perchance scribble in this journal, (or, possibly, sleep!) and otherwise suffer Time to loiter onward at his own pleasure, till the dinner-hour. In pleasant days, the chief event of the afternoon, and the happiest one of the day, is a walk with my wife; she must describe these walks; for where she and I have enjoyed anything together, I always deem my pen unworthy and inadequate to record it. Then comes the night; and I look back upon a day spent in what the world would call idleness, and for which I can myself suggest no more appropriate epithet; and which, nevertheless, I cannot feel to have been spent amiss. True; it might be a sin and shame, in such a world as ours, to spend a life-time in this manner; but, for a few summer-weeks, it is good to live as if this world were Heaven. And so it is, and so it shall be; although, in a little while, a flitting shadow of earthly care and toil will mingle itself with our realities.

Monday, August 15th, [1842].

George Hillard and his wife arrived from Boston, in the dusk of Saturday evening, to spend Sunday with us.[39] It was a pleasant sensation when the coach rumbled up our avenue, and wheeled round at the door; for then I felt that I was regarded as a man with a wife and a household—a man having a tangible existence and locality in the world—when friends came to avail themselves of our hospitality. It was a sort of acknowledgement and reception of us into the corps of married people—a sanction by no means essential to our peace and well-being, but yet agreeable enough to receive. So my wife and I welcomed them cordially at the door, and ushered them into our parlor, and soon into the supper-room—and afterwards, in due season, to bed. Then came my dear little wife to her husband's bosom, and slept sweetly, I trust; for she is a beloved woman—which is more than can be said of every wife in the world. Pray Heaven that Mrs. Hillard had a good night's rest in our guest-chamber; but I hardly think that she slept so sweetly as my lily. However, the night flitted over us all, and passed away, and uprose a gray and sullen morning, which would have saddened me, only that my sunny wife shone into my heart, and made it warm and bright. We had a splendid breakfast of flapjacks—(or *slap*jacks, as my wife insists upon calling them)—of flap-jacks or slap-jacks, and of whortleberries, which we gathered on a neighboring hill, and of perch, bream, and pouts, which I hooked out of the river, the evening before. About nine o'clock, Hillard and I set out for a walk to Walden Pond, calling by the way at Mr. Emerson's, to obtain his guidance or directions. He, from a scruple of his external conscience, detained us till after the people had got into church, and then accompanied us in his own illustrious person. We turned aside a little from our way to visit a Mr. Edmund Hosmer, a yeoman of whose homely and self-acquired wisdom Mr. Emerson has a very high opinion.[40] We found him walking in his fields—a short, but stalwart and sturdy personage of middle age, somewhat uncouth and ugly to look at, but with a face of shrewd and kind expression, and manners of natural courtesy.

He seemed to have a very free flow of talk, and not much diffidence about his own opinions; for, with a little induction from Mr. Emerson, he began to discourse about the state of the nation, agriculture, and business in general—uttering thoughts that had come to him at the plough, and which had a sort of flavor and smell of the fresh earth about them. I was not impressed with any remarkable originality in his views; but they were sensible and characteristic, and had grown in the soil where we found them. Methought, however, the good yeoman was not quite so natural as he may have been at a former period; the simplicity of his character has probably suffered, in some degree, by his detecting the impression which he makes on those around him. There is a circle, I suppose, who look up to him as an oracle; and so he inevitably assumes the oracular manner, and speaks as if truth and wisdom were uttering themselves by his voice. Mr. Emerson has risked the doing him much mischief, by putting him in print—a trial which few persons can sustain, without losing their unconsciousness. But, after all, a man gifted with thought and expression, whatever his rank in life, and his mode of uttering himself, whether by pen or tongue, cannot be expected to go through the world, without finding himself out—and as all such self-discoveries are partial and imperfect, they do more harm than good to the character. Mr. Hosmer is more natural than ninety-nine men out of a hundred; and he is certainly a man of intellectual and moral substance, a sturdy fact, a reality, something to be felt and touched. It would be amusing to draw a parallel between him and his admirer. Mr. Emerson—the mystic, stretching his hand out of cloud-land, in vain search for something real; and the man of sturdy sense, all whose ideas seem to be dug out of his mind, hard and substantial, as he digs potatoes, beets, carrots, and turnips, out of the earth. Mr. Emerson is a great searcher for facts; but they seem to melt away and become unsubstantial in his grasp.

After leaving Mr. Hosmer, we proceeded through woodpaths to Walden Pond, picking blackberries of enormous size along the way. The pond itself was beautiful and refreshing to my soul, after such long and exclusive familiarity with our tawny and sluggish river. It lies embosomed among wooded hills, not very extensive, but large enough for waves to dance upon its surface, and to look like a piece of blue firmament, earth-encircled. The shore has a narrow, pebbly strand, which it was worth a day's journey to look at, for the sake of the contrast between it and the weedy, slimy, oozy margin of the river. Farther within its depths, you perceive a bottom of pure white sand, sparkling through the transparent water, which, methought, was the very purest liquid in the world. After Mr. Emerson left us, Hillard and I bathed in the pond; and it does really seem as if not only my corporeal person, but my moral self, had received a cleansing from that bath. A good deal of mud and river-slime had accumulated on my soul; but those bright waters washed it all away.

We returned home in due season for dinner, at which my wife presided with all imaginable grace and lady-likeness. On her part, she bears testimony to my air of dignified hospitality at the other end of the table; so that there can be no reasonable doubt that we were a most accomplished host and hostess.... On our return, we found my sweetest wife entertaining Mr. and Mrs. Storer and Elizabeth Hoar, who shortly took their leave; and we sate up till after ten o'clock telling ghost-stories.[41] This morning, at seven o'clock, our friends left us; and, at this present moment, being I know not what hour in the forenoon, my little wife is, or ought to be, sleeping off the fatigues of her hospitality. We were both pleased with the visit; and so, I think, were our guests,—and pleased were we, likewise, as my dear wife is kind enough to say, to be left again to one another. If she wants a better chronicle of yesterday's events, she must ever write it herself.

Tuesday, August 16th, [1842].

I have been examining old Doctor Ripley's library, which (or, at least, a portion of it) is deposited in one of our outhouses, where it fills two bookcases.[42] The Doctor, of course, succeeded to the erudite tomes, as well as to the mansion and widow of the Reverend Mr. Emerson of ante-revolutionary memory; and a considerable number of the volumes would seem to have been transmitted to that long-ago deceased worthy from divines of a much elder day. There are dark old folios, containing a thousand pages apiece, or thereabouts, some of them in Latin by Catholic authors, others demolishing Papistical doctrines with a sledge-hammer, in plain English. A dissertation on the book of Job fills, I should think, some score of small, chunky quartos, proceeding at the rate of a volume to one or two chapters. Job himself, methinks, would have found it the severest trial of his patience to read this immeasurable dissertation. Then there is a great folio body of Divinity—too corpulent a body, I should fear, to contain much of a soul. The quarto is the most prevalent form of these ancient volumes, square, and almost as thick as they are broad and long, giving the idea of an immense number of sturdy, closely-printed pages to be waded through—a hard, heavy, lumpish mass of learning, which it might give the intellectual stomach an indigestion even to think of. Books of this form generally date two hundred years back, or more, and are bound in black leather, very solemn, and have much such an aspect as I should attribute to books of magic. Others, of equal antiquity, are very small volumes, such as might easily have been deposited in the large waistcoat pockets of old times—small, but as black as their larger brethren, and printed in minute type, largely interfused with Latin and Greek quotations. Somehow or other, these little old volumes always impress me as if they had been intended for very large ones, but had been blighted in an early stage of their growth, and so were stunted and withered. Several of the works are collections of sermons by the elder divines of New-England, men famous in their generation, but whose writings would now be found nowhere, save in a library derived, at one or two removes, from clergymen of their own epoch. In the blank leaves of many of the old books are written names of former possessors, who vacated their pulpits above a century ago—some, perhaps, who were among the early pilgrims, and others, certainly, who were born before the pilgrims had passed from their earthly labors. On some of the blank leaves, there are pages of writing in short hand, perhaps containing very deep wisdom and most important truth, but for which the world will never be the better, inasmuch as nobody can read it. Doctor Ripley's own additions to the library are not of a very interesting character. Volumes of the Christian Examiner and Liberal Preacher, modern sermons, the controversial works of Unitarian ministers, and all such trash; but which, I suppose, express fairly enough, when compared with the elder portion of the library, the difference between the cold, lifeless, vaguely liberal clergyman of our own day, and the narrow but earnest cushion-thumper of puritanical times. On the whole, I prefer the last-mentioned variety of the black-coated tribe.

[Monday, August 22d, 1842.]

I took a walk through the woods, yesterday afternoon, to Mr. Emerson's, with a book which Margaret Fuller had left behind her, after a call on Saturday eve.[43] I missed the nearest way, and wandered into a very secluded portion of the forest—for forest it might justly be called, so dense and sombre was the shade of oaks and pines. Once I wandered into a tract so overgrown with bushes and underbrush that I could scarcely force a passage through. Nothing is more annoying than a walk of this kind—to be tormented to death by an innumerable host of petty impediments; it incenses and depresses me at the same time. Always when I flounder into the midst of a tract of bushes, which cross and intertwine themselves about my legs, and brush my face, and seize hold of my clothes with a multitudinous gripe—always, in such a difficulty, I feel as if it were almost as well to lie down and die in rage and despair, as to go one step further. It is laughable, after I have got out of the scrape, to think how miserably it affected me for the moment; but I had better learn patience betimes; for there are many such bushy tracts in this vicinity, on the margins of meadows; and my walks will often lead me into them. Escaping from the bushes, I soon came to an open space among the woods—a very lonely spot, with the tall old trees standing around, as quietly as if nobody had intruded there throughout the whole summer. A company of crows were holding their sabbath in the tops of some of the trees; apparently they felt themselves injured or insulted by my presence; for, with one consent, they began to caw—caw—caw—and launching themselves sullenly on the air, took flight to some securer solitude.... There was no other sound, except the song of the crickets, which is but an audible stillness; for though it be very loud, and heard afar, yet the mind does not take note of it as a sound, so entirely does it mingle and lose its individuality among the other characteristics of coming Autumn. Alas, for the summer! The grass is still verdant on the hills and in the vallies; the foliage of the trees is as dense as ever, and as green; the flowers are abundant along the margin of the river, and in the hedge-rows, and deep among the woods; the days, too, are as fervid as they were a month ago—and yet, in every breath of wind, and in every beam of sunshine, there is an autumnal influence. I know not how to describe it;—methinks there is a sort of coolness amid all the heat, and a mildness in the brightest of the sunshine. A breeze cannot stir, without thrilling me with the breath of autumn; and I behold its pensive glory in the far golden gleams, among the long shadows of the trees. The flowers—even the brightest of them—the Golden-Rod, and the gorgeous Cardinals, all the most glorious flowers of the year, have this gentle sadness amid their pomp. Pensive Autumn is expressed in the glow of every one of them. I have felt this influence earlier in some years than in others—sometimes Autumn may be perceived even in the early days of July. There is no other feeling like what is caused by this faint, doubtful, yet real perception, or rather prophecy, of the year's decay—so deliciously sweet and sad in the same breath.

After leaving the book at Mr. Emerson's, I returned through the woods, and entering Sleepy Hollow, I perceived a lady reclining near the path which bends along its verge. It was Margaret herself. She had been there the whole afternoon, meditating or reading; for she had a book in her hand, with some strange title, which I did not understand and have forgotten. She said that nobody had broken her solitude, and was just giving utterance to a theory that no inhabitant of Concord ever visited Sleepy Hollow, when we saw a whole group of people entering the sacred precincts. Most of them followed a path that led them remote from us; but an old man passed near us, and smiled to see Margaret lying on the ground, and me sitting by her side. He made some remark about the beauty of the afternoon, and withdrew himself into the shadow of the wood. Then we talked about Autumn—and about the pleasures of getting lost in the woods—and about the crows, whose voices Margaret had heard—and about the experiences of early childhood, whose influence remains upon the character after the collection of them has passed away—and about the sight of mountains from a distance, and the view from their summits—and about other matters of high and low philosophy. In the midst of our talk, we heard footsteps above us, on the high bank; and while the intruder was still hidden among the trees, he called to Margaret, of whom he had gotten a glimpse. Then he emerged from the green shade; and, behold, it was Mr. Emerson, who, in spite of his clerical consecration, had found no better way of spending the Sabbath than to ramble among the woods. He appeared to have had a pleasant time; for he said that there were Muses in the woods to-day, and whispers to be heard in the breezes. It being now nearly six o'clock, we separated, Mr. Emerson and Margaret towards his house, and I towards mine, where my little wife was very busy getting tea. By the bye, Mr. Emerson gave me an invitation to dinner to-day, to be complied with or not, as might suit my convenience at the time; and it happens not to suit. He likewise communicated an invitation from Mrs. Ripley of Waltham for my wife and me to attend a party at her house, next Thursday evening—an annual party, I believe, on the evening after the Φ.B.K. celebration.[44] If my wife chooses, she shall go, and stay all night, away from her poor desolate husband.

Last evening there was the most beautiful moonlight that ever hallowed this earthly world; and when I went to bathe in the river, which was as calm as death, it seemed like plunging down into the sky. But I had rather be on earth than even in the seventh Heaven, just now.

Sunday, August 28th, [1842].

Still another rainy day—the heaviest rain, I believe, that has fallen since we came to Concord. There never was a more sombre aspect of all external nature....

In this sombre weather, when ordinary mortals almost forget that there ever was any golden sunshine, or ever will be any hereafter, my little wife seems absolutely to radiate it from her own heart and mind. The gloom cannot pervade her; she conquers it, and drives it quite out of her sphere, and creates a moral rain-bow of hope upon the blackest cloud. As for myself, I am little other than a cloud, at such seasons; but she contrives to make me a sunny one; for she gets into the remotest recesses of my heart, and shines all through me. And thus, even without the support of a stated occupation, I survive these sullen days, and am happy. This morning, my wife read us the Sermon on the Mount, most beautifully; so that methinks even the Author of it might be satisfied with such an utterance. In the course of the forenoon, the rain abated for a season; and I went out and gathered some corn and summer-squashes for our dinner, and picked up the windfalls of apples and pears, and peaches.... How inhospitable Nature is, during a rain! In the fervid heat of sunny days, she still retains some degree of mercy for us;—she has shady spots, whither the sun cannot come; but she provides no shelter against her storms. It makes one shiver to think how dripping with wet are those deep, umbrageous nooks—those over-shadowed banks—where we find such enjoyment during sultry afternoons. And what becomes of the birds, in such a soaking rain as this? Is hope, and an instinctive faith, so mixed up with their nature, that they can be cheered by the thought that the sunshine will return?—or do they think, as I almost do, that there is to be no sunshine any more? Very disconsolate must they be, among the dripping leaves; and when a single summer makes so important a portion of their lives, it seems hard that so much of it should be dissolved in rain. I, likewise, am greedy of the summer-days for my own sake; the life of man does not contain so many of them that even one can be spared without regret.

Tuesday, August 30th, [1842].

My wife promised, in the midst of Sunday's rain, that yesterday should be fair; and behold! the sun came back to us, and brought one of the most perfect days that ever was made, since Adam was driven out of Paradise. By the bye, was there ever any rain in Paradise? If so, how comfortless must Eve's bower have been!—and what a wretched and rheumatic time must they have had on their bed of wet roses! It makes me shiver to think of it. Well; it seemed as if the world was newly created, yesterday morning; and I beheld its birth; for I had risen before the sun was over the hill, and had gone forth to fish. How instantaneously did all dreariness and heaviness of the earth's spirit flit away, before one smile of the beneficent sun. This proves that all gloom is but a dream and a shadow, and that cheerfulness is the real truth....

In the afternoon, Mr. Emerson called, bringing Mr. Frost, the colleague and successor of Dr. Ripley.[45] He is a good sort of hum-drum parson enough, and well fitted to increase the stock of manuscript sermons, of which there must be a fearful quantity already in the world. I find that my respect for clerical people, as such, and my faith in the utility of their office, decreases daily. We certainly do need a new revelation—a new system—for there seems to be no life in the old one. Mr. Frost, however, is probably one of the best and most useful of his class; because no suspicion of the necessity of his profession, constituted as it now is, to mankind, and of his own usefulness and success in it, has hitherto disturbed him; and therefore he labors with faith and confidence, as ministers did a hundred years ago, when they had really something to do in the world. I do not remember any points of interest in our conversation....

Thursday, September 1st, [1842].

Mr. Thorow dined with us yesterday. He is a singular character—a young man with much of wild original nature still remaining in him; and so far as he is sophisticated, it is in a way and method of his own. He is as ugly as sin, long-nosed, queer-mouthed, and with uncouth and somewhat rustic, although courteous manners, corresponding very well with such an exterior. But his ugliness is of an honest and agreeable fashion, and becomes him much better than beauty. He was educated, I believe, at Cambridge, and formerly kept school in this town; but for two or three years back, he has repudiated all regular modes of getting a living, and seems inclined to lead a sort of Indian life among civilized men—an Indian life, I mean, as respects the absence of any systematic effort for a livelihood. He has been for sometime an inmate of Mr. Emerson's family; and, in requital, he labors in the garden, and performs such other offices as may suit him—being entertained by Mr. Emerson for the sake of what true manhood there is in him. Mr. Thorow is a keen and delicate observer of nature—a genuine observer, which, I suspect, is almost as rare a character as even an original poet; and Nature, in return for his love, seems to adopt him as her especial child, and shows him secrets which few others are allowed to witness. He is familiar with beast, fish, fowl, and reptile, and has strange stories to tell of adventures, and friendly passages with these lower brethren of mortality. Herb and flower, likewise, wherever they grow, whether in garden or wild wood, are his familiar friends. He is also on intimate terms with the clouds, and can tell the portents of storms. It is a characteristic trait, that he has a great regard for the memory of the Indian tribes, whose wild life would have suited him so well; and strange to say, he seldom walks over a ploughed field without picking up an arrow-point, a spear-head, or other relic of the red men—as if their spirits willed him to be the inheritor of their simple wealth.

With all this he has more than a tincture of literature—a deep and true taste for poetry, especially the elder poets, although more exclusive than is desirable, like all other Transcendentalists, so far as I am acquainted with them. He is a good writer—at least, he has written one good article, a rambling disquisition on Natural History in the last Dial,—which, he says, was chiefly made up from journals of his own observations.[46] Methinks this article gives a very fair image of his mind and character—so true, minute, and literal in observation, yet giving the spirit as well as letter of what he sees, even as a lake reflects its wooded banks, showing every leaf, yet giving the wild beauty of the whole scene;—then there are passages in the article of cloudy and dreamy metaphysics, partly affected, and partly the natural exhalations of his intellect;—and also passages where his thoughts seem to measure and attune themselves into spontaneous verse, as they rightfully may, since there is real poetry in him. There is a basis of good sense and moral truth, too, throughout the article, which also is a reflection of his character; for he is not unwise to think and feel, however imperfect in his own mode of action. On the whole, I find him a healthy and wholesome man to know.

After dinner (at which we cut the first water-melon and musk melon that our garden has ripened) Mr. Thorow and I walked up the bank of the river; and, at a certain point, he shouted for his boat. Forthwith, a young man paddled it across the river, and Mr. Thorow and I voyaged further up the stream, which soon became more beautiful than any picture, with its dark and quiet sheet of water, half shaded, half sunny, between high and wooded banks. The late rains have swollen the stream so much, that many trees are standing up to their knees, as it were, in the water; and boughs, which lately swung high in air, now dip and drink deep of the passing wave. As to the poor cardinals, which glowed upon the bank, a few days since, I could see only a few of their scarlet caps, peeping above the water. Mr. Thorow managed the boat so perfectly, either with two paddles or with one, that it seemed instinct with his own will, and to require no physical effort to guide it. He said that, when some Indians visited Concord a few years since, he found that he had acquired, without a teacher, their precise method of propelling and steering a canoe. Nevertheless, being in want of money, the poor fellow was desirous of selling the boat, of which he is so fit a pilot, and which was built by his own hands; so I agreed to give him his price (only seven dollars) and accordingly became possessor of the Musketaquid. I wish I could acquire the aquatic skill of its original owner at as reasonable a rate.

Friday, September 2d, [1842].

Yesterday afternoon, while my wife, and Louisa, and I, were gathering the windfallen apples in our orchard, Mr. Thorow arrived with the boat.[47]

The adjacent meadow being overflowed by the rise of the stream, he had rowed directly to the foot of the orchard, and landed at the bars, after floating over forty or fifty yards of water, where people were making hay, a week or two since. I entered the boat with him, in order to have the benefit of a lesson in rowing and paddling. My little wife, who was looking on, cannot feel very proud of her husband's proficiency. I managed, indeed, to propel the boat by rowing with two oars; but the use of the single paddle is quite beyond my present skill. Mr. Thorow had assured me that it was only necessary to will the boat to go in any particular direction, and she would immediately take that course, as if imbued with the spirit of the steersman. It may be so with him, but certainly not with me; the boat seemed to be bewitched, and turned its head to every point of the compass except the right one. He then took the paddle himself, and though I could observe nothing peculiar in his management of it, the Musketaquid immediately became as docile as a trained steed. I suspect that she has not yet transferred her affections from her old master to her new one. By and bye, when we are better acquainted, she will grow more tractable; especially after she shall have had the honor of bearing my little wife, who is loved by all things, living or inanimate. We propose to change her name from Musketaquid (the Indian name of Concord river, meaning the river of meadows) to the Pond Lily—which will be very beautiful and appropriate, as, during the summer season, she will bring home many a cargo of pond lilies from along the river's weedy shore. It is not very likely that I shall make such long voyages in her as Mr. Thorow has. He once followed our river down to the Merrimack, and thence, I believe, to Newburyport—a voyage of about eighty miles, in this little vessel.

In the evening, Ellery Channing called to see us, wishing to talk with me about the Boston Miscellany,[48] of which he had heard that I was to be Editor, and to which he desired to contribute. He is one of those queer and clever young men whom Mr. Emerson (that everlasting rejecter of all that is, and seeker for he knows not what) is continually picking up by way of a genius. There is nothing very peculiar about him—some originality and self-inspiration in his character, but none, or very little, in his intellect. Nevertheless, the lad himself seems to feel as if he were a genius; and, ridiculously enough, looks upon his own verses as too sacred to be sold for money. Prose he will sell to the highest bidder, but measured feet and jingling lines are not to be exchanged for gold—which, indeed, is not very likely to be offered for them. I like him well enough, however; but after all, these originals in a small way, after one has seen a few of them, become more dull and common-place than even those who keep the ordinary pathway of life. They have a rule and a routine, which they follow with as little variety as other people do *their* rule and routine; and when once we have fathomed their mystery, nothing can be more wearisome. An innate perception and reflection of truth gives the only sort of originality that does not finally grow intolerable.

Sunday, September 4th, [1842].

I made a voyage in the Pond Lily all by myself, yesterday morning, and was much encouraged by my success in causing the boat to go whither I would. I have always liked to be afloat; but I think I have never adequately conceived of the enjoyment till now, when I begin to feel a power over that which supports me. I suppose I must have felt something like this sense of triumph, long years ago, when I first learned to swim; but I have forgotten it. Oh that I could run wild!—that is, that I could put myself into a true relation with nature, and be on friendly terms with all congenial elements.

We had a thunder-storm, last evening; and today has been a cool, breezy, north-west, autumnal day, such as my soul and body love. My wife went to church in the forenoon;—but not so her husband. He loves the Sabbath, however, though he has no set way of observing of it; but it seldom comes and goes without—but here are some visitors; so this disquisition must rest among the things that never will be written. They are Miss Fuller and Mr. Sam Ward, I believe.[49]

Sunday, September 18th, [1842].

How the summer-time flits away—even while it seems to be loitering onward, arm in arm with autumn! Of late, I have walked but little over the hills and through the woods,—my leisure being chiefly occupied with my boat, which I have now learned to manage with tolerable skill. Yesterday afternoon (my dearest wife having gone to Mr. Emerson's with her mother) I made a voyage alone up the North Branch of Concord river. There was a strong north-west wind blowing dead against me, which, together with the current, increased by the height of the water, made the first part of the passage pretty toilsome. The black river was all dimpled over with little eddies and whirl-pools; and the breeze, moreover, caused the billows to beat against the bow of the boat, with a sound like the flapping of a bird's wing. The water-weeds, where they were discernible through the tawny water, were straight outstretched by the force of the current, looking as if they were forced to hold on to their roots with all their might. If, for a moment, I desisted from paddling, the head of the boat was swept round by the combined might of wind and tide. However, I toiled onward stoutly, and, entering the North Branch, soon found myself floating quietly along a tranquil stream, sheltered from the breeze by the woods and a lofty hill. The current, likewise, lingered along so gently, that it was merely a pleasure to propel the boat against it. I never could have conceived that there was so beautiful a river-scene in Concord, as this of the North Branch. The stream flows through the midmost privacy and deepest heart of a wood, which, as if but half satisfied with its intrusion, calm, gentle, and unobtrusive as it is, seems to crowd upon it, and barely to allow it passage; for the trees are rooted on the very verge of the water, and dip their pendent branches into it.... I scarcely remember a scene of more complete and lovely seclusion than the passage of the river through this wood; even an Indian canoe, in olden times, could not have floated onward in more complete solitude than mine did. I have never elsewhere had such an opportunity to observe how much more beautiful reflection is than what we call reality. The sky, and the clustering foliage on either hand, and the effect of sunlight as it found its way through the shade, giving lightsome hues in contrast with the quiet depth of the prevailing tints—all these seemed unsurpassably beautiful, when beheld in upper air. But, on gazing downward, there they were, the same even to the minutest particular, yet arrayed in ideal beauty, which satisfied the spirit incomparably more than the actual scene. I am half convinced that the reflection is indeed the reality—the real thing which Nature imperfectly images to our grosser sense. At all events, the disembodied shadow is nearest to the soul.

There were many tokens of autumn in this beautiful scene. Two or three of the trees were actually arrayed in their coats of many colors, the real scarlet and gold which they wear before they put on mourning....

On my return, I suffered the boat to float almost at its own will down the stream, and caught fish enough for this morning's breakfast. But, partly from a qualm of conscience, and partly, I believe, because I eschewed the trouble of cleaning them, I finally put them all into the water again, and saw them swim away as if nothing had happened.

Monday, October 10th, [1842].

A long while, indeed, since my last date. But the weather has generally been sunny and pleasant; though often very cold; and I cannot endure to waste anything so precious as autumnal sunshine by staying in the house. So I have spent almost all the daylight hours in the open air. My chief amusement has been boating up and down the river. A week or two ago (September 27th and 28th) I went on a pedestrian excursion with Mr.

Emerson, and was gone two days and one night—it being the first and only night that I slept away from my belovedest wife. We spent the night at the village of Harvard, and the next morning walked three miles further to the Shaker village, where we breakfasted. Mr. Emerson held a theological discussion with two of the Shaker brethren; but the particulars of it have faded from my memory; and all the other adventures of the tour have now so lost their freshness that I cannot adequately recall them. Wherefore let them rest untold. I recollect nothing so well as the aspect of some fringed gentians, which we saw growing by the roadside, and which were so beautiful that I longed to turn back, and bring them to my little wife. After our arduous journey, we arrived safe home in the afternoon of the second day—the first time that I ever came home in my life; for I never had a home before.

Tuesday, November 8th, [1842].

I am sorry that our journal has fallen so into neglect; but unless my naughty little wife will take the matter in hand, I see no chance of amendment. All my scribbling propensities will be far more than gratified in writing nonsense for the press; so that any gratuitous labor of the pen becomes peculiarly distasteful. Since the last date, we have paid a visit of nine days to Boston and Salem, whence we returned a week ago yesterday. Thus we lost above a week of delicious autumnal weather, which should have been spent in the woods, or upon the river. Ever since our return, however, until to-day, there has been a succession of genuine Indian summer days, with gentle winds, or none at all, and a misty atmosphere, which idealizes all nature, and a mild, beneficent sunshine, inviting one to lie down in a nook and forget all earthly care. Today, the sky is dark and lowering, and occasionally lets fall a few sullen tears. I suppose we must bid farewell to Indian summer, now, and expect no more love and tenderness from Mother Nature till next spring be well advanced. She has already made herself as unlovely, in outward aspect, as can well be. My wife and I took a walk to Sleepy Hollow yesterday, and beheld scarcely a green thing—except the everlasting verdure of the family of pines; which, indeed, are trees to thank God for, at this season....

During the last week, we have had three stoves put up; and henceforth, no light of a cheerful fire will gladden us at even tide. Stoves are detestable in every respect, except that they keep us perfectly comfortable. ["Fire-Worship"]

Thursday, November 24th, [1842].

This is Thanksgiving Day—a good old festival; and my wife and I have kept it with our hearts, and besides have made good cheer upon our turkey, and pudding, and pies, and custards, although none sat at our board but our two selves. There was a new and livelier sense, I think, that we have at last found a home, and that a new family has been gathered since the last Thanksgiving Day.

There have been many bright, cold days, latterly—so cold that it has required a pretty rapid pace to keep one warm in walking.... We wander among the wood-paths, which are very pleasant in the sunshine of the afternoons—the trees looking rich and warm, such of them, I mean, as have retained their russet leaves; and where the leaves are strewn along the paths, or heaped plentifully into some hollow of the hills, the effect is not without a charm. To-day, the morning rose with rain, which has since changed to snow and sleet; and now the landscape is as dreary as can well be imagined—white, with the brownness of the soil and withered grass every where peeping out. The swollen river, of a leaden hue, drags itself sullenly along; and this may be termed the first winter's day.

Friday, March 31st, 1843.

The first month of Spring is already gone; and still the snow lies deep on hill and valley; and the river is still frozen from bank to bank; although a late rain has caused pools of water to stand on the surface of the ice, and the meadows are overflowed into broad lakes. Such a protracted winter has not been known for twenty years at least. I have almost forgotten the wood-paths and shady places, which I used to know so well, last summer; and my views are so much confined to the interior of our home, that sometimes, looking out of the window, I am surprised to catch a glimpse of houses at no great distance, which had quite passed out of my recollection. From present appearances, another month may scarcely suffice to wash away all the snow from the open country; and in the woods and hollows, it may linger yet longer. The winter will not have been a day less than five months long; and it would not be unfair to call it seven. A great space, indeed, to miss the smile of Nature, in a single year of human life. Even out of the midst of happiness, I have sometimes sighed and groaned; for I love the sunshine and the green woods, and the sparkling blue water; and it seems as if the picture of our inward bliss should be set in a beautiful frame of outward nature. My dear little wife bears it infinitely better than I; and except on my account, I do believe that she has not once wished for summer. But she is sunshine, and delicate Spring and delightful Summer, in her own person; else the winter would have been dreary indeed. One grief we have had—that which she herself has recorded in the preceding pages; all else has been happiness.[50] Nor did the grief penetrate to the reality of our life. We do not feel as if our promised child were taken from us forever; but only as if his coming had been delayed for a season; and that, by-and-by, we shall welcome that very same little stranger, whom we had expected to gladden our home at an earlier period. The longer we live together—the deeper we penetrate into one another, and become mutually interfused—the happier we are. God will surely crown our union with children, because it fulfils the highest conditions of marriage.

As to the daily course of our life, I have written with pretty commendable diligence, averaging from two to four hours a day; and the result is seen in various Magazines. I might have written more, if it had seemed worth while; but I was content to earn only so much gold as might suffice for our immediate wants, having prospects of official station and emolument, which would do away the necessity of writing for bread. Those prospects have not yet had their fulfilment; and we are well content to wait; because an office would inevitably remove us from our present happy home—at least from an outward home; for there is an inner one that will accompany us wherever we go. Meantime, the Magazine people do not pay their debts; so that we taste some of the inconveniences of poverty, and the mortification—only temporary, however—of owing money, with empty pockets. It is an annoyance; not a trouble.[51]

Every day, I trudge through snow and slosh to the village, look into the Post Office, and spend an hour at the reading-room; and then return home, generally without having spoken a word to any human being. My wife is, in the strictest sense, my sole companion; and I need no other—there is no vacancy in my mind, any more than in my heart. In truth, I have spent so many years in total seclusion from all human society, that it is no wonder if I now feel all my desires satisfied by this sole intercourse. But my Dove has come to me from the midst of many friends, and a large circle of acquaintance; yet she lives from day-to-day in this solitude, seeing nobody but myself and our Molly, while the snow of our avenue is untrodden for weeks by any footstep save mine; yet she is always cheerful, and far more than cheerful. Thank God that I suffice for her boundless heart!

In the way of exercise, I saw and split wood; and physically I never was in so good condition as now. This is chiefly owing, doubtless, to a satisfied heart,—in aid of which comes the exercise above-mentioned, and about a fair proportion of intellectual labor, and a diet in which apples form a considerable part; though not to the exclusion of more substantial viands.

On the 9th of this month, we left home on a visit to Boston and Salem—at least, my wife stopt at the former place, and I went to the latter, where I resumed all my bachelor habits for nearly a fortnight, leading the same life in which ten years of my youth flitted away like a dream. But how much changed was I!—at last, I had caught hold of a reality, which never could be taken from me. It was good thus to get apart from my happiness, for the sake of contemplating it.

Friday, April 7th, [1843].

My belovedest wife has deserted her poor husband; she has this day gone to Boston to see her sister Mary, who is to marry Mr. Mann in two or three weeks, and then immediately to visit Europe for six months.[53] A wagon came at about eleven o'clock to carry my Dove to the stage-house. I helped her in, and stood watching her, on the door-step, till she was out of sight. Then I betook myself to sawing and splitting wood; there being an inward inquietness, which demanded active exercise; and I sawed, I think, more briskly than ever before. When I re-entered the house, it was with somewhat of a desolate feeling; yet not without an intermingled pleasure, as being the more conscious that all separation was temporary, and scarcely real even for the little time that it may last. After my solitary dinner, I lay down, with the Dial in my hand, and attempted to sleep; but sleep would not come,—for the sufficient reason, perhaps, that my little wife was at that very moment jolting most uncomfortably over a rough road. So I arose, and began this record in the Journal, almost at the commencement of which I was interrupted by a visit from Mr. Thoreau, who came to return a book, and to announce his purpose of going to reside at Staten Island, as private tutor in the family of Mr. Emerson's brother. We had some conversation upon this subject, and upon the spiritual advantages of change of place, and upon the Dial, and upon Mr. Alcott, and other kindred or concatenated subjects.[54] I am glad, on Mr. Thoreau's own account, that he is going away; as he is physically out of health, and, morally and intellectually, seems not to have found exactly the guiding clue; and in all these respects, he may be benefitted by his removal;—also, it is one step towards a circumstantial position in the world. On my account, I should like to have him remain here; he being one of the few persons, I think, with whom to hold intercourse is like hearing the wind among the boughs of a forest-tree; and with all this wild freedom, there is high and classic cultivation in him too. He says that Ellery Channing is coming back to Concord, and that he (Mr. Thoreau) has concluded a bargain, in his behalf, for the hire of a small house, with land attached, at $55 per year. I am rather glad than otherwise; but Ellery, so far as he has been developed to my observation, is but a poor substitute for Mr. Thoreau.

I had a purpose, if circumstances would permit, of passing the whole term of my wife's absence without speaking a word to any human being; but now my Pythagorean vow has been broken,[55] within three or four hours after my departure—*her* departure, I should have said; but *my* will do as well.

Saturday, April 8th, [1843].

After journalizing yesterday afternoon, I went out and sawed and split wood, till supper-time; then studied German, (translating Lenore,) with an occasional glance at a beautiful sunset, which I could not enjoy sufficiently, by myself, to induce me to lay aside the book. After lamp-light, finished Lenore, and drowsed over Voltaire's Candide, occasionally refreshing myself with a tune from Mr. Thoreau's musical-box, which he had left in my keeping. The evening was but a dull one. How much more essential than lamp-light or fire-light is the presence of my brightest little wife! I bathed and went to bed, soon after nine. Where was my little wife then? I felt some apprehension that the old Doctor's ghost would take this opportunity to visit me; but I rather think his former visitations have been intended for my wife, and that I am not sufficiently spiritual for ghostly communication. At all events, I met with no disturbance of the kind, and slept soundly enough till six o'clock, or thereabouts. Before seven, there being nothing to detain me in bed, I arose. The fore-noon was spent with the pen in my hand; and sometimes I had the glimmering of an idea, and endeavored to materialize it in words; but, on the whole, my mind was idly vagrant, and refused to work to any systematic purpose.... After dinner, I lay down on the couch, with the Dial as a soporific, and had a short nap; then began to journalize.

Mr. Emerson came, with a sunbeam in his face; and we had as good a talk as I ever remember experiencing with him. My little wife, I know, will demand to know every word that was spoken; but she knows me too well to anticipate anything of the kind. He seemed fullest of Margaret Fuller, who, he says, has risen perceptibly into a higher state, since their last meeting. He apotheosized her as the greatest woman, I believe, of ancient or modern times, and the one figure in the world worth considering. (There rings the supper-bell.) Then we spoke of Ellery Channing, a volume of whose poems is to be immediately published, with revisions by Mr. Emerson himself, and Mr. Sam Ward.[56] He seems to anticipate no very wide reception for them; he calls them "poetry for poets," and thinks that perhaps a hundred persons may admire them very much; while, to the rest of the world, they will be little or nothing. Next Mr. Thoreau was discussed, and his approaching departure; in respect to which we agreed pretty well; but Mr. Emerson appears to have suffered some inconveniency from his experience of Mr. Thoreau as an inmate. It may well be that such a sturdy and uncompromising person is fitter to meet occasionally in the open air, than to have as a permanent guest at table and fireside. We talked of Brook Farm, and the singular moral aspects which it presents, and the great desirability that its progress and developements should be observed, and its history written.... Various other matters were discussed or glanced at; and finally, between five and six o'clock, Mr. Emerson took his leave, threatening to come again, unless I call on him very soon. I then went out to chop wood, my allotted space for which had been very much abridged by his visit; but, on the whole, I was not sorry. I went on with the journal for a few minutes before supper; and have finished the present record in the setting sunshine and gathering dusk. I would like to see my wife!

Tuesday, April 25th, [1843].

Spring is advancing, sometimes with sunny days, and sometimes—as is the case now—with chill, moist, sullen ones. There is an influence in the season that makes it almost impossible for me to bring my mind down to literary employment—perhaps because several months' pretty constant work has exhausted that species of energy—perhaps because, in Spring, it is more natural to labor actively than to think. But my impulse is to be idle altogether;—to lie in the sun, or wander about and look at the revival of Nature from her death-like slumber;—or to be borne down the current of the river in my boat. If I had wings I would gladly fly; yet would prefer to be wafted along by a breeze, sometimes alighting on a patch of green grass, then gently whirled away to a still sunnier spot. [...] But here I linger upon earth, very happy, it is true, at bottom, but a good deal troubled with the sense of imbecility—one of the dismallest sensations, methinks, that mortal can experience—the consciousness of a blunted pen, benumbed figures, and a mind no longer capable of a vigorous grasp. My torpidity of intellect makes me irritable; [...]

Oh, how blest should I be, were there nothing to do! Then I would watch every inch and hair's breadth of the progress of the season; and not a leaf should put itself forth, in the vicinity of our old mansion, without my noting it. But now, with the burthen of a continual task upon me, I have not freedom of mind to make such observations. I merely see what is going on, in a very general way....

Wednesday, April 26th, [1843].

Here is another misty day, muffling the sun. The lilac-shrubs, under my study-window, are almost in leaf; in two or three days more, I may put forth my hand and pluck a green bough. These lilacs appear to be very aged, and have lost the luxuriant foliage of their prime. Old age has a singular aspect in lilacs, rose-bushes, and other ornamental shrubs; it seems as if such things, as they grow only for beauty, ought to flourish in immortal youth, or, at least, to die before their decrepitude. They are trees of Paradise, and therefore not naturally subject to decay, but have lost their birthright by being transplanted hither. But there is a kind of ludicrous unfitness in the idea of a venerable rose-bush; and there is something analogous to this in human life. Persons who can only be graceful and ornamental—who can give the world nothing but flowers—should die young, and never be seen with grey hairs and wrinkles, any more than the flower-shrubs with mossy bark and scanty foliage, like the lilacs under my window. Not that beauty is not worthy of immortality—nothing else, indeed, is worthy of it—and thence, perhaps, the sense of impropriety, when we see it triumphed over by time. Apple-trees, on the other hand, grow old without reproach; let them live as long as they may, and contort themselves in whatever fashion they please, they are still respectable, even if they afford us only an apple or two in a season, or none at all. Human flower-shrubs, if they will grow old on earth, should, beside their lovely blossoms, bear some kind of fruit that will satisfy earthly appetites; else men will not be satisfied that the moss should gather on them.

Winter and spring are now struggling for the mastery in my study; and I yield somewhat to each, and wholly to neither. The window is open; and there is a fire in the stove. The day when the window is first thrown open should be an epoch in the year; but I have forgotten to record it.... Methinks my little wife is twin-sister of the Spring; so they should greet one another tenderly; for they both are fresh and dewy, both full of hope and cheerfulness, both have bird-voices always singing out of their hearts, both are sometimes overcast with flitting mists, which only make the flowers bloom brighter; and both have a power to renew and re-create the weary spirit. I have married the Spring!—I am husband to the month of May!

It is remarkable how much uncleanness Winter brings with it, or leaves behind it. My dearest wife has almost toiled herself to death with endeavors to purify her empire within the house; and the yard, garden, and avenue, which should be my department, require a still greater amount of labor. . . . It is a pity that the world cannot be really made over anew, every spring.

Friday, June 23d, [1843].

Summer has come at last;—the longest days, and the blazing sunshine and fervid heat. Yesterday glowed like molten brass; last night was the most uncomfortably and unsleepably sultry that we have experienced since our residence in Concord; and to-day is another scorcher. I have a sort of enjoyment in these seven-times heated furnaces of mid-summer, even though they make me droop like a thirsty plant. The sunshine can scarcely be too much or too intense for my taste; but I am no enemy to summer showers. Could I only have the freedom to be perfectly idle now—no duty to fulfil—no mental or physical labor to perform—I could be as happy as a squash, and much in the same mode. But the necessity of keeping my brain at work eats into my comfort as the squash-bugs do into the heart of the vines. I keep myself uneasy, and produce little, and almost nothing that is worth producing.

Sunday, July 9th, [1843].

Dearest love, I know not what to say, and yet cannot be satisfied without marking with a word or two this holiest anniversary of our life. But life now heaves and swells beneath me like a brim-full ocean; and the endeavor to comprise any portion of it in words, is like trying to dip up the ocean in a goblet. We never were so happy as now—never such wide capacity for happiness, yet overflowing with all that the day and every moment brings to us. Methinks this birthday of our married life is like a cape, which we have now doubled, and find a more infinite ocean of love stretching out before us. God bless us and keep us; for there is something more awful in happiness than in sorrow—the latter being earthly and finite, the former composed of the texture and substance of eternity, so that spirits still embodied may well tremble at it.[57]

Friday, July 28th, [1843].

...There has been no rain, except one moderate shower, for many weeks; and the earth appears to be wasting away in a slow fever. This weather, I think, affects the temper and spirits very unfavorably;—there is an irksomeness, a restlessness, a pervading dissatisfaction, together with an absolute incapacity to bend the mind to any serious effort. With me, as regards literary production, the summer has been idle and unprofitable; and I can only hope that my forces are recruiting themselves for the autumn and winter. For the future, I shall endeavor to be so diligent during nine months of the year, that I may allow myself a free and full vacation of the other three.

Sunday, September 24th, [1843].

...This is a glorious day, bright, very warm, yet with an unspeakable gentleness both in its warmth and brightness. On such days, it is impossible not to love Nature; for she evidently loves us. At other seasons, she does not give me this impression; or only at very rare intervals; but in these happy autumnal days, when she has perfected her harvests, and accomplished every necessary thing that she had to do, she overflows with a blessed superfluity of love. It is good to be alive now. Thank God for breath—yes, for mere breath!—when it is made up of such a heavenly breeze as this. It comes to the cheek with a real kiss; it would linger fondly around us, if it might; but since it must be gone, it caresses us with its whole kindly heart, and passes onward, to caress likewise the next thing that it meets. There is a pervading blessing diffused all over the world. I look out of the window, and think—"Oh perfect day! Oh beautiful world! Oh good God!" And such a day is the promise of a blissful Eternity; our Creator would never have made such weather, and have given us the deep hearts to enjoy it above and beyond all thought, if He had not meant us to be immortal. It opens the gates of Heaven, and gives us glimpses far inward.[58]

Friday, October 6th, [1843].

Yesterday afternoon (leaving wifie with my sister Louisa, who has been with us two or three days) I took a solitary walk to Walden Pond. It was a cool, north-west windy day, with heavy clouds rolling and tumbling about the sky, but still a prevalence of genial autumn sunshine. The fields are still green, and the great masses of the woods have not yet assumed their many-colored garments; but here and there, are solitary oaks of a deep, substantial red, or maples of a more brilliant hue, or chesnuts, either yellow or of a tenderer green than in summer. Some trees seem to return to their hue of May or early June, before they put on the brighter autumnal tints. In some places, along the borders of low and moist land, a whole range of trees were clothed in the perfect gorgeousness of autumn, of all shades of brilliant color, looking like the palette on which Nature was arranging the tints wherewith to paint a picture. These hues appeared to be thrown together without design; and yet there was perfect harmony among them, and a softness and delicacy made up of a thousand different brightnesses. There is not, I think, so much contrast among these colors as might at first appear; the more you consider them, the more they seem to have one element among them all—which is the reason that the most brilliant display of them soothes the observer, instead of exciting him. And I know not whether it be more a moral effect, or a physical one operating merely on the eye, but it is a pensive gaiety, which causes a sigh often, but never a smile. We never fancy, for instance, that these gaily-clad trees should be changed into young damsels in holiday attire, and betake themselves to dancing on the plain. If they were to undergo such a transformation, they would surely arrange themselves in a funeral procession, and go sadly along with their purple, and scarlet, and golden garments trailing over the withering grass. When the sunshine falls upon them, they seem to smile; but it is as if they were heart-broken. But it is in vain for me to attempt to describe these autumnal brilliancies, or to convey the impression which they make on me. I have tried a thousand times, and always without the slightest self-satisfaction. Luckily, there is no need of such a record; for Nature renews the scene, year after year; and even when we shall have passed away from the world, we can spiritually create these scenes; so that we may dispense now and hereafter with all further efforts to put them into words.

    Walden Pond was clear and beautiful, as usual. It tempted me to bathe; and though the water was thrillingly cold, it was like the thrill of a happy death. Never was there such transparent water as this. I threw sticks into it, and saw them float suspended on an almost invisible medium; it seemed as if the pure air was beneath them, as well as above. If I were to be baptized, it should be in this pond; but then one would not wish to pollute it by washing off his sins into it. None but angels should bathe there. It would be a fit bathing-place for my little wife; and sometime or other, I hope, our blessed baby shall be dipt into its bosom.[59]

    In a small and secluded dell, that opens upon the most beautiful cove of the whole lake, there is a little hamlet of huts or shanties, inhabited by the

Irish people who are at work upon the rail-road. There are three or four of these habitations, the very rudest, I should imagine, that civilized men ever made for themselves, constructed of rough boards, with protruding ends. Against some of them the earth is heaped up to the roof, or nearly so; and when the grass has had time to sprout upon them, they will look like small natural hillocks, or a species of ant-hill, or something in which Nature has a larger share than man. These huts are placed beneath the trees, (oaks, walnuts, and white pines) wherever the trunks give them space to stand; and by thus adapting themselves to natural interstices instead of making new ones, they do not break or disturb the solitude and seclusion of the place. Voices are heard, and the shouts and laughter of children, who play about like the sunbeams that come down through the branches. Women are washing beneath the trees, and long lines of whitened clothes are extended from tree to tree, fluttering and gamboling in the breeze. A pig, in a stye even more extemporary than the shanties, is grunting, and poking his snout through the clefts of his habitation. The household pots and kettles are seen at the doors, and a glance within shows the rough benches that serve for chairs, and the bed upon the floor. The visiter's nose takes note of the fragrance of a pipe. And yet, with all these homely items, the repose and sanctity of the old wood do not seem to be destroyed or prophaned; she overshadows these poor people, and assimilates them, somehow or other, to the character of her natural inhabitants. Their presence did not shock me, any more than if I had merely discovered a squirrel's nest in a tree. To be sure, it is a torment to see the great, high, ugly embankment of the rail-road, which is here protruding itself into the lake, or along its margin, in close vicinity to this picturesque little hamlet. I have seldom seen anything more beautiful than the cove, on the border of which the huts are situated; and the more I looked, the lovelier it grew. The trees overshadowed it deeply; but on one side there was some brilliant shrubbery which seemed to light up the whole picture with the effect of a sweet and melancholy smile. I felt as if spirits were there—or as if these shrubs had a spiritual life—in short, the impression was undefinable; and after gazing and musing a good while, I retraced my steps through the Irish hamlet, and plodded on along a wood-path.

[Saturday, July 27th, 1844.]

To sit down in a solitary place (or a busy and bustling one, if you please) and await such little events as may happen, or observe such noticeable points as the eyes fall upon around you. For instance, I sat down to-day—July 27th, 1844, at about ten o'clock in the forenoon—in Sleepy

Hollow,[60] a shallow space scooped out among the woods, which surround it on all sides, it being pretty nearly circular, or oval, and two or three hundred yards—perhaps four or five hundred—in diameter. The present season, a thriving field of Indian corn, now in its most perfect growth, and tasselled out, occupies nearly half of the hollow; and it is like the lap of bounteous Nature, filled with bread stuff. On one verge of this hollow, skirting it, is a terraced pathway, broad enough for a wheel-track, overshadowed with oaks, stretching their long, knotted, rude, rough arms between earth and sky; the gray skeletons, as you look upward, are strikingly prominent amid the green foliage; likewise, there are chesnuts, growing up in a more regular and pyramidal shape; white pines, also; and a shrubbery composed of the shoots of all these trees, overspreading and softening the bank on which the parent stems are growing;—these latter being intermingled with coarse grass. Observe the pathway; it is strewn over with little bits of dry twigs and decayed branches, and the sear and brown oak-leaves of last year, that have been moistened by snow and rain, and whirled about by harsh and gentle winds, since their departed verdure; the needle-like leaves of the pine, that are never noticed in falling—that fall, yet never leave the tree bare—are likewise on the paths; and with these are pebbles, the remains of what was once a gravelled surface, but which the soil accumulating from the decay of leaves, and washing down from the bank, has now almost covered. The sunshine comes down on the pathway with the bright glow of noon, at certain points; in other places, there is a shadow as deep as the glow; but along the greater portion, sunshine glimmers through shadow, and shadow effaces sun-shine, imaging that pleasant mood of mind where gaiety and pensiveness intermingle.... Were we to sit here all day, a week, a month, and doubtless a lifetime, objects would thus still be presenting themselves as new, though there would seem to be no reason why we should not have detected them all at the first moment.

Now a cat-bird is mewing at no great distance. Then the shadow of a bird flitted across a sunny spot; there is a peculiar impressiveness in this mode of being made acquainted with the flight of a bird; it affects the mind more than if the eye had actually seen it. As we look round to catch a glimpse of the winged creature, we behold the living blue of the sky, and the brilliant disk of the sun, broken and made tolerable to the eye by the intervening foliage. Now, when you are not thinking of it, the fragrance of the white pines is suddenly wafted to you by a slight, almost imperceptible breeze, which has begun to stir. Now the breeze is the gentlest sigh imaginable, yet with a spiritual potency, insomuch that it seems to penetrate, with its mild, ethereal coolness, through the outward clay, and breathe upon the spirit itself, which shivers with gentle delight; now the breeze strengthens so much as to shake all the leaves, making them rustle sharply, but has lost its most ethereal power. And now, again, the shadows of the boughs lie as motionless as if they were painted on the pathway. Now, in this stillness, is heard the long, melancholy note of a bird, complaining alone, of some wrong or sorrow, that worm, or her own kind, or the immitigable doom of human affairs has inflicted upon her. A complaining, but unresisting sufferer. And now, all of a sudden, we hear the sharp, shrill chirrup of a red squirrel, angry, it seems, with somebody, perhaps with ourselves for having intruded into what he is pleased to consider as his own domain.... Now we hear the striking of the village-clock, distant, but yet so near that each stroke is distinctly impressed upon the air. This is a sound that does not disturb the repose of the scene; it does not break our Sabbath; for like a Sabbath seems this place, and the more so on account of the cornfield rustling at our feet. It tells of human labor, but being so solitary now, it seems as if it were on account of the sacredness of the Sabbath. Yet it is not so, for we hear at a distance, mowers whetting their scythes; but these sounds of labor, when at a proper remoteness, do but increase the quiet of one who lies at his ease, all in a mist of his own musings. There is the tinkling of a cow-bell—a noise how peevishly dissonant, were it close at hand, but even musical now. But, hark! There is the whistle of the locomotive—the long shriek, harsh, above all other harshness, for the space of a mile cannot mollify it into harmony. It tells a story of busy men, citizens, from the hot street, who have come to spend a day in a country village; men of business; in short of all unquietness; and no wonder that it gives such a startling shriek, since it brings the noisy world into the midst of our slumbrous peace. As our thoughts repose again, after this interruption, we find ourselves gazing up at the leaves, and comparing their different aspect, the beautiful diversity of green, as the sunlight is diffused through them as a medium, or reflected from their glossy surface. You see, too, here and there, dead, leafless branches, which you had no more been aware of before, than if they had assumed this old and dry decay since you sat down upon the bank. Look at our feet; and here likewise are objects as good as new. There are two little round white fungi, which probably sprung from the ground in the course of last night, curious productions of the mushroom tribe, and which and by will be those little things, with smoke in them, which children call puff-balls. Is there nothing else? Yes; here is a whole colony of little ant-hills, a real village of them; they are small, round hillocks, formed of minute particles of gravel, with an entrance in the centre; and through some of them blades of grass or small shrubs have sprouted up, producing an effect not unlike that of trees overshadowing a homestead. Here is a type of domestic industry—perhaps, too, something of municipal institutions—perhaps, likewise (who knows) the very model of a community, which Fourierites and others are stumbling in pursuit of. Possibly, the student of such philosophies should go to the ant, and find that nature has given him his lesson there. Meantime, like a malevolent genius, I drop a few grains of sand into the entrance of one of these dwellings, and thus quite obliterate it. And, behold, here comes one of the inhabitants, who has been abroad upon some public or private business, or perhaps to enjoy a fantastic walk—and cannot any longer find his own door. What surprise, what hurry, what confusion of mind, are expressed in all his movements! How inexplicable to him must be the agency that has effected this mischief. The incident will probably be long remembered in the annals of the ant-colony, and be talked of in the winter days, when they are making merry over their hoarded provisions. But come, it is time to move. The sun has shifted his position, and has found a vacant space through the branches, by means of which he levels his rays full upon my head. Yet now, as I arise, a cloud has come across him, and makes everything gently sombre in an instant. Many clouds, voluminous and heavy, are scattered about the sky, like the shattered ruins of a dreamer's Utopia; but we will not send our thoughts thitherward now, nor take one of them into our present observations. The clouds of any one day, are material enough, alone, for the observation either of an idle man or a philosopher.

And now how narrow, scanty, and meagre, is this record of observation, compared with the immensity that was to be observed, within the bounds which I prescribed to myself. How shallow and scanty a stream of thought, too,—of distinct and expressed thought—compared with the broad tide of dim emotions, ideas, associations, which were flowing through the haunted regions of imagination, intellect, and sentiment, sometimes excited by what was around me, sometimes with no perceptible connection with them. When we see how little we can express, it is a wonder that any man ever takes up a pen a second time.

The search of an investigator for the Unpardonable Sin;—he at last finds it in his own heart and practice. ["Ethan Brand"]

The trees reflected in the river;—they are unconscious of a spiritual world so near them. So are we.

The Unpardonable Sin might consist in a want of love and reverence for the Human Soul; in consequence of which, the investigator pried into its dark depths, not with a hope or purpose of making it better, but from a cold philosophical curiosity;—content that it should be wicked in whatever kind or degree, and only desiring to study it out. Would not this, in other words, be the separation of the intellect from the heart? ["Ethan Brand"]

People who write about themselves and their feelings, as Byron did, may be said to serve up their own hearts, duly spiced, and with brain-sauce out of their own heads, as a repast for the public.[61]

The life of a woman, who, by the old colony law, was condemned always to wear the letter A, sewed on her garment, in token of her having committed adultery.[62]

[Friday], May 9th, 1845.

On the night of July 9th, a search for the dead body of a drowned girl.[63] She was a Miss Hunt, about nineteen years old; a girl of education and refinement, but depressed and miserable for want of sympathy—her family being an affectionate one, but uncultivated, and incapable of responding to her demands. She was of a melancholic temperament, accustomed to solitary walks in the woods. At this time, she had the superintendence of one of the district-schools, comprising sixty scholars, particularly difficult of management. Well; Ellery Channing knocked at the door, between 9 and 10 in the evening, in order to get my boat, to go in search of this girl's drowned body. He took the oars, and I the paddle, and we went rapidly down the river, until, a good distance below the bridge, we saw lights on the bank, and the dim figures of a number of people waiting for us. Her bonnet and shoes had already been found on this spot, and her handkerchief, I believe, on the edge of the water; so that the body was probably at no great distance, unless the current (which is gentle, and almost imperceptible) had swept her down.
We took in General Buttrick,[64] and a young man in a blue frock, and commenced the search; the general and the other man having long poles with hooks at the end, and Ellery a hay-rake, while I steered the boat. It was a very eligible place to drown one's self. On the verge of the river, there were water-weeds; but after a few steps, the bank goes off very abruptly, and the water speedily becomes fifteen or twenty feet deep. It must be one of the deepest spots in the whole river; and, holding a lantern over it, it was black as midnight, smooth, impenetrable, and keeping its secrets from the eye as perfectly as mid-ocean could. We caused the boat to float once or twice past the spot where the bonnet &c had been found; carefully searching the bottom at different distances from the shore—but, for a considerable time

without success. Once or twice the poles or the rake caught in bunches of water-weed, which, in the star-light, looked like garments; and once Ellery and the General struck some substance at the bottom, which they at first mistook for the body; but it was probably a sod that had rolled in from the bank. All this time, the persons on the bank were anxiously waiting, and sometimes giving us their advice to search higher or lower, or at such and such a point. I now paddled the boat again past the point where she was supposed to have entered the river, and then turned it, so as to let it float broadside downwards, about midway from bank to bank. The young fellow in the blue frock sat on the next seat to me, plying his long pole.

We had drifted a little distance below the group of men on the bank, when this fellow gave a sudden start—"What's this?" cried he. I felt in a moment what it was; and I suppose the same electric shock went through everybody in the boat. "Yes; I've got her!" said he; and heaving up his pole with difficulty, there was an appearance of light garments on the surface of the water; he made a strong effort, and brought so much of the body above the surface, that there could be no doubt about it. He drew her towards the boat, grasped her arm or hand; and I steered the boat to the bank, all the while looking at this dead girl, whose limbs were swaying in the water, close at the boat's side. The fellow evidently had the same sort of feeling in his success as if he had caught a particularly fine fish; though mingled, no doubt, with horror. For my own part, I felt my voice tremble a little, when I spoke, at the first shock of the discovery; and at seeing the body come to the surface, dimly in the starlight. When close to the bank, some of the men stepped into the water and drew out the body; and then, by their lanterns, I could see how rigid it was. There was nothing flexible about it; she did not droop over the arms of those who supported her, with her hair hanging down, as a painter would have represented her; but was all as stiff as marble. And it was evident that her wet garments covered limbs perfectly inflexible. They took her out of the water, and deposited her under an oak-tree; and by the time we had got ashore, they were examining her by the light of two or three lanterns.

I never saw nor imagined a spectacle of such perfect horror. The rigidity, above spoken of, was dreadful to behold. Her arms had stiffened in the act of struggling; and were bent before her, with the hands clenched. She was the very image of a death-agony; and when the men tried to compose her figure, her arms would still return to that same position; indeed it was almost impossible to force them out of it for an instant. One of the men put his foot upon her arm, for the purpose of reducing it by her side; but, in a moment, it rose again. The lower part of the body had stiffened into a more quiet attitude; the legs were slightly bent, and the feet close together.

But that rigidity!—it is impossible to express the effect of it; it seemed as if she would keep the same posture in the grave, and that her skeleton would keep it too, and that when she rose at the day of Judgment, it would be in the same attitude.

As soon as she was taken out of the water, the blood began to stream from her nose. Something seemed to have injured her eye, too; perhaps it was the pole when it first struck the body. The complexion was a dark red, almost purple; the hands were white, with the same rigidity in their clench as in all the rest of the body. Two of the men got water, and began to wash away the blood from her face; but it flowed and flowed, and continued to flow; and an old carpenter, who seemed to be skilful in such matters, said that this was always the case, and that she would continue to "purge" as he called it, in this manner, until her burial, I believe. He said, too, that the body would swell, by morning, so that nobody would know her. Let it take what change it might, it could scarcely look more horrible than it did now, in its rigidity; certainly, she did not look as if she had gotten grace in the world whither she had precipitated herself; but rather, her stiffened death-agony was an emblem of inflexible judgment pronounced upon her. If she could have foreseen, while she stood, at 5 o'clock that morning, on the bank of the river, how her maiden corpse would have looked, eighteen hours afterwards, and how coarse men would strive with hand and foot to reduce it to a decent aspect, and all in vain—it would surely have saved her from this deed. So horribly did she look, that a middle-aged man, David Buttrick,[65] absolutely fainted away, and was found lying on the grass, at a little distance, perfectly insensible. It required much rubbing of hands and limbs to restore him.

Meantime, General Buttrick had gone to give notice to the family that the body was found; and others had gone in search of rails, to make a bier. Another boat now arrived, and added two or three more horror-struck spectators. There was a dog with them, who looked at the body, as it seemed to me, with pretty much the same feelings as the rest of us—horror and curiosity. A young brother of the deceased, apparently about twelve or fourteen years old, had been on the spot from the beginning. He seemed not much moved, externally, but answered questions about his sister, and the number of the brothers and sisters, (ten in all,) with composure. No doubt, however, he was stunned and bewildered with the scene—to see his sister lying there, in such terrific guise, at midnight, under an oak, on the verge of the black river, with strangers clustering about her, holding their lanterns over her face; and that old carpenter washing the blood away, which still flowed forth, though from a frozen fountain. Never was there a wilder scene. All the while, we were talking about the circumstances, and about an inquest, and whether or no it was necessary, and of how many it should consist; and the old carpenter was talking of dead people, and how he would as lief handle them as living ones.

By this time, two rails had been procured, across which were laid some boards or broken oars from the bottom of a boat; and the body, being wrapt in an old quilt, was laid upon this rude bier. All of us took part in bearing the corpse, or in steadying it. From the bank of the river to her father's house, there was nearly half a mile of pasture-ground, on the ascent of the hill; and our burthen grew very heavy before we reached the door. What a midnight procession it was! How strange and fearful it would have seemed, if it could have been foretold, a day beforehand, that I should help carry a dead body along that track! At last, we reached the door, where appeared an old gray-haired man, holding a light; he said nothing, seemed calm, and after the body was laid upon a large table, in what seemed to be the kitchen, the old man disappeared. This was the grandfather. Good Mrs. Pratt was in the room,[66] having been sent for to assist in laying out the body; but she seemed wholly at a loss how to proceed; and no wonder—for it was an absurd idea to think of composing that rigidly distorted figure into the decent quiet of the coffin. A Mrs. Lee had likewise been summoned, and shortly appeared, a withered, skin-and-bone looking woman; but she, too, though a woman of skill, was in despair at the job, and confessed her ignorance how to set about it. Whether the poor girl did finally get laid out, I know not, but can scarcely think it possible. I have since been told that, on stripping the body, they found a strong cord wound round the waist, and drawn tight—for what purpose is impossible to guess.

"Ah, poor child!"—that was the exclamation of an elderly man, as he helped draw her out of the water. I suppose one friend would have saved her; but she died for want of sympathy—a severe penalty for having cultivated and refined herself out of the sphere of her natural connections.

She is said to have gone down to the river at 5 in the morning, and to have been seen walking to and fro on the bank, so late as 7—there being all that space of final struggle with her misery. She left a diary, which is said to exhibit (as her whole life did) many high and remarkable traits. The idea of suicide was not a new one with her; she had before attempted, walking up to her chin into the water, but coming out again, in compassion to the agony of a sister, who stood on the bank. She appears to have been religious, and of a high morality.

The reason, probably, that the body remained so near the spot where she drowned herself, was, that it had sunk to the bottom of perhaps the deepest spot in the river, and so was out of the action of the current.

After three years at the Old Manse, Hawthorne returned to his native Salem and took up the position of surveyor of customs at the Salem Custom House. He remained in Salem even after his "decapitation" as surveyor in the summer of 1849. That same summer Hawthorne's mother died at Salem. In the spring of the following year, Hawthorne and his family moved to a small cottage in Lenox, Massachusetts, where he resided until November 1851.

[Wednesday], November 17th, 1847.

A story of the effects of revenge, in diabolizing him who indulges in it.[67]

[Friday], October 13th, 1848.

During this moon, I have two or three evenings, sat sometime in our sitting-room, without light, except from the coal-fire and the moon. Moonlight produces a very beautiful effect in the room; falling so white upon the carpet, and showing its figures so distinctly; and making all the room so visible, and yet so different from a morning or noontide visibility. There are all the familiar things;—every chair, the tables, the couch, the bookcase, all the things that we are accustomed to in the daytime; but now it seems as if we were remembering them through a lapse of years rather than seeing them with the immediate eye. A child's shoe—the doll, sitting in her little wicker-carriage—all objects, that have been used or played with during the day, though still as familiar as ever, are invested with something like strangeness and remoteness. I cannot in any measure express it. Then the somewhat dim coal-fire throws its unobtrusive tinge through the room—a faint ruddiness upon the wall—which has a not unpleasant effect in taking from the colder spirituality of the moonbeams. Between both these lights, such a medium is created that the room seems just fit for the ghosts of persons very dear, who have lived in the room with us, to glide noiselessly in, and sit quietly down, without affrighting us. It would be like a matter of course, to look round, and find some familiar form in one of the chairs. If one of the white curtains happen to be down before the windows, the moonlight makes a delicate tracery with the branches of the trees, the leaves somewhat thinned by the progress of autumn, but still pretty abundant. It is strange how utterly I have failed to give anything of the effect of moonlight in a room.

The fire-light diffuses a mild, heart-warm influence through the room; but is scarcely visible, unless you particularly look for it—and then you become conscious of a faint tinge upon the ceiling, of a reflected gleam from the mahogany furniture; and if your eyes fall on the glass, deep within it you perceive the glow of the burning anthracite.

I hate to leave such a scene; and when retiring to bed, after closing the sitting-room door, I re-open it, again and again, to peep back at the warm, cheerful, solemn repose, the white light, the faint ruddiness, the dimness,—all like a dream, and which makes me feel as if I were in a conscious dream.[68]

Sunday, January 28th, 1849, 10 o'clock A.M.

The sitting room all in confusion, with little building-blocks and alphabet-blocks strewn about the floor; a hay-cart standing on the carpet; the horse that belongs to it on the book case. Julian playing on the couch with a little set of crockery ware; Una dressing her nails with a pair of scissors. She goes to Julian, and, from mere contrariness, takes away one of the little cups; at which he loudly remonstrates. Then there is a dispute about Dolly, whom Julian has brought out of the closet. Una looks cloudy; her aspect is ominous of a gusty day. Julian has taken the great, round, wooden cushion of the couch, and converts it into a baby, lugging it with difficulty about the room. Children always seem to like a very wide scope for imagination, as respects their babies, or indeed any playthings; this cushion, or a rolling-pin, or a nine-pin, or any casual thing, seems to answer the purpose of a doll, better than the nicest little wax figure that the art of man can contrive.

They are now enacting a sort of drama, in which Julian personates a grandmother, Una the daughter, and Dolly her little baby. The plot is too vague to be put on paper. Julian sits wrapt in a red shawl, continually breaking out into smiles, which have the effect of sunshine on his rosy little phiz; but doing nothing nor saying anything in character. Una acts her part better; but, if any little dispute occurs, she puts on a frown that is anything but dutiful towards her parent in the red shawl. However, she treats her dramatic mother quite as well as she is accustomed to treat her real one.

Here has been an interval, during which Julian has been entreating for my pen, and I have made much mirth by inking his nose and Una's. Now they sit down together to write on a slate—both on the same broken slate—it being their fate always to want to do the same thing, with the same toy, at the same time.

Julian has a great deal of the comic element in his nature, and delights to cause laughter; he puts himself into the most absurd postures, and makes the queerest grimaces, with no other end; and yet they are not what we can call extravagant—there is still a human nature, a natural warmth and joy in them. Una, I think, does not possess humor, nor anything of the truly comic; she cannot at all bear to be laughed at, for anything funny that she perpetrates unawares; and when she tries to be funny, the result is seldom anything but an [ ] eccentricity—a wild grimace—a [ ], unnatural tone. Her natural bent is towards the passionate and tragic. Her life, at present, is a tempestuous day, with blinks of sunshine gushing between the rifts of cloud; she is as full oftentimes of acerbity as an unripe apple, that may be perfected to a mellow deliciousness hereafter—[. . .]

. . . [Una] has a very strong craving for sympathy, and yet, a hundred times a day, she seems to defy sympathy, and puts herself in a position where she knows she cannot receive it. If she can but make an impression—produce a perceptible effect—it partly satisfies her craving.

It is one of Una's characteristics never to shut the door. Yet this does not seem exactly to indicate a loose, harum-scarum disposition; for I think she is rather troubled by any want of regularity in matters about her. She sometimes puts the room in order, and sets things to right very effectively. When she leaves anything loose, it is owing to a hasty, headlong mood, intent upon the end, and rushing at once towards it. It is Julian's characteristic, on the other hand, *always* to shut the door, whatever hurry he may be in. It does not seem to interfere with the settled purpose wherewith he pursues his object; although, indeed, he is not so strenuous in his purposes as Una, and it seems to cost him little or no sacrifice of feeling to give them up. "Well," he says, benignly, after being reasoned or remonstrated with, and turns joyfully to something else. Nevertheless, he is patient of difficulties, and unwearied in his efforts to accomplish his enterprises—as, for instance, in building a house of blocks, where he renews the structure again and again, however often it may tumble down, only smiling at each new catastrophe; when Una would have blazed up in a passion, and tossed her building-materials to the other side of the room. Her mother thinks that her not shutting the door is owing to laziness. She *has* a great fund of laziness, like most people who move with an impetus.

. . . [Una's] beauty is the most flitting, transitory, most uncertain and unaccountable affair, that ever had a real existence; it beams out when nobody expects it; it has mysteriously passed away, when you think yourself sure of it;—if you glance sideways at her, you perhaps think it is illuminating her face, but, turning full round to enjoy it, it is gone again. Her mother sees it much oftener than I do; yet, neither is the revelation always withheld from me. When really visible, it is rare and precious as the vision of an angel; it is a transfiguration—a grace, delicacy, an ethereal fineness, which, at once, in my secret soul, makes me give up all severe opinions that I may have begun to form respecting her. It is but fair to conclude, that, on these occasions, we see her real soul; when she seems less lovely, we merely see something external. But, in truth, one manifestation belongs to her as much as another; for, before the establishment of principles, what is character but the series and succession of moods?

Tuesday, February 6, [1849].

Two o'clock. Mamma has gone out shopping, and to take the air; Una is building an extensive edifice of blocks; Julian asleep. Una is in a quieter humor than usual, to-day; < ... > She has left the blocks, and gone to the blackboard, and is complaining that she cannot draw what she wishes. I amuse her by building all the blocks into an edifice which supplies the long desideratum of an American style of architecture. I take up my pen, and she comes to the table and stands beside me—weary, it seems to me, from mere idleness, and the want of a purpose in life. If there were not so many strong objections, it would be an excellent thing to send her to school; we should see no more of this premature ennui—her mind would be filled, with very questionable matter, no doubt, but still it would be filled. Her heart, too, would expand, and gather to itself good as well as evil; and—what I greatly desire—she would have a much happier childhood than, I fear, we can secure to her by a home-education. Still, I know that there are reasons of greater weight on the other side; and unless an angel should come down from Heaven for the purpose, I should hardly be willing to trust her to any schoolmistress.

Sunday, July 29th, 1849, ½ past 9 o'clock A.M.

A beautiful, fresh summer morning. All my journals of the children, hitherto, have been written at fireside seasons, when their daily life was spent within doors. Now, it is a time of open doors and windows, when they run in and out at will, and their voices are heard in the sunshine, like the song of birds. Our metes and bounds are rather narrow; but still there is fair room for them to play under the elms, the pear-tree, and the two or three plum trees, that overshadow our brick avenue and little grass-plot. There is air, too, as good almost as country-air, from across the North-river; and so our little people flourish in the unrestrained freedom which they enjoy within these limits. They are inactive hardly for a moment throughout the day—living a life as full of motion as the summer insects, who are compelled to crowd their whole existence into this one summer.

This morning, however, my journal begins with discord and trouble; for Una is shut up in the drawing-room and crying bitterly for her mamma,—who is compelled to be in grandmamma's sick-chamber. Julian looks very sad and dolorous, and puckers up his little face, in sympathy with his sister's outcries; and being himself on the point of bursting into tears, I tell him to go to the drawing-room door, and release Una from imprisonment. So he departs on his mission, and forthwith returns, leading Una by the hand, with the tears all over her discolored face, but in peaceful mood. I kiss her forehead; and the sun shines out again, with a bright rainbow in the sky. Little Julian seems to be exhausted by the interest which he has taken in this scene, and lies down on the couch, saying, "Father, I'm so tired!" He gets up for a moment, and Una immediately runs and takes possession of the couch; so that there ensues a dispute for it, which, beginning with complaints, seems likely to end in violence, unless I interpose my supreme authority. I settle the matter, by inviting Una to come and sit in my lap. In a moment, Julian likewise desires to exchange the couch for the same place; but I forbid him.

Una makes infinite complaint, and whining, and teazing about her hair, which has not been combed and put in order this morning—everybody being busy with grandmamma. At last comes in Dora, and takes her into the little room, where I hear her busily prattling about various matters, while Dora combs her hair. Julian, who, I think, has remarkable sensibility to musical sounds, sits on the floor, playing a sort of tune, by pulling a string across a bar of iron. Soon, he gets up and runs into the little room to talk with Dora and Una. His mother making a momentary and flitting appearance, he requests to go up to see grandmamma with her; being refused, he asks for a kiss, and, while receiving it, still offers up a gentle and mournful petition to be allowed to go with his mother. As this cannot be, he remains behind, with a most woeful countenance and some few quiet tears; the shower, however, is averted by Dora's telling him a story, while she continues to fix Una's hair. Julian has too much tenderness, love, and sensibility in his nature; he needs to be hardened and tempered. I would not take a particle of the love out of him; but methinks it is highly desirable that some sterner quality should be interfused throughout the softness of his heart; else, in course of time, the hard intercourse of the world, and the many knocks and bruises he will receive, will cause a morbid crust of callousness to grow over his heart; so that, for at least a portion of his life, he will have less sympathy and love for his fellow-beings than those who began life with a much smaller portion. After a lapse of years, indeed, if he have native vigor enough, there may be a second growth of love and benevolence; but the first crop, with its wild luxuriance, stands a good chance of being blighted.

"Well, father!" cries Una, coming out of the little room, with her hair nicely combed, and looking into the glass with an approving glance. This is not one of her beautiful days, nevertheless; but it is highly possible that some evanescent and intangible cause may, at any moment, make her look lovely; for such changes come and go, as unaccountably as the changes of aspect caused by the atmosphere in mountain scenery. A queer comparison, however—a family of mountains on one side, and Una's little phiz on the other.

Una is describing grandmamma's sickness to Julian. "Oh you don't know how sick she is, Julian; she is sick as I was, when I had the scarlet-fever in Boston." What a contrast between that childish disease, and these last heavy throbbings—this funeral-march—of my mother's heart. Death is never beautiful but in children. How strange! For then Nature breaks her promise, violates her pledge, and like a pettish child, destroys her own prettiest playthings; whereas, the death of old age is the consummation of life, and yet there is so much gloom and ambiguity about it, that it opens no vista for us into Heaven. But we seem to see the flight of a dead child upward, like a butterfly's.

... At about five o'clock, I went to my mother's chamber, and was shocked to see such an alteration since my last visit, the day before yesterday. I love my mother; but there has been, ever since my boyhood, a sort of coldness of intercourse between us, such as is apt to come between persons of strong feelings, if they are not managed rightly. I did not expect to be much moved at the time—that is to say, not to feel any overpowering emotion struggling, just then—though I knew that I should deeply remember and regret her. Mrs. Dike was in the chamber.[69] Louisa pointed to a chair near the bed; but I was moved to kneel down close by my mother, and take her hand. She knew me, but could only murmur a few indistinct words—among which I understood an injunction to take care of my sisters. Mrs. Dike left the chamber, and then I found the tears slowly gathering in my eyes. I tried to keep them down; but it would not be—I kept filling up, till, for a few moments, I shook with sobs. For a long time, I knelt there, holding her hand; and surely it is the darkest hour I ever lived. Afterwards, I stood by the open window, and looked through the crevice of the curtain. The shouts, laughter, and cries of the two children had come up into the chamber, from the open air, making a strange contrast with the death-bed scene. And now, through the crevice of the curtain, I saw my little Una of the golden locks, looking very beautiful; and so full of spirit and life, that she was life itself. And then I looked at my poor dying mother; and seemed to see the whole of human existence at once, standing in the dusty midst of it.[70] Oh what a mockery, if what I saw were all,—let the interval between extreme youth and dying age be filled up with what happiness it might! But God would not have made the close so dark and wretched, if there were nothing beyond; for then it would have been a fiend that created us, and measured out our existence, and not God. It would be something beyond wrong—it would be insult—to be thrust out of life into annihilation in this miserable way. So, out of the very bitterness of death, I gather the sweet assurance of a better state of being.

At one moment, little Una's voice came up, very clear and distinct, into the chamber—"Yes;—she is going to die." I wish she had said "going to God"—which is her idea and usual expression of death; it would have been so hopeful and comforting, uttered in that bright young voice. She must have been repeating or enforcing the words of some elder person who had just spoken.

[Monday], July 30th, [1849], ½ past 10 o'clock.

Another bright forenoon, warmer than yesterday, with flies buzzing through the sunny air. Mother still lives, but is gradually growing weaker, and appears to be scarcely sensible.[71] Julian is playing quietly about, and is now out of doors, probably hanging on the gate. Una takes a strong and strange interest in poor mother's condition, and can hardly be kept out of the chamber—endeavoring to thrust herself into the door, whenever it is opened, and continually teazing me to be permitted to go up. This is partly the intense curiosity of her active mind—partly, I suppose, natural affection. I know not what she supposes is to be the final result to which grandmamma is approaching. She talks of her being soon to go to God, and probably thinks that she will be taken away bodily. Would to God it were to be so! Faith and trust would be far easier than they are now. But, to return to Una, there is something that almost frightens me about the child—I know not whether elfish or angelic, but, at all events, supernatural. She steps so boldly into the midst of everything, shrinks from nothing, has such a comprehension of everything, seems at times to have but little delicacy, and anon shows that she possesses the finest essence of it; now so hard, now so tender; now so perfectly unreasonable, soon again so wise. In short, I now and then catch an aspect of her, in which I cannot believe her to be my own human child, but a spirit strangely mingled with good and evil, haunting the house where I dwell. The little boy is always the same child, and never varies in his relation to me.

3 o'clock, P.M. Julian is now lying on the couch in the character of sick grandmamma, while Una waits on him as Mrs. Dike. She prompts him

in the performance, showing a quite perfect idea of how it should all be. "Now, stretch out your hands to be held." "Will you have some of this jelly!" Julian starts up to take the imaginary jelly. "No; grandmamma lies still." He smacks his lips. "You must not move your lips so hard." "Do you think Una had better come up?" "No!" "You feel so, don't you?" His round, curly head, and rosy face, with a twinkling smile upon it, do not look the character very well. Now, Una is transformed into grandmamma, and Julian is mamma, taking care of her. She groans, and speaks with difficulty, and moves herself feebly and wearisomely—then lies perfectly still, as if in an insensible state. Then rouses herself, and calls for wine. Then lies down on her back, with clasped hands—then puts them to her head. It recalls the scene of yesterday to me, with a frightful distinctness; and out of the midst of it, little Una looks at me with a smile of glee. Again, Julian assumes the character. "You're dying now," says Una, "so you must lie still." "I shall walk, if I'm dying," answers Julian; whereupon he gets up, and stumps about the room with heavy steps. Meantime, Una lies down on the couch, and is again grandmamma, stretching out her hand, in search of some tender grasp, to assure herself that she is still on the hither side of the grave. All of a sudden, Julian is Dr. Pearson, and Una is apparently mamma, receiving him, and making excuses for not ushering him into the sick-chamber. Here ensues a long talk about the patient's condition, and symptoms. Una tells the Doctor plainly, that she thinks we had better have Dr. Cummins; whereupon, Doctor Pearson replies, "We can't have any more talking. I must go!" The next instant, Una transforms him into Dr. Cummins—one of the greatest miracles that was ever performed, this instantaneous conversion from allopathy to homeopathy.

Tuesday, October 23d, [1849].

To inherit a great fortune. To inherit a great misfortune.[72]

The sunbeam that comes through a round-hole in the shutter of a darkened room, where a dead man sits in solitude.

∼

In the summer of 1850, Hawthorne left Salem and moved to Lenox in the Berkshire Mountains.

∼

[Tuesday], May 7th, [1850].

I did not go out yesterday afternoon, but after tea I went to Parker's.[76] The drinking and smoking shop is no bad place to see one kind of life. The front apartment is for drinking. The door opens into Court Square, and is denoted, usually, by some choice specimens of dainties exhibited in the windows, or hanging beside the door-post; as, for instance, a pair of canvas-back ducks, distinguishable by their delicately mottled feathers; an admirable cut of raw beefsteak; a ham, ready boiled, and with curious figures traced in spices on its outward fat; a half, or perchance the whole, of a large salmon, when in season; a bunch of partridges, &c, &c. A screen stands directly before the door, so as to conceal the interior from an outside barbarian. At the counter stand, at almost all hours,—certainly at all hours when I have chanced to observe,—tipplers, either taking a solitary glass, or treating all round, veteran topers, flashy young men, visitors from the country, the various petty officers connected with the law, whom the vicinity of the Court-House brings hither. Chiefly, they drink plain liquors, gin, brandy, or whiskey, sometimes a Tom and Jerry, a gin cocktail (which the bar-tender makes artistically, tossing it in a large parabola from one tumbler to another, until fit for drinking), a brandy-smash, and numerous other concoctions. All this toping goes forward with little or no apparent exhilaration of spirits; nor does this seem to be the object sought,—it being either, I imagine, to create a titillation of the coats of the stomach and a general sense of invigoration, without affecting the brain. Very seldom does a man grow wild and unruly.[77]

The inner room is hung round with pictures and engravings of various kinds,—a painting of a premium ox, a lithograph of a Turk and of a Turkish lady, [...] and various showily engraved tailors' advertisements, and other shop bills; among them all, a small painting of a drunken toper, sleeping on a bench beside the grog-shop,—a ragged, half-hatless, bloated, red-nosed, jolly, miserable-looking devil, very well done, and strangely suitable to the room in which it hangs. Round the walls are placed some half a dozen marble-topped tables, and a center-table in the midst; most of them strewn with theatrical and other show-bills; and the large theatre bills, with their type of gigantic solidity and blackness, hung against the walls.

Last evening, when I entered, there was one guest somewhat overcome with liquor, and slumbering with his chair tipped against one of the marble tables. In the course of a quarter of an hour, he roused himself, a plain, middle-aged man, and went out, with rather an unsteady step, and a hot, red face. One or two others were smoking, and looking over the papers, or glancing at a play-bill. From the centre of the cieling descended a branch with two gas-burners, which sufficiently illuminated every corner of the room. Nothing is so remarkable in these bar-rooms and drinking-places as the perfect order that prevails there; if a man gets drunk, it is no otherwise perceptible than by his going to sleep, or inability to walk....

I take an interest in all the nooks and crannies and every developement of cities; so here I try to make a description of the view from the back windows of a house in the centre of Boston, at which I glance in the intervals of writing. The view is bounded, at perhaps thirty yards distance (or perhaps not so much,) by a row of opposite brick dwellings, standing, I think, on Temple-place; houses of the better order, with tokens of genteel families visible in all the rooms betwixt the basements and the attic windows in the roof; plate-glass in the rear drawing-rooms, flower-pots in some of the windows of the upper stories; occasionally, a lady's figure, either seated, or appearing with a flitting grace, or dimly manifest farther within the obscurity of the room. A balcony with a wrought iron fence running along under the row of drawing-room windows above the basement. In the space betwixt this opposite row of dwellings, and that in which I am situated, are the low out-houses of the above described dwellings, with flat-roofs; or solid brick walls, with walks on them, and high railings, for the convenience of the washerwomen in hanging out their clothes. In the intervals betwixt these ranges of out houses or walks, are grass-plots, already green, because so sheltered; and fruit-trees, now beginning to put forth their leaves, and one of them, a cherry tree, almost in full blossom. Birds flutter and sing among these trees. I should judge it a good site for the growth of delicate fruit; for quite enclosed on all sides by houses; the blighting winds cannot molest the trees; they have sunshine on them a good part of the day, though the shadow must come early; and I suppose there is a rich soil about their roots. I see grape vines clambering against one wall, and also peeping over another, where the main body of the vine is invisible to me. In another place, a frame is erected for a grape vine, and probably it will produce as rich clusters as the vines of Madeira, here in the heart of the city, in this little spot of fructifying earth, while the thunder of wheels rolls about it on every side. The trees are not all fruit-trees; one pretty well-grown buttonwood tree aspires upward above the roofs of the houses. In the full verdure of summer, there will be quite a mass or curtain of foliage, between the hither and the thither row of houses.[78]

[Wednesday], May 8th, [1850].

I went, last night, to the National Theatre to see a pantomime; it was

Jack the Giant Killer, and somewhat heavy and tedious. The audience was more noteworthy than the play. The theatre itself is for the middling and lower classes; and I had not taken my seat in the most aristocratic part of the house; so that I found myself surrounded chiefly by young sailors, Hanover-street shopmen, mechanics, and other people of that kidney. It is wonderful the difference that exists in the personal aspect and dress, and no less in the manners, of people in this quarter of the city, as compared with others. One would think that Oak Hall should give a common garb and air to the great mass of the Boston population;[79] but it seems not to be so; and perhaps what is most singular is, that the natural make of the men has a conformity and suitableness to their dress. Glazed caps and Palo Alto hats were much worn.[80] It is a pity that this picturesque and comparatively graceful hat should not have been generally adopted, instead of falling to the exclusive use of a rowdy class.

In the next box to me were two young women, with an infant of perhaps three or four months old (if so much) but to which of them appertaining, I could not at first discover. One was a large, plump girl, with a heavy face, a snub nose, coarse looking, but good-natured, and with no traits of evil; save, indeed, that she had on the vilest gown—of dirty white cotton, so pervadingly dingy that it was white no longer, as it seemed to me—the sleeves short, and ragged at the borders—and an old faded shawl, which she took off on account of the heat—the shabbiest and dirtiest dress, in a word, that I ever saw a woman wear. Yet she was plump, as aforesaid, and looked comfortable in body and mind. I imagine that she must have had a better dress at home, but had come to the theatre extemporaneously, and not going to the dress-circle, considered her ordinary gown good enough for the occasion. The other girl seemed as young, or younger than herself; she was small, with a particularly intelligent and pleasant face, not handsome, perhaps, but as good or better than if it were. It was mobile with whatever sentiment chanced to be in her mind; as quick and vivacious a face in its movements as I have ever seen; cheerful, too, and indicative of a sunny, though I should think it might be a hasty temper. She was dressed in a dark gown, (chintz, I suppose the women call it,) a good homely dress, proper enough for the fireside, but a strange one to appear at a theatre in. Both these girls appeared to enjoy themselves very much; the large and heavy one, in her own duller mode; the smaller manifesting her interest by gestures, pointing at the stage, and so vivid a talk of countenance that I could sympathize precisely as well as if she had spoken. She was not a brunette; and this made her vivacity of expression the more agreeable. Her companion, on the other hand, was so dark that I rather suspected her to have a tinge of African blood.

There were two men who seemed to have some connection with these girls; one an elderly, gray-headed personage, well stricken in liquor, talking loudly and foolishly, but good-humouredly; the other a young man, sober, and doing his best to keep his older friend quiet. The girls seemed to give themselves no uneasiness about the matter. Both the men wore Palo Alto hats. I could not make out whether either of the men were the father of the child, or what was the nature of the union among them; though I was inclined to set it down as a family-party.

As the play went on, the house became crowded, and oppressively warm; and the poor little baby grew dark red, or purple almost, with the uncomfortable heat in its small body. It must have been accustomed to discomfort, and have concluded it to be the condition of mortal life; else it never would have remained so quiet; for [ ] its rather inconvenient time, it seemed [ ] to [ ] itself through [its] dinner time. Perhaps it had been quieted with a sleeping potion. The two young women were not negligent of it, but passed it to-and-fro between them, each willingly putting herself to inconvenience for the sake of tending it. But I really feared it might die in some kind of a fit; so hot was the theatre; so purple with heat, yet strangely quiet, was the child. I was glad to hear it cry, at last; but it did not cry with any great rage and vigor, as it should, but in a stupid kind of way. Hereupon, the smaller of the two girls, after a little inefficacious dandling, at once settled the question of maternity, by uncovering her bosom, and presenting it to the child, with so little care of concealment that I saw, and anybody might have seen, the whole breast, and the apex which the infant's little lips compressed. Yet there was nothing indecent in this; but a perfect naturalness. The child sucked a moment or two, and then became quiet, but still looked very purple. Children must be hard to kill, however injudicious the treatment. The two girls, and their cavaliers, remained till nearly the close of the play. I should like well to know who they are—of what condition in life—and whether reputable as members of the class to which they belong. My own judgement is, that they are so.

Throughout the evening, drunken young sailors kept stumbling into and out of the boxes, calling to one another from different parts of the house, shouting to the performers, and singing the burthens of songs. It was a scene of life in the rough.

Monday, August 5th, [1850].

Rode with Fields & wife to Stockbridge, being thereto invited by Mr. Field of S.—in order to ascend Monument mountain. Found at Mr. F's Dr.

Holmes, Mr. Duyckink of New-York, also Messrs. Cornelius Mathews & Herman Melville. Ascended the mountain—that is to say, Mrs. Fields & Miss Jenny Field—Messrs. Field & Fields—Dr. Holmes, Messrs. Duyckinck, Mathews, Melville, Mr. Henry Sedgwick, & I.—and were caught in a shower. Dined at Mr. F's. Afternoon, under guidance of J. T. Headley, the party scrambled through the Ice Glen. Left Stockbridge and arrived at home, about 8 P.M.[73]

Wednesday, August 7th, [1850].

Messrs. Duyckinck, Mathews, Melville, & Melville, Jr., called in the forenoon. Gave them a couple of bottles of Mr. Mansfield's champaigne, and walked down to the lake with them. At twilight, Mr. Edwin P. Whipple and wife called, from Lenox.[74]

Tuesday, September 3d, [1850].

Herman Melville came, in the forenoon.

[Wednesday], September 4th, [1850].

Rode with Mr. Tappan & Melville (in T's wagon) to Pittsfield;[75] left T. there, to take the cars for Albany; and spent the day with Melville at his cousin's, near Pittsfield. Reached home, with Melville, at about 8 p.m.

Saturday, September 7th, [1850].

Herman Melville went away, after breakfast.

[Thursday], December 19th, 1850.

If we consider the lives of the lower animals, we shall see in them a close parallelism to those of mortals;—toil, struggle, danger, privation, mingled with glimpses of peace and ease; enmity, affection, a continual hope of bettering themselves, although their objects lie at less distance before them than our own do. Thus, no argument from the imperfect character of our existence, and its delusory promises, and its injustice, can be drawn in reference to our immortality, without, in a degree, being applicable to our brute brethren.

∽

In July 1851, Sophia went to visit her family, taking Una and the Hawthornes' third child, Rose, with her and leaving Hawthorne with Julian.

∽

Twenty Days with Julian & Little Bunny
By Papa

Lenox, Monday, July 28th, 1851.

At seven o'clock, a.m. Wife, E. P. P.,[81] Una, and Rosebud, took their departure, leaving Julian and me in possession of the Red Shanty. The first observation which the old gentle-man made thereupon, was—"Father, isn't it nice to have baby gone?" His perfect confidence of my sympathy in this feeling was very queer. "Why is it nice?" I inquired. "Because now I can shout and squeal just as loud as I please!" answered he. And for the next half hour he exercised his lungs to his heart's content, and almost split the welkin thereby. Then he hammered on an empty box, and appeared to have high enjoyment of the racket which he created. In the course of the forenoon, however, he fell into a deep reverie, and looked very pensive. I asked what he was thinking of, and he said, "Oh, about Mama's going away. I do not like to be away from her;"—and then he romanticized about getting horses and galloping after her. He declared, likewise, that he likes Una, and that she never troubled him. [. . .]

I hardly know how we got through the forenoon-bath; [. . .], and [. . .] [such] kinds of rational employment. It is impossible to write, read, think, or even to sleep (in the daytime) so constant are his appeals to me in one way or another; still he is such a genial and good-humored little man that there is certainly an enjoyment intermixed with all the annoyance.

In the afternoon we walked down to the lake, and amused ourself with flinging in stones, until the gathering clouds warned us homeward. In the wood, mid-way home, a shower overtook us; and we sat on an old decayed log, while the drops pattered plentifully on the trees overhead. He enjoyed the shower, and favored me with a great many weatherwise remarks, for it is to be observed, that he has a marvellous opinion of his own wisdom, and thinks himself beyond a comparison sager and more experienced than his father. It continued showery all the rest of the day; so that I do not recollect of his going out afterwards.

For an in-door playmate, there was Bunny, who does not turn out to be a very interesting companion, and makes me more trouble than he is worth. There ought to be two rabbits, in order to bring out each other's remarkable qualities—if any there be. Undoubtedly, they have the least feature and characteristic prominence of any creatures that God has made. With no playfulness, as silent as a fish, inactive, Bunny's life passes between a torpid half-slumber, and the nibbling of clover-tops, lettuce, plantain-leaves, pigweed, and crumbs of bread. Sometimes, indeed, he is seized with a little impulse of friskiness; but it does not appear to be sportive, but nervous. Bunny has a singular countenance—like somebody's I have seen, but whose I forget. It is rather imposing and aristocratic, on a cursory glance, but examining it more closely, it is found to be laughably vague. Julian pays him very little attention now, and leaves me to take the whole labor of gathering leaves for him; else the poor little beast would be likely to starve. I am strongly tempted of the Evil One to murder him privately; and I wish with all my heart that Mrs. Peters would drown him.

Friday, August 1st, [1851].

We had, to-day, the first string beans of the season; the earliest product of our garden, indeed, except currants and lettuce. At three o'clock, came Julian home. He said that he had tomatoes, beans, and asparagus, for dinner, and that he liked them very much, and had had a good time. I dressed him and myself for a walk to the village, and we set out at four. . . . Returning to the Post office, I got Mr. Tappan's mail and my own, and proceeded homeward, but clambered over the fence and sat down in Love Grove, to read the papers. While thus engaged, a cavalier on horseback came along the road, and saluted me in Spanish; to which I replied by touching my hat, and went on with the newspaper. But the cavalier renewing his salutation, I regarded him more attentively, and saw that it was Herman Melville! So, hereupon, Julian and I hastened to the road, where ensued a greeting, and we all went homeward together, talking as we went. Soon, Mr. Melville alighted, and put Julian into the saddle; and the little man was highly pleased, and sat on the horse with the freedom and fearlessness of an old equestrian, and had a ride of at least a mile homeward.

I asked Mrs. Peters to make some tea for Herman Melville;[82] and so she did, and he drank a cup, but was afraid to drink much, because it would keep him awake. After supper, I put Julian to bed; and Melville and I had a talk about time and eternity, things of this world and of the next, and books, and publishers, and all possible and impossible matters, that lasted pretty deep into the night; and if truth must be told, we smoked cigars even within the sacred precincts of the sitting-room. At last, he arose, and saddled his horse (whom we had put into the barn) and rode off for his own domicile; and I hastened to make the most of what little sleeping-time remained for me.

Saturday, August 2d, [1851].

I forgot to say, in the record of last night, that Herman Melville invited me to bring Julian and spend several days at his house, next week, when E. A. Duyckinck and his brother are to be there. I accepted for at least one night; and so Melville is to come for us.

Friday, August 8th, [1851].

... Between eleven and twelve, came Herman Melville, and the two Duyckincks, in a barouche and pair. Melville had spoken, when he was here, of bringing these two expected guests of his to call on me; and I intended, should it be anywise practicable, to ask them to stay to dinner; but we had nothing whatever in the house today. It passed well enough, however; for they proposed a ride and a pic-nic, to which I readily consented. In the first place, however, I produced our only remaining bottle of Mr. Mansfield's champaigne; after which we set out, taking Julian, of course. It was an admirable day; neither too cold nor too hot—with some little shadow of clouds, but no appearance of impending rain. We took the road over the mountain towards Hudson, and by and by came to a pleasant grove, where we alighted and arranged matters for our pic-nic.

After all, I suspect they had considered the possibility, if not probability, of my giving them a dinner; for the repast was neither splendid nor particularly abundant—only some sandwiches and gingerbread. There was nothing whatever for Julian, except the gingerbread; for the bread, which encased the sandwiches, was buttered, and moreover had mustard on it. So I had to make the little man acquainted, for the first time in his life,

PART I: THE AMERICAN NOTEBOOKS

with gingerbread; and he seemed to be greatly pleased until he had eaten a considerable quantity—when he began to discover that it was not quite the thing to make a meal of. However, his hunger was satisfied and no harm done; besides that there were a few nuts and raisins at the bottom of the basket, whereof he ate and was contented. He enjoyed the ride and the whole thing exceedingly, and behaved like a man experienced in pic-nics.

After a smoke under the trees, and talk about literature and other things, we set forth again, and resolved to go and visit the Shaker establishment at Hancock,[83] which was but two or three miles off. I don't know what Julian expected to see—some strange sort of quadruped or other, I suppose—at any rate, the term "Shakers" was evidently a subject of great puzzlement with him; and probably he was a little disappointed when I pointed out an old man in a gown and a gray, broad-brimmed hat, as a Shaker. This old man was one of the fathers and rulers of the village; and under his guidance, we visited the principal dwelling-house in the village. It was a large brick edifice, with admirably convenient arrangements, and floors and walls of polished wood, and plaster as smooth as marble, and everything so neat that it was a pain and constraint to look at it; especially as it did not imply any real delicacy or moral purity in the occupants of the house. There were spit-boxes (bearing no appearance of ever being used, it is true) at equal distances up and down the long and broad entries. The sleeping apartments of the two sexes had an entry between them, on one side of which hung the hats of the men, on the other the bonnets of the women. In each chamber were two particularly narrow beds, hardly wide enough for one sleeper, but in each of which, the old elder told us, two people slept. There were no bathing or washing conveniences in the chambers; but in the entry there was a sink and wash-bowl, where all their attempts at purification were to be performed. The fact shows that all their miserable pretence of cleanliness and neatness is the thinnest superficiality; and that the Shakers are and must needs be a filthy set. And then their utter and systematic lack of privacy; their close junction of man with man, and supervision of one man over another—it is hateful and disgusting to think of; and the sooner the sect is extinct the better—a consummation which, I am happy to hear, is thought to be not a great many years distant.

In the great house, we saw an old woman—a round, fat, cheerful little old sister—and two girls, from nine to twelve years old; these looked at us and at Julian with great curiosity, though slily and with side glances. At the doors of other dwellings, we saw women sewing or otherwise at work; and there seemed to be a kind of comfort among them, but of no higher kind than is enjoyed by their beasts of burden. Also, the women looked pale, and none of the men had a jolly aspect. They are certainly the most singular and bedevilled set of people that ever existed in a civilized land; and one of these days, when their sect and system shall have passed away, a History of the Shakers will be a very curious book. All through this outlandish village went our little man hopping and dancing, in excellent spirits; nor had he been long there before he desired to confer with himself—neither was I unwilling that he should bestow such a mark of his consideration (being the one of which they were most worthy) on the system and establishment of these foolish Shakers.

I think it was about five o'clock when we left the village. Lenox was probably seven or eight miles distant; but we mistook the road, and went up hill and down, through unknown regions, over at least twice as much ground as there was any need. It was by far the most picturesque ride that I ever had in Berkshire. On one height, just before sunset, we had a view for miles and miles around, with the Kaatskills blue and far on the horizon. Then the road ran along the verge of a deep gulf—deep, deep, deep, and filled with foliage of trees that could not reach half way up to us; and on the other side of the chasm uprose a mountainous precipice. This continued for a good distance; and on the other side of the road there were occasional openings through the forest, that showed the low country at the base of the mountain. If I could find the way, I should like to go back to this scene on foot; for I had no idea that there was such a region within a few miles of us.

By and by, we saw Monument Mountain, and Rattlesnake hill, and all the familiar features of our own landscape, except the lake, which (by some witchcraft that I cannot possibly explain to myself) had utterly vanished. It appeared as if we ought to see the lake, and our little red-house, and Highwood; but none of these objects were discoverable, although the scene was certainly that of which they make a part. It was now after sunset; and we found that as we went we were approaching the village of Lenox from the west, and must pass through it before reaching home. I got out at the post office, and received, among other things, a letter from Phoebe. By the time we were out of the village, it was beyond twilight; indeed, but for the full moon, it would have been quite dark. The little man behaved himself still like an old traveller; but sometimes he looked round at me from the front seat (where he sat between Herman Melville and Evert Duyckinck) and smiled at me with a peculiar expression, and put back his hand to touch me. It was a method of establishing a sympathy in what doubtless appeared to him the wildest and unprecedentedest series of adventures that had ever befallen mortal travellers. Anon, we drew up at the little gate of the old red house.

Saturday, August 9th, [1851].

Julian awoke in bright condition, this morning; and we arose at about seven. I felt the better for the expedition of yesterday; and asking Julian whether he had a good time, he answered with great enthusiasm in the affirmative, and that he wanted to go again, and that he loved Mr. Melville as well as me, and as mamma, and as Una.

PART II

The English Notebooks

Thursday, August 4th [1853]. A month, lacking two days, since we left America;—a fortnight, and some odd days, since we arrived in England.[1] I began my services (such as they are) on Monday last, August 1st; and here I sit in my private room at the Consulate, while the Vice Consul and clerk are carrying on affairs in the outer office. Every morning, I find the entry thronged with the most rascally set of sailors that ever were seen—dirty, desperate, and altogether pirate-like in aspect. What the devil they want here, is beyond my present knowledge; but probably they have been shipwrecked, or otherwise thrown at large on the world, and wish for assistance in some shape. Daily, half a dozen or so of these rogues are distributed among the American vessels to be sent back to their native country;—or rather, to their adopted one; for not one in ten of them are really Americans, but outcasts of all the maritime nations on earth, in a uniform of dirty red-baize shirts.[2]

The pleasantest incident of the day, is when Mr. Pierce (the vice-consul or head-clerk) makes his appearance with the account books, containing the receipts and expenditures of the preceding day, and deposits on my desk a little rouleau of the Queen's coin, wrapt up in a piece of paper. This morning, there were eight sovereigns, four half-crowns, and a shilling—a pretty fair day's work, though not more than the average ought to be.

This forenoon, thus far, I have had two calls, not of business—one from an American captain, Foster, and his son, a boy—another from Mr. H. A. Bright, whom I met in America, and who has showed us great attention here.[3] He has arranged for us to go to the Theatre with his family, this evening.

My office consists of two rooms in an edifice called Washington buildings, and so named from the circumstance of the consulate being located here. It is near the docks, and on the corner of Brunswick-street; and from my window, across the narrow street, I have a view of a tall, dismal, smoke-blackened, ugly brick warehouse,—uglier than any building I ever saw in America; and from one or another of the various stories, bags of salt are often being raised or lowered, swinging and vibrating in the air. There is a continual rumble of heavy wheels, which makes conversation rather difficult, although I am gradually getting accustomed to it. My apartment (about twelve feet by fifteen, and of a good height) is hung with a map of the United States, and another of Europe; there is a hideous colored lithograph of General Taylor,[4] life-size, and one or two smaller engraved portraits; also three representations of American naval victories; a lithograph of the Tennessee state-house, and another of the steamer Empire State. The mantelpiece is adorned with the American Eagle, painted on the wood; and on shelves there are a number of volumes, bound in sheepskin, of the laws of the United States and the Statutes at Large. Thus the consular office is a little patch of America, with English life encompassing it on all sides. One truly English object, however, is the Barometer hanging on the wall, and which, today, for a wonder, points to Fair. Since I have been in Liverpool, we have hardly had a day, until yesterday, without more or less of rain; and so cold and shivery that life was miserable. I am not warm enough, even now, but am gradually getting acclimated in that respect.

August 8th [1853]. Day before yesterday, I escorted my family to Rockferry,[5] two miles either up or down the Mersey (and I really don't know which) by steamer, which runs every half-hour. There are other steamers going continually to Birkenhead and other landings, and almost always a great many passengers on the transit. On this occasion the boat was crowded so as to afford scanty standing room; it being Saturday, and therefore a kind of gala-day. I think I have never seen a populace before coming to England; but this crowd afforded a specimen of one, both male and female.[6] The women were the most remarkable; there is almost always something ladylike and delicate about an American woman; but in these, though they seemed not disreputable, there was a coarseness, a freedom, an—I don't know what—that was purely English. In fact, men and women do things that would at least make them ridiculous in America; they are not afraid to enjoy themselves in their own way, and have no pseudo gentility to support. Some girls danced upon the crowded deck, to the miserable music of a little fragment of a band, which goes up and down the river on each trip of the boat. Just before the termination of the voyage, a man goes round with a bugle turned wide end upward, to receive the half elemosynary pence and half-pence of the passengers. I gave one of them, the other day, a silver four-pence; which fell into the vitals of the instrument, and compelled the man to take it to pieces.[7] At Rockferry, there was a great throng, forming a scene not unlike one of our muster-days or Fourth of July; and there were bands of music, and banners, with small processions after them; and there was a school of charity-children, I believe, enjoying a festival; and there was a club of respectable persons, playing at bowls on the bowling-green of the hotel; and there were children, infants riding on donkies, at a penny a ride, while their mothers walked alongside, to prevent a fall.

August 15th [1853]. Many scenes which I should have liked to record have occurred; but the pressure of business has prevented me from recording them from day-to day. On Thursday, I went, on invitation from Mr. Bright, in the prodigious Steamer Great Britain down the harbor, and some miles into the sea, to see her off on her voyage to Australia. There is an immense enthusiasm amongst the English people, about this ship, on account of her being the largest in the world. The shores were lined with people to see her sail; and there were innumerable small steamers, crowded with people, all the way out into the ocean. Nothing seems to touch the English nearer than this question of nautical superiority; and if we wish to hit them on the *raw*, we must hit them there.

On Friday, at 7 P.M. I went to dine with the Mayor.[8] It was a dinner given to the Judges and the Grand Jury. The Judges of England, during the time of holding an Assize, are the persons first in rank in the Kingdom.[9] They take precedence of everybody else—of the highest military officers—of the Lord Lieutenants—of the Archbishops—of the Prince of Wales—of all except the Sovereign; whose authority and dignity they represent. In case of a royal dinner, the Judge would lead the Queen to the table.

The dinner was at the Town-Hall; and the rooms, and the whole affair, were all in the most splendid style. Nothing struck me more than the footmen in the city-livery; they really looked more magnificent, in their gold-lace, and breeches, and white silk stockings, than any officers of state whom I have ever seen. The rooms were beautiful; gorgeously painted and gilded, gorgeously lighted, gorgeously hung with paintings, gorgeously illuminated—the plate gorgeous, the dinner gorgeous, in the English fashion. As to the company, they had a kind of roughness, that seems to be the characteristic of all Englishmen so far as I have yet seen them;—elderly

John Bulls—and there is hardly a less beautiful object than the elderly John Bull, with his large body, protruding paunch, short legs, and mottled, double-chinned, irregular-featured aspect. They are men of the world, at home in society, easy in their manners, but without refinement; nor are they especially what one thinks of, under the appelation of gentleman.

After the removal of the cloth, the Mayor gave various toasts, prefacing each with some remarks—the first of course, the Sovereign, after which "God Save the Queen" was sung; and there was something rather ludicrous in seeing the company stand up and join in the chorus, their ample faces glowing with wine, enthusiasm, perspiration, and loyalty. There certainly is a vein of the ridiculous running through these people; nor does it take away from their respectability. Afterwards the Bar, and various other dignities and institutions were toasted; and by-and-by came a toast to the United States and me as their representative. Hereupon, either "Hail Columbia" or "Yankee Doodle," or some other of our national tunes (but Heaven knows which) was played; and at the conclusion—being cornered, and with no alternative—I got upon my legs and made a response. They received me and listened to my nonsense with a good deal of rapping; and my speech seemed to give great satisfaction. My chief difficulty lay in not knowing how to pitch my voice to the size of the room; as for the matter, it is not of the slightest consequence. Any body may make an after-dinner speech, who will be content to talk onward without saying anything. My speech was not more than two or three inches long;—and considering that I did not know a soul there, except the Mayor himself, and that I am wholly unpractised in all sorts of oratory, and that I had nothing to say, it was quite successful.[10] I hardly thought it was in me; but being once on my legs, I felt no embarrassment, and went through it as coolly as if I were going to be hanged.

Yesterday, after dinner, I took a walk with my family. We went through by-ways and private roads, and saw more of rural England, with its hedgerows, its grassy fields, and its white-washed old stone cottages, than we have before seen since our arrival.

August 20th [1853]. This being Saturday, there early commenced a throng of visitants to Rock Ferry. The boat, in which I came over, brought from the city a multitude of factory-people, male and female. They had bands of music, and banners inscribed with the Mills they belonged to, and other devices; pale-looking people, but not looking exactly as if they were underfed. They are brought on reduced terms by the railways and steamers, and come from considerable distances in the interior. These, I believe, were from Preston.[11] I have not yet had an opportunity of observing how they amuse themselves during these excursions.

Almost every day, I take walks about Liverpool; preferring the darker and dingier streets, inhabited by the poorer classes. The scenes there are very picturesque in their way; at every two or three steps, a gin-shop; also [*five lines excised*] [fil]thy in clothes and person, ragged, pale, often afflicted with humors; women, nursing their babies at dirty bosoms; men haggard, drunken, care-worn, hopeless, but with a kind of patience, as if all this were the rule of their life; groups stand or sit talking together, around the door-steps, or in the descent of a cellar; often a quarrel is going on in one group, for which the next group cares little or nothing. Sometimes, a decent woman may be seen sewing or knitting at the entrance of her poor dwelling, a glance at which shows dismal poverty. I never walk through these streets without feeling as if I should catch some disease; but yet there is a strong interest in such walks; and moreover there is a bustle, a sense of being in the midst of life, and of having got hold of something real, which I do not find in the better streets of the city. Doubtless, this noon-day and open life of theirs is entirely the best aspect of their existence; and if I were to see them within doors, at their meals, or in bed, it would be unspeakably worse. They appear to wash their clothes occasionally; for I have seen them hanging out to dry in the street.

At the dock, the other day, the steamer arrived from Rock Ferry with a countless multitude of female children in coarse blue-gowns, who, as they landed, formed in procession and walked up the dock. These girls had been taken from the work-houses, and educated at a charity-school, and would by-and-by be apprenticed as servants. I should not have conceived it possible that so many children could have been collected together, without a single trace of beauty, or scarcely of intelligence, in so much as one individual; such mean, coarse, vulgar features and figures, betraying unmistakeably a low origin, and ignorant and brutal parents. They did not appear wicked, but only stupid, animal, and soulless. It must require many generations of better life to elicit a soul in them. All America could not show the like.[12]

August 24th [1853]. From 1 °clock till 2, to-day, I have spent in rambling along the streets, Tythe Barn street, Scotland road, and that vicinity. I never saw, of course, nor imagined from any description, what squalor there is in the inhabitants of these streets, as seen along the sidewalks. All these avenues (the quotation occurs to me continually; and I suppose I have made it two or three times already) are "with dreadful faces thronged."[13] Women with young figures, but old and wrinkled countenances; young girls, without any maiden neatness and trimness, barefooted, with dirty legs, compelling the imaginative eye to seek the delightful region. Women of all ages, even elderly, go along with great, bare, ugly feet; many have baskets and other burdens on their heads. All along the street, with their wares at the edge of the sidewalk, and their own seats fairly in the carriage-way, you see women with fruit to sell, or combs and cheap jewelry, or chamber pots and other coarse crockery, or oysters, or the devil knows what; and sometimes the woman is sewing, meanwhile. This life and domestic occupation in the street is very striking, in all these meaner quarters of the city—nursing of babies, sewing and knitting, sometimes even reading. In a drama of low life, the street might fairly and truly be the one scene where everything should take place—courtship, quarrels, plot and counter-plot, and what not besides. My God, what dirty, dirty children! And the grown people are the flowers of these buds, physically and morally. At every ten steps, too, there are "Spirit Vaults," and often "Beds" are advertized on a placard, in connection with the liquor-trade.

Little children are often seen taking care of littler children; and it seems to me that they take good and faithful care of them. To-day, I heard a dirty mother laughing and priding herself on the pretty ways of her dirty infant—just as a Christian mother might in a nursery or drawing-room. I must study this street-life more, and think of it more deeply.

August 25th [1853]. Further items of street-rambles:—little gray donkeys, dragging along disproportionately large carts;—the disagreeable vista of feeble, thin little babies, legs and arms bare, [*word obliterated*], or having hopes for;—the anomalous aspect of cleanly dressed and healthy looking young women, whom one sometimes sees talking together in the street, evidently residing in some contiguous house;—the apparition, now and then, of a bright, intelligent, merry, child's face, with dark, knowing eyes, gleaming through the dirt like sunshine through a dusty window-pane; at provision-shops, the little bits of meat, ready for poor customers, and little heaps of selvages and corners, snipt off from joints and steaks;—the kindliness with which a little boy leads and lugs along his little sister;—a pale, hollow-cheeked, large-eyed girl of 12, or less, paying a sad, cheerless attention to an infant;—a milkwoman, with a wooden yoke over her shoulder, and a large pail on each side;—in a more reputable street, respectably dressed women going into an ale and spirit-vault, evidently to drink there;—the police-men loitering along, with observant eye, holding converse with none and seldom having occasion to interfere with anybody;—the multitudinousness and continual motion of all this kind of life. The people are as numerous as maggots in cheese; you behold them, disgusting, and all moving about, as when you raise a plank or log that has long lain on the ground, and find many vivacious bugs and insects beneath it.

Septr 2^d [1853]. We got into our new house in Rock Park, yesterday.[14] It is quite a good house, with three apartments, besides kitchen and pantry on the lower floor; and three stories high, with four good chambers in each story. It is a stone edifice, like almost all the modern English houses, and handsome in its design—much more so than most of the American houses. The rent, without furniture, would probably have been £100;—furnished, it is £160. Rock Park, as the locality is called, is private property, and is now nearly covered with residences for professional people, merchants, and others of the upper middling class, the houses being mostly built, I suppose, on speculation, and let to those who occupy them. It is the quietest place imaginable; there being a police station at the entrance; and the officer on duty admits no ragged or ill looking person to pass. There being a toll, it precludes all unnecessary passage of carriages; and never were there more noiseless streets than those that give access to these pretty residences. On either side, there is thick shrubbery, with glimpses through it at the ornamented portals, or into the trim gardens, with smooth shaven lawns, of no large extent, but still affording reasonable breathing space. They are really an improvement on anything save what the very rich can enjoy, in America. The former occupants (a Mrs. Campbell and family) of our house having been fond of flowers, there are many rare varieties in the garden; and we are told that there is scarcely a month of the year in which a flower will not be found there.

The house is respectably, though not elegantly furnished. It was a dismal rainy day, yesterday; and we had a coal fire in the sitting-room; beside which I sat, last evening, as twilight came on, and thought rather sadly how many times we have changed our home, since we were married. In the first place, our three years at the Old Manse; then a brief residence at Salem, then at Boston, then two or three years at Salem again; then at Lenox, then at West Newton, and then again at Concord, where we imagined that we were fixed for life, but spent only a year. Then this farther flight to England, where we expect to spend four years, and afterwards another year in Italy—during all which time we shall have no real home.[15] For, as I sat in this English house, with the chill, rainy English twilight brooding over the lawn, and a coal-fire to keep me comfortable on the first evening of September; and the picture of a stranger (the dead husband of Mrs Campbell) gazing down at me from above the mantel-piece, I felt that I never should be quite at home here. Nevertheless, the fire was very comfortable to look at; and the shape of the fire-place, an arch, with a deep cavity, was an improvement on the square, shallow opening of an American coal-grate.

Septr 22^d [1853]. Nothing very important has happened lately. Some days ago, an American captain came to the office, and told how he had shot one of his crew, shortly after sailing from New Orleans, and while the ship was still in the river. As he described the event, he was in peril of his life from this man, who was an Irishman; and he only fired his pistol, when the man was coming upon him with a knife in one hand, and some other weapon of offence in the other;—the captain, at the same time, struggling with one or two more of the crew. At the time, he was weak, having just recovered from the yellow fever. The shot struck him in the pit of the stomach, and he only lived about a quarter of an hour.

No magistrate in England has a right to arrest or examine the captain, unless by a warrant from the Secretary of State on the charge of murder. After his statement to me, the mother of the slain man went to the police officer, and accused him of killing her son. Two or three days since, moreover, two of the sailors came before me, and gave their account of the matter; and it looked very different from that of the captain. According to them, the man had no idea of attacking the captain, and was so drunk that he could not keep himself upright, without assistance. One of these two men was actually holding him up, when the captain fired two barrels of his pistol, one immediately after the other, and lodged two balls in the pit of his stomach. The man immediately sank down, saying, "Jack, I'm killed,"—and died very shortly. Meanwhile, the captain drove this man away, under threat of shooting him, likewise. Both the seamen described the captain's conduct, both then and during the whole voyage, as outrageous; and I do not much doubt that it was so. They gave their evidence (under oath) like men who wished to tell the truth, and were moved by no more than a natural indignation at the captain's wrong.

I did not much like the captain, from the first; a hard, rough man, with little education—nothing of the gentleman about him; a red face, a loud voice. He seemed a good deal excited, and talked fast and much about the event, but yet not as if it had sunk deeply into him. He observed that he would not have had it happen for a "thousand dollars"—that being the amount of detriment which he conceives himself to suffer by the ineffaceable blood-stain on his hand. In my opinion, it is little short of murder, if at all; but then what would be murder, on shore, is almost a natural occurrence, when done in such a hell on earth as one of these ships, in the first hours of her voyage. The men are then all drunk, some of them often in delirium tremens; and the captain feels no safety for his life, except in making himself as terrible as a fiend. It is the universal testimony, that there is a worse set of sailors in these short voyages between Liverpool and America, than in any other trade whatever.

There is no probability that the captain will ever be called to account for this deed. He gave, at the time, his own version of the affair in his logbook; and this was signed by the entire crew, with the exception of one man, who had hidden himself in the hold in terror of the captain. His mates will sustain his side of the question; and none of the sailors would be within reach of the American courts, even should they be sought for.

Septr 24 [1853]. The women of England are capable of being more atrociously ugly than any other human beings; and I have not as yet seen one whom we should distinguish as beautiful in America. They are very apt to be dowdy. Ladies often look like cooks and housemaids, both in figure and complexion;—at least, to a superficial observer, although a closer inspection shows a kind of dignity, resulting from their quiet good opinion of themselves and consciousness of their position in society. I do not find in them those characteristics of robust health, in which they are said so much to exceed our countrywomen. Some have that appearance, and thereby are well repaid for the coarseness which it gives their figures and faces; others, however, are yellow and haggard, and evidently ailing women. As a general rule, they are not very desirable objects in youth, and, in many instances, become perfectly grotesque after middle-age;—so massive, not seemingly with pure fat, but with solid beef, making an awful ponderosity of frame. You think of them as composed of sirloins, and with broad and thick steaks on their immense rears. They sit down on a great round space of God's footstool, and look as if nothing could ever move them; and indeed they must have a vast amount of physical strength to be able to move themselves.[16] Nothing of the gossamer about them; they are elephantine, and create awe and respect by the muchness of their personalities. Then as to their faces, they are stern, not always positively forbidding, yet calmly terrible, not merely by their breadth and weight of feature, but because they show so much self-reliance, such acquaintance with the world, its trials, troubles, dangers, and such internal means of defence;—such *à plombe*;—I can't get at my exact idea; but without anything salient and offensive, or unjustly terrible to their neighbors, they seem like seventy-four gun ships in time of peace;—you know that you are in no danger from them, but cannot help thinking how perilous would be their attack, if pugnaciously inclined,—and how hopeless the attempt to injure them. Really they are not women at all;—not that they are masculine, either, though more formidable than any man I ever saw. They are invariably, I think, clad in black. I have not happened to see any thin, lady-like old women, such as are so frequent among ourselves; but sometimes, even in these broadly developed old persons, you see a face that indicates cultivation, and even refinement, although, even in such cases, I am generally disturbed by the absence of sex. They certainly look much better able to take care of themselves than our women; but I see no reason to suppose that they really have greater strength of character than they. They are only strong, I suspect, in society, and in the common route of things.

I have not succeeded in getting my idea of the English dowager into the above;—beefy, not pulpy.[17]

October 19th [1853]. Coming to the ferry, this morning, a few minutes before the boat arrived from town, I went into the Ferry House (a small stone edifice) and found there an Irishman, his wife, and three children,—the oldest eight or nine years old, and all girls. There was a good fire burning in the room, and the family were clustered round it, apparently enjoying the warmth very much; but when I came in, both husband and wife very hospitably asked me to come to the fire, although there was not more than room at it for their own party. I declined, on the plea that I was warm enough; and then the woman said that they were very cold, having been long on the road. The man was gray haired and gray-bearded, clad in an old drab over-coat, and had a huge bag, which seemed to contain bed-clothing or something of the kind. The woman was pale, with a thin, anxious, wrinkled face, but a good and kind expression. The children were quite pretty, with delicate faces, and a look of patience and endurance in them, but yet as if they had suffered as little as they possibly could. The two elder were cuddled up close to the father; the youngest, about four years old, sat in its mother's lap, and she had taken off its little shoes and stockings, and was warming its feet at the fire. Their little voices had a sweet and kindly sound, as they talked in low tones to their parents and one another. They all looked very shabby, but yet had a decency about them; and it was touching to see how they made themselves at home at this casual fireside, and got all the comfort they could out of the circumstances. By and by, two or three market-women came in, and looked kindly at them, and said a word or two to the children.

They did not beg of me, as I partly expected they would; but after looking at them awhile, I pulled out a sixpence, and handed it to one of the little girls. She took it very readily, as if she partly expected it; and then the father and mother thanked me, and said they had been travelling a long distance, and had nothing to live upon, but what they picked up on the road. They found it impossible to live in England, and were now on their way to Liverpool, hoping to get a passage back to Ireland, where, I suppose, extreme poverty is rather better off than here. I heard the little girl say that she should buy a loaf with the money. There is not much that can be caught in the description of this scene; but it made me understand, better than before, how poor people feel, wandering about in such destitute circumstances, and how they suffer, and yet how they know a life not quite miserable, after all; and how family love goes along with them. Soon, the boat arrived at the pier; and we all went on board; and as I sat in the cabin, looking up through a broken pane in the skylight, I saw the woman's thin face, with its anxious, motherly aspect, and the youngest child in her arms, shrinking from the chill wind, but yet not impatiently; and the eldest of the girls standing close by, with her expression of childish endurance—but yet so bright and intelligent, that it would evidently take but a few days to make a happy and playful child of her. Somehow or other, I got into the interior of this poor family, and understand, through sympathy, more of them than I can tell. They were much better, I think, and more delicate, than if they had been English.

I am getting to possess some of the English indifference as to beggars and poor people; but still, whenever I come face to face with them, and have any intercourse, it seems as if they ought to be the better for me. I wish, instead of sixpence, I had given this poor family ten shillings, and denied it to a begging subscriptionist, who has just fleeced me to that amount. How silly a man feels, in this latter predicament!

Decr 31st [1853]. Among the beggars of Liverpool, the hardest to encounter is a man without any legs, and, if I mistake not, likewise deficient in arms.[18] You see him before you all at once, as if he had sprouted half-way out of the earth, and would sink down and re-appear in some other place, the moment he has done with you. His countenance is large, fresh, and very intelligent; but his great power lies in his fixed gaze, which is inconceivably difficult to bear. He never once removes his eye from you, till you are quite past his range; and you feel it all the same, although you do not meet his glance. He is perfectly respectful; but the intentness and directness of his silent appeal is far worse than any impudence. In fact, it is the very flower of impudence. I would rather go a mile about than pass before his battery. I feel wronged by him, and yet unutterably ashamed. There must be great force in the man, to produce such an effect. There is nothing of the customary squalidness of beggary about him, but remarkable trimness and cleanliness. A girl of twenty, or thereabouts, who vagabondizes about the city on her hands and knees, possesses, to a considerable degree, the same characteristics. I think they hit their victims the more effectually, from being below the common level of vision.

Jany 6th, 1854.

If mankind were all intellect, they would be continually changing, so that one age would be entirely unlike another. The great conservative is the heart, which remains the same in all ages; so that common-places of a thousand years standing are as effective as ever.

Feb 23^d '54. There came to see me the other day a young gentleman with a moustache and a blue cloak (of rather coarse texture) who announced himself as William Allingham, and handed me a copy of his poems, in a thin volume with paper-covers, published by Routledge.[19] I thought I remembered hearing his name, but had never seen any of his works. His face was intelligent, dark, rather pleasing, and not at all John Bullish. He said that he had been employed in the Customs in Ireland, and was now going to London to live by literature—to be connected with some newspaper, I imagine. He had been in London before, and was acquainted with some of the principal literary people—among others, Carlyle and Tennyson.[20] He seemed to have been on rather intimate terms with the latter; and I gathered from what he said that Tennyson is a moody man, though genial with his friends. He says Tennyson told him that if he were sure there were no hereafter, he would go and fling himself over London bridge;—a foolish thing to do or to say; but perhaps he might have said a wiser thing to a wiser man. Tennyson is a very shy man, and thinks everybody stares at him on account of his strange appearance, on railways and everywhere else, even in the seclusion of his own garden. This, I judge, has no reference to the notice drawn on him by his poetry, but is the natural morbidness of a man who shirks society. Tennyson's wife seems to be a good person, not handsome, but cheerful, capable of appreciating him and fit to make him comfortable. Her mode seems to be a gentle and good-humored raillery of his peculiarities. Allingham says that they have a fine boy and that it would have been better for Tennyson to have been married fifteen years ago, instead of three or four. We talked awhile in my dingy and dusky consulate, and he then took leave. His manners are good, and he appears to possess independence of mind. On looking over his poems, I find some good things among them.

March 16th [1854].

A woman's chastity consists, like an onion, of a series of coats. You may strip off the outer ones without doing much mischief, perhaps none at all; but you keep taking off one after another, in expectation of coming to the inner nucleus, including the whole value of the matter. It proves, however, that there is no such nucleus, and that Chastity is diffused through the whole series of coats, is lessened with the removal of each, and vanishes with the final one, which you supposed would introduce you to the hidden pearl.

September 26th [1854]. On Saturday evening, my wife and I went to a soiree, given by the Mayor and Mrs. Lloyd at the Town Hall. It was quite brilliant; the public rooms being really magnificent; and adorned for the occasion with a large collection of pictures, belonging to Mr Naylor.[21] They were mostly (I believe entirely) of modern artists, comprising some of Turner, Wilkie, Landseer, and others of the best English painters.[22] Turner's seemed too airy to have been done by mortal hands.

The British scientific association being now in session here, many distinguished strangers were present. What chiefly struck me, however, was the lack of beauty in the women, and the horrible ugliness of not a few of them. I have heard a good deal of the tenacity with which English women retain their personal charms to a late period of life; but my experience is, that an English lady of forty or fifty is apt to become the most hideous animal that ever pretended to human shape. No caricature could do justice to some of their figures and features; so puffed out, so huge, so without limit, with such hanging dewlaps, and all manner of fleshly abomination—dressed, too, in a way to show all these points to the worst advantage, and walking about with entire self-satisfaction, unconscious of the wrong they are doing to one's idea of womanhood. They are gross, gross, gross. Who would not shrink from such a mother! Who would not abhor such a wife! I really pitied the respectable elderly gentlemen whom I saw walking about with such atrocities hanging on their arms—the grim, red-faced monsters! Surely, a man would be justified in murdering them—in taking a sharp knife and cutting away their mountainous flesh, until he had brought them into reasonable shape, as a sculptor seeks for the beautiful form of woman in a shapeless block of marble. The husband must feel that something alien has grown over and incrusted the slender creature whom he married, and that he is horribly wronged by having all this flabby flesh imposed upon him as his wife. "Flesh of his flesh," indeed![23] And this ugliness surely need not be, at least to such a dreadful extent; it must be, in great part, the penalty of a life of gross feeding—of much ale-guzzling and beef-eating. Nor is it possible to conceive of any delicacy and grace of soul existing within; or if there be such, the creature ought to be killed, in order to release the spirit so vilely imprisoned. Flee away then, fugitive of the past! I really and truly believe that the entire body of American washerwomen would present more grace than the entire body of English ladies, were both to be shown up together. American women, of all ranks, when past their prime, generally look thin, worn, care-begone, as if they may have led a life of much trouble and few enjoyments; but English women look as if they had fed upon the fat of meat, and made themselves gross and earthy in all sorts of ways. As a point of taste, I prefer my own countrywomen; though it is a pity that we must choose between a greasy animal and an anxious skeleton.

January 3ᵈ 1855. The progress of the age is trampling over the aristocratic institutions of England, and they crumble beneath it. The war has given the country a vast impulse towards democracy.[24] The nobility will never hereafter, I think, assume, or be permitted, to rule the nation in peace, or command armies in war, on any ground except the individual ability which may appertain to one of their number, as well as to a commoner. And yet the nobles were never positively more noble than now—never, perhaps, so chivalrous, so honorable, so highly cultivated; but, relatively to the rest of the world, they do not maintain their old place. The pressure of the war has tested and proved this fact, at home and abroad. At this moment, it would be an absurdity in the nobles to pretend to the position which was quietly conceded to them a year ago. This one year has done the work of fifty ordinary ones;—or more accurately, perhaps, it has made apparent what has long been preparing itself.

January 6ᵗʰ 1855. Mr. Buchanan called on me today, and staid a good while—an hour or two.[25] He is now staying at Mr. Wᵐ Brown's at Richmond Hill, having come to this region to bring his niece, who is to be bridesmaid at a wedding of an American girl. I like Mr. Buchanan; he cannot exactly be called gentlemanly in his manners, there being a sort of rusticity about him;—moreover, a habit of squinting one eye, and an aukward carriage of his head; but, withal, a dignity in his large, white-headed person, and a consciousness of high position and importance, which gives him ease and freedom. Very simple and frank in his address; he may be as crafty as other diplomatists are said to be; but I see only good sense and plainness of speech—appreciative, too, and genial enough to make himself conversible. He talked very freely of himself and other public people, and American and English affairs. He returns to America, he says, next October, and then retires forever from public life, being sixty-four years of age, and having now no desire except to write memoirs of his times—and especially of the administration of Mr. Polk. I suggested a doubt whether the people would permit him to retire; and he immediately responded to my hint as regards his prospects for the Presidency. He said that his mind was fully made up, and that he would never be a candidate, and that he had expressed this intention to his friends in such a way as to put out of his own power to change it. He acknowledged that he should have been glad of the nomination for Presidency in 1852, but that it was now too late, and that he was too old;—and, in short, he seemed to be quite sincere in his nolo episcopari; although, really, he is the only Democrat, at this moment, whom it would not be absurd to talk of for the office. As he talked, his face flushed, and he seemed to get inwardly excited. Doubtless, it was the high vision of half his lifetime which he here relinquished. I cannot question that he is sincere; but, of course, should the people insist upon having him for President, he is too good a patriot to disobey. I wonder whether he can have had any object in saying all this to me. He might see that it would be perfectly natural for me to tell it to General Pierce. But it is a very vulgar idea—this of seeing craft and subtlety, where there is a plain and honest aspect.

April 12th [1855]. In my Romance ["The American Claimant," never completed], the original emigrant to America may have carried away with him a family-secret, whereby it was in his power (had he so chosen) to have brought about the ruin of the family. This secret he transmits to his American progeny, by whom it is inherited throughout all the intervening generations. At last, the hero of the Romance comes to England, and finds that, by means of this secret, he still has it in his power to procure the downfal of the family. It would be something similar to the story of Meleager, whose fate depended on the firebrand that his mother had snatched out of the flames.[26]

Tuesday, April 24th 55. On Saturday, I was present at a dejeûner on board the Donald Mackay (a new American ship, built for James Baines & Co) the principal guest being Mr. Layard, M.P.[27] There were several hundred people present, quite filling the between decks of the ship, which was converted into a saloon for the nonce. I sat next to Mr. Layard, at the head of the table—or rather, at the cross-table—and so had a good opportunity of seeing and getting acquainted with him. He is a man in early middle-age (with hair a very little frosted, I think) of a somewhat plebeian aspect, as Englishmen are so apt to be; of middle stature, with an open, frank, intelligent, kindly face, but no very intellectual or refined lines in it. His forehead is not expansive, but is prominent in the perceptive regions, and retreats a good deal; his mouth is fleshy. I liked him from the first, but, had I met him in America, should have set him down as an intelligent mechanic;—not that there is any lack of good-breeding, but only the usual English homeliness, and unpolished surface. Yet he has a French shrug; which I don't like to see. He was very kind and complimentary to me, and made me promise to come and see him in London.

It would have been a very pleasant entertainment; only that my pleasure in it was much marred by having to acknowledge a toast in honor of the President;—however, such things don't trouble me nearly so much as they did, and I came through it tolerably enough. Mr. Layard's speech was the great affair of the day. He speaks (though he assured me that he had to put great force upon himself to speak publickly) with much fluency; and, as he warms up, seems to speak with his whole moral and physical man, and to be quite possessed with what he has to say. His evident earnestness and good-faith make him eloquent, and stand him in stead of oratorical graces—of which (as a matter of study and acquisition) he does not seem to have any. His view of the position of England and the prospects of the war were as dark as well could be; in fact, there never was a better specimen of English grumbling than his whole speech—and it was exceedingly to the purpose, full of common sense, and with not one word of clap-trap. Judging from its effect upon the audience, he spoke the voice of the whole English people—although an English baronet, who sat next below me, seemed to dissent, or at least to think that it was not exactly the thing for a stranger to hear it. The speech concluded amidst great cheering. Mr. Layard appears to me a true Englishman, not remarkably bright intellectually, but with a moral force, and strength of character, and earnestness of purpose, and fullness of common sense, such as have always served England's turn in her past successes; but rather fit for resistance than for progress. No doubt, he is a good and very able man; but I question whether he could get England out of the difficulties which he sees so clearly, or could do much better than Lord Palmerston, whom he so decries.[28] The truth is, there is a spirit lacking in England, which *we* do not lack, and for the want of which she will have to resign a foremost position among the nations, even if there were not enough other circumstances to compel her to do so. Her good qualities are getting out of date;—at all events, there should be something added to them, in the present stage of the world.

May 24th [1855]. A week or two ago, there called on me a Doctor of Divinity from New Orleans, who had just arrived in a sailing vessel; he was a good-looking, gentlemanly, middle-aged man, and seemed all right, except perhaps a little excited, as most Americans are, on first setting foot in England.[29] He took a large bundle of letters, which had come to hand in anticipation of his arrival, and went away. A day or two after, Captain Emerson (in whose vessel he had arrived) came to me and said that the Doctor had disappeared—not having been seen by him since his visit to my office. From this Captain's communications, I learned that the Reverend Doctor was a man of rather sad experience, having been divorced from his second wife, and having been in a lunatic asylum, and being also liable to fits of terrible intemperance. It was therefore obvious to suppose that he had allowed himself to lapse into one of these fits. I had some thoughts of setting the police on his track, but concluded that it might be as well to let matters take their course, as he would probably turn up when his money was spent. Accordingly, precisely a week after his disappearance, he was brought back to Captain Emerson's ship, in a state of delirium tremens, by a woman of the town! He was in a filthy and horrible condition, the Captain told me, and said that he had been robbed of five hundred dollars—which was more than he had ever had.

There is a Dr. Macauley, our Consul at Venice, now in Liverpool; and as he is likewise from New Orleans, I mentioned the Reverend Doctor's case in confidence to him.[30] It turned out that Dr. Macauley is an old acquaintance; and as he seems to be a most humane and good little, simple-hearted man, he immediately undertook to take charge of him, and get him back to America, if possible. Yesterday, while Dr. Macauley was sitting with me (having already visited Doctor R., and been joyfully received by him) there came into my office, a tall, middle-aged, mustachioed gentleman, of rather a military aspect, in a blue surtout, closely buttoned. He addressed me as if previously acquainted; and at his first word, and my first glance at his face, I could see that he was under the influence of liquor—a very rowdy-looking gentleman, indeed. I bowed coolly, and observed that I had not the pleasure of knowing him. "Am I then so changed!" he cried, with a vast depth of tragic intonation; and, after a little more blind talk, behold! I recognized him as the reverend gentleman himself. If I had meditated a scene, or a *coup de theatre*, I could not have contrived a more effectual one than by this simple non-recognition; for the poor man—his nerves being all in a devil's tremble—thought that he must have almost lost his personal identity in the space of one little week. To say the truth, he did look as if he had been dragged through hell, and changed from a decorous clergyman into a rowdy military man; but I should probably have known him, had I taken any particular note of his aspect, at our first interview. Seeing how good an effect had been produced, I maintained my austerity of manner, only granting him a cold recognition; and took occasion to represent to him the deplorable condition to which he had reduced himself, inasmuch as he could no longer be known for the same person whom I had seen a week ago; and exhorted him to refrain from such evil courses hereafter—a lecture which I never dreamed of having an opportunity to bestow on a Doctor of Divinity. It was really a very tragic scene; and an actor might have taken a lesson in his art from him; for all his emotions, and all the external movement and expression of them, by voice, face, and gesture, were exaggerated by the tremendous vibration of nerves remaining from his delirium tremens. Poor, Reverend devil! Drunkard! Whoremaster! Doctor of Divinity! He is very powerfully eloquent, I am told, in sermon and prayer.

June 22ᵈ Thursday [1855]. In the forenoon of yesterday, wife, Una and I took a walk through what looked like a park, but seemed to be a sort of semi-public tract on the outskirts of the town—hill and glade, with a fair gravel path through it, and most stately and beautiful trees overshadowing it. Here and there benches were set beneath the trees. These old, vigorous, well-nurtured trees, are fine beyond description; and in this leafy month of June,[31] they certainly surpass my recollections of American trees—so tall, with such an aspect of age-long life. But I suppose what we know of English trees, of the care bestowed on them, the value at which they are estimated, their being traditional, and connected with the fortunes of old families—these moral considerations inevitably enter into physical admiration of them. They are individuals—which few American trees have the happiness to be. The English elm is more beautiful in shape and growth than I had imagined; but I think our own elm is still more so. Julian compared an English oak, which we saw on our journey, to a cauliflower; and its shape, its regular, compact rotundity, makes it very like one;—there is a certain John-Bullism about it. Its leaf, too, is much smaller than our own oak; and with similar advantages of age and cultivation, the latter would be far the noblest and most majestic form of a tree. But in verdure, in the rich aspect of the country, nothing surely can equal England; and I never enjoyed weather anywhere so delightful as such a day as yesterday; so warm and genial, and yet not oppressive—the sun a very little too warm, while walking beneath it, but only enough too warm to assure us that it was warm enough. And, after all, there was an unconquered freshness in the atmosphere, which each little motion of the air made evident to us. I suppose there is still latent in us Americans (even of two centuries date, and more, like myself) an adaptation to the English climate, which makes it like native soil and air to us.[32]

∼

Hawthorne and his family visit Shakespeare's Stratford-upon-Avon.

∼

June 27ᵗʰ, Thursday [1855]. This day promising to be a very fair one, we devoted it to our pilgrimage to Stratford on Avon; and Mamma,

Una, Julian, and I, set out in a phaeton, at about ½ past 9. It was really a bright morning, warm, genial and delightful; so that we saw English scenery under almost an American sun, and the combination made something very like perfection. Our road lay through Warwick; and I observed, on the wall of an old chapel in the High-street, some fox-glove flowers growing, as also grass and little shrubs, all at the height of perhaps twenty feet above the ground. Adjacent to this chapel (which stands almost across the street, with an archway for foot passengers beneath it, and causing the carriage track to swerve aside in passing it) there is an ancient edifice, in excellent repair, and with coats of arms and the cognizance of the Bear and Ragged Staff painted on its front. This turns out to be Leicester's Hospital,[33] an institution for the support of twelve poor brethren; and I think we saw the better part of a dozen old faces, idly contemplating us from the windows or about the doors of the old house. I must try to get a better knowledge of this institution.

The road from Warwick to Stratford is most beautiful; not that it owes any remarkable features to Nature; for the country thereabouts is a succession of the gentlest swells and subsidences, here and there affording wide and far glimpses of champagne scenery; and near Stratford it becomes quite level. Altogether, throwing in a few higher hills, and opening the eye of the scene, here and there, by a sheet of water, like Walden-pond, it would look a good deal like the country near Concord—so far as its natural features are concerned. But the charm of the English scene is its old and high cultivation, its richness of verdure, its stately trees, with their trunks clustered about by creeping shrubs;—a great deal of which man has done, and in which he could be partly rivalled in America; but much, too, is due to the moisture of the climate, and the gentle sunshine. At any rate, the effect is beyond all description, and seen, as I have just said, under an American sun (that is to say, once or twice a year) nothing more could be asked by mortals, in the way of rural beauty. All along the way, there were cottages of old date, many so old that Shakespeare might have passed them in his walks, or entered their low doors; a few modern-villas, too; and perhaps mansions of gentility or nobility hidden among the trees—for such houses seldom show themselves from the road.

There is nothing remarkable in the approach to Stratford. The spire of Shakespeare's church shows itself among the trees, at a little distance from the town. Then comes shabby old houses, intermixed with more modern ones, mostly mean-looking; and the streets being quite level, the effect on the whole is tame and quite unpicturesque. I think I might ride into such a town, even in America, and not be much struck by many peculiarities. Here and there, however, there are very queer dwellings, that seem to have been growing queerer and odder during the three or four centuries of their existence; and there appear to be more old people, tottering about and leaning on sticks—old people in breeches, and retaining all the traditional costume of the last century—than could be found anywhere on our side of the water. Old places seem to produce old people; or perhaps the secret is, that old age has a natural tendency to hide itself, when it is brought into contact with new edifices, and new things, but comes freely out, and feels itself in sympathy, and is not ashamed to face the eye of man, in a decaying town. There is a sense of propriety in this.

We stopt at the Red Lion, a hotel of no great pretensions, and immediately set out on our rambles about town. After wandering through two or three streets, we found Shakespeare's birth-place, which is almost a worse house than anybody could dream it to be; but it did not surprise me, because I had seen a full-sized fac-simile of it in the Zoological-gardens at Liverpool.[34] It is exceedingly small—at least, the portion of it which had anything to do with Shakespeare. The old, worn, butcher's counter, on which the meat used to be laid, is still at the window. The upper half of the door was open; and on my rapping at it, a girl dressed in black soon made her appearance and opened it. She was a lady like girl, not a menial, but I suppose the daughter of the old lady who shows the house. This first room has a pavement of gray slabs of stone, which, no doubt, were rudely squared when the house was new, but they are all cracked and broken, now, in a curious way. One does not see how any ordinary usage, for whatever length of time, should have cracked them thus; it is as if the devil had been stamping on them, long ago, with an iron hoof, and the tread of other persons had ever since been reducing them to an even surface again. The room is white-washed, and very clean, but woefully shabby and dingy, coarsely built, and such as it is not very easy to idealize. In the rear of this room is the kitchen, a still smaller room, of the same dingy character; it has a great, rough fire-place, with an immense passage way for the smoke, and room for a large family under the blackened opening of the chimney. I stood under it, without stooping; and doubtless Shakespeare may have stood on the same spot, both as child and man. A great fire might of course make the kitchen cheerful; but it gives a depressing idea of the humble, mean, sombre character of the life that could have been led in such a dwelling as this—with no conveniences, all higgledy-piggledy, no retirement, the whole family, old and young, brought into too close contact to be comfortable together. To be sure, they say the house used to be much larger than now, in Shakespeare's time; but what we see of it is consistent in itself, and does not look as if it ever could have been a portion of a large and respectable house.

Thence we proceeded upstairs to the room in which Shakespeare is supposed to have been born, and which is over the front lower room, or butcher's shop. It has one broad window, with old irregular panes of glass; the floor is of very rudely hewn planks; the naked beams and rafters at the sides and over head bear all the marks of the builder's axe; and the room, besides, is very small—a circumstance more difficult to reconcile one's self to, as regards places that we have heard and thought much about, than any other part of a mistaken ideal. I could easily touch the ceiling, and could have done so had it been a good deal higher; indeed, the ceiling was entirely written over with names in pencil, by persons, I suppose, of all varieties of stature; so was every inch of the wall, into the obscurest nooks and corners; so was every pane of glass—and Walter Scott's name was said to be on one of the panes; but so many people had sought to immortalize themselves in close vicinity to him, that I really could not trace out his signature. I did not write my own name.

This room, and the whole house, so far as I saw it, was white-washed and very clean; and it had not the aged, musty smell, with which Chester makes one familiar, and which I suspect is natural to old houses, and must render them unwholesome. The woman who showed us up stairs had the manners and aspect of a gentlewoman, and talked intelligently about Shakespeare. Arranged on a table and in chairs, there were various prints, views of houses and scenes connected with Shakespeare's memory, editions of his works, and local publications relative to him—all for sale, and from which, no doubt, this old gentlewoman realizes a good deal of profit. We bought several shillings' worth, partly as thinking it the civillest method of requiting her for the trouble of showing the house. On taking our leave, I most ungenerously imposed on Sophia the duty of offering an additional fee to the lady like girl who first admitted us; but there seemed to be no scruple, on her part, as to accepting it. I felt no emotion whatever in Shakespeare's house—not the slightest—nor any quickening of the imagination. It is agreeable enough to reflect that I have seen it; and I think I can form, now, a more sensible and vivid idea of him as a flesh-and-blood man; but I am not quite sure that this latter effect is altogether desirable.

From Shakespeare's house (after doing a little shopping and buying some toys for Rosebud) we inquired out the church—the Church of the Holy Trinity—where he lies buried....[35] We were admitted into the church by a respectable-looking man in black, who was already exhibiting the Shakespeare monuments to two or three visitors; and other parties came in while we were there. The poet and his family seem to have the best burial-places that the church affords—or, at least, as good as any. They lie in a row, right across the breadth of the chancel, the foot of each gravestone being close to the elevated floor about the altar. Nearest to the side wall, beneath Shakespeare's bust, is the slab of stone bearing an inscription to his wife; then his own, with the old anathematizing stanza upon it; then, I think, the stone of Thomas Nash, who married his granddaughter; then that of Dr. Hall, the husband of his daughter Susannah; then Susannah's own.[36] Shakespeare's grave stone is the commonest looking slab of all, just such a flagstone as a sidewalk of the street might be paved with. Unlike the other monuments of the family, it has no name whatever upon it; and I do not see on what authority it is absolutely determined to be his. To be sure, being in a range with his wife and children, it might naturally be guessed that it was his; but then he had another daughter, and a son, who would need a grave somewhere. Perhaps, however, as his name was on the bust, above, and as his wife, when he was buried, had not yet taken her place between him and the church-wall, his name was thought unnecessary. . . .

Now, as for the bust of Shakespeare, it is affixed to the northern wall of the church, the base of it being about a man's height (or more) above the floor of the chancel.[37] The bust is quite unlike any portrait, or any other bust of Shakespeare, that I have ever seen, and compels one to root up all old ideas of his aspect, and adopt an entirely different one. For my part, I am loth to give up the beautiful, lofty-browed, noble picture of him which I have hitherto had in my mind; for this bust does not represent a beautiful face, or a noble head. And yet it clutches hold of one's sense of reality, and you feel that this was the man. I don't know what the phrenologists say to this bust; its forehead is but moderately developed, and retreats somewhat; the upper part of the skull seems rather contracted; the eyes are rather prominent. The upper lip is so long that it must have been almost a deformity; the showman of the church said that Sir Walter Scott's upper lip was longer, but I doubt it. On the whole, Shakespeare must have had a singular, rather than a striking face; and it is wonderful how, with this bust before its eyes, the world has insisted on forming an erroneous idea of his appearance, permitting painters and sculptors to foist their idealized nonsense upon mankind, instead of the genuine Shakespeare. But as for myself, I am henceforth to see in my mind's eye a red-faced personage, with a moderately capacious brow, an intelligent eye, a nose curved very slightly outward, a long, queer upper lip, with the mouth a little unclosed beneath it, and cheeks very much developed in the lower part of the face.[38]

∽

Hawthorne makes another pilgrimage, this one to Lichfield, Staffordshire, the town of Samuel Johnson.

Wednesday, July 4th 1855.

My ride to Rugby, and thence to Lichfield, presented nothing to be noted;—the same rich, verdant country, and old trees, which I had grown accustomed to, in a fortnight past....

The streets of Lichfield are very crooked, and the town stands on an ascending surface. There are not so many old gabled houses as in Coventry, but still a great many of them;—and very few of the edifices, I suspect, are really and fundamentally new. They hide their age behind spruce fronts, but are old at heart. The people have an old-fashioned way with them, and stare at a stranger, as if the railway had not yet quite accustomed them to visitors and novelty. The old women, in one or two instances, dropt me a curtsey, as I passed them;—perhaps it was a mere obeisance to one whom, in their antique way, they acknowledged as their better;—perhaps they looked for sixpence at my hands. I gave them the benefit of the doubt, and kept my money.

The Swan Hotel stands, I believe, in Bird-street. At my first sally forth, I turned a corner at a venture, and soon saw a church before me. At this point, the street widens so much (though not very much either) as to be called Saint Mary's square; and adjacent to it stands the market-house. In this square, not quite in the middle of it, is a statue of Dr. Johnson, on a stone pedestal, some ten or twelve feet high; the statue is colossal (though perhaps not much bigger than the mountainous Doctor) and sits in a chair, with big books underneath it, looking down on the spectator with a broad, heavy, benignant countenance, very like those of Johnson's portraits. The figure is immensely broad and massive—a ponderosity of stone, not fully humanized, nor finely spiritualized, but yet I liked it well enough, though it looked more like a great boulder than a man. On the pedestal were three bas-reliefs;[39]—the first, Johnson sitting on an old man's shoulders, a mere baby, and resting his chin on the bald head which he embraces with his arms, and listening to Dr. Sacheverell preaching; the second, Johnson carried on the shoulders of two boys to school, another boy supporting him behind; the third, Johnson doing penance at Uttoxeter, the wind and rain beating hard against him, very sad and woe-begone, while some market-people and children gaze in his face, and behind are two old people with clasped hands, praying for him. I think these last must be the spirits of his father and mother; though, in queer proximity, there are dead and living ducks. I never heard of this statue before; it seems to have no reputation as a work of art, and probably may deserve none;—nevertheless, I found it somewhat touching and effective. The statue faces towards the house in which Johnson was born, which stands not more than twenty to forty yards off, on the corner of a street which divides it from the church. It is a tall, three-story house, with a square front, and a roof rising steep and high; on a side view, the house appears to have been cut in two in the midst, there being no slope of the roof on that side. The house is plaistered, and there was a high ladder against it, and painters at work on the front. In the basement corner apartment, what we should call a dry-good store (and the English, I believe, a haberdasher's shop) is kept. There is a side, private entrance, on the cross-street between the house and the church, with much-worn stone steps, and an iron balustrade. I set my foot on the worn steps, and laid my hand on the wall of the house, because Johnson's hand and foot might have been in those same places....

The Cathedral of Lichfield seemed to me very beautiful indeed. I have heretofore seen no cathedral save that of Chester, and one or two little ones, unworthy of the name, in Wales. No doubt, there may be much more magnificent cathedrals, in England and elsewhere, than this of Litchfield; but if there were no other, I should be pretty well satisfied with this; such beautiful shapes it takes, from all points of view, with its peaks and pinnacles, and its three towers and their lofty spires, one loftier than its fellows; so rich it is with external ornament, of carved stone-work, and statues in a great many niches, though many more are vacant, which I suppose were once filled. I had no idea before (nor, possibly, have I now) what intricate and multitudinous adornment was bestowed on the front of a Gothic church. Above the chief entrance, there is a row of statues of saints, angels, martyrs, or kings, running along that whole front, to the number, no doubt, of more than a score, sculptured in red stone. Then there are such strange, delightful recesses in the great figure of the Cathedral; it is so difficult to melt it all into one idea, and comprehend it in that way; and yet it is all so consonant in its intricacy—it seems to me a Gothic Cathedral may be the greatest work man has yet achieved—a great stone poem. I hated to leave gazing at it, because I felt that I did not a hundredth part take it in and comprehend it; and yet I wanted to leave off, because I knew I never should adequately comprehend its beauty and grandeur. Perhaps you must live with the Cathedral in order to know it; but yet the clerical people connected with it do not seem oppressed with reverence for the edifice....

At about 11, I left Lichfield for Uttoxeter, on a purely sentimental pilgrimage, to see the spot where Johnson performed his penance....

On arriving at the rail-way station, the first thing I saw, in a convenient vicinity, was the tower and tall gray spire of a church. It is but a very short walk from the station up into the town. It was my impression that the market-place of Uttoxeter lay round the church; and if I remember the incident aright, Johnson mentions that his father's bookstall had stood in the market-place, close by the church. But this is not the case. The church has a street, of ordinary width, passing around it; while the market-place, though near at hand, is not really contiguous to the church, nor would there probably be much of the bustle of the market about this edifice, now-a-days. Still a minute's walk would bring a person from the centre of the market-place to the door of the church; and Michael Johnson may very well have had his stall in the angle of the tower and body of it;—not now, indeed, because there is an iron railing round it. The tower and spire of the church look old; but the walls have evidently been renewed since Johnson's time. The market-place is rather spacious, and is surrounded by houses and shops, some old, with red-tiled roofs, others with a pretence of newness, but probably as old as the rest. Unless it were by the church, I could not fix on any one spot more than another, likely to have been the spot where Johnson stood to do his penance. How strange and stupid, that there should be no local memorial of this incident—as beautiful and touching an incident as can be cited out of any human life—no inscription of it on the wall of the church, no statue of the venerable and illustrious penitent in the market-place, to throw a wholesome awe over its earthly business. Such a statue ought almost to have grown up out of the pavement, (and thus have shown me the spot) of its own accord, in the place that was watered by his remorseful tears, and by the rain that dripped from him.

...I spent I know not how many hours in Uttoxeter, and, to say the truth, was heartily tired of it; my penance being a great deal longer than Dr. Johnson's. It is a pity I did not take the opportunity to repent of my own sins; but I forgot all about them till it was too late. No train passed the town by which I could get away, till five °clock. As I sat waiting for its appearance, I asked a boy who sat near me—(a school-boy, of some twelve or thirteen years, he seemed to me; and I should take him for a clergy-man's son)—I asked him whether he had ever heard the story of Dr. Johnson's standing an hour by that church, whose spire rose before us. He said "no." I asked if no such story was known or talked about in Uttoxeter. He answered, "No, not that he ever heard of." Just think of the absurd little town, knowing nothing about the incident which sanctifies it to the heart of a stranger from three thousand miles over the sea!—just think of the fathers and mothers of the town, never telling the children this sad and lovely story, which might have such a blessed influence on their young days, and spare them so many a pang hereafter!

July 8th, Sunday [1855]. At the Consulate, yesterday, a queer, stupid, good-natured, fat-faced individual came in, dressed in a sky blue, coarse, cut-away coat, and mixed pantaloons, which (both coat and trowsers,) seemed rather too small for his goodly size.[40] He turned out to be the Yankee who came to England, a few weeks ago, to see the Queen, on the strength of having sent her his own and his wife's daguerreotype, and having received a note of thanks from her secretary. Having been swindled by a fellow-passenger, he has loafed about here ever since his arrival, unable to get home—and, indeed, unwilling, until he shall have gone to London to see the Queen; and, to support himself, he has parted with all the clothes he brought with him, and thrusts himself into the narrow limits of this sky-blue coat and mixed pantaloons. It is certainly a very odd-looking dress; and he hinted, with a melancholy, stupid smile, that he did not look quite fit to see the Queen now. Of course, he wanted my assistance; but it is marvellous, the pertinacity with which he clings to his idea of going to court, and, though starving, will not think of endeavoring to get home, till that has been effected. I laid his absurdity before him, in the plainest terms. "My dear man!" quoth he, with good-natured, simple stubbornness, "if you could but enter into my feelings, and see the business from beginning to end, as I see it!" And this he repeated over and over again. He wished me, if I would not help him myself, to give me the names of some American merchants, to whom he might apply for means to get to London; but I refused to interfere with his affairs in any way, unless he promised to go back immediately to the United States, in case I could get him a passage. Besides his desire to see the Queen, he has likewise (like so many of his countrymen) a fantasy that he is one of the legal heirs of a great English inheritance. No doubt, this dream about the Queen and his English estate has haunted his poor, foolish mind for years and years; and he deems it the strangest and mournfullest perversity of fate, and awfullest cruelty in me, that now—when he has reached England, and has wealth and royal honors almost within his grasp—he must turn back, a poor, penniless, be-fooled simpleton, merely because I will not lend him thirty shillings to get to London. I had never such a perception of a complete booby before, in my life; it made me feel kindly towards him, and yet impatient that such a fool should exist. Finally (as he had not a penny in his pocket, and no means of getting anything to eat) I gave him a couple of shillings, and told him not to let me see him again, till he had made up his mind to get back to America—when I would beg a passage for him if I could. He thanked me, and went away, half-crying, and yet with some thing like a dull, good-natured smile on his face; still fixed in his inveterate purpose of getting to London to see the Queen!

August 12th, Sunday [1855].

For the last week or two, I have passed my time between the Hotel and the Consulate; and a weary life it is, and one that leaves little of profit behind it. I am sick to death of my office;—brutal captains and brutish sailors;—continual complaints of mutual wrong, which I have no power to set right, and which, indeed, seem to have no right on either side;—calls of idleness or ceremony from my travelling countrymen, who seldom know what they are in search of, at the commencement of their tour, and never have attained any desirable end, at the close of it;—beggars, cheats, simpletons, unfortunates, so mixed up that it is impossible to distinguish one from another, and so, in self-defense, the consul distrusts them all. I see many specimens of mankind, but come to the conclusion that there is but little variety among them, after all.

August 17th Friday [1855].

Yesterday afternoon, Julian and I went to Birkenhead Park. It is a large enclosure, open to the public, and is pretty well beautified with shrubbery, and a pond, and pretty bridges, and here and there a statue, such as Mazeppa,[41] and others of no particular merit, among the trees. There are broad open spaces, where people may play cricket and otherwise disport themselves; also, a camera obscura; and, of course, a refreshment room—where, however, there is nothing better, of a drinkable order, than ginger-beer and British wines. And here the respectable middle-classes—the lower-middling—come to spend a summer afternoon, wandering up and down the winding gravel-paths, feeding the swans off the bridges, nibbling buns and gingerbread and polka-ing (girls with girls) to the music of a hand-organ. It so happened that yesterday there was a large school spending its holiday there; a school of girls of the lower classes, to the number of some hundred & fifty, who disported themselves on the green, under the direction of their schoolmistresses, and of an old gentleman. It struck me, as it always has, to observe how the lower orders of this country indicate their birth and station by their aspect and features. In America, there would be a good deal of grace and beauty among one hundred and fifty children and budding girls, belonging to whatever rank of life; but here they had universally a most plebian look—stubbed, sturdy figures, round, coarse faces, snubnoses—the most evident specimens of the brown bread of human nature. They looked wholesome, and good enough, and fit to sustain their rough share of life; but it would have been impossible to make a lady out of any one of them. Climate, no doubt, has most to do with diffusing a slender elegance over American young-womanhood;

but something, perhaps, is also due to the circumstance that classes are not kept apart there, as they are here; they cross-breed together, amid the continual ups-and-downs of our social life; and so, in the lowest stratum of life, you may see the refining influence of <u>gentler blood</u>. At all events, it is only necessary to look at such an assemblage of children as I saw yesterday, to be convinced that birth and blood do produce certain characteristics. To be sure, I have seen no similar evidence, in England or elsewhere, that old gentility refines and elevates the race.

August 25th Saturday [1855]. On Thursday, I went by invitation to Smithills Hall, at Bolton le Moors, to dine and spend the night. The hall is two or three miles from the town of Bolton where I arrived by railway from Liverpool, and which seems to be a pretty large town, though the houses are generally modern, or with modernized fronts of brick or stucco. It is a manufacturing town; and the tall brick chimneys rise numerously in the neighborhood, and are so near Smithills Hall that, I suspect, the atmosphere is sometimes impregnated with their breath. Mr Ainsworth comforts himself, however, with the rent which he receives from the factories erected on his own grounds; and I suppose the value of his estate has greatly increased by the growth of manufactures; although, unless he wishes to sell it, I do not see what good this can do him.[42]

Smithills Hall is one of the oldest residences in England, and still retains very much the aspect that it must have had, several centuries ago....

The peculiarity of this house is what is called "The Bloody Footstep."[43] In the time of Bloody Mary, a protestant clergyman (George Marsh by name) was examined before the then proprietor of the Hall (Sir Roger Barton, I think it was) and committed to prison for his heretical opinions, and ultimately burned at the stake. As his guards were conducting him from the justice-room, through the stone-paved passage that leads from front to rear of Smithills Hall, he stamped his foot upon one of the flag-stones, in earnest protestation against the wrong which he was undergoing. The foot, as some say, left a bloody mark in the stone; others have it, that the stone yielded like wax under his foot, and that there has been a shallow cavity ever since. This miraculous footprint is still extant; and Mrs. Ainsworth showed it to me, before her husband took me round the estate. It is almost at the threshold of the door opening from the rear of the house, a stone two or three feet square, set among similar ones, that seem to have been worn by the tread of many generations. The footprint is a dark-brown stain in the smooth gray surface of the flag-stone; and looking sidelong at it, there is a shallow cavity perceptible, which Mrs. Ainsworth accounted for as having been worn by people setting their feet just at this place, so as to tread at the very spot where the martyr wrought the miracle. The mark is longer than any mortal foot, as if caused by sliding along the stone, rather than sinking into it; and it might be supposed to have been made by a pointed shoe, being blunt at the heel, and decreasing towards the toe. The blood-stain version of the story is more consistent with the appearance of the mark, than the imprint would be; for if the martyr's blood oozed out through his shoe and stocking, it might have made his foot slide along the stone, and thus have lengthened the shape.

Of course, it is all a humbug—a darker vein cropping up through the gray flag-stone; but it is probably fact (and, for aught I know, may be found in Fox)[44] that George Marsh underwent an examination in this house; and the tradition may have connected itself with the stone within a short time after the martyrdom. Or perhaps, when the old persecuting knight departed this life and Bloody Mary was also dead, people who had stood a little distance from the hall door, and had seen George Marsh lift his hands and stamp his foot, just at this spot—perhaps they remembered this action and gesture, and really believed that Providence had thus made an indelible record of it on the stone; although the very stone and the very mark might have lain there at the threshold, hundreds of years before. But, even if it had been always there, the footprint might, after the fact, be looked upon as a prophecy, from the time when the foundation of this old house was laid, that a holy and persecuted man should one day set his foot here, on the way that was to lead him to the stake. At any rate, the legend is a good one.

Septr 12th, Wednesday [1855]. Yesterday forenoon, my wife and I (taking Julian with us) went to Westminster Abbey. Approaching it down Whitehall and Parliament street, you pass the Abbey, and see "Poets' Corner" on the corner-house of a little lane, leading up in the rear of the edifice. The entrance-door is at the south-eastern end of the South Transept—not a spacious arch, but a small, lowly door—and as soon as you are within it, you see the busts of poets looking down upon you from the wall.[45] Great poets, too; for Ben Jonson is right behind the door; and Spenser's tablet is next; and Butler on the same wall of the transept; and Milton's (which you know at once by its resemblance to one of his portraits, though it looks older, more wrinkled, and sadder than the portrait) is close by it, with a profile medallion of Gray beneath it. It is a very delightful feeling, to find yourself at once among them;—the consciousness (mingled with a pleasant awe) of kind and friendly presences, who are anything but strangers to you, though heretofore you have never personally encountered them. I never felt this kind of interest in any other tomb-stones, or in the presence of any other dead people, and one is pleased, too, at finding them all there together, however separated by distant generations, or by personal hostility or other circumstances, while they lived.

The South Transept is divided lengthwise by a screen (as I think they call these partition-walls in a church,) and there are monuments against the wall of the screen, on both sides, as well as against those of the church. All are in excellent preservation—indeed, just as good as if put up yesterday—except that the older marbles are somewhat yellow. There seems to be scarcely an inch of space to put up any more; although room has been found, recently, for a bust of Southy, and a full length statue of Campbell.[46] It is but a little portion of the Abbey, after all, that is dedicated to poets, literary men, musical composers, and others of that gentle breed; and even in Poets' Corner, and in the portion of it properest to poets, men of other kinds of eminence have intruded themselves; generals, statesmen, noblemen, at whom one looks askance, and would willingly turn them out, even if deserving of honorable graves elsewhere. Yet it shows aptly and truly enough what portion of the world's regard and honor has hitherto been awarded to literature, in comparison with other modes of greatness—this little nook in the vast Minster (nor even that more than half to themselves) the walls of which are sheathed and hidden behind the marble that has been sculptured for men once prominent enough, but now forgotten. Nevertheless, it would hardly be worth while to quarrel with the world on account of the scanty space and little honor it awards to poets; for even their own special Corner contains some whom one does not care to meet; and, I suppose, all the literary people who really make a part of one's inner life—reckoning since English literature first existed—might lie together, along one side of the Transept, and be separately and splendidly emblazoned against that one wall. But we must not look at the matter in just this way; and I should be willing that small poets, as well as great ones, all who are anywise known by tale or song, or who have even striven to be so, should meet here.

Sept'r 13th, Thursday [1855]. Mr Buchanan (American Minister) called on me on Tuesday, and left his card; an intimation that I ought to have paid my respects sooner; so, yesterday forenoon, I set out to find his residence, 56, Harley-street. It is a street out of Cavendish Square, in a fashionable quarter, although fashion is said to be ebbing away from it. The ambassador seems to intend some little state in his arrangements; but, no doubt, the establishment compares shabbily enough with the legations of other great countries, and with the houses of the English aristocracy. A servant—not in livery (or in a very unrecognizable one) opened the door for me, and gave my card to a sort of upper servant, who took it into Mr. Buchanan. He had three gentlemen with him; so desired that I should be shown into the office of the legation, until he should be able to receive me. Here I found Mr. Moran, a clerk or attaché, who has been two or three years on this side of the water; an intelligent person, who seems to be in correspondence (I know not whether more than occasionally) with the New York "Courier and Enquirer." By and by, came in another American to get a passport for the Continent; and soon the three previous gentlemen took leave of the Ambassador, and I was invited to his presence.

The tall, large figure of Mr. Buchanan has a certain air of state and dignity; he carries his head in a very aukward way, (in consequence, as the old scandal says, of having once attempted to cut his throat,) but still looks like a man of long and high authority, and, with his white hair, is now quite venerable.[47] There is certainly a lack of polish, a kind of rusticity; notwithstanding which, you feel him to be a man of the world. I should think he might succeed very tolerably in English society, being heavy and sensible, cool, kindly and good-humored, and with a great deal of experience of life. We talked about various matters, politics among the rest; and he observed that if the President had taken the advice which he gave him in two long letters, before his inauguration, he would have had a perfectly quiet and successful term of office. The advice was, to form a perfectly homogeneous cabinet of Union men, and to satisfy the extremes of the party by a fair distribution of minor offices; whereas Pierce formed his cabinet of extreme men, on both sides, and gave the minor offices to moderate ones. But the anti-slavery people, surely, had no representative in the cabinet. Mr. Buchanan further observed, that he thought Pierce has a fair chance of re-nomination, for that the South could not in honor desert him;—to which I replied, that the South had been guilty of such things, heretofore.[48] He (Buchanan) thinks that the next Presidential term will be more important and critical, both as to our foreign relations and internal affairs, than any preceding one;—which I should judge likely enough to be the case, although I heard the same prophecy often made respecting the present term.

Mr. Buchanan was very kind in his inquiries about my wife, with whom he is acquainted, from having dined at our house, a year or two ago. I always feel as if he were a man of heart, feeling, and simplicity, and certainly it would be unjust to conclude otherwise, merely from the fact (very suspicious, it is true) of his having been a life-long politician. After we had got through a little matter of business (respecting a young American who has enlisted, at Liverpool) the minister rang his bell, and ordered another visitor to be admitted; and so I took my leave.

March 27th [1856], Thursday. Yesterday, I went out at about twelve, and visited the British Museum; an exceedingly tiresome affair. It quite crushes a person to see so much at once; and I wandered from hall to hall, with a weary and heavy heart, wishing (Heaven forgive me!) that the Elgin marbles and the frieze of the Parthenon were all burnt into lime, and that the granite Egyptian statues were hewn and squared into building-stones, and that the mummies had all turned to dust, two thousand years ago; and, in fine, that all the material relics of so many successive ages had disappeared with the generations that produced them. The present is burthened too much with the past. We have not time, in our earthly existence, to appreciate what is warm with life, and immediately around us; yet we heap up all these old shells, out of which human life has long emerged, casting them off forever. I do not see how future ages are to stagger onward under all this dead weight, with the additions that will be continually made to it.

April 13th, Sunday [1856]. I remember nothing particular that happened the day after our visit to Firfield, until about five o'clock, when I went to Bennoch's;[49] for he was to accompany me to dine at the Mansion-House, in compliance with the Lord Mayor's invitation. We went thither at ½ past six, and were received in a great entrance-hall by some of the most gorgeously dressed footmen I ever saw. Their livery is blue and buff, and they look something like American revolutionary generals, only far more splendid. Two officers of his Lordship's household were busy in assigning to the guests the seats that they were to occupy in the dining-room; a list of all the guests and their places lying on the table before them. These two officers were dressed in scarlet coats, with epaulets, and looked precisely like military men. In fact there is a great deal of state and ceremony in this palace of the city-king; and the Mansion House itself (which I believe was built in Queen Anne's time) is worthy of its inhabitant, were he really the greatest man of this great city. After finding out where our places were to be, we passed into the reception-room; and our names being announced, the Lord Mayor met me and shook hands with me, close by the door; introducing me also to the Lady Mayoress, whom (as she will never hear what I think of her) I shall be bold to call a short and ugly old Jewess. As for his lordship, he is a tall, hard-looking, white-headed old Jew, of plain deportment, but rather hearty than otherwise in his address. He said little to me, except that I must hold myself in readiness to respond to a toast which he meant to give; and though I hinted that I would much rather be spared, he showed no signs of mercy.

There are two reception-rooms, or one large one, connected by folding-doors; and, though in an old style, they are very handsome apartments, with carved cielings and walls, and at each end a magnificent fire-place of marble, ornamented with wreaths of flowers and foliage, and other sculpture. Both rooms were crowded with guests, principally, I suppose, city-magnates with their wives or daughters; and, however it may have happened, I must own that I saw here more comeliness of womankind than I have before seen in England. I soon met with Mr. S. C. Hall, who introduced me to all the noted people he knew. The only one I had heard of before was the Rev. Mr. Gleig, Chaplain General of the army; a tall, rather stern-looking, military man of God, in clerical attire. Mrs. Hall was likewise present, and it was arranged that we were to sit together. The company consisted of about three hundred; and at a given signal, we all found our way into an immense hall (called, I know not why, the Egyptian Hall, though its architecture is classic) brilliantly lighted, and presenting quite a splendid spectacle, when all the tables were full. A band (but Mrs Hall said the music was very bad) played inspiringly; and truly there were all the circumstances and accompaniments of a stately feast. There was a cross-table, and two others (at one of which I sat) extending along the length of the hall.[50]

The first thing produced, after a blessing had been asked, was, of course, turtle-soup, of which everybody was allowed to help themselves twice, or, no doubt, as many times as they chose, and could get it. Being not very fond of turtle-soup, I took it only once, although it must be supposed to be better (such a civic dainty as this) at the Lord Mayor's table than anywhere else. With the soup was taken a small sip of rum-punch, in a very little tumbler. The rest of the dinner was catalogued upon a bill of fare, printed within a border of gold and green on delicate white paper, and was very good, and of variety enough, though not better than those given by the Mayors of Liverpool, or perhaps, than those given by the landlords of American Hotels. I do not remember eating anything but some red mullets, some potted ptarmigan, and some stewed mushrooms; and I have often enjoyed a mutton-chop (or, in my vegetable days, some roasted potatoes and salt) as much as I did these delicacies. The dishes were all put upon the table, and helped by guests at the table; an inconvenient arrangement in so great a party. There were decanters of sherry, from which the guests helped themselves, on the table; and the servants came round pretty frequently with champagne and hock. The band kept playing, at intervals, all the time; and, when not talking with Mrs Hall, or my neighbor on the other side (some city dignitary) my eyes were mostly drawn to a young lady who sat nearly opposite me, across the table.[51] She was, I suppose, dark, and yet not dark, but rather seemed to be of pure white marble, yet not white; but the purest and finest complexion (without a shade of color in it, yet anything but sallow or sickly) that I ever beheld. Her hair was a wonderful deep, raven black, black as night, black as death; not raven black, for that has a shiny gloss, and her's had not; but it was hair never to be painted, nor described—wonderful hair, Jewish hair. Her nose had a beautiful outline, though I could see that it was Jewish too; and that, and all her features, were so fine that sculpture seemed a despicable art beside her; and certainly my pen is good for nothing. If any likeness of her could be given, it must be by sculpture, not painting. She was slender, and youthful, but yet had a stately and cold, though soft and womanly grace; and, looking at her, I saw what were the wives of the old patriarchs, in their maiden or early married days—what Rachel was, when Jacob wooed her seven years, and seven more—what Judith was; for, womanly as she looked, I doubt not she could have slain a man, in a good cause—what Bathsheba was; only she seemed to have no sin in her—perhaps what Eve was, though one could hardly think her weak enough to eat the apple. I never should have thought of touching her, nor desired to touch her; for, whether owing to distinctness of race, my sense that she was a Jewess, or whatever else, I felt a sort of repugnance, simultaneously with my perception that she was an admirable creature. But, at the right hand of this miraculous Jewess, there sat the very Jew of Jews; the distilled essence of all the Jews that have been born since Jacob's time; he was Judas Iscariot; he was the Wandering Jew; he was the worst, and at the same time, the truest type of his race, and contained within himself, I have no doubt, every old prophet and every old clothesman, that ever the tribes produced; and he must have been circumcised as much as ten times over.[52] I never beheld anything so ugly and disagreeable, and preposterous, and laughable, as the outline of his profile; it was so hideously Jewish, and so cruel, and so keen; and he had such an immense beard that you could see no trace of a mouth, until he opened it to speak, or to eat his dinner,—and then, indeed, you were aware of a cave, in this density of beard. And yet his manners and aspect, in spite of all, were those of a man of the world, and a gentleman. Well; it is as hard to give an idea of this ugly Jew, as of the beautiful Jewess. He was the Lord Mayor's brother, and an elderly man, though he looked in his prime, with his wig and dyed beard; and Rachel, or Judith, or whatever her name be, was his wife! I rejoiced exceedingly in this Shylock, this Iscariot; for the sight of him justified me in the repugnance I have always felt towards his race.

The dishes being removed, grace was said; and then an official personage, behind the Lord Mayor's chair, made a proclamation. I ought to have mentioned that there stood a man in a helmet, in accordance with an ancient custom of the city, behind his lordship's chair, but it was not he who now made the proclamation. In the first place, he enumerated the names of the principal guests, comprising two or three noblemen, some baronets, members of parliament, aldermen, and other of the illustrious, (among whom was enrolled a certain gentleman of consular rank) and ended in some such way as this—"and all others, gentlemen and ladies, here present, the Lord Mayor drinks to you all in a Loving Cup, and sends it round among you." And forthwith the Loving Cup (or rather two of them, on either side of the table) came slowly down, with all the antique ceremony. The fashion of it is thus;—the Lord Mayor presents the covered cup to the guest at his elbow, standing up, in order that the guest should remove the cover; his lordship then drinks, the guest replaces the cover, takes the cup into his own hands, and presents it to his next neighbor, for the cover to be again removed, so that he may take his own draught. His next neighbor goes through the same form with the person below him; and thus the whole company are finally interlinked in one long chain of love. When the cup came to me, I found it to be an old and richly ornamented goblet of silver, capable of containing about a quart of wine; and, indeed, there was nearly that quantity in it, for I doubt whether the guests do much more than make a pretense of drinking; so that the goblets never need replenishing. I drank a sip, however, being curious to know what the liquor was, and found it to be claret, spiced and sweetened, and hardly preferable to sweetened water.

After this, the toasts began, and there were several very poor speeches; one from the young Earl of Grannard, his maiden speech, and promising nothing very wonderful in future; and I forget who else spoke, but all as dull as could well be.[53] Before each toast, the man behind the Lord Mayor made proclamation that his Lordship was going to give a toast; after the toast, and his lordship's accompanying remarks, the band played an appropriate tune; then the herald, or whatever he was, proclaimed that such or such a person was about to respond to the Lord Mayor's toast and speech; then another air, I think, from the band; and then the doomed person got up and proceeded to make a fool of himself. Now I had by no means forgotten his lordship's threat of calling me up, and conscious that, if toasted at all, it would be discourteous not to do it early in the evening, I bethought me, in some trepidation, what could be said in reply; and this was rather difficult, because I did not know what the drift of the Lord Mayor's remarks might be. However, I communicated my dilemma to Mr. S. C. Hall, who sat next his wife; and if I had sought the whole world over, I could not have found a better artist in whip-syllabub and flummery; and, without an instant's hesitation, he suggested a whole rivulet of lukewarm stuff, which I saw would be sufficiently to the purpose, if I could but remember it. Really, he is one of the kindest and best men in the world, and I felt grateful to him in my heart.

Well; in due time, the Lord Mayor began some remarks which I quickly perceived to be drifting in my direction; and after paying me some high

PART II: THE ENGLISH NOTEBOOKS

compliments in reference to my works (I don't believe he ever read a word of them) he drank prosperity to my country, and my own health, which was received with great applause. Then, I suppose, the band played 'Hail Columbia!' (but it might have been 'God Save the Queen,' without my being the wiser) the herald proclaimed that I was going to respond, and I rose amid much cheering, so screwed up to the point that I did not care what happened next. The Lord Mayor might have fired a pistol, instead of a speech, at me, and I should not have flinched. As a starting point, I took some of Mr. Hall's flummery, and clothing it in my own words, it really did very well indeed; and this I joined and interwove with two or three points of my own, and thus tinkered up and amalgamated a very tolerable little speech, which was much helped along by the cheers that broke in between the sentences. Certainly, there was a very kind feeling in the audience; and it is wonderful how conscious the speaker is of sympathy, and how it warms and animates him. When I sat down, Bennoch, and Mr. and Mrs. Hall were loud in their praises, and so were many other persons, in the course of the evening; and I was glad to have got out of the scrape so well. But one quickly cools down after these efforts; and I soon felt—indeed, I had never ceased to feel—that I, like the other orators of the evening, had made a fool of myself, and that it is altogether a ridiculous custom to talk in one's cups. Nor has this feeling been lessened, since I have read various reports of what I said, none of them correct, all obliterating the best points, and all exaggerating the sentiment of international kindness, which I myself had too strongly expressed. This speech was sent down to Liverpool by electric telegraph, posted in the Exchange, and has since been printed all over the kingdom; and, in the shape in which it appears before the public, it is nothing short of ridiculous. But it is an absurd world; so let this absurdity pass with the rest. I should not care for England; but America will read it too.

Shortly after this great event of the evening, the ladies retired from table. There were a good many more toasts and speechifyings among the gentlemen; but I think we all went to get our coffee by eleven °clock, or thereabouts. Losing Bennoch and my other acquaintances, in the crowd, I took my departure; and not being able to find a cab, rode homeward as far as Charing Cross in an omnibus.[54]

Hawthorne visits the home of Sir Walter Scott, a favorite author of his youth.

Friday, May 10th, '56.

We were not long in reaching Abbotsford.[55] The house (which is more compact, and of considerably less extent than I anticipated) stands in full view from the road, and at only a short distance from it, lower down towards the river. Its aspect disappointed me; but so does everything. It is but a villa, after all; no castle, nor even a large manor-house, and very unsatisfactory when you consider it in that light. Indeed, it impressed me not as a real house, intended for the home of human beings—a house to die in, or to be born in—but as a plaything, something in the same category as Horace Walpole's Strawberry Hill.[56] The present owner seems to have found it insufficient for the actual purposes of life; for he is adding a wing which promises to be as extensive as the original structure.

We rang at the front-door (the family being now absent) and were speedily admitted by a middle-aged or somewhat elderly man—the butler, I suppose, or some upper servant—who at once acceded to our request to be permitted to see the house. We stept from the porch immediately into the entrance hall; and having the great hall of Battle Abbey, I believe, in my memory, and the ideal of a baronial hall in my mind, I was quite taken aback at the smallness, and narrowness, and lowness of this—which, however, is a very fine one on its own little scale.[57] In truth, it is not much more than a vestibule. The cieling is carved; and every inch of the walls is covered with claymores, targets, and other weapons and armor, or old-time curiosities, tastefully arranged, many of which, no doubt, have a history attached to them—or had, in Sir Walter's own mind. Our attendant was a very intelligent person, and pointed out much that was interesting; but, in such a multitudinous variety, it was almost impossible to fix the eye upon any one thing. Probably the apartment looked smaller than it really was, on account of being so wainscoted and festooned with curiosities. I remember nothing particularly, unless it be the coal-grate in the fireplace, which was one formerly used by Archbishop Sharpe, the prelate whom Balfour of Burley murdered. Either in this room or the next one, however, there was a glass-case, containing the suit of clothes last worn by Scott—a short green coat, somewhat worn, with silvered buttons, a pair of gray tartan trowsers, and a white hat. It *was* in the hall that we saw these things; for there, too, I recollect, were a good many walking sticks that had been used by Scott, and the hatchet with which he was in the habit of lopping branches from his trees, as he walked among them.

From the hall we passed into the study, a small room lined with the books which Sir Walter, no doubt, was most frequently accustomed to refer to; and our guide pointed out some volumes of the Moniteur, which he used while writing the History of Napoleon.[58] Probably these were the driest and dullest volumes in his whole library. About mid-height of the walls of the study, there is a gallery with a short flight of steps, for the convenience of getting at the upper books. A study-table occupies the centre of the room, and at one end of the table stands an easy chair, covered with morocco, and with ample space to fling one's self back. The servant told me that I might sit down in this chair, for that Sir Walter sat there while writing his romances; "and perhaps," quoth the man, smiling, "you may catch some inspiration!" What a bitter word this would have been, if he had known me to be a romance-writer! "No, I never shall be inspired to write romances," I answered, as if such an idea had never occurred to me. I sat down, however. This study quite satisfies me, being planned on principles of common sense, and made to work in, and without any fantastic adaptation of old forms to modern uses.

Next to the study is the library, an apartment of respectable size, and containing as many books as it can hold, all protected by wirework. I did not observe what or whose works were here; but the attendant showed us one whole compartment, full of volumes having reference to ghosts, witchcraft, and the supernatural generally. It is remarkable that Scott should have felt interested in such subjects, being such a worldly and earthly man as he was; but, then, indeed, almost all forms of popular superstition do clothe the ethereal with earthly attributes, and so make it grossly perceptible. The library, like the study, suited me well—merely the fashion of the apartment, I mean—and I doubt not it contains as many curious volumes as are anywhere to be met with, within a similar space. The drawing-room adjoins it; and here we saw a beautiful ebony cabinet, which was presented to Sir Walter by George IV.; and some pictures of much interest—one of Scott himself, at thirty five, rather portly, with a heavy face, but shrewd eyes, which seem to observe you closely. There is a full length of his eldest son, an officer of dragoons, leaning on his charger; and a portrait of Lady Scott, a brunette, with black hair and eyes, very pretty, warm, vivacious, and un-English in her aspect.[59] I am not quite sure whether I saw all these pictures in the drawing-room, or some of them in the dining-room; but the one that struck me most—and very much indeed—was the head of Mary Queen of Scotts, literally, the head, cut off, and lying in a dish. It is said to have been painted by an Italian or French artist, two days after her death. The black hair curls or flows all about it; the face is of a deathlike hue, but has an expression of quiet after much pain and trouble, very beautiful, very sweet and sad; and it affected me strongly with the horror and strangeness of such a head being severed from its body. Methinks I should not like to have it always in the room with me. I thought of the lovely picture of Mary that I had seen at Edinburgh Castle, and thought what a symbol it would be—how expressive of a human being having her destiny in her own hands—if that beautiful young Queen were painted as carrying this vessel, containing her own woeful head, and perhaps casting a curious and pitiful glance down upon it, as if it were not her own.

Also, in the drawing-room, (if I mistake not,) there was a plaster-cast of Sir Walter's face, taken after death; the only one in existence, as our guide assured us. It is not often that one sees a homelier set of features than this; no elevation, no dignity, whether bestowed by nature, or thrown over them by age or death; sunken cheeks, the bridge of the nose depressed, and the end turned up; the mouth puckered up, and no chin whatever, or hardly any. The expression was not calm and happy, but rather as if he were in a perturbed slumber, perhaps nothing short of nightmare. I wonder that the family allow this cast to be shown; the last record that there is of Scott's personal reality, and conveying such a wretched & unworthy idea of it.

Adjoining the drawing-room is the dining-room, in one corner of which, between two windows, Scott died. It is now a quarter of a century since his death; but it seemed to me that we spoke with a sort of hush in our voices, as if he were still dying here, or but just departed. I remember nothing else in this room. The next one is the armory, which is the smallest of all that we had passed through; but its walls gleam with the steel blades of swords, and the barrels of pistols, matchlocks, firelocks, and all manner of deadly weapons, whether European or oriental; for there are many trophies here of East Indian warfare. I saw Rob Roy's gun, rifled, and of very large bore; and a beautiful pistol, formerly Claverhouse's; and the sword of Montrose, given him by King Charles, the silver hilt of which I grasped.[60] There was also a superb claymore, in an elaborately wrought silver sheath, made for Sir Walter Scott, and presented to him by the Highland Society, for his services in marshalling the clans, when George IV. came to Scotland.[61] There were a thousand other things, which I knew must be most curious, yet did not ask nor care about them; because so many curiosities drive one crazy, and fret one's heart to death. On the whole, there is no simple and great impression left by Abbotsford; and I felt angry and dissatisfied with myself for not feeling something which I did not and could not feel. But it is just like going to a museum, if you look into particulars; and one learns from it, too, that Scott could not have been really a wise man, nor an earnest one, nor one that grasped the truth of life—he did but play, and the play grew very sad towards its close. In a certain way, however, I understand his romances the better for having seen his house; and his house the better, for having read his romances. They throw light on one another.

We had now gone through all the show-rooms; and the next door admitted us again into the entrance-hall, where we recorded our names in the visitor's book. It contains more names of Americans, (I should judge, from casting my eyes back over last year's record) than of all other people in the world, including Great Britain. Bidding farewell to Abbotsford, I cannot but confess a sentiment of remorse for having visited the dwelling-place—as, just before, I visited the grave—of the mighty minstrel and romancer, with so cold a heart, and in so critical a mood;—*his* dwelling-place and *his* grave, whom I had so admired and loved, and who had done so much for my happiness, when I was young. But I, and the world generally, now look at him from a different point of view; and, besides, these visits to the actual haunts of famous people, though long dead, have the effect of making us sensible, in some degree, to their human imperfections, as if we actually saw them alive. I felt this effect, to a certain extent, even with respect to Shakespeare, when I visited Stratford-on-Avon. As for Scott, I still cherish him in a warm place, and I do not know that I have any pleasanter anticipation (as regards books) than that of reading all his novels over again, after we get back to the Wayside.

July 13th, Sunday [1856]. On Friday morning at 9 °clock, (having first fortified myself with some coffee and cold beef) I took the rail into town, to breakfast with R. M. Milnes....[62]

... Mrs. Milnes greeted me very kindly; and Mr. Milnes came towards me with an old gentleman in a blue coat and gray pantaloons—with a long, rather thin, homely visage, exceedingly shaggy eyebrows, though no great weight of brow, and thin gray hair—and introduced me to the Marquess of Lansdowne.[63] The Marquess had his right hand wrapt up in a black silk handkerchief; so he gave me his left, and, from some awkwardness in meeting it, when I expected the right, I gave him only three of my fingers;—a thing I never did before to any person, and it is queer that I should have done it to a Marquess. He addressed me with great simplicity and natural kindness, complimenting me on my works, and speaking, if I remember aright, about the society of Liverpool in former days. Lord Lansdowne was the friend of Moore, and has about him the fragrance communicated by the memories of many illustrious people, with whom he has associated.[64]

Mr. Ticknor, the Historian of Spanish Literature, now greeted me.[65] He looks greyer than when I saw him in Boston, but in good preservation. Mr. Milnes introduced me to Mrs. Browning, and assigned her to me to conduct into the breakfast-room; she is a small, delicate woman, with ringlets of black hair, (I think they were ringlets, and am sure they were black) a pleasant, intelligent, sensitive face, and a low, agreeable voice.[66] She is more youthful and comely than I supposed, and very gentle and ladylike. And so we proceeded to the breakfast-room, which is hung round with pictures; and in the middle of it stood an immense round table, worthy to have been King Arthur's, and here we seated ourselves without any question of precedence or ceremony. On one side of me was an elderly lady with a very fine countenance, and altogether more agreeable to look at than most English dames of her age; and, in the course of breakfast, I discovered her to be the mother of Florence Nightingale. One of her daughters (not *the* daughter) was likewise present.[67] Mrs. Milnes, Mrs. Browning, Mrs. Nightingale, and her daughter, were the only ladies at table; and I think there were as many as eight or ten gentlemen, whose names—as I came so late—I was to find out for myself, or to leave unknown.

It was a pleasant and sociable meal; and, thanks to my cold beef and coffee at home, I had no occasion to trouble myself much about the fare; so I just ate some delicate chicken, and a very small cutlet, and a slice of dry toast, and thereupon surceased from my labors. Mrs. Browning seems to be a vegetarian; at least, she ate nothing but an egg. We talked a good deal during breakfast; for she is of that quickly appreciative and responsive order of women, with whom I can talk more freely than with any men; and she has, besides, her own originality wherewith to help on conversation; though, I should say, not of a loquacious tendency. She introduced the subject of spiritualism, which, she says, interests her very much; indeed, she seems to be a believer.[68] Her husband, she told me, utterly rejects the subject, and will not believe even in the outward manifestations, of which there is such overwhelming evidence. We also talked of Miss Bacon; and I developed something of that lady's theory respecting Shakspeare,[69] greatly to the horror of Mrs. Browning and that of her next neighbor—some nobleman, whose name I did not know. On the whole, I like her the better for loving the man Shakspeare with a personal love. We talked, too, of Margaret Fuller, who spent her last night in Italy with the Brownings; and of William Story,[70] with whom they have been intimate, and who, Mrs. Browning says, is much stirred up about Spiritualism. Really, I cannot help wondering that so fine a spirit as hers should not reject the matter, till, at least, it is forced upon her. But I like her very much—a great deal better than her poetry, which I could hardly suppose to have been written by such a quiet little person as she.

Mrs. Nightingale had been talking at first with Lord Lansdowne, who sat next her; but by and by she turned to me, and began to speak of London smoke. She is a nice old lady, very intelligent—that is, very sensible—but with no saliency of ideas; a lady born and bred, evidently, for—unless with that advantage—all English women have a certain nonsense about them, even more inevitably than the men. Then (there being a discussion about Lord Byron, on the other side of the table) she spoke to me about Lady Byron, whom she knows intimately, characterizing her as a most excellent and exemplary person, high-principled, unselfish, and now devoting herself to the care of her two grandchildren; their mother (Byron's daughter) being dead.[71] Lady Byron, she says, writes beautiful verses. Somehow or other, all this praise, and more of the same kind, gave me the idea of an intolerably irreproachable person; and I asked Mrs. Nightingale if Lady Byron was warm-hearted. With some hesitation, or mental reservation—at all events, not quite out-spokenly—she answered that she was.

I was too much engaged with these personal talks to attend much to what was going on elsewhere; but all through breakfast, I had been more and more impressed by the aspect of one of the guests, sitting next to Milnes. He was a man of large presence—a portly personage—gray haired, but scarcely as yet aged; and his face had a remarkable intelligence, not vivid nor sparkling, but conjoined with great quietude; and if it gleamed or brightened, at one time more than another, it was like the sheen over a broad surface of sea. There was a somewhat careless self-possession, large and broad enough to be called dignity; and the more I looked at him, the more I knew that he was somebody, and wondered who. He might have been a minister of state; only there is not one of them who has any right to such a face and presence. At last—I do not know how the conviction came—but I became aware that it was Macauley, and began to see some slight resemblance to his portraits.[72] But I have never seen any that is not wretchedly unworthy of the original. As soon as I knew him, I began to listen to his conversation; but he did not talk a great deal—contrary to his usual custom, for I am told he is apt to engross all the talk to himself. Probably he may have been restrained by the presence of Ticknor and Mr. Palfrey,[73] who were among his auditors and interlocutors; and as the conversation seemed to turn much on American subjects, he could not well have assumed to talk them down. Well, I am glad to have seen him—a face fit for a scholar, a man of the world, a cultivated intelligence.

After we got up from table, and went into the library, Mr. Browning introduced himself to me; a younger man than I expected to see, handsome, with brown hair, a very little frosted. He is very simple and agreeable in manner, gently impulsive, talking as if his heart were uppermost. He spoke of his pleasure in meeting me, and his appreciation of my books; and (which has not often happened to me) mentioned that the Blithedale Romance was the one he admired most. I wonder why. I hope I showed as much pleasure at his praise as he did at mine; for I was glad to see how pleasantly it moved him. After this I talked with Ticknor and Milnes, and with Mr. Palfrey, to whom I had been introduced, very long ago, by George

Hillard, and had never seen him since.[74] We looked at some autographs, of which Mr. Milnes has two or three large volumes. I recollect a leaf from Swift's Journal to Stella; a letter from Addison; one from Chatterton, in a most neat and legible hand;[75] and a characteristic sentence or two and signature of Oliver Cromwell written in a religious book. There seemed to be many curious volumes in the library; but I had not time to look at them.

I liked greatly the manners of almost all—yes, all, as far as I observed—all the people at this breakfast; and it was doubtless owing to their being all people either of high rank, or remarkable intellect, or both. An Englishman can hardly be a gentleman, unless he enjoys one or the other of these advantages; and perhaps the surest way to give him good manners is, to make a lord of him—or rather, of his grandfather, or great-grandfather. In the third generation—scarcely sooner—he will be polished into simplicity and elegance, and his deportment will be all the better for the homely material out of which it is wrought and refined. The Marquess of Lansdowne, for instance, would have been a very common-place man in the common ranks of life, but it has done him good to be a nobleman. Not that I consider his tact quite perfect. In going up to breakfast, he made me precede him; in returning to the library, he did the same, although I drew back, till he impelled me up the first stair, with gentle persistence. By insisting upon it, he showed his sense of condescension, much more than if—when he saw me unwilling to take precedence—he had passed forward, as if the point were not worth either asserting or yielding. Heaven knows, it was in no humility that I would have trod behind him. But he is a kind old man, and I am willing to believe of the English aristocracy generally that they are kind, and of beautiful deportment; for certainly there never can have been mortals in a position more advantageous for becoming so. If any, they must be Americans; and, really, I hope there may come a time when we shall be so, and I already know Americans whose noble and delicate manners may compare well with any I have seen.

∽

Hawthorne calls upon Delia Bacon, proponent of a theory about the authorship of Shakespeare's plays.

∽

July 29th Tuesday [1856].

Yesterday, at about ten, I walked across the heath, and through Greenwich Park, to the Thames' side, and took the Steamer to town. The trip up the river to London Bridge, occupies about half an hour, or perhaps less.... I took a cab to Miss Bacon's lodgings, 12, Spring-street, Sussex Gardens. It is a pleasant part of London enough, at no great distance from the Park, and seems to be modern. The basement of the house, where Miss B. lodges, is occupied by a grocer, who is likewise her landlord—a portly, middle-aged, civil and kindly man, who seemed to feel a personal kindness towards his lodger. At least, this was the impression made on me by the few words I heard from him, when I stept into the shop to inquire if she lived there.

The girl of the house took up my card, and then ushered me up two (and, I rather believe, three) pair of stairs, into a parlor—plain, but neat enough—and told me that Miss Bacon would come soon. There were a number of books on the table; and, looking into them, I found that every one had some reference to her Shakspearian theory;—there was a volume of Raleigh's History of the World, a volume of Montaigne, a volume of Bacon's letters, a volume of Shakspeare's plays;—and, on another table, there was the manuscript of part of her work. To be sure, there was a pocket-Bible; but everything else referred to this one idea of hers; and, no doubt, as it has engrossed her whole soul, the Bible has reference to it likewise. I took up Montaigne (it was Hazlitt's translation) and read his Journey to Italy for a good while, until I heard a chamber on the same floor open, and Miss Bacon appeared. I expected to see a very homely, uncouth, elderly personage, and was rather pleasantly disappointed by her aspect. She is rather uncommonly tall, and has a striking and expressive face—dark hair, dark eyes, which shone as she spoke; and, by and by, a color came into her cheeks. She must be over forty years old—perhaps, towards fifty—and, making allowance for years and ill health, she may be supposed to have been handsome once. There was little or no embarrassment in her manner; and we immediately took a friendly and familiar tone together, and began to talk as if we had known one another a long while. Our previous correspondence had smoothed the way; and we had a definite topic, in my proposal to offer her book to Routledge. She thought well of this, and at once acceded.

She was very communicative about her theory, and would have been more so, had I desired it; but I thought it best to repress, rather than to draw her out. Unquestionably, she is a monomaniac; this great idea has completely thrown her off her balance; but, at the same time, it has wonderfully developed her intellect, and made her what she could not otherwise have been. I had heard, long ago, that she believed that the confirmation of her theory was to be found buried in Shakspeare's grave. Recently, as I understood her, this idea has been modified and fully developed in her mind; she now believes that she has found, in Lord Bacon's letters, the key and clue to the whole mystery—definite and minute instructions how to find a will and other documents, relating to this new philosophy, which are concealed in a hollow space in the under surface of Shakspeare's gravestone. These instructions, she intimates, go completely and precisely to the point, and obviate all difficulties in the way of coming at the treasure, and even, I believe, secure her from any troublesome consequence likely to result from disturbing the grave. All that she now stays in England for—indeed, the object for which she came here, and which has kept her here these three years past—is, to discover these material and unquestionable proofs of the truth of her theory.

She communicated all this strange matter in a low, quiet tone, and, for my part, I listened as quietly, and without any expression of dissent. It would have shut her up at once, and without in the least weakening her faith in the existence of these things; and, if it were possible to convince her of their non-existence, I apprehend that she would collapse and die at once. She says herself that she cannot now bear the society of those who do not sympathize with her; and, finding little sympathy or none, she entirely secludes herself from the world. In all these years, she has seen Mrs. Farrar a few times, but has long ago given her up; Carlyle, once or twice, but not of late; Mr. Buchanan, while minister, once called on her; and General Campbell two or three times, on business;—with these exceptions, she has lived in complete solitude.[76] She never walks out; she suffers much from neuralgia; she is in difficult circumstances, pecuniarily; and yet, she tells me, she is perfectly happy. I can well conceive of this; for she feels sure that she has a great object to accomplish, and that Providence is specially busy, not only in what promotes her progress, but in what seems to impede it. For instance, she thinks that she was providentially led to this lodging-house, and put in relation with this landlord and his family; and, to say the truth, considering what London lodging-house keepers usually are—and in view of her pecuniary embarrassments—the kindness of this man and his household is little less than miraculous. Evidently, too, she thinks that Providence has brought me forward at this critical juncture, when she could not have done without me.

For my part, I would rather that Providence would have employed some other instrument; but still I have little or no scruple or doubt about what I ought to do. Her book is a most remarkable one, and well deserves publication; and towards that end, she shall have every assistance that I can render. Her relatives are endeavoring to force her home, by withholding from her all means of support in England; but, in my opinion, if taken from England now, she would go home as a raving maniac, and I shall write to them and suggest this view of the case. Meanwhile, as she must be kept alive, it devolves on me to supply her with some small means for that purpose. As to her designs on Shakespeare's grave, I see no way but to ignore them entirely, and leave Providence to manage that matter in its own way. If I had it in my power to draw her out of her delusions, on that point, I should not venture to do so;—it is the condition on which she lives, in comfort and joy, and exercises great intellectual power; and it would be no business of mine to annihilate her, for this world, by showing her a miserable fact. I am not quite sure, that she will not be practically wiser, in this particular matter, than her theory seems to indicate;—there is a ladylike feeling of propriety, and a New England orderliness, and probably a sturdy common sense at bottom, which may begin to act at the right time. And, at all events, it is still the safest course to allow her her own way, till she brings up against an impossibility.

My interview with her may have lasted about an hour, and she flowed out freely, as to the first friend whom she had met in a long while. She is a very good talker, considering how long she has held her tongue for want of a listener—pleasant, sunny and shadowy, often piquant, suggesting all a woman's various moods and humours; and beneath all there is a deep undercurrent of earnestness, which does not fail to produce, on the listener's part, something like a temporary faith in what she believes so strongly.

From her own account, it appears she did at one time lose her reason; it was on finding that the philosophy, which she found under the surface of the plays, was running counter to the religious doctrines in which she had been educated. I think there is no other instance of anything like this; a system growing up in a person's mind without the volition—contrary to the volition—and substituting itself in place of everything that originally grew there. It is really more wonderful that she should have fancied this philosophy, than if she had really found it.

∽

Melville visits Hawthorne in Liverpool in November 1856, en route to the Middle East—a trip funded by his father-in-law, Judge Lemuel Shaw, in response to family concerns about Melville's physical and mental health. Melville had recently completed The Confidence-Man *(1857), which would prove to be the last piece of fiction he would publish in his lifetime. Hawthorne's characterization of Melville's religious plight has been enormously influential on interpretations of Melville.*

∽

November 20th, Thursday [1856]. A week ago last Monday, Herman Melville came to see me at the Consulate, looking much as he used to do (a little paler, and perhaps a little sadder), in a rough outside coat, and with his characteristic gravity and reserve of manner. He had crossed from New York to Glasgow in a screw steamer, about a fortnight before, and had since been seeing Edinburgh and other interesting places. I felt rather awkward, at first; because this is the first time I have met him since my ineffectual attempt to get him a consular appointment from General Pierce. However, I failed only from real lack of power to serve him; so there was no reason to be ashamed, and we soon found ourselves on pretty much our former terms of sociability and confidence. Melville has not been well, of late; he has been affected with neuralgic complaints in his head and limbs, and no doubt has suffered from too constant literary occupation, pursued without much success, latterly; and his writings, for a long while past, have indicated a morbid state of mind. So he left his place at Pittsfield, and has established his wife and family, I believe, with his father-in-law in Boston, and is thus far on his way to Constantinople. I do not wonder that he found it necessary to take an airing through the world, after so many years of toilsome pen-labor and domestic life, following upon so wild and adventurous a youth as his was. I invited him to come and stay with us at Southport, as long as he might remain in this vicinity; and, accordingly, he did come, the next day, taking with him, by way of baggage, the least little bit of a bundle, which, he told me, contained a night-shirt and a toothbrush. He is a person of very gentlemanly instincts in every respect, save that he is a little heterodox in the matter of clean linen.

He stayed with us from Tuesday till Thursday; and, on the intervening day, we took a pretty long walk together, and sat down in a hollow among the sand hills (sheltering ourselves from the high, cool wind) and smoked a cigar. Melville, as he always does, began to reason of Providence and futurity, and of everything that lies beyond human ken, and informed me that he had "pretty much made up his mind to be annihilated"; but still he does not seem to rest in that anticipation; and, I think, will never rest until he gets hold of a definite belief. It is strange how he persists—and has persisted ever since I knew him, and probably long before—in wandering to-and-fro over these deserts, as dismal and monotonous as the sand hills amid which we were sitting. He can neither believe, nor be comfortable in his unbelief; and he is too honest and courageous not to try to do one or the other. If he were a religious man, he would be one of the most truly religious and reverential; he has a very high and noble nature, and better worth immortality than most of us.

He went back with me to Liverpool, on Thursday; and, the next day, Henry Bright met him at my office, and showed him whatever was worth seeing in town. On Saturday, Melville and I went to Chester together. I love to take every opportunity of going to Chester; it being the one only place, within easy reach of Liverpool, which possesses any old English interest....

We left Chester at about four °clock; and I took the rail for Southport at half-past six, parting from Melville at a corner in Liverpool, in the rainy evening. I saw him again on Monday, however. He said that he already felt much better than in America; but observed that he did not anticipate much pleasure in his rambles, for that the spirit of adventure is gone out of him. He certainly is much overshadowed since I saw him last; but I hope he will brighten as he goes onward. He sailed from Liverpool in a steamer on Tuesday, leaving his trunk behind him at my consulate, and taking only a carpet-bag to hold all his travelling-gear. This is the next best thing to going naked; and as he wears his beard and moustache, and so needs no dressing-case—nothing but a toothbrush—I do not know a more independent personage. He learned his travelling-habits by drifting about, all over the South Sea, with no other clothes or equipage than a red flannel shirt and a pair of duck trowzers. Yet we seldom see men of less criticizable manners than he.

July 26th Sunday [1857], Old Trafford. Day before yesterday, I went with my wife to the Arts Exhibition, of which I do not think that I have a great deal to say.[77] The edifice, being built more for convenience than show, appears better in the interior than from without—long vaulted vistas, lighted from above, extending far away, all hung with pictures, and, on the floor below, statues, knights in armour, cabinets, vases, and all manner of curious and beautiful things, in a regular arrangement. Scatter five thousand people through the scene; and I do not know how to make a better outline sketch. I was unquiet, from a hopelessness of being able fully to enjoy it. Nothing is more depressing than the sight of a great many pictures together; it is like having innumerable books open before you at once, and being able to read a sentence or two in each. They bedazzle one another with cross-lights. There never should be more than one picture in a room, nor more than one picture to be studied in one day; galleries of pictures are surely the greatest absurdities that ever were contrived; there being no excuse for them, except that it is the only way in which pictures can be made generally available and accessible. We went first into the gallery of British Painters, where there were hundreds of pictures; any one of which would have interested me by itself; but I could not fix my mind on one more than another; so I left my wife there, and wandered away by myself, to get a general idea of the exhibition. Truly, it is very fine; truly, also, every great show is a kind of humbug. I doubt whether there were half a dozen people there who got the kind of enjoyment that it was intended to create; very respectable people they seemed to be, and very well behaved, but all skimming the surface, as I did, and none of them so feeding on what was beautiful as to digest it, and make it a part of themselves. Such a quantity of objects must be utterly rejected, before you can get any real profit from one! It seemed like throwing away time to look twice even at whatever was most precious; and it was dreary to think of not fully enjoying this collection, the very flower of Time, which never bloomed before, and never by any possibility can bloom again. Viewed hastily, moreover, it is somewhat sad to think that mankind, after centuries of cultivation of the beautiful arts, can produce no more splendid spectacle than this. It is not so very grand, although, poor as it is, I lack capacity to take in even the whole of this.

Wednesday, July 28th, Old Trafford [1857]. Day before yesterday, I paid a second visit to the Exhibition, and devoted the day mainly to seeing the works of British painters, which fill a very large space—two or three great saloons on the right side of the nave. Among the earliest are Hogarth's pictures,[78] including the Sigismunda, which I remember to have seen before, with her lover's heart in her hand, looking like a monstrous strawberry; and the March to Finchley, than which nothing truer to English life and character was ever painted, nor ever can be; and a large, stately portrait of Captain Coram, and several others, all excellent in proportion as they come near to ordinary life, and are wrought out through its forms. All English painters seem to resemble Hogarth in this respect; they cannot paint anything high, heroic, and ideal, and their attempts in that direction are wearisome to look at; but they sometimes produce good effects by means of awkward figures in ill-made coats and small-clothes, and hard, coarse-complexioned faces, such as they might see anywhere in the street. They are strong in homeliness and ugliness; weak in their efforts at the beautiful. Sir Thomas Lawrence, for instance, attains a sort of grace, which you feel to be a trick, and therefore get disgusted with it. Reynolds is not quite genuine, though certainly he has produced some noble and beautiful heads.[79] But Hogarth is the only English painter, except in the landscape department; there is no other (unless it be some of the modern pre-Raphaelites) who interprets life to me at all. Pretty village-scenes of common life—pleasant domestic passages, with a touch of easy humor in them—little pathoses and fancyness—are abundant enough; and Wilkie, to be sure, has done more than this, though not a great deal more....

No doubt, I am doing vast injustice to a great many gifted men, in what I have here written; as, for instance, Copley,[80] who certainly has painted a slain man to the life; and to a crowd of landscape-painters, who have made wonderful reproductions of little English streams and shrubbery, and cottage-doors, and country-lanes. And there is a picture called the "Evening Gun" by Danby,[81] a ship of war on a calm, glassy tide, at sunset, with the cannon-smoke puffing from her port-hole; it is very beautiful, and so effective that you can even hear the report, breaking upon the stillness with so grand a roar that it is almost like stillness too. As for Turner, I care no more for his light-colored pictures than for so much lacquered ware, or painted gingerbread. Doubtless, this is my fault—my own deficiency—but I cannot help it; not, at least, without sophisticating myself by the effort.

Hawthorne visits the Exhibition once again and observes Tennyson in one of the rooms.

Thursday, July 30th Old Trafford [1857].

After getting through the portrait-gallery, I went among the engravings and photographs, and then glanced along the Old Masters, but without seriously looking at anything. While I was among the Dutch painters, a gentleman accosted me; it was Mr. Ireland, the Editor of the Manchester Examiner, whom I once met at dinner with Bennoch.[82] He told me that the Poet Laureate (and it was rather English that he should designate him by this fantastic dignity, instead of by his name) was in the Exhibition Rooms; and as I expressed great interest, Mr. Ireland was good enough to go in quest of him. Not for the purpose of introduction, however; for he was not acquainted with Tennyson, and I was rather glad of it than otherwise. Soon, Mr. Ireland returned to tell me that he had found the Poet Laureate; and going into the saloon of Old Masters, we saw him there, in company with Mr. Woolner, whose bust of him is now in the Exhibition.[83] Tennyson is the most picturesque figure, without affectation, that I ever saw; of middle-size, rather slouching, dressed entirely in black, and with nothing white about him except the collar of his shirt, which methought might have been clean the day before. He had on a black wide-awake hat, with round crown and wide, irregular brim, beneath which came down his long black hair, looking terribly tangled; he had a long, pointed beard, too, a little browner than the hair, and not so abundant as to incumber any of the expression of his face. His frock coat was buttoned across the breast, though the afternoon was warm. His face was very dark, and not exactly a smooth face, but worn, and expressing great sensitiveness, though not, at that moment, the pain and sorrow which is seen in his bust. His eyes were black; but I know little of them, as they did not rest on me, nor on anything but the pictures. He seemed as if he did not see the crowd nor think of them, but as if he defended himself from them by ignoring them altogether; nor did anybody but myself cast a glance at him. Mr. Woolner was as unlike Tennyson as could well be imagined; a small, smug man, in a blue frock and brown pantaloons. They talked about the pictures, and passed pretty rapidly from one to another, Tennyson looking at them through a pair of spectacles which he held in his hand, and then standing a minute before those that interested him, with his hands folded behind his back. There was an entire absence of stiffness in his figure; no set-up in him at all; no nicety or trimness; and if there had been, it would have spoilt his whole aspect. Gazing at him with all my eyes, I liked him well, and rejoiced more in him than in all the other wonders of the Exhibition.

Knowing how much my wife would delight to see him, I went in search of her, and found her and the rest of us under the music-gallery; and we all, Fanny and Rosebud included, went back to the saloon of Old Masters. So rapid was his glance at the pictures, that, in this little interval, Tennyson had got half-way along the other side of the saloon; and, as it happened, an acquaintance had met him, an elderly gentleman and lady, and he was talking to them as we approached. I heard his voice; a bass voice, but not of a resounding depth; a voice rather broken, as it were, and ragged about the edges, but pleasant to the ear. His manner, while conversing with these people, was not in the least that of an awkward man, unaccustomed to society; but he shook hands and parted with them, evidently as soon as he courteously could, and shuffled away quicker than before. He betrayed his shy and secluded habits more in this, than in anything else that I observed; though, indeed, in his whole presence, I was indescribably sensible of a morbid painfulness in him, a something not to be meddled with. Very soon, he left the saloon, shuffling along the floor with short irregular steps, a very queer gait, as if he were walking in slippers too loose for him. I had observed that he seemed to turn his feet slightly inward, after the fashion of Indians. How strange, that in these two or three pages I cannot get one single touch that may call him up hereafter!

I would most gladly have seen more of this one poet of our day, but forbore to follow him; for I must own that it seemed mean to be dogging him through the saloons, or even to have looked at him, since it was to be done stealthily, if at all. I should be glad to smoke a cigar with him.... He might well enough pass for a madman at any time, there being a wildness in his aspect, which doubtless might readily pass from quietude to frenzy. He is exceedingly nervous, and altogether as un-English as possible; indeed, an Englishman of genius usually lacks the national characteristics, and is great abnormally, and through disease. Even their great sailor, Nelson, was unlike his countrymen in the qualities that constituted him a hero; he was not the perfection of an Englishman, but a creature of another kind, sensitive, nervous, excitable, and really more like a Frenchman.

Un-English as he was, and sallow, and unhealthy, Tennyson had not, however, an American look. I cannot well describe the difference; but there was something more mellow in him, softer, sweeter, broader, more simple, than we are apt to be. Living apart from men, as he does, would hurt any one of us more than it does him. I may as well leave him here; for I cannot touch the central point.

November 8th Monday [1857]. All this month, we have had genuine, English November weather; much of it profusely rainy, and the rest overcast and foggy, making it a desperate matter to venture out for a walk. Since my last record—describing a visit to Warwick—I have taken only a few strolls up and down the Parade, or in the immediate neighborhood of the town. Yesterday afternoon, being merely damp, chill, and foggy, I made a little longer stretch of my tether, and walked to Whitnash Church, with Miss Shepard, Una, and Julian. This is one of the small, old churches of the vicinity, and stands in the midst of a village that retains as much of its primitive aspect as any one that I have seen; the dwellings being mostly the old, timber and plaister cottages and farmhouses, with thatched roofs; and though there are a few new brick buildings, the air of antiquity prevails. In front of the church tower is a small, rude and irregular space, in the midst of which grows a very ancient tree, with a huge, hollow trunk, and a still verdant head of foliage growing out of its mutilated decay. I should not wonder if this tree were many centuries old, and a contemporary of the gray, Norman tower before which it has flourished and decayed; perhaps even older than that. The old, rustic dwellings of the village stand about the church; and the churchyard with its graves is especially central and contiguous to the living village; so that the old familiar forms and faces have had but a little way to go in order to lie down in their last sleep; and there they rest, close to their own thresholds, with their children and successors all about them, chatting, laughing, and doing business within hearing of their grave-stones. It makes death strangely familiar, and brings the centuries together in a lump. But methinks it must be weary, weary, weary, this rusty, unchangeable village-life, where men grow up, grow old, and die, in their fathers' dwellings, and are buried in their grandsires' very graves, the old skulls, and cross-bones being thrown out to make room for them, and shovelled in on the tops of their coffins. Such a village must, in former times, have been a stagnant pool, and may be little better even now, when the rush of the main current of life has probably created a little movement. We went a few paces into the church-yard, and heard the indistinct, dull drone of the parson within the church, but thought it not best to enter the church. Passing through the village, we paused to look at a venerable farm-house—spacious and dignified enough, indeed, to have been a manor-house—with projecting bay-windows, an old, square portal, a lawn, shadowy with great trees, and an aspect of ancient peace diffused all around. It was a timber and plaster house, the timber-frame marked out in black on the white plaster, and, if I mistake not, a thatched roof, though the house was two stories high and very extensive. These thatched roofs are very beautiful, when time has made them verdant; it makes the house seem to be a part of Nature, and, so far as man has anything to do with it, as simple as a nest.

24 Gt Russell-street, Decr 6th, Sunday [1857]. All these days, since my last date, have been marked by nothing very well worthy of detail and description. I have walked the streets a great deal, in the dull November days, and always take a certain pleasure in being in the midst of human life—as closely encompassed by it as it is possible to be, anywhere in this world; and, in that way of viewing it, there is a dull and sombre enjoyment always to be had in Holborn, Fleet-street, Cheapside, and the other thronged parts of London. It is human life; it is this material world; it is a grim and heavy reality. I have never had the same sense of being surrounded by materialism, and hemmed in with the grossness of this earthly life, anywhere else; these broad, thronged streets are so evidently the veins and arteries of an enormous city. London is evidenced in every one of them, just as a Megatherium is in each of its separate bones, even if they be small ones.[84] Thus I never fail of a sort of self-congratulation in finding myself, for instance, passing along Ludgate Hill; but, in spite of this, it is really an ungladdened life, to wander through these huge, thronged ways, over a pavement foul with mud, ground into it by a million of footsteps; jostling against people who do not seem to be individuals, but all one mass, so homogeneous is the street-walking aspect of them; the roar of vehicles pervading me, wearisome cabs and omnibusses; everywhere, the dingy brick edifices heaving themselves up, and shutting out all but a strip of sullen cloud that serves London for a sky;—in short, a general impression of grime and sordidness, and, at this season, always a fog scattered along the vista of streets, sometimes so densely as almost to spiritualize the materialism and make the scene resemble the other world of worldly people, gross even in ghostliness. It is strange how little splendor and brilliancy one sees in London-streets; in the city, almost none, though some in the shops of Regent-street.

PART III

The French and Italian Notebooks

Arriving in Paris on January 6, 1858, Hawthorne settled into the Hôtel du Louvre. His initial journal entry describes the journey of the family and governess Ada Shepard from England to Boulogne, through Amiens, to Paris across a frigid countryside reminiscent of "the December aspect of my dear native-land.... My impression of France will always be, that it is an Arctic region" (CE XIV: 6).

Hôtel du Louvre, Paris, Jany 6th, Wednesday.

We left Amiens at ½ past one; and I can tell as little of the country between that place and Paris, as between Boulogne and Amiens.... At five, we reached Paris, and were suffered to take a conveyance to the Hôtel du Louvre, without any examination of the little luggage we had with us. Arriving at the Hôtel we took a suite of apartments *au troisieme*, which will cost a little more than 25 francs per day; and the waiter immediately lighted a wax candle in each separate room, thereby saddling us with four francs more. We might have dined at the table d'hôte, but preferred the restaurant connected with the hotel. It is a terrible business, feeding so many mouths, and especially children, and most especially a boy, at a French table. We had a soup, some lamb-cutlets (and a very young and diminutive lamb it must have been,) and a chicken with truffles, ending with some ice-cream, which I little thought to have eaten in this Arctic weather. For drink, a half bottle of Burgundy. All the dishes were very delicate, and a vast change from the simple English system, with its joints, shoulders, beef-steakes and chops; but I doubt whether English cookery, for the very reason that it is so gross, is not better for man's moral and spiritual nature, than French. In the former case, you know that you are gratifying your coarsest animal needs and propensities, and are duly ashamed of it; but, in dealing with these French delicacies, you delude yourself into the idea that you are cultivating your taste while filling your belly. This last, however, it needs a good deal of perseverance to accomplish.

Hôtel du Louvre, Jan 8th, Friday.

The splendor of Paris, so far as I have seen, takes me altogether by surprise; such stately edifices, prolonging themselves in unwearying magnificence and beauty, and, ever and anon, a long vista of a street, with a column rising at the end of it, or a triumphal arch, wrought in memory of some grand event. The light stone, or stucco, wholly untarnished by smoke and soot, puts London to the blush, if a blush could be seen through its dingy face; but, indeed, London is paltry, despicable, not to be mentioned in the same day, nor compared even for the purpose of ridiculing it, with Paris. I never knew what a palace was, till I had a glimpse of the Louvre and the Tuilleries;—never had any idea of a city gratified, till I trod these stately streets. The life of the scene, too, is infinitely more picturesque than London, with its monotonous throng of smug faces and black coats; whereas, here, you see soldiers and priests; policemen in cocked hats; Zouaves, with turbans, long mantles, and bronzed, half-Moorish faces; and a great many people whom you perceive to be outside of your experience, and know them ugly to look at, and fancy them villainous. Truly, I have no sympathies towards the French people; their eyes do not win me, nor do their glances melt and mingle with mine. But they do grand and beautiful things, in the architectural way; and I am grateful for it. The Place de la Concord is the most splendid square, large enough for a nation to erect trophies of all its triumphs there; and one side of it is the Tuilleries, on the opposite side the Champ Elyssée, and on a third the Seine, adown which we saw large cakes of ice floating beneath the arches of a bridge. The Champ Elysée, so far as I saw it, had not a grassy soil beneath its trees, but the bare earth, white and dusty. The very dust, if I saw nothing else, would assure me that I was out of England. We had time only to take this little walk, when it began to grow dusk; and being so pitilessly cold, we hurried back to our Hôtel. Thus far, I think, what I have seen of Paris is wholly unlike what I expected, but very like an imaginary picture which I had conceived of Saint Petersburg; new, bright, magnificent, and desperately cold. A great part of this architectural splendor is due to the present Emperor, who has wrought a great change on the aspect of the city within a very few years. A traveller, if he look at the thing selfishly, ought to wish him a long reign, and arbitrary power; since he makes it his policy to illustrate his capital with palatial edifices, which are better for a stranger to look at than for his own people to pay for.

We have spent to-day chiefly in seeing, or glimpsing, at some of the galleries of the Louvre. I will not be fool enough to attempt a description; but I must confess that the vast and beautiful edifice struck me far more than the pictures, sculpture, and curiosities which it contains; the shell more than the meat inside. I never saw (nor could have seen, as none such exist elsewhere) such noble suites of rooms and halls as those through which we first passed, containing Egyptian, and, farther onward, Greek and Roman antiquities; the walls cased with variegated marbles, the cielings glowing with beautiful pictures, the whole prolonged into infinite vistas by looking-glasses, that seemed like vacancy, and multiplied everything forever. The picture-rooms are not so splendid, and the pictures themselves did not greatly win upon me, in this one day. Many artists were employed in copying them, especially in the rooms hung with the productions of French painters; not a few of these copyists were females; most of them were young men, picturesquely moustached and bearded, but some were elderly, who, it was pitiful to think, had passed through life without so much success as now to paint pictures of their own.

Hôtel du Louvre, Jany 10th, Sunday.

This morning, Paris looked as bleak as London, with clouds and rain; and when we issued forth, it seemed as if a cold, sullen agony were interposed between each separate atom of our bodies. In all my experience of bad atmospheres, methinks I never knew anything so atrocious as this. England has nothing to be compared with it. We had purposed going to the Cathedral of Notre Dame to-day; but the weather and walking were too unfavorable for a distant expedition; so Mamma, Julian, and I, merely went across the street to the Louvre, while Una, who was much wearied with yesterday's rambles, staid at home in our saloon. Baby and Miss Shepard had gone together to visit Miss Macdaniel, intending to dine at a Restaurant by themselves.[1]

Our principal object, to-day, was to see the pencil-drawings by eminent artists. Of these the Louvre has a very rich collection, occupying many apartments, and comprising sketches by Annibal Caracci, Claude, Raphael, Leonardo di Vinci, Michael Angelo, Rubens, Rembrandt, and almost all the other great masters, whether French, Italian, Dutch, or whatever else;[2] the earliest drawings of their great pictures, when they had the glory of their pristine idea directly before their mind's eye—that idea which inevitably became overlaid with their own handling of it, in the finished painting. No doubt, the painters themselves had often a happiness in these rude, off-hand sketches, which they never felt again in the same work, and which resulted in disappointment after they had done their best. To an artist, the collection must be intensely interesting; to myself, it was merely curious, and soon grew wearisome. In the same suite of apartments, there is a collection of miniatures, some of them very exquisite, and absolutely life-like, on their small scale. I observed two of Franklin, both good, and picturesque; one of them especially so, with its cloudlike white hair.[3] I do not think we have produced a man so interesting to contemplate, in many points of view, as he. Most of our great men are of a character that I find it impossible to warm into life by thought, and by lavishing any amount of sympathy upon them; not so Franklin, who had a great deal of common and uncommon human-nature in him. Much of the time, while my wife was looking at the drawings, I sat observing the crowd of Sunday visitors.... I did not much like any of these French faces; and yet I am not sure that there is not more resemblance between them and the American physiognomy, than between the latter and the English. The women are not pretty; but in all ranks above the lowest, they have a trained expression that supplies the place of beauty.

I was wearied to death with the drawings, and began to have that dreary and desperate feeling which has often come upon me, when the sights last longer than my capacity for receiving them....

By this time, poor Julian (who, with his taste for art yet undeveloped, is [*word deleted*] the companion of all our visits to sculpture and picture galleries.) ... We returned to the Hôtel; and it being too damp and raw to go *out* to our Restaurant d'Eschelle, we took Una and Julian down with us to the Restaurant of the Hotel. In my opinion, it would require less time to cultivate one's gastronomic tastes, than taste of any other kind; and, on the whole, I am not sure that a man could do a better thing than to afford himself a little discipline in this line. It is certainly throwing away the bounties of Providence to treat them as the English do, producing, from better materials than the French have to work upon, nothing but sirloins, joints, joints, steaks, steaks, steaks, chops, chops, chops, chops! We ate a soup, in which twenty kinds of vegetables were represented, and manifested each its own aroma; a fillet of stewed beef, which was ordered principally for Julian's benefit; and a fowl, in some form of delicate fricassée. We had a bottle of Chablis, and renewed ourselves, at the close of the banquet, with a plate of Chateaubriand ice. It was all very good, and we respected ourselves far more than if we had gorged a quantity of red roast-beef; but I am not quite sure that we were right.

Hôtel du Louvre, Jany 12th, Tuesday.

...Julian and I walked to Nôtre Dame, the rich and magnificent front of which I viewed with more attention than yesterday.... I must again speak of the horrible muddiness, not only of this part of the city [an old quarter behind Nôtre Dame], but of all Paris, so far as I have traversed it to-day. My ways, since I came to Europe, have often lain through nastiness; but I never before saw a pavement so universally overspread with mud-pudding, as that of Paris. It is difficult to imagine where so much filth comes from.

We dined in the Restaurant de L'Echelle; but already we are getting to be connoisseurs in French cookery, and we found nothing very admirable in the dishes of to-day. After dinner, I walked through the gardens of the Tuileries.... The trees in the Champs Elysées, and, I presume, in the gardens of the Tuileries, are said to need renewing, every few years. The same is true of the human race; families becoming extinct after a generation or two of residence in Paris. Nothing really thrives here; and vegetables have but an artificial life, like flowers stuck in a little mould, but never taking root. I am quite tired of Paris, and never longed for a home so much.

Leaving Paris, Hawthorne journeyed to Marseilles, which rivaled New England for its "bold, picturesque headlands" and views of the sea but exceeded anything in his "heretofore experience" for its "human nastiness, as an abode of men" (CE XIV: 43). From Marseilles he sailed to Genoa.

37, Via Porta Pinciana, Rome, Jany 24th, Sunday.

I went to bed immediately after my last record, and was rocked to sleep pleasantly enough by the billows of the Mediterranean; and coming on deck about sunrise, next morning, found the steamer approaching Genoa.

PART III: THE FRENCH AND ITALIAN NOTEBOOKS

We saw the city lying at the foot of a range of hills, and stretching a little way up their slopes; the hills sweeping round it in the segment of a circle, and looking like an island rising abruptly out of the sea; for no connection with the mainland was visible on either side. There was snow scattered on their summits, and streaking their sides a good way down; they looked bold and barren, and brown except where the snow streaked them. The city did not impress us with much expectation of size or magnificence. Shortly after coming into the port, our whole party landed, and found ourselves at once in the midst of a crowd of cab-drivers, hotel-runners, and commissionaires, who assaulted us with a volley of French, Italian, and broken English, which beat pitilessly about our ears; for really it seemed as if all the dictionaries in the world had been torn to pieces, and blown around us by a hurricane. I never heard such a pother. We took a commissionaire, a respectable-looking man in a cloak, who said his name was Salvator Rosa; and he engaged to show us whatever was interesting in Genoa. In the first place, he took us through narrow streets (mere gullies, as it were, between lines of tall stone houses, and chill as death with the eternal shade that broods in them) to an old church, the name of which I have forgotten, and indeed its peculiar features; but I know that I found it more magnificent than anything I had before seen or imagined; its whole interior being cased in polished marble, of various kind and colors, its cieling painted, and its chapels adorned with pictures.[4] However, this church was dazzled out of sight by the Cathedral of San Lorenzo, to which we afterwards were conducted, the exterior front of which is covered with alternate slabs of black and white marble, which were brought, either in whole or in part, from Jerusalem. Within, there was an immense richness of precious marbles, and a pillar, if I mistake not, from Solomon's Temple, and a picture of the Virgin by Saint Luke, and others (rather more intrinsically valuable, I imagine) by old Masters, set in magnificent marble frames, within the arches of the Chapels. I used to try to imagine how splendidly the English Cathedrals must have looked in their primeval glory, before the Reformation, and before the whitewash of Cromwell's time had overlaid their marble pillars; but I never imagined anything at all approaching what my eyes now beheld; this sheen of polished variegated marble, covering every inch of the walls; this glow of brilliant frescoes all over the roof, and up within the domes; these beautiful pictures by great masters, painted for the places which they now occupied, and making an actual portion of the edifice; this wealth of silver, gold, and gems, that adorned the shrines of the saints, before which wax candles burned, and were kept burning, I suppose, from years' end to years' end; in short, there is no imagining or remembering a hundredth part of this magnificence. And even the Cathedral (though I give it up as indescribable) was nothing in comparison with a church to which the Commissionaire afterwards led us; a church that had been built, four or five hundred years ago, by a pirate, in expiation of his sins and out of the profit of his rapine. This last edifice, in its interior, absolutely shone with burnished gold, and glowed with pictures; its walls were a quarry of precious stones, so valuable were the marbles out of which they were wrought; its columns and pillars were of inconceivable value; its pavement was a mosaic of wonderful beauty. There were four twisted pillars made out of stalactites. I am ashamed of my folly in trying even to make myself remember how much I was dazzled by this church. Perhaps the best way to form some dim conception of it, is to imagine a little casket, all inlaid, in its inside, with precious stones, so that there shall not a hair's breadth be left un-precious-stoned; and then imagine this little bit of a casket increased to the magnitude of a great church, without losing anything of the intense glory that was compressed into its original small compass, but all its pretty lustre made sublime and magnificent by the immensity. At any rate, nobody who has not seen a church like this (if there be another such) can imagine what a splendid religion it was that reared it. In the Cathedral, and in all the churches, we saw priests, and many persons kneeling at their devotions; and our Salvator Rosa, whenever we passed a chapel or shrine, failed not to touch the pavement with one knee, crossing himself the while; and once, when a priest was going through some form of devotion, he stopt a few moments to share in it.

He conducted us, too, to the Balbi palace, the stateliest and most magnificent residence that I had ever seen, but not more so than another which he afterwards showed us nor perhaps than many others which exist in Genoa the superb. The painted cielings in these palaces are a glorious adornment; the walls of the saloons, encrusted with various-colored marbles, give an idea of splendor which I never gained from anything else; the floors wrought in mosaic, seem too precious to tread upon. In the royal palace, many of the floors were wrought of inlaid woods, by an English artist, and looked like a magnification of some exquisite piece of Tunbridge ware; but, in all respect, this palace was inferior to others which we saw. I say nothing of the immense pictorial treasures which hung upon the walls of all the rooms through which we passed: for I soon grew so weary of admirable things that I could neither enjoy nor understand them. My receptive faculty is very limited; and when the utmost of its small capacity is full, I become perfectly miserable, and the more so, the better worth seeing are the things I am forced to reject. I do not know a greater misery; to see sights after such repletion is, to the mind, what it would be to the body to have dainties forced down the throat long after the appetite was satiated.

37, Via Porta Pinciana, Rome, February 3ᵈ 1858, Wednesday.

We have been in Rome, I believe, a fortnight to day; or rather at eleven °clock to night; and I have seldom or never spent so wretched a time anywhere. Our impressions were very unfortunate, arriving at midnight, half-frozen, in the wintry rain, and being received into a cold and cheerless hotel, where we shivered during two or three days; meanwhile, seeking lodging, amongst the sunless, dreary alleys which are called streets in Rome. One cold, bright day after another has pierced me to the heart and cut me in twain, as with a sword, keen and sharp, and poisoned at point and edge. I did not think cold weather could have made me so very miserable; upon my word, having caught a feverish cold, I was glad of being muffled up comfortably in the fever-heat. The atmosphere certainly has a peculiar quality of malignancy. After a day or two, we settled ourselves in a suite of ten rooms, comprehending one flat, or what is called the second piano of this house.[5] The rooms, thus far, have been very cold and uncomfortable, it being impossible to warm them by means of the deep, old-fashioned, inartificial fireplaces, unless we had the great logs of a New England forest to burn in them; so I have sat in my corner by the fireside, with more clothes on than ever I wore before, and my thickest great coat. In the middle of the day, I generally venture out for an hour or two, but have only once been warm enough even in the sunshine; and out of the sun, it is as chill as death. I understand, now, the force of that story of Alexander and Diogenes, when the latter asked the conqueror, as the only favor he could do him, to stand out of his sunshine; there being such a difference, in these Southern climes of Europe, between sun and shade.[6] You stand within the sunshine, though on its very verge, and are comfortably warm; you make one step beyond, and are smitten as with the edge of cold steel. If my wits had not been too much congealed, and my fingers too numb, I should like to have kept a minute journal of my feelings and impressions, during the past fortnight; it would have shown up modern Rome in an aspect in which it has never yet been depicted. But I have now grown somewhat acclimated, and the first freshness of my discomfort has worn off; so that I shall never be able to express how I dislike the place, and how wretched I have been in it; and soon, I suppose, warmer weather will come, and perhaps reconcile me to Rome against my will. Cold, nastiness, evil smells, narrow lanes between tall, ugly, mean-looking, white-washed houses, sour bread, pavement, most uncomfortable to the feet, enormous prices for poor living, beggars, pickpockets, ancient temples and broken monuments with filth at the base, and clothes hanging to dry about them, French soldiers, monks, and priests of every degree, a shabby population smoking bad cigars—these would have been some of the points of my description.[7] Of course there are better and truer things to be said; but old Rome does seem to lie here like a dead and mostly decayed corpse, retaining here and there a trace of the noble shape it was, but with a sort of fungous growth upon it, and no life but of the worms that creep in and out.[8]

It would be idle for me to attempt any sketches of these famous sites and edifices—Saint Peter's for example—which have been described by a thousand people, though none of them have ever given me an idea what sort of place Rome is. Saint Peter's disappointed me terribly by its want of effect, and the little justice it does to its real magnitude, externally; but the interior blazed upon me with altogether unexpected magnificence; so brilliant is it with picture, gilding, variegated and polished marbles, and all that splendor which I tried in vain to describe in the churches of Genoa. I had expected something vast and dim, like the great English Cathedrals, only more vast, and dim, and gray; but there is as much difference as between noonday and twilight. I never saw nor imagined so bright and splendid an interior as that of this immense church; but I am not sure that it would not be more grand and majestic if it were less magnificent, though I should be sorry to see the experiment tried.[9] The Coliseum was very much what I had pre-conceived it, though I was not prepared to find it turned into a sort of Christian church, with a pulpit on the verge of the open space. Right in the center, there is a great iron cross, on which is advertized, in Italian, an indulgence of two hundred days to whoever shall kiss it. While I sat on a stone, under one of the arches, I saw two women prick their way through the mud and kiss this cross, and then go away repeating their prayers aloud. The French soldiers (who keep guard within the Coliseum, as in most other public places in Rome) have an excellent opportunity to secure the welfare of their souls.

Rome, Feby 7th, Sunday.

I cannot get fairly into the current of my Journal, since we arrived in Rome; and already I perceive that the nice peculiarities of Roman life are passing from my notice before I have recorded them. It is a very great pity. During this past week, I have plodded daily, for an hour or two, through the narrow, stony streets, that look worse than the worst backside lanes of any other city; indescribably ugly and disagreeable they are; so cold, so alley-like, so uncomfortably paved with little square stones, without side walks, but provided with a line of larger squares, set cornerwise to each other, along which there is somewhat less uneasy walking. Along these lanes, or gullies, a chill wind blows; down into their depths the sun never falls; they are bestrewn with horse dung and the filth of the adjacent houses, which rise on each side to the height of five or six stories, generally plastered and white-washed and looking neither old nor new. Probably these houses have the brick and stone of old Rome in them—the Coliseum, and many another stately structure—but they themselves look like magnified hovels. Ever and anon, even in the meanest streets (though, generally speaking, one can hardly be called meaner than another) we pass a palace, extending far along the narrow way on the line with the other houses, but distinguished by its architectural windows, iron-barred on the basement story, and by its portal arch through which we have glimpses sometimes of a filthy courtyard, or perhaps an ornamented one, with trees, a colonnade, a fountain and a statue in the vista; though, more likely, it resembles the entrance to a stable, and may perhaps really be one. The lower regions of palaces come to strange uses in Rome; a cobler or a tinker perhaps exercizes his craft under the archway; a work-shop may be established in one of the apartments; and in the basement story of the Barberini palace a regiment of French cavalry seems to be quartered, while, no doubt, princes have magnificent domiciles above. Be it palace or whatever other dwelling, the inmates climb through stink and nastiness to the comforts, such as they may be, that await them above. I vainly try to get down upon paper the dreariness and ugliness, nastiness, discomfort, shabbiness, un-home-likeness, of a Roman street.... If an antiquary were to accompany me through the streets, no doubt he would point out ten thousand interesting objects, that I now pass over unnoticed, so general is the surface of plaster, white-wash, and shabbiness; but often I can see fragments of antiquity built into the walls, or perhaps a church that was a Roman temple, or a basement of ponderous stones, that were laid above twenty centuries ago. It is strange how our ideas of what antiquity is become altered here in Rome; the sixteenth century, in which many of the churches and fountains seem to have been built or re-edified, seems close at hand, even like our own days; a thousand years, or the days of the latter empire, is but a modern date; and scarcely interests us; and nothing is really venerable of a more recent epoch than the reign of Constantine.[10] The Egyptian obelisks that stand in several of the piazzas, put even the Augustan or Republican antiquities to shame.[11] I remember reading in a New York newspaper an account of one of the public buildings of that city—a relic of the "olden time," the writer called it; for it was erected in 1825! I am glad I saw the castles and Gothic churches and cathedrals of England before visiting Rome; or I never could have felt that delightful reverence for their gray and ivy-hung antiquity, after seeing these so much older remains. But indeed, old things are not so beautiful in this dry climate and clear atmosphere as in moist England. The marble, it is true, grows black or brown, and shows its age in that manner; but it remains hard and sharp, and does not become again a part of Nature, as stone walls do in England; some dry and dusty grass sprouts along the ledges of a ruin, as in the Coliseum, but there is no green mantle of ivy kindly spreading itself over the gray dilapidation. Whatever beauty there may be in a Roman ruin is the remnant of what was beautiful originally, whereas an English ruin is more beautiful, often, in its decay than ever it was in its primal strength. If we ever build such noble structures as these Roman ones, we can have just as good ruins after two thousand years, in the United States; but we never can have a Furness Abbey or a Kenilworth....[12]

I have not yet fairly begun the sight-seeing of Rome; the weather being so cold that I shiver at the thought of each new thing. I have been three or four times to Saint Peters' and always with pleasure, because there is such a delightful, summer-like warmth the moment we pass beneath the heavy, padded, leather curtains, that protect the entrances. It is almost impossible not to believe that this genial temperature is the result of furnace heat; but really it is the warmth of last summer, which will be included within those massive walls, and in that vast immensity of space, till, six months hence, this winter's chill will just have made its way thither.... Saint Peter's offers itself as a place of worship and religious comfort for the whole human race; and in one of the transepts I found a range of confessionals, where the penitent might tell his sins in the tongue of his own country, whether French, German, Polish, English, or what not. If I had had a murder on my conscience or any other great sin, I think I should have been inclined to kneel down there, and pour it into the safe secrecy of the confessional.[13] What an institution that is! Man needs it so, that it seems as if God must have ordained it. This popish religion certainly does apply itself most closely and comfortably to human occasions; and I cannot but think that a great many people find their spiritual advantage in it, who would find none at all in our formless mode of worship. You cannot think it is all a farce when you see peasant, citizen, and soldier, coming into the church, each on his own hook, and kneeling for moments or for hours, directing his silent devotions to some particular shrine; too humble to approach his God directly, and therefore asking the mediation of some saint, who stands beside his infinite presence. In the church of San Paulo yesterday I saw a young man standing before a shrine, writhing and wringing his hands in an agony of grief and contrition. If he had been a protestant, I think he would have shut all that up within his heart, and let it burn there till it seared him....

My wife and I went yesterday to the Pantheon,[14] which stands in the central intricacy and nastiness of Roman lanes. Its portico, with ranges of vast granite columns, is greatly admired by architects, and no doubt justly. Its interior is most noble and beautiful, yet with a strange, half-heathenish aspect, which seems to be caused chiefly by a great circular opening in the center of its dome, through which comes all the light that illuminates the edifice. It is open to the sky, and, when we were there, the pavement beneath was plashy with the rain that had fallen through. All round the great circle of the Pantheon there are arches and stately altars, formerly dedicated to heathen gods and now to Saints, who step with ludicrous composure into every vacant niche in Rome, just as if it had been made for them. Up as far as the commencement of the curve of the dome, the walls are encrusted with precious marbles, which, together with the marble pillar and pilasters, must once have been most gorgeous; as also the mosaic pavement of colored marble and porphyry. I know not whether all this marble has laid over the walls, since the Pantheon became a Christian church, or whether it has remained from old Roman times, but I think the latter can hardly have been the case. The Pantheon has been Christianized more than twelve centuries; so that there has been time for its Christian decorations to grow dingy and weather-worn, especially as the waters have had free access through the circular skylight. The interior of the dome, which is now bare and stony, was formerly overlaid with bronze. The tomb of Raphael is in this church, or temple, but we did not see it, and must go again for that purpose. I think the Pantheon has impressed me more than anything else I have seen in Rome; the more for its dust and dinginess, and for that one circumstance of its gray roof open to the sky, so unlike the snugness of all our modern civilization. I must not forget, as characteristic of the spirit of modern Rome, that there are pasteboard statues, as large as life, aloft beneath the dome; so well done it is true, that they deceived me at first, in the dim cloudy light that came through the circular opening, on that rainy day. Also there are tin-hearts and other adornments of that kind hanging at the shrines of the Saints. I do not believe that the old heathen deities were ever cheated with similar sham jewellery. People were kneeling in devotion at several of the shrines. When I first came to Rome I felt embarrassed, and unwilling to pass with my heresy and unbelief, between a devotee and his saint; for they often shoot their prayers at a shrine almost quite across the church. But there seems to be no violation of etiquette in so doing. A woman begged of us in the Pantheon, and accused my wife of impiety, for not giving her an alms. Beggars are extremely numerous in Rome; and people of very decent appearance are often unexpectedly converted into beggars, as you approach them, but, in general, they take a "No" at once.

Rome, February 13th, Saturday.

Day before yesterday, we took a carriage—Mamma, Julian, Rosebud and I—and went to see the Carnival by driving up and down the Corso. Una and Miss Shepard were spectators from a window with Miss Mitchell.[15] It was as ugly a day, as respects weather, as has befallen us since we came to Rome, cloudy, with an indecisive little wet, which finally settled into a rain; and people say that such is generally the weather in Carnival-time. There is very little to be said about the spectacle. Sunshine would have improved it, no doubt; but a person must have very broad sunshine within himself to be very joyous on such shallow provocation. The street, at all events, would have looked rather brilliant under a sunny sky, the balconies being hung with bright-colored draperies, which were also flung out of some of the windows. The balconies were mostly filled with ladies; some of whom sat nearly on a level with the passers by, in full dress, with deep colored Italian faces, ready to encounter whatever the chances of the Carnival might bring them. The upper balconies (and there was sometimes a third, if not a fourth tier) were occupied, I think, chiefly by foreigners, English or Americans; nor, I fancy, do the Roman ladies of rank and respectability generally display themselves at this time. At least, the festival seems to me to have sunk from the upper classes to the lower ones; and probably it is only kept alive by tradition, and the curiosity which impels foreigners to join in it.

. . . I never in my life knew a shallower joke than the Carnival at Rome; such a rainy and muddy day, too! Greenwich Fair (at the very last of which I assisted) was worth a hundred of it. . . . On comparing notes with Julian and Rosebud—indeed, with Una too—I find that they all enjoyed the Carnival much more than I did. Only the young ought to write descriptions of such scenes. My cold criticism chills the life out of it.

Rome, February 14th, Sunday.

Friday was a sunny day, the first that we had had for some time; and my wife and I went forth to see sights, as well as to make some calls that had long been due. . . .

We called into the Barberini Palace, where William Story has established himself and family for the next seven years, on the third piano, in apartments that afford a very fine look-out over Rome, and (which is more important) have the sun in them through most of the day. . . .[16] [We] found him at work on a sitting statue of Cleopatra.[17] William Story looks thin and worn, already a little bald and a very little gray, but quite as vivid—in a graver way—as when I saw him last, a young man. He can yet, methinks, be scarcely thirty-seven.[18] His perplexing variety of talents and accomplishments—a poet, a prose-writer, a lawyer, a painter, a sculptor—seems now to be concentrating itself into this latter vocation; and I cannot see why he should not achieve something very good. He has a beautiful statue, already finished, of Goethe's Margaret pulling a flower to pieces to discover whether Faust loves her; a very type of virginity and simplicity.[19] The statue of Cleopatra, now only fourteen days advanced in the clay, is as wide a step from the little maidenly Margaret as any artist could take; it is a grand subject, and he appears to be conceiving it with depth and power, and working it out with adequate skill. He certainly is sensible of something deeper in his art than merely to make beautiful nudities and baptize them by classic names.

Rome, February 15th, Monday.

To-day has been very rainy. I went out in the forenoon, and took a sitting at Miss Lander's studio, she having done me the honor to request me to sit for my bust.[20] Her rooms are those formerly occupied by Canova;[21] the one where she models being large, high, and dreary, from the want of carpet, furniture, or anything but clay and plaster. A sculptor's studio has not the picturesque charm of a painter's, where there is color, warmth, cheerfulness, and where the artist continually turns towards you the glow of some picture which is resting against the wall. Miss Lander is from my own native town, and appears to have genuine talent, and spirit and independence enough to give it fair play. She is living here quite alone, in delightful freedom, and has sculptured two or three things that may probably make her favorably known. "Virginia Dare" is certainly very beautiful.[22] During the sitting, I talked a good deal with Miss Lander, being a little inclined to take a similar freedom with her moral likeness to that which she was taking with my physical one. There are very available points about her and her position; a young woman, living in almost perfect independence, thousands of miles from her New England home, going fearlessly about these mysterious streets, by night as well as by day, with no household ties, no rule or law but that within her; yet acting with quietness and simplicity, and keeping, after all, within a homely line of right. In her studio, she wears a sort of pea-jacket, buttoned across her breast, and a little foraging-cap, just covering the top of her head. She asked me not to look at the bust at the close of the sitting, and, of course, I obeyed; though I have a vague idea of a heavy-browed physiognomy, something like what I have seen in the glass, but looking strangely in that guise of clay. Miss Lander has become strongly attached to Rome, and says that, when she dreams of home, it is merely of paying a short visit, and coming back before her trunk is unpacked. This is a strange fascination that Rome exercises upon artists; there is clay elsewhere, and marble enough, and heads to model; and ideas may be made sensible objects at home as well as here. I think it is the peculiar mode of life, and its freedom from the enthralments of society, more than the artistic advantages which Rome offers; and then, no doubt, though the artists care little about one another's works, yet they keep one another warm by the presence of so many of them.

Rome, February 17th, Wednesday.

Yesterday morning was perfectly sunny; and my wife and I went betimes to see churches, going first to the Capuchin church (I forget its individual title) close by the Piazza Barbarini.[23] It is now, I believe, the church of a convent of Capuchin monks. On entering, we found it not very large, but of good architecture, with a vaulted roof over the nave, and rows of chapels on either side, instead of aisles. The pavement seemed old and worn, and was much patched with brick tiles as well as with mediaeval tombstones; and we were startled to see—right in the middle of the pavement, and in the centre of the nave, on a bier, with three candles burning on each side, and one at the head and another at the feet—a dead monk! He was dressed, as when alive, in the brown woollen frock of his order, with the hood drawn over his head, but so as to leave his face uncovered, as well as part of his gray beard. His beads and cross hung by his side; his hands were folded over his breast; his feet were bare both of shoes and stockings, and seemed to be tied together with a black ribbon. He certainly was a dead monk, and had once been alive; though, at first, I was in some doubt whether he might not be a wax figure, so strange was it to see him displayed in such guise. Meanwhile, his brother monks were singing or chanting some deep, lugubrious strain—a *de profundis*, I believe—in the vaults under the church, where the dead man was soon to be laid, in earth brought long ago from Jerusalem, but which has been the bed, over and over again, of deceased members of the fraternity. For it is the custom of this convent, when one of its monks dies, to take the bones that have been longest buried out of the oldest grave, and remove them to a common ossuary, putting the newly deceased into the vacant bed. It is rather hard upon these poor fathers, that they cannot call even their graves their own. We walked round the church, which contains pictures and frescoes by Guido and Domenichino;[24] but pictures in the side-chapels of churches are quite lost, in nine cases out of ten, by the bad light, or the no light, in which they must be seen. Much the most interesting object to me was still the dead monk, with his bare feet, those old, worn feet, that had walked to and fro over the hard pavements of Rome, and along the dreary corridors of his convent, for so many years, and now stuck forth so stiffly from beneath his frock. He had been a somewhat short and punchy personage, this poor monk, and perhaps had died of apoplexy; for his face did not look pale, but had almost, or quite, the natural flush of life, though the feet were of such a yellow, waxy hue. His gray eyebrows were very thick, and my wife had a fancy that she saw him contort them. . . . By and by, as we moved round from chapel to chapel, still with our eyes turning often to the dead monk, we saw some blood oozing from his nostrils! Perhaps his murderer—or his doctor—had just then come into the church and drawn nigh the bier; at all events, it was about as queer a thing as ever I witnessed. We soon came away and left him lying there; a sight which I shall never forget.

∼

Hawthorne visits the sculpture gallery in the Vatican and the Roman Forum.

∼

Rome, February 19th. Friday.

. . . After wandering to and fro, a good while, I at last found myself in a long, long gallery, on each side of which were innumerable inscriptions, in Greek and Latin, on slabs of marble, built into the walls; and classic altars and tablets were ranged along the gallery, from end to end. At the extremity was a closed iron-grating, from which I was turning back; but a French gentleman accosted me, with the information that the Custode would admit us, if I chose, and would accompany us through the sculpture department of the Vatican. I acceded, and thus took my first view of those innumerable art-treasures, passing from one object to another, at any easy pace, pausing hardly a moment anywhere, and dismissing even the Apollo, and the Laocoon, and the torso of Hercules, in the space of half a dozen breaths.[25] I was well enough content to do so, in order to get a general idea of the contents of the galleries, before settling down upon individual objects. Most of these world-famous sculptures presented themselves to my eye with a kind of familiarity, through the copies and casts which I had seen; but I found the originals were different than I anticipated. The

Apollo, for instance, has a face which I have never seen in any cast or copy. I must confess, however—taking such transient glimpses as I did—I was more impressed with the extent of the Vatican, and the beautiful order in which it is kept, and its great, sunny, open courts, with fountains, grass, and shrubs, and the views of Rome and the Campagna from its windows—more impressed with these, and with certain vastly capacious vases, and two great sarcophagi, than with the statuary. Thus we went round the whole, and were dismissed through the grated barrier into the gallery of inscriptions again; and after a little more wandering, I found my way out of the palace....

Yesterday, I went out betimes, and strayed through some portion of ancient Rome,—to the column of Trajan, to the forum, thence along the Tarpeian way, after which I lost myself among the intricacies of the streets, and finally came out at the bridge of St. Angelo. The first observation which a stranger is led to make, in the neighborhood of Roman ruins, is, that the inhabitants seem to be strangely addicted to the washing of clothes; for all the precincts of Trajan's forum, and of the Roman forum, and wherever else an iron railing affords opportunity to hang them, were whitened with sheets and other linen and cotton, drying in the sun. It must be that washerwomen burrow among the old temples. The second observation is not quite so favorable to the cleanly character of the modern Romans; indeed, it is so very unfavorable that I hardly know how to express it. But the fact is, that, through the forum, and along the base of any ancient wall, and anywhere else, out of the commonest foot-track and road-way, you must look well to your steps, or they will be defiled with unutterable nastiness. If you tread beneath the triumphal arch of Titus or Constantine, you had better look downward than upward, whatever be the merit of the sculptures aloft; and, in my opinion, the Romans of today consider these ancient relics as existing for no other purpose than that they may turn aside to them in their necessity. They appear to have no other places of need, and to need them ten times as much as other people.[26] After awhile, the visitant finds himself getting accustomed to this horrible state of things, and the associations of moral sublimity and beauty seem to throw a veil over the physical meannesses to which I allude. Perhaps there is something in the mind of the people of these countries that enables them quite to dissever small ugliness from great sublimity and beauty. They spit on the glorious pavement of St Peter's, and wherever else they like; they place mean-looking wooden confessionals beneath its sublime arches, and ornament them with cheap little colored prints of the crucifixion; they hang tin hearts and other tinsel and trumpery at the gorgeous shrines of the saints, in chapels that are encrusted with gems, or marbles almost as precious; they put pasteboard statues of Saints beneath the dome of the Pantheon; in short they let the sublime and the ridiculous come close together, and are not in the least troubled by the proximity. It must be that their sense of the beautiful is stronger than in the Anglo Saxon mind, and that it observes only what is fit to gratify it.

Rome, February 20th, Saturday.

This morning, after breakfast, I walked across the city, making a pretty straight course to the Pantheon, and thence to the Bridge of St Angelo, and to Saint Peter's. It had been my purpose to go to the Fontana Paolina,[27] but finding that the distance was too great, and being weighed down with a Roman lassitude, I concluded to go into St Peter's. Here I looked at Michael Angelo's *Pieta;* a representation of the dead Christ, naked in his mother's lap.[28] Then I strolled round the great church, and find that it continues to grow upon me both in magnitude and beauty, by comparison with the many interiors of sacred edifices, which I have lately seen. At times, a single, casual, momentary glimpse of its magnificence gleams upon my soul, as it were, when I happen to glance at arch opening beyond arch, and I am surprised into admiration when I think least of it. I have experienced that a landscape, and the sky, unfold their deepest beauty in a similar way, not when they are gazed at of set purpose, but when the spectator looks suddenly through a peep-hole among a crowd of other thoughts. Passing near the confessionals for foreigners, to day, I saw a Spaniard, who had just come out of the one devoted to his native tongue, taking leave of his confessor, with an affectionate reverence which—as well as the benign dignity of the good Father—it was good to behold. The relation between the confessor and his penitent might, and ought to be, one of great tenderness and beauty; and the more I see of the Catholic church, the more I wonder at the exuberance with which it responds to the demands of human infirmity. If its ministers were themselves a little more than human, they might fulfill their office, and supply all that men need.

    I returned home early, in order to go with my wife to the Barberini Palace, at two °clock. . . . The entrance to the picture gallery is by the door on the right hand, affording us a sight of a beautiful spiral staircase, which goes circling upward from the very basement to the very summit of the palace with a perfectly easy ascent, yet confining its sweep within a moderate compass. We looked up through the interior of the spiral, as through a tube, from the bottom to the top. The pictures are contained in three contiguous rooms of the lower story, and are few in number, comprising barely half-a-dozen which I should care to see again, though doubtless all have value in their way. One that attracted our attention was a picture of Christ disputing with the Doctors, by Albert Durer, in which was represented the ugliest, most evil-minded, stubborn, pragmatical, and contentious old Jew, that ever lived under the law of Moses; and he and the child Jesus were arguing not only with their tongues, but making hieroglyphics, as it were, by the motion of their hands and fingers.[29] It is a very queer, as well as a very remarkable picture. But we passed hastily by this, and almost all the other pictures, being eager to see the two which chiefly make the collection famous.—These are Raphael's Fornarini, and Guido's portrait of Beatrice Cenci.[30] These we found in the last of the three rooms; and as regards Beatrice Cenci, I might as well not try to say anything, for its spell is indefinable, and the painter has wrought it in a way more like magic than anything else I have known. It is a very youthful, girlish, perfectly beautiful face, with white drapery all around it, and quite enveloping the form. One or two locks of auburn hair stray out. The eyes are large and brown, and meet those of the spectator; and there is, I think, a little red about the eyelids, but it is very slightly indicated. The whole face is perfectly quiet; no distortion nor disturbance of any single feature; nor can I see why it should not be cheerful, nor why an imperceptible touch of the painter's brush should not suffice to brighten it into joyousness. Yet it is the very saddest picture that ever was painted, or conceived; there is an unfathomable depth and sorrow in the eyes; the sense of it comes to you by a sort of intuition. It is a sorrow that removes her out of the sphere of humanity; and yet she looks so innocent, that you feel as if it were only this sorrow, with its weight and darkness, that keeps her down upon the earth and brings within our reach at all. She is like a fallen angel, fallen, without sin. It is infinitely pitiful to meet her eyes, and feel that nothing can be done to help or comfort her; not that she appeals to you for help and comfort, but is more conscious than we can be that there is none in reserve for her. It is the most profoundly wrought picture in the world; no artist did it, or could do it again. Guido may have held the brush, but he painted better than he knew. I wish, however, it were possible for some spectator, of deep sensibility, to see the picture without knowing anything of its subject or history; for no doubt we bring all our knowledge of the Cenci tragedy to the interpretation of the picture.

Close beside Beatrice Cenci hangs the Fornarina, a brunette, with a deep, bright glow in her face, naked below the navel and well pleased to be so for the sake of your admiration—ready for any extent of nudity, for love or money,—the brazen trollope that she is. Raphael must have been capable of great sensuality, to have painted this picture of his own accord and lovingly.

PART III: THE FRENCH AND ITALIAN NOTEBOOKS

Rome, February 21st, Sunday.

I went along the Via di Ripetta, and through other streets, stepping into two or three churches, one of which was the Pantheon. When I last saw it, the sun was coming through the circular opening in its dome; now the sunshine fell side-long through it, and threw a large span of light on the hollow curve; and it seemed well to have such a skyward door for good spirits to float down through, and for prayers to ascend. It is truly a noble edifice; and it is curious to see how well the Heathen temple has adapted itself to Christian and Catholic purposes, supplying more shrines and chapels than any other form of building possibly could. There are, I think, seven deep, pillared recesses around the circumference, each of which becomes a sufficiently spacious chapel; and, alternately with these chapels, there is a marble structure, like the architecture of a doorway, beneath which is the shrine of a saint; so that the whole circle of the Pantheon is filled up with the seven chapels and seven shrines. A number of persons were sitting or kneeling around; others came in while I was there, dipping their fingers in the holy water, and bending their knee as they passed the shrines and chapels, until they reached the one which, apparently, they had selected as the particular altar for their devotions. Everybody seemed so devout, and in a frame of mind so suited to the day and place, that it really made me feel a little awkward not to be able to kneel down along with them. Unlike the worshippers in our own churches, each individual here seems to do his own individual acts of worship, and I cannot but think it better so than to make a joint-stock concern of it, as we do. It is my opinion that a great deal of devout and reverential feeling is kept alive in people's hearts by the Catholic mode of worship....

I reached home at about twelve, and, at one °clock, set out again with my wife towards St Peter's, where we meant to stay till after vespers.... I suppose there was hardly a man or woman who had not heard mass, confessed, and said their prayers; a thing which—the prayer, I mean—it would be absurd to predicate of London, or New York, or any Protestant city. In however adulterated a guise, the Catholics do get a draught of devotion to slake the thirst of their souls, and methinks it must needs do them good, even if not quite so pure as if it came from better cisterns, or from the original fountain-head.

Arriving at St Peter's shortly after two, we walked round the whole church, looking at all the pictures and most of the monuments.... We passed quite round the whole circumference of the church, and paused longest before Guido's picture (its mosaic copy, rather) of the archangel Michael overcoming Lucifer.[31] This is surely one of the most beautiful things in the world; one of the human conceptions that are imbued most largely with the celestial. These old painters were wonderful men, and have done great things for the Church of Rome—great things, we may say, for the church of Christ and the cause of good; for the moral of this picture (the immortal youth and loveliness of virtue; and its irresistible might against evil) is as much directed to a Puritan as to a Catholic.

Rome, February 23rd, Tuesday.

Yesterday at noon, mamma and I set out for the Capitol....[32] [W]e went into the Museum, in an edifice on our left, entering the Piazza, and here in the vestibule we found various old statues and relics of which there remains hardly the slightest trace in my memory. Ascending the stairs, we passed through a long gallery, of the contents of which I can make no better record, and turning to our left, examined somewhat more carefully a suite of rooms running parallel with the gallery. The first of these contained busts of the Caesars and their kindred, from the epoch of the mightiest Julius downward, eighty-three, I believe, in all.[33] I had seen a bust of Julius Caesar, in the British Museum, and was surprised at its thin and withered aspect; but this head is of a very ugly old man indeed, wrinkled, puckered, shrunken, lacking breadth and substance, care-worn, grim, as if he had fought hard with life, and had suffered in the conflict; a man of schemes, and of eager effort to bring his schemes to pass. His profile is by no means good, advancing from the top of his forehead to the tip of his nose, and retreating, at about the same angle, from the latter point to the bottom of his chin, which seems to be thrust forcibly down into his shrunken neck. Not that he pokes his head forward, for it is particularly erect. The head of Augustus is very beautiful, and appears to be that of a meditative, philosophic man, saddened with the sense that it is not very much worth while to be at the summit of human greatness, after all. It is a sorrowful thing to trace the decay of civilization through this series of busts, and to observe how the artistic skill, so exquisite at first, went on declining through the dreary dynasty of the Caesars, till at length the master of the world could not get his head carved in better style than the figure-head of a ship.

In the next room, there were better statues than we had yet seen, but neither do I retain any vivid recollection of these, nor yet of those in the succeeding apartment; but, in the last room of the range, we found the Dying Gladiator, of which I had already caught a glimpse, in passing by the open door.[34] It had made all the other treasures of the gallery tedious, in my eagerness to come to that. I was not in a very fit state to see it, for that most miserable sense of satiety—the mind's repletion when too much rich or delicate food has been forced upon it—had got possession of me, though I had really done little more than glance at objects. Still, I had life enough left to admire this statue, and was more impressed by it than by anything of marble that I ever saw. I do not believe that so much pathos is wrought into any other block of stone. Like all other works of the highest excellence, however, it makes great demands upon the spectator; he must make a generous gift of his sympathies to the sculptor, and help out his skill with all his heart, or else he will see little more than a skillfully wrought surface. It suggests far more than it shows. I looked long at this statue, and little at anything else, though, among other famous works, a statue of Antinous was in the same room.[35]

I was glad when we left the Museum, which, by the by, was awfully chill, as if the multitude of statues radiated cold out of their marble substance. We might have gone to see the pictures in the Palace of the Conservators;[36] and my wife (whose receptivity is unlimited, and forever fresh) would willingly have done so; but I objected, and so we went towards the Forum.

Rome, February 25th, Thursday.

We went, this forenoon, to the Palazzo Borghese, which is situated on a street that runs at right angles with the Corso, and very near the latter....[37]

As to the pictures, I do not propose to say much about them. The collection is one of the most celebrated in the world, and contains between eight and nine hundred pictures, many of which are esteemed master-pieces. I think I was not in a frame for admiration, to-day, nor could achieve that free and generous surrender of myself, which I have already said is essential to the proper estimate of anything excellent. Besides, how is it possible to give one's soul, or any considerable part of it, to a single picture, seen for the first time, among a thousand others, all of which set forth their own claims in an equally good light! Furthermore, there is an external weariness and sense of thousand-fold sameness to be overcome, before we can begin to enjoy a gallery of the old Italian masters. There is such a terrible lack of variety in their subjects....[38] These old painters seldom treated their subjects in a homely way; they were above life, or on one side of it; and if they ever touched the heart, it was by the help of the religious sentiment, which we Protestants can not call up, to eke out our profane admiration. I can hardly think they really had the sentiments themselves; for evidently they were just as ready, or more so, to paint a lewd and naked woman, and call her Venus, as to imagine whatever is purest in womanhood, as the mother of their Saviour.... Raphael, and other great painters, have done wonders with sacred subjects; but the greatest wonder is, how they could ever paint them at all, and always they paint from the outside, and not from within.

I was glad, in the very last of the twelve rooms, to come upon some Dutch and Flemish pictures, very few, but very welcome; Rubens, Rembrandt, Vandyke, Paul Potter, Teniers, and other—men of flesh and blood, with warm fists, and human hearts.[39] As compared with them, these mighty Italian masters seem men of polished steel, not human, nor addressing themselves so much to human sympathies as to a formed intellectual taste.

Rome, March 10th, Wednesday.

On Monday, my wife, Una, Julian, and I, went to the Sculpture Gallery of the Vatican, and saw as much of the sculpture as we could in the three hours during which the public are admissible.[40] There were a few things which I really enjoyed, and a few moments during which I really seemed to see them; but it is in vain to attempt giving the impression produced by masterpieces of art, and most in vain when we see them best. They are a language in themselves; and if they could be expressed any way except by themselves, there would have been no need of expressing those particular ideas and sentiments by sculpture. I saw the Apollo Belvidere as something ethereal and godlike; only for a flitting moment, however, and as if he had alighted from heaven, or shone suddenly out of the sunlight, and then had withdrawn himself again. I felt the Laocoon, too, very powerfully, though very quietly; an immortal agony, with a strange calmness diffused through it, so that it resembles the vast rage of the sea, calm on account of its immensity, or the tumult of Niagara, which does not seem to be tumult because it keeps pouring on, forever and ever. I have not had so good a day as this (among works of art) since we came to Rome; and I impute it partly to the magnificence of the arrangements of the Vatican—its long vistas, and beautiful courts, and the aspect of immortality which marble statues acquire by being kept free from dust. Julian was very hungry, and seeing a vast porphyry vase, forty-four feet in circumference, he wished that he had it full of soup.

Rome, March 23rd, Tuesday.

Yesterday, mamma and I went to the sculpture-gallery of the Vatican. I think I enjoy these noble galleries, and their contents, and beautiful arrangement, better than anything else in the way of art; and, sometimes, I seem to have a deep feeling of something wonderful in what I look at. The Laocoon, on this visit, impressed me not less than before; there was such a type of human beings struggling with inextricable trouble, and entangled in a complication which they can never free themselves from by their own efforts, and out of which Heaven will not help them....[41] I was interested in looking at the busts of the Triumvirs, Antony, Augustus, and Lepidus. The two first are men of intellect, evidently, though they do not recommend themselves to one's affections by their physiognomy; but Lepidus has the strangest common-place countenance that can be imagined, small-featured, weak, such a face as you meet anywhere in a man of no mark, but are amazed to find in one of the three foremost men of the world. I suppose that it is these weak and shallow men, when chance raises them above their proper sphere, that commit enormous crimes without any such restraint as stronger men would feel, and without any retribution in the depths of their conscience. These old Roman busts, of which there are so many in the Vatican, have often a most life like aspect, a striking individuality. One recognizes them as faithful portraits, just as certainly as if the living originals were standing beside them. The arrangement of the hair and beard, too, in many cases, is just what we see now; the fashions of two thousand years ago having come round again.

April 3rd, Saturday. Rome.

A few days ago, my wife and I visited the studio of Mr. Mozier, an American, who seems to have a good deal of vogue as a sculptor....[42]

He called to see us last night, and talked for about two hours in a very amusing and interesting style; his topics being taken from his own experience, and shrewdly treated. He spoke much of Greenough, whom he described as an excellent critic of art, but possessed of not the slightest inventive genius....[43] From Greenough, Mr. Mozier passed to Margaret Fuller,[44] whom he knew well, she having been an inmate of his during a part of her residence in Italy. His developements about poor Margaret were very curious. He says that Ossoli's family, though technically noble, is really of no rank whatever; the elder brother, with the title of Marquis, being at this very time a working brick-layer, and the sisters walking the streets without bonnets—that is, being in the station of peasant-girls, or the female populace of Rome. Ossoli himself, to the best of his belief, was Margaret's servant, or had something to do with the care of her apartments. He was the handsomest man whom Mr. Mozier ever saw, but entirely ignorant even of his own language, scarcely able to read at all, destitute of manners; in short, half an idiot, and without any pretensions to be a gentleman. At Margaret's request, Mr Mozier had taken him into his studio, with a view to ascertain whether he was capable of instruction in sculpture; but, after four months' labor, Ossoli produced a thing intended to be a copy of a human foot; but the "big toe" was on the wrong side. He could not possibly have had the least appreciation of Margaret; and the wonder is, what attraction she found in this boor, this hymen without the intellectual spark—she that had always shown such a cruel and bitter scorn of intellectual deficiency. As from her towards him, I do not understand what feeling there could have been, except it were purely sensual; as from him towards her, there could hardly have been even this, for she had not the charm of womanhood. But she was a woman anxious to try all things, and fill up her experience in all directions; she had a strong and coarse nature, too, which she had done her utmost to refine, with infinite pains, but which of course could only be superficially changed. The solution of the riddle lies in this direction; nor does one's conscience revolt at the idea of thus solving it; for—at least, this is my own experience—Margaret has not left, in the hearts and minds of those who knew her, any deep witness for her integrity and purity. She was a great humbug; of course with much talent, and much moral reality, or else she could not have been so great a humbug. But she had stuck herself full of borrowed qualities which she chose to provide herself with, but which had no root in her.

Mr. Mozier added, that Margaret had quite lost all power of literary production, before she left Rome, though occasionally the charm and power of her conversation would re-appear. To his certain knowledge, she had no important manuscripts with her when she sailed, (she having shown him all she had, with a view to his procuring their publication in America;) and the History of the Roman Revolution, about which there was so much lamentation, in the belief that it had been lost with her, never had existence. Thus there appears to have been a total collapse in poor Margaret, morally and intellectually; and tragic as her catastrophe was, Providence was, after all, kind in putting her, and her clownish husband, and their child, on board that fated ship. There never was such a tragedy as her whole story; the sadder and sterner, because so much of the ridiculous was mixed up with it, and because she could bear anything better than to be ridiculous. It was such an awful joke, that she should have resolved—in all sincerity, no doubt—to make herself the greatest, wisest, best woman of the age; and, to that end, she set to work on her strong, heavy, unpliable, and, in many respects, defective and evil nature, and adorned it with a mosaic of admirable qualities, such as she chose to possess; putting in here a splendid talent, and there a moral excellence, and polishing each separate piece, and the whole together, till it seemed to shine afar and dazzle all who saw it. She took credit to herself for having been her own Redeemer, if not her own Creator; and, indeed, she was far more a work of art than any of Mr. Mozier's statues. But she was not working on an inanimate substance, like marble or clay; there was something within her that she could not possibly come at, to re-create and refine it; and, by and by, this rude old potency bestirred itself, and undid all her labor in the twinkling of an eye. On the whole, I do not know but I like her the better for it;—the better, because she proved herself a very woman, after all, and fell as the weakest of her sisters might.

To-day, my wife, Rosebud, and I, went to see Miss Hosmer; and as her studio seems to be mixed up with Gibson's, we had an opportunity of glancing at some of his beautiful works.[45] We saw a Venus and a Cupid, both of them tinted, and, side by side with them, other statues identical with these, except that the marble was left in its pure whiteness. The tint of the Venus seemed to be a very delicate, almost imperceptible, shade of yellow, I think, or buff; that of the Cupid was a more decided yellow; and the eyes and hair of both, and especially the Cupid, were colored so as to indicate life rather than imitate it. The apple in Venus's hand was brightly gilt. I must say, there was something fascinating and delectable in the warm, yet delicate tint of the beautiful nude Venus, although I should have preferred to dispense with the colouring of the eyes and hair; nor am I at all certain that I should not, in the end, like the snowy whiteness better for the whole statue. Indeed, I am almost sure I should; for this lascivious warmth of hue quite demoralizes the chastity of the marble, and makes one feel ashamed to look at the naked limbs in the company of women. There is not the least question about the eyes and hair; their effect is shocking, in proportion to the depth of tint.[46]

Rome, April 15th, Thursday.

Yesterday, I went with Julian to the Forum, and descended into the excavations at the base of the Capitol, and on the site of the Basilica of Julia.[47] The essential elements of old Rome are there; columns, single, or in groupes of two or three, still erect, but battered and bruised, at some forgotten time, with infinite pains and labor; fragments of other columns lying prostrate, together with rich capitals and friezes; the bust of a colossal female statue, showing the bosom and upper part of the arms, but headless; a long, winding space of pavement, forming part of the ancient ascent to the Capitol, still as firm and solid as ever; the foundation of the Capitol itself, wonderfully massive, built of immense square blocks of stone, doubtless nearly three thousand years old, and durable for whatever may be the lifetime of the world.... The level of these excavations is about fifteen feet, I should judge, below the present level along which the street passes through the forum, and only a very small part of this alien surface has been removed, though there can be no doubt that it hides immense treasures of art and monuments of history. Yet these remains do not make that impression of antiquity upon me, which Gothic ruins do. Perhaps it is because they belong to quite another system of society and epoch of time; and in view of them, we forget all that has intervened betwixt them and us, being morally unlike, and disconnected with them, and not belonging to the same train of thought; so that we look across a gulf to these Roman times, and do not realize how wide the gulf is. Yet in that intervening valley, lie Christianity, the dark ages, the feudal system, chivalry and Romance, and a deeper life of the human race than Rome brought to the verge of the gulf.[48]

Rome, April 18th 1858, Sunday.

Yesterday, at noon, the whole family of us set out on a visit to the Villa Borghese and its grounds, the entrance to which is just outside of the Porta del Popolo....[49]

Saturday being, I believe, the only day of the week on which visitors are admitted to the Casino, there were many parties in carriages, artists on foot, gentlemen on horseback, and miscellaneous people, to all of whom the door was opened by a Custode, on ringing a bell. The whole of the basement floor of the Casino, comprising a suite of beautiful rooms, is filled with statuary.... Many of the specimens of Sculpture, displayed in these rooms, are fine, but none of them, I think, possess the highest merit; an Apollo is beautiful; a group of a fighting Amazon, and her enemies trampled under her horse's feet, is very impressive; a Faun, copied from that of Praxiteles, and another, who seems to be dancing, are exceedingly pleasant to look at.[50] I like these strange, sweet, playful, rustic creatures, almost entirely human as they are, yet linked so prettily, without monstrosity, to the lower tribes by the long, furry ears, or by a modest tail; indicating a strain of honest wildness in them. Their character has never, that I know of, been wrought out in literature; and something very good, funny, and philosophical, as well as poetic, might very likely be educed from them. In my mind, they connect themselves with that ugly, bearded woman, who was lately exhibited in England, and by some supposed to have been engendered betwixt a human mother and an orangoutang; but she was a wretched monster—the faun, a natural and delightful link betwixt human and brute life, and with something of a divine character intermingled.

Rome, April 22ᵈ, Thursday.

We have been, recently, to the studio of G. L. Brown, the American landscape painter, and were altogether surprised and delighted at his pictures....[51]

We have likewise been to Mr. Bartholomew's studio,[52] where we saw several pretty statues and busts, and among them an Eve, after the fall, with her wreath of fig-leaves lying across her poor nudity; pretty in some points, but with an awful volume of thighs and calves. I do not altogether see the necessity of ever sculpturing another nakedness. Man is no longer a naked animal; his clothes are as natural to him as his skin, and sculptors have no more right to undress him than to flay him. Also, we have seen again William Story's Cleopatra; a work of genuine thought and energy, representing a terribly dangerous woman, quiet enough for the moment, but very likely to spring upon you like a tigress. It is delightful to escape from this universal prettiness, which seems to be the highest conception of the herd of modern sculptors, and which they almost invariably attain....

To-day, my wife and I have been at the Picture and Sculpture Galleries of the Capitol. I rather enjoyed looking at several of the pictures....

We afterwards went into the Sculpture Gallery, where I looked at the faun of Praxitiles, and was sensible of a peculiar charm in it; a sylvan beauty and homeliness, friendly and wild at once. Its lengthened, but not preposterous ears, and the little tail which we infer, behind, have an exquisite effect, and make the spectator smile in his very heart. This race of fauns was the most delightful of all that antiquity imagined. It seems to me that a story, with all sorts of fun and pathos in it, might be contrived on the idea of their species having become intermingled with the human race; a family, with the faun blood in them, having prolonged itself from the classic era till our own days. The tail might have disappeared by dint of constant intermarriages with ordinary mortals; but the pretty, hairy ears should occasionally reappear in members of the family; and the moral instincts and intellectual characteristics of the faun might be most picturesquely brought out, without detriment to the human interest of the story. Fancy this combination in the person of a young lady!

Hawthorne views Raphael's The Transfiguration, *considered the greatest painting of the Italian Renaissance.*

∽

Rome, April 25th, Sunday.

The Transfiguration is finished with great minuteness and detail; the weeds and blades of grass in the foreground being as distinct as if they were growing in a natural soil. A partly decayed stick of wood, with the bark, is likewise given in close imitation of nature. The reflection of one of the apostles' foot is seen in a pool of water, at the verge of the picture. One or two hands and arms seem almost to project from the canvass; there is great lifelikeness and reality, as well as higher qualities. The face of Jesus, being so high aloft, and so small in the distance, I could not well see, but am impressed with the idea that it looks too much like human flesh and blood to be in keeping with the celestial aspect of the figure, or with the probabilities of the scene, when the divinity and immortality of the Savior beamed from within him through the earthly features that ordinarily shaded him. As regards the composition of the picture, I am not convinced of the propriety of its being in two so distinctly separate parts; the upper portion not thinking of the lower, and the lower portion not being aware of the higher. It symbolizes, however, the spiritual shortsightedness of mankind, that, amid the trouble and grief of the lower picture, not a single individual, either of those who seek help or those who would willingly afford it, lifts his eyes to that region one glimpse of which would set everything right. One or two of the disciples point upward, but without really knowing what abundance of help is to be had there.

Rome, April 30th, Friday.

I went yesterday to the Sculpture Gallery of the Capitol, and looked pretty thoroughly through the busts of the Illustrious Men, and less particularly at those of the Emperors and their relatives. I likewise took particular note of the Faun of Praxitiles; because the idea keeps recurring to me of writing a little Romance about it, and for that reason I shall endeavor to set down a somewhat minutely itemized detail of the statue and its surroundings. The faun is the image of a young man, leaning with one arm upon the trunk or stump of a tree; he has a pipe, or some such instrument of music, in the hand which rests upon the tree, and the other, I think, hangs carelessly by his side.[53] His only garment falls half way down his back, but leaves his whole front, and all the rest of his person, exposed, displaying a very beautiful form, but clad in more flesh, with more full and rounded outlines, and less developement of muscle, than the old sculptors were wont to assign to masculine beauty. The figure is not fat, but neither has it the attribute of slender grace. The face has a character corresponding with that of the form; beautiful and most agreeable features, but rounded, especially about the throat and chin; a nose almost straight, yet very curving inward, a voluptuous mouth, that seems almost (not quite) to smile outright;—in short, the whole person conveys the idea of an amiable and sensual nature, easy, mirthful, apt for jollity, yet not incapable of being touched by pathos. The faun has no principle, nor could comprehend it, yet is true and honest by virtue of his simplicity; very capable, too, of affection. He might be refined through his feelings, so that the coarser, animal part of his nature would be thrown into the back ground, though liable to assert itself at any time. Praxitiles has only expressed this animal nature by one (or rather two) definite signs—the two ears—which go up in a little peak, not likely to be discovered on slight inspection, and, I suppose, are covered with fine, downy fur. A tail is probably hidden under his garment. Only a sculptor of the finest imagination, most delicate taste, and sweetest feeling could have dreamed of representing a Faun in this guise; and if you brood over it long enough, all the pleasantness of sylvan life, and all the genial and happy characteristics of the brute creation, seemed to be mixed in him with humanity—trees, grass, flowers, cattle, deer, and unsophisticated man.

Rome, May 1st, Saturday.

This morning, I wandered, for the thousandth time, through some of the narrow intricacies of Rome, stepping here and there into a church. I do not know the name of the first one; nor had it anything remarkable here; though, till I came to Rome, I was not aware that any such churches existed.... Two or three persons are kneeling at separate shrines; there are several wooden confessionals placed against the walls, at one of which kneels a lady, confessing to a priest who sits within; the tapers are lighted at the high altar, and at one of the shrines; an attendant is scrubbing the marble pavement with a broom and water—a process, I should think, seldom practiced in most of the Roman churches. By and by, the lady finishes her confession, kisses the priest's hand, and sits down in one of the chairs which are set about the floor; while the priest (in a black robe, with a short, loose, white jacket over his shoulders) disappears by a side-door out of the church. I, likewise, finding nothing attractive in the pictures, take my departure. But, really, to good Catholics, it must be a blessed convenience—this facility of finding a cool, quiet, silent, beautiful place of worship in even the hottest and most bustling street, into which they may step, leaving the fret and trouble of the world at the threshold, purifying themselves with a touch of holy water as they enter, and kneeling down to hold communion with some saint, their awful friend; or perhaps confessing all their sins to a priest, laying the whole dark burthen at the foot of the cross, and coming forth in the freshness and elasticity of innocence. It is for Protestants to inquire whether some of these inestimable advantages are not compatible with a purified faith, and do not indeed belong to Christianity, making part of the blessings it was meant to bring. It would be a good time to suggest and institute some of them, now that the American public seems to be stirred by a Revival, hitherto unexampled in extent. Protestantism needs a new Apostle to convert it into something positive.[54]

After leaving this church, I soon saw before me the great, dark, pillars forming the portico of the Pantheon. I went in, and was impressed anew with the large, free space of the interior, wholly unencumbered from side to side of the vast circle; and, above, that great eye continually gazing straight upward to the seventh heaven. The world has nothing else like the Pantheon. It is very grand; so grand, that the paste-board statues, between the rotunda and the commencement of the dome, do not in the least disturb the effect, any more than the tin crowns and hearts and the faded artificial flowers, and all manner of trumpery gewgaws, hanging at some of the shrines....

In the Pantheon, it was pleasant, looking up to the circular opening, to see the clouds flitting across it; sometimes covering it quite over, then permitting a glimpse of sky, then showing all the circle of sunny blue. Then would come the ragged edge of a cloud, brightened throughout with sunshine; all, whether sun or shadow, passing and changing quickly, not that the divine smile was not always the same, but continually variable through the medium of earthly influences. The great slanting beam of sunshine was visible all the way down to the pavement, falling upon motes of dust or a thin smoke of incense, imperceptible in the shadow. Insects were playing to-and-fro in the beam, high up toward the opening. There is a wonderful charm in the naturalness of all this; and it is natural enough to fancy a swarm of cherubs coming down through the opening, and sporting in the broad sunbeam, to gladden the faith of worshippers on the pavement beneath; or angels, bearing prayers upward, or bringing down responses to them, visible with dim brightness as they pass through that pathway of heaven's radiance, even the many hues of their wings discernible by a trusting eye; though, as they pass into the shadow, they vanish as the motes do. So the sunbeam would represent those rays of divine intelligence which enable us to see wonders, and to know that they are natural things.

Rome, May 16th, Sunday.

My wife and I went yesterday to the Sistine Chapel, it being my first visit. It is a room of noble proportions, lofty and long, though divided in the midst by a screen or partition of white marble, which rises high enough to break the effect of spacious unity....

There can be no doubt that, while these frescoes remained in their perfection, there was nothing else in the world to be compared with the magnificent and solemn beauty of this chapel. Enough of ruined splendour still remains to convince the spectator of all that has departed; but methinks I have seen hardly anything else so forlorn and depressing as it is now; all dusky and dim, even the very lights having passed into shadows, and the shadows into utter blackness; so that it needs a sunshiny day, under this bright Italian sky, to make the designs perceptible at all. As we sat in the chapel, there were clouds flitting across the sky; when the clouds came, the pictures vanished; when the sunshine broke forth, the figures sadly glimmered into something like visibility—the Almighty bestirring himself in Chaos, the noble shape of Adam, the beautiful Eve; and, beneath, where the roof curves, the mighty figures of Sybils and Prophets, looking as if they were necessarily so gigantic, because the thought within them was so massive. In the Last Judgment, the scene of the greater part of the picture lies in the upper sky, the blue of which glows through betwixt the groups of naked figures; and above sits Jesus, not looking in the least like the Savior of the world, but with uplifted arm denouncing eternal misery on those whom he came to save. I fear I am myself among the wicked, for I found myself inevitably taking their part, and asking for at least a little pity, some few regrets, and not such a stern denunciatory spirit on the part of Him who had thought us worth dying for. Around him stand grim Saints, and, far beneath, people are getting up sleepily out of their graves, not well knowing what is about to happen; many of them, however, finding themselves clutched by demons before they are half-awake. It would be a very terrible picture to one who should really see Jesus, the Savior, in that inexorable Judge; but it seems to me very undesirable that he should ever be represented in that aspect, when it is so essential to our religion to believe him infinitely kinder and better towards us than we deserve. At the Last Day, I presume—that is, in all future days, when we see ourselves as we are—man's only inexorable Judge will be himself, and the punishment of his sins will be the perception of them.

∼

Hawthorne prepares to leave Rome during the long summer, the season of malaria.

∼

Rome, May 23ᵈ, Sunday.

This evening, Una and I took a farewell walk in the Pincian gardens, to see the sunset, and found the hill crowded with people, promenading, and listening to the music of the French band.[55] It was the feast of Whitsunday, which probably brought a greater throng than usual abroad. When the sun was down, we descended into the Piazza del Popolo, and thence into the Via di Ripetta, and emerged through a gate to the shore of the Tiber, along which there is a pleasant walk beneath a grove of trees. We traversed it once, and back again, looking at the rapid river, which still kept its mud-puddly aspect even in the clear twilight and beneath the brightening moon. The great bell of Saint Peter's tolled with a deep boom, a grand and solemn sound; the moon gleamed through the branches of the trees above us; and Una spoke with somewhat alarming fervor of her love for Rome and regret at leaving it. We shall have done the poor child no good office in bringing her here, if the rest of her life is to be a dream of this 'city of the soul,' and an unsatisfied yearning to come back.[56] On the other hand, nothing elevating and refining can be really injurious; and so I hope she will always be the better for Rome, even if her life should be spent where there are no pictures, no statues, nothing but the dryness and meagreness of a New England village.

Foligno, May 26ᵗʰ, Wednesday.

At six °clock this morning, we packed ourselves into our vetturo, my wife and I occupying the coupé (or whatever the seat in front is called,) and drove out of the city-gate of Terni.... Our way lay now through the vale of Terni, as I believe it is called, where we saw somewhat of the fertility of Italy; vines trained on poles, or twining round mulberry and other trees, ranged regularly like orchards; groves of olives, and fields of grain.... The road soon began to wind among the hills, which rose steep and lofty from the scanty level space that lay between; they continually thrust themselves across the passage, and appeared as if determined to shut us completely in; a great hill would put its foot right before us, but, at the last moment, would grudgingly withdraw it, and allow us room enough to creep by. Adown their sides we discerned the dry beds of mountain torrents, which had lived too fierce a life to let it be a long one. On here and there a hill-side or a promontory, we saw a ruined castle or a convent, looking down from its commanding height upon the road, which very likely some robber-knight had formerly infested with his banditti, retreating with his booty to the security of such strongholds. We came, once in a while, to wretched villages, where there was no token of prosperity or comfort, but perhaps may have been more than we could appreciate; for the Italians do not seem to have any of that sort of pride which we find in New England villages, where every man, according to his taste and means, endeavors to make his homestead an ornament to the place. We miss nothing in Italy more than the neat door-steps and pleasant porches and thresholds, and delightful lawns or grass-plats, which hospitably invite the imagination into a sweet domestic interior. Everything—however sunny and luxuriant may be the scene around—is especially dreary and disheartening in the immediate vicinity of an Italian home.[57]

Perugia, May 28th, Friday.

As I said last night, we left Foligno betimes in the morning, which was bleak, chill, and very threatening; there being very little blue sky anywhere, and the clouds lying heavily on some of the mountain ridges....

By and by we reached Assisi, which is magnificently situated for pictorial purposes; with a gray castle above it, and a gray wall around it; itself on a mountain, and looking over the great plain which we had been traversing, and through which lay our onward way....

... The aspect of everything was awfully old; a thousand years would be but a middle age for one of those houses, built so massively, with great stones, and solid arches, that I do not see how they ever are to tumble down, or to be less fit for human habitation than they are now. The streets crept between them, and beneath arched passages, and up and down steps of stone or ancient brick; for it would be altogether impossible for a carriage to ascend above the Great Piazza, though possibly a donkey or a charman's mule might find foothold. The city seems like a sort of stony growth out of the hill-side, or a fossilized city, so old and strange it is, without enough life and juiciness in it to be susceptible of decay.[58] An earthquake is the only chance of its ever being ruined, beyond its present ruin. Nothing is more strange than to think that this now dead city—dead, as regards the purposes for which men live, now-a-days—was, centuries ago, the seat, and birth-place almost, of art, the only art in which the beautiful part of the human mind then developed itself. How came that flower to grow among these wild mountains?[59] I do not conceive, however, that the people of Assisi were ever much more enlightened, or cultivated on the side of art, than they are at present. The ecclesiastics were then the only patrons; and the flower grew here, because there was a great ecclesiastical garden in which it was sheltered and fostered. But it is very curious to think of Assisi, a school of art within, and mountains and wilderness without.

Perugia,[60] May 29th, Saturday.

This morning, at about 9 °clock, my wife and I, with Julian and Rosebud, went out and visited the church of the Dominicans, where we saw some quaint pictures by Fra Angelico with a good deal of religious sincerity in them;[61] also, a picture of Saint Columba by Perugino, which unquestionably is very good....

It was market day, and the principal piazza, with the neighboring streets, was crowded with people, and blocked up with petty dealers and their merchandize; baskets of vegetables, donkeys and mules with panniers, stalls, some of which had books for sale, chiefly paper-covered little volumes in Italian, and a few in French, as Paul de Kock's novels, for example; also, ink and writing materials.[62] Cheap jewelry and cutlery made a considerable show; shoes, hats, and caps; and I know not what else. The scene was livelier than any I have seen in Rome, the people appearing more vivacious, in this mountain air, than the populace of the eternal city, and the whole piazza babbling with a multitudinous voice. I noticed to-day, more than yesterday, the curious and picturesque architecture of the principal streets, especially that of the grand piazza; the great Gothic arch of the door of the vast edifice in which the Exchange is situated, elaborately wreathed around with one sculptured semi-circle within another; an open gallery running along the same edifice, on the second story, looking out on the piazza through arched and stone-mullioned windows.[63] The quaint old front, too, of the Cathedral-church of San Lorenzo (it is the same which we visited yesterday and which I called the church of San Luigi)[64] is in keeping with the Gothic aspect of the piazza; as is likewise a large and beautiful fountain, consisting of a great marble basin, carved all round with angels, I believe. Within a short distance, there is a bronze statue of Pope Julius III, in his pontificals; one of the best statues, I think, that I ever saw in a public square.[65] He seems to have life and observation in him, and impresses the spectator as if he might rise up from his chair, should any public exigency demand it, and encourage or restrain the people by the dignity and awe of his presence. I wish I could in any way catch and confine within words my idea of the venerableness and stateliness, the air of long-past time subsisting into the present, which remains upon my mind with the recollection of these mediæval antiquities of Perugia. When I am absolutely looking at them, I do not feel it so much as when remembering them; for there is, of course, a good deal of the modern and common-place that obtrudes into the actual scene. The people themselves are not very picturesque; though there are some figures with cloaks (even in this summer weather) and broad-brimmed, slouching hats that a painter might make something of.

∼

Hawthorne settles in Florence in the late spring of 1858; he will spend the warm months there before returning to Rome in the fall.

∼

Florence, June 2ᵈ, 1858.

...Our afternoon's drive was through scenery less striking than some which we had traversed, but still picturesque and beautiful; we saw deep vallies and ravines, with streams at the bottom; long, wooded hill-sides, rising far and high, and dotted with white dwellings, well towards the summits. By and by, we had a distant glimpse of Florence, showing its great dome and some of its towers out of a side-long valley, as it were between two great waves of the tumultuous sea of hills; while, far beyond, rose out of the distance the blue peaks of three or four of the Appenines, just on the remote horizon.[66]—There being a haziness in the atmosphere, however, Florence was little more distinct to us than the Celestial City was to Christian and Hopeful, when they spied at it from the Delectable Mountains.[67] Keeping stedfastly onward, we ascended a winding road, and passed a grand villa, standing very high, and surrounded with extensive grounds....

From this point, we descended, and drove along an ugly, dusty avenue, with a high brick wall on one side or both, till we reached the gate of Florence, into which we were admitted with as little trouble as Custom-

House officers, soldiers, and policemen, can possibly give.... As we hoped that the Casa del Bello had been taken for us, we drove thither in the first place, but found that the bargain had not been concluded. As the house and studio of Mr. Powers were just on the opposite side of the street, I went thither, but found him too much engaged to see me at the moment; so I returned to the vettura, and we told Gaetano to carry us to a Hotel.[68] He established us at the Albergo della Fontana, a good and comfortable house, and, as it proved, very moderate in its charges. Mr. Powers called in the evening—a plain, homely personage, characterized by strong simplicity and warm kindliness, with an impending brow, and large, light eyes, which kindle as he speaks. He is gray and slightly bald, but does not seem elderly, nor past his prime. I accept him at once as an honest and trust-worthy man, and shall not vary from this judgment. Through his good offices, the next day, we engaged the Casa del Bello at a rent of fifty dollars a month; and I shall take another opportunity (my fingers and head being tired now) to write about the house, and Mr. Powers, and what appertains to him, and about the beautiful city of Florence. At present, I shall only further say, that this journey from Rome has been one of the brightest and most uncareful interludes of my life; we have all enjoyed it exceedingly; and I am happy that our younger companions have it to look back upon.

Florence June 4th, Friday.

At our visit to Powers's studio, on Tuesday, we saw a marble copy of the fisher-boy, holding a shell to his ear, and of the bust of Proserpina, and two or three other ideal busts; besides casts of most of the ideal statues and portrait-busts which he has executed.[69] He talks very freely about his works, and is no exception to the rule that an artist is not apt to speak in a very laudatory style of a brother-artist....

... [Powers] appears to consider himself neglected by his country—by the Government of it, at least—and talks with indignation of the by-ways and political intrigue which he thinks, win the rewards which ought to be bestowed exclusively on merit.... Not that Powers is made sour or bitter by these wrongs, as he considers them; he talks of them with the frankness of his disposition, when the topic comes in his way, and seems to be pleasant, kindly, and sunny when he has done with it. His long absence from our country has made him think worse of us than we deserve; and it is an effect of which I myself am sensible, in my shorter exile,—the most piercing shriek, the wildest yell, and all the ugly sounds of popular turmoil, inseparable from the life of a republic, being a million times more audible than the peaceful hum of prosperity and content, which is going on all the while. He talks of going home, but says that he has been talking of it every year since he first came to Italy; and between his pleasant life of congenial labor here, and his idea of moral deterioration in America, I think it doubtful whether he ever crosses the sea again. Like most twenty-year exiles, he has lost his native country without finding another; but then it is as well to recognize the truth, that an individual country is by no means essential to one's comfort....

When we had sufficiently looked at the sculpture, Powers proposed that we should now go across the street and see the Casa del Bello.... The Casa del Bello is a palace of three pianos, the topmost of which is occupied by an English lady, and an Italian count, her husband; the two lower pianos are to let, and we looked at both. The upper one would have suited us well enough, and might have been had for forty dollars a month; but the lower has a terrace, with a rustic summer-house over it, and is connected with a garden, where there are arbors, and a willow-tree, and a little wilderness of shrubbery and roses, with a fountain in its midst. It has likewise an immense suite of rooms around the four sides of a small court, spacious, lofty, with frescoed cielings and rich paper hangings, and abundantly furnished with arm-chairs, sofas, marble-tables, and great looking-glasses. Not that these last are a great temptation; but, in our wandering life, I wished to be perfectly comfortable myself, and to make my family so, for just this summer; and so I have taken the lower piano, the price being only fifty dollars per month. Certainly, this is something like the Paradise of cheapness which we were told of, and which we vainly sought in Rome.... The weather is delightful; too warm to walk, but perfectly fit to do nothing in, in the coolness of these great rooms. Every day I shall write a little, perhaps—and probably take a brief nap, somewhere between breakfast and tea—but go to see pictures and statues occasionally, and so assuage and mollify myself a little, after that uncongenial life of the Consulate, and before going back to my own hard and dusty New-England.

Florence, June 5th, Saturday.

For two or three mornings, after breakfast, I have rambled a little about the city, till the shade grows narrow beneath the walls of the houses, and the heat makes it uncomfortable to be in motion.... Florence at first struck me as having the aspect of a very new city, in comparison with Rome; but on closer acquaintance, I find that many of the buildings are antique and massive, though still the clear atmosphere, the bright sunshine, the light cheerful hues of the stucco, and—as much as anything else perhaps—the vivacious character of the human life in the streets, take away the sense of its being an ancient city. The streets are delightful to walk in, after so many penitential pilgrimages as I have made over those little square, uneven blocks of the Roman pavement, which wear out the boots and torment the soul. I absolutely walk on the smooth flags of Florence for the mere pleasure of walking, and live in its atmosphere for the mere pleasure of living, and, warm as the weather is getting to be, I never feel that inclination to sink down in a heap and never stir again, which was my dull torment and misery as long as I staid in Rome. I hardly think there can be a place in the world where life is more delicious for its own simple sake than here.

Florence, June 8th, Tuesday.

I went this morning to the Uffizzi Gallery....[70]

I at first travelled slowly through the whole extent of this long, long gallery, which occupies the whole length of the palace on both sides of the court, and is full of sculpture and pictures. The latter, being opposite to the light, are not seen to the best advantage; but it is the most perfect collection, in a chronological series, that I have seen, comprehending specimens of all the masters since painting began to be an art. Here are Giotto, and Cimabue, and Botticcelli, and Fra Angelico, and Phillippo Lippi, and a hundred others, who have haunted me in churches and galleries ever since I came to Italy, and who ought to interest me a great deal more than they do.[71] Occasionally, to-day, I was sensible of a certain degree of emotion in looking at an old picture; as, for example, by a large, dark, ugly picture of Christ bearing the cross, and sinking beneath it, where, somehow or other, a sense of his agony, and the fearful wrong that mankind did to its Redeemer, and the scorn of his enemies and sorrow of those that loved him, came knocking at my heart, and partly got entrance.[72] Once more, I deem it a pity that Protestantism should have entirely laid aside this mode of appealing to the religious sentiment.

I chiefly paid attention to the sculpture, and was interested in a long series of busts of the Emperors, and the members of their families, and of some of the great men of Rome.... Generally, these wicked old fellows, and their wicked wives and daughters, are not so hideous as we might expect.... The bust of Nero might almost be called handsome here, though bearing his likeness unmistakeably. I wish some competent person would undertake to analyze and develop his character, and how and by what necessity—with all his elegant tastes, his love of the beautiful, his artist nature—he grew to be such a monster. Nero has never yet had justice done him, nor have any of the wicked Emperors; not that I suppose them to have been any less monstrous than history represents them; but there must surely have been something in their position and circumstances to render the terrible moral disease, which seized upon them so generally, almost inevitable. A wise and profound man, tender and reverent of the human soul, and capable of appreciating it in its height and depth, has a great field here for the exercize of his powers. It has struck me, in reading the history of the Italian republics, that many of the tyrants, who sprung up after the destruction of their liberties, resembled the worst of the Roman emperors. This subject of Nero and his brethren has often perplexed me with vain desires to come at the truth.[73]

There were many beautiful specimens of antique, ideal sculpture, all along the gallery; Apollos, Bacchuses, Venuses, Mercuries, Fauns, with the general character of all of which I was familiar enough to recognize them at a glance. The mystery and wonder of the gallery, however—the Venus de Medici—I could nowhere see, and indeed was almost afraid to see it: for I somewhat apprehended the extinction of another of those lights that shine along a man's pathway, and go out in a snuff the instant he comes within eye-shot. My European experience has blown out a great many such. I was pretty well contented, therefore, not to find the famous statue, in the whole of my long journey from end to end of the gallery, which terminates on the opposite side of the court from that where it commences....

I could not quite believe that I was not to find the Venus de Medici;[74] and still, as I passed from one room to another, my breath rose and fell a little, with the half-hope, half-fear, that she might stand before me. Really, I did not know that I cared so much about Venus, or any possible woman of marble. At last—when I had come from among the Dutchmen, I believe, and was looking at some works of Italian artists, chiefly Florentines—I caught a glimpse of her, through the door of the next room. It is the best room of the whole series, octagonal in shape, and hung with red damask; and the light comes down from a row of windows passing quite round, beneath an octagonal dome. The Venus stands somewhat aside from the centre of the room, and is surrounded by an iron-railing, a pace or two from her pedestal in front, and less behind. I think she might safely be left to the reverence her womanhood would win, without any other protection. She is very beautiful; very satisfactory; and has a fresh and new charm about her, unreached by any cast or copy that I have seen. The hue of the marble is just so much mellowed by time as to do for her all that Gibson tries, or ought, to try, to do for his statues by color; softening her, warming her almost imperceptibly, making her an inmate of the heart as well as a spiritual existence. I felt a kind of tenderness for her; an affection, not as if she were one woman, but all womankind in one. Her modest attitude—which, before I saw her, I had not liked, deeming that it might be an artificial shame—is partly what unmakes her as the heathen goddess, and softens her into woman. There is a slight degree of alarm too, in her face; not that she really thinks anybody is looking at her, yet the idea has flitted through her mind and startled her a little. Her face is so beautiful and intellectual, that it is not dazzled out of sight by her body. Methinks this was a triumph for the sculptor to achieve. I may as well stop here. It is of no use to throw heaps of words upon her; for they all fall away and leave her standing in chaste and naked grace, as untouched as when I began.

... On the wall of the room, and to be taken in at the same glance, is a painted Venus by Titian, reclining on a couch, naked and lustful.[75]

Florence, June 9th, Wednesday.

Mamma, Miss Shepard and I, went last evening, at eight °clock, to see the Brownings;[76] and after some search and inquiry, we found the Casa Guidi, which is a palace in a street nor very far from our own.... [Browning] came into the ante-room to greet us; as did his little boy, Robert, whom they nickname Penny for fondness. This latter cognomen is a diminutive of Apennine, bestowed upon him at his first advent into the world, because he was so very small; there being a statue in Florence nicknamed Apennine, because it is so huge.[77] I never saw such a boy as this before; so slender, fragile, and spritelike, not as if he were actually in ill-health, but as if he had little or nothing to do with human flesh and blood. His face is very pretty and most intelligent, and exceedingly like his mother's, whose constitutional lack of stamina I suppose he inherits. He is nine years old, and seems at once less childlike and less manly than would befit that age. I should not quite like to be the father of such a boy; and should fear to stake so much interest and affection on him as he cannot fail to inspire. I wonder what is to become of him;—whether he will ever grow to be a man;—whether it is desirable that he should. His parents ought to turn their whole attention to making him gross and earthly, and giving him a thicker scabbard to sheathe his spirit in. He was born in Florence, and prides himself on being a Florentine, and is indeed as un-English a production as if he were native in another planet.

Mrs. Browning met us at the door of the drawing-room and greeted us most kindly; a pale little woman, scarcely embodied at all; at any rate, only substantial enough to put forth her slender fingers to be grasped and to speak with a shrill, yet sweet, tenuity of voice. Really, I do not see how Mr. Browning can suppose that he has an earthly wife, any more than an earthly child; both are of the elfin-breed, and will flit away from him, some day when he least thinks of it. She is a good and kind fairy, however, and sweetly disposed towards the human race, although only remotely akin to it. It is wonderful to see how small she is; how diminutive, and peaked, as it were, her face, without being ugly; how pale her cheek; how bright and dark her eyes. There is not such another figure in this world; and her black ringlets cluster down into her neck and make her face look the whiter by their sable profusion. I could not form any judgment about her age; it may range any where within the limits of human life, or elfin-life. When I met her in London, at Mr. Milnes's breakfast-table, she did not impress me so strangely; for the morning light is more prosaic than the dim illumination of their great, tapestried drawing room; and besides, sitting next to her, she did not then have occasion to raise her voice in speaking, and I was not sensible what a slender pipe she has. It is as if a grasshopper should speak. It is marvelous to me how so extraordinary, so acute, so sensitive a creature, can impress us, as she does, with the certainty of her benevolence. It seems to me there were a million chances to one that she would have been a miracle of acidity and bitterness.

Florence, June 11th Friday.

I paid another visit to the Uffizzi gallery, this morning, and found that the Venus is one of the things, the charm of which does not diminish on better acquaintance. The world has not grown weary of her in all these ages; and mortal man may look on her with new delight from infancy to old age, and keep the memory of her, I should imagine, as one of the treasures of spiritual existence hereafter. Surely, it makes one more ready to believe in the high destinies of the human race, to think that this beautiful form is but Nature's plan for all womankind, and that the nearer the actual woman approaches to it, the more natural she is. I do not, and cannot, think of her as a senseless image, but as a being that lives to gladden the world, incapable of decay and death; as young and fair to day as she was three thousand years ago, and still to be young and fair, as long as a beautiful thought shall require physical embodiment. I wonder how any sculptor has had the impertinence to aim at any other presentation of female beauty. I mean no disrespect to Gibson, or Powers, or a hundred other men who people the world with nudities, all of which are abortive as compared with her; but I think the world would be all the richer if their Venuses, their

Greek Slaves, their Eves, were burnt into quick-lime, leaving us only this statue as our image of the beautiful. I observed to day (what my wife had already remarked) that the eyes of the statue are slightly hollowed out, in a peculiar way, so as to give them a look of depth and intelligence. She is a miracle. The sculptor must have wrought religiously, and have felt that something far beyond his own skill was working through his hand. I mean to leave off speaking of the Venus hereafter, in utter despair of saying what I wish; especially as the contemplation of the statue will refine and elevate my taste, and make it continually more difficult to express my sense of its excellence, as the perception of it grows upon me. If, at any time, I become less sensible of it, it will be my deterioration, not any defect in the statue.

Florence, June 13th, Sunday.

Wife and I called at the Powers', yesterday morning, to leave Rosebud there for an hour or two's play with the children; and it being not yet quite time for the Pitti Palace, we stept into the studio. Soon, Mr. Powers made his appearance, in his dressing-gown and slippers, and sculptor's cap, smoking a cigar, which by the by was none of the best. He was very cordial and pleasant, as I have always found him, and began immediately to be communicative about his own works or on any other subject that came up. There were two casts of the Venus de Medici in the studio, which he said were valuable in a commercial point of view, being genuine casts from the mould taken from the statue. He then gave us a quite unexpected but most interesting lecture on the Venus, demonstrating it as he proceeded by reference to the points which he criticized. The figure, he seemed to allow, was admirable, though I rather think he hardly classes it so high as his own Greek Slave or Eve; but the face, he began with saying, was that of an idiot. Then, leaning on the pedestal of the cast, he continued—"It is rather a bold thing to say, isn't it, that the sculptor of the Venus de Medici did not know what he was about?" Truly, it appeared to me so; but Powers went on remorselessly, and showed, in the first place, that the eye was not like any eye that Nature ever made; and, indeed, being examined closely, and abstracted from the rest of the face, it has a very queer look—less like a human eye than a half-worn buttonhole. Then he attacked the ear, which he affirmed, and demonstrated, was placed a great deal too low on the head, thereby giving an artificial and monstrous height to the portion of the head above it. The forehead met with no better treatment in his hands, and as to the mouth, it was altogether wrong, as well in its general make, as in such niceties as the junction of the skin of the lips to the common skin around them. In a word, the poor face was battered all to pieces and utterly demolished; nor was it possible to doubt or question that it fell by its own demerits—all that could be urged in its defense (and even *that* I did not urge) being that this very face had affected me, only the day before, with a sense of higher beauty and intelligence than I had ever till then received from sculpture, and that its expression seemed to accord with that of the whole figure, as if it were the sweetest note of the same music. There must be something in this; the sculptor disregarded technicalities and the imitation of actual nature, the better to produce the effect which he really does produce, in somewhat the same way as a painter works his magical illusions by touches that have no relation to the truth, if looked at from the wrong point of view. But Powers considers it certain that the old sculptor had bestowed all his care on the study of the human figure, and really did not know how to make a face. I myself used to think that the face was a much less important thing with the Greeks, among whom the entire beauty of the form was familiarly seen, than with ourselves, who allow no other nudity.

After annihilating this poor visage, Powers showed us his two busts of Proserpine and Psyche, and continued his lecture by showing the truth to nature with which these are modelled. I freely acknowledge the fact; there is no sort of comparison to be made between the beauty, intelligence, feeling, and accuracy of representation, in these two faces, and in that of the Venus de Medici. A light—the light of a soul proper to each individual character—seems to shine from the interior of the marble and beam forth from the features, chiefly from their eyes. Still insisting upon the eye, and hitting the poor Venus another, and another, and still another blow on that unhappy feature, Mr. Powers, turned up, and turned inward, and turned outward, his own Titanic orb (the biggest by far that ever I saw in mortal head) and made us see and confess that there was nothing right in the Venus, and everything right in Psyche and Proserpine. To say the truth, their marble eyes have life, and, placing yourself in the proper position towards them, you can meet their glances, and feel theirs mingle with your own. Powers is a great man, and also a tender and delicate one, massive and rude of surface as he looks; and it is rather absurd to feel how he impresses his auditor, for the time being, with his own evident idea that nobody else is worthy to touch marble.

Florence, June 15th, Tuesday.

Yesterday, my wife and I went to the Uffizzi gallery; and of course I took the opportunity to look again at the Venus de Medici, after Powers' attack upon her face. Some of the defects he attributed to her I could not see in the statue; for instance, the ear appeared to be in accordance with his own rule; the lowest part of it being about in a straight line with the upper lip. The eyes must be given up, as not, when closely viewed, having the shape, the curve outwards, the formation of the lids, that eyes ought to have; but still, at a proper distance, they seemed to have intelligence in them, beneath the shadow cast by the brow. I cannot help thinking that the sculptor intentionally made every feature what it is, and calculated them all with a view to the desired effect. Whatever rules may be transgressed, it is a noble and beautiful face; more so, perhaps, than if all rules had been obeyed. I wish Powers would do his best to fit the Venus de Medici's figure (which he does not deny to be admirable) with a face which he would deem equally admirable, and in accordance with the sentiment of the form.

We looked pretty thoroughly through the gallery, and I saw many pictures that impressed me; but, among such a multitude, with only one poor mind to take note of them, the stamp of each new impression helps to obliterate a former one. I am sensible, however, that a process is going on—and has been, ever since I came to Italy—that puts me in a state to see pictures with less toil, and more pleasure, and makes me more fastidious, yet more sensible of beauty where I saw none before. It is the sign, I presume, of a taste still very defective, that I take singular pleasure in the elaborate imitations of Van Mieris, Gerard Duow, and other old Dutch wizards who painted such brass-pots that you can see your face in them, and such earthen jugs that they will surely hold water; and who spent weeks and months in turning a foot or two of canvass into a perfect, microscopic illusion of some homely scene.[78] For my part, I wish Raphael had painted the Transfiguration in this style, at the same time preserving his breadth and grandeur of design; nor do I believe that there is any real impediment to the combination of the two styles, except that no possible span of human life would suffice to cover a quarter part of the canvas of the Transfiguration with such touches as Gerard Duow's. But one feels the vast scope of this wonderful art, when we think of two excellences so far apart as that of this last painter and Raphael. I pause a good while, too, before the Dutch paintings of fruit and flowers, where tulips and roses acquire an immortal bloom; and grapes have kept the freshest juice in them for two or three hundred years. Often, in these pictures, there is a bird's nest, every straw perfectly represented, and the stray feather, or the down that the mother-bird plucked from her bosom, with the three or four small, speckled eggs, that seem as if they might be yet warm. These petty miracles have their use in assuring us that painters really can do something that takes hold of us in our most matter of fact moods; whereas, the merits of the grander style of art may be beyond our ordinary appreciation, and leave us in doubt (nine times out of ten that we look at them) whether we have not befooled ourselves with a false admiration. Until we learn to appreciate the cherubs and angels that Raphael scatters through the blessed air, in a picture of the Nativity, it is not amiss to look at a Dutch fly settling on a peach, or a humble-bee burying himself in a flower.

Florence, June 21st, Monday.

This morning, my wife and I went to the Pitti Palace....

It was useless to try to see the pictures; all the artists, engaged in copying, laid aside their brushes; and we all looked out of the windows into the square before the palace, where a mighty wind sprang up, and quickly raised a prodigious cloud of dust. It hid the opposite side of the street, and was carried in a great dusky whirl higher than the roofs of the houses, higher than the tip top of the Pitti Palace itself. The thunder muttered and grumbled; the lightning emitted now and then a flash; and a few raindrops pattered against the windows; but, for a long time, the shower held off. At last, it came down in a stream, and lightened the air to such a degree that we could see some of the pictures, especially those of Rubens, and the illuminated parts of Salvator Rosa's,[79] and best of all, Titian's Magdelene, the one with the golden hair clustering round her naked body. The golden hair, indeed, seemed to throw out a glory of its own. This Magdelene is very coarse and sensual, with only an impudent assumption of penitence and religious sentiment, scarcely so deep as the eyelids; but it is a splendid picture, nevertheless, with those naked, lifelike arms, and the hands that press the rich locks about her, and so carefully let those two voluptuous breasts be seen. She a penitent! She would shake off all pretence to it, as easily as she would shake aside that clustering hair and offer her nude front to the next comer. Titian must have been a very good-for-nothing old man.

Villa Montauto, September 1st, Wednesday.

Few things journalizable have happened during the past month, because Florence and the neighborhood have lost their novelty; and, furthermore, I usually spend the whole day at home, having been engaged in planning and sketching out a Romance. I have now done with this for the present, and mean to employ the rest of the time we stay here chiefly in re-visiting the galleries, and seeing what remains to be seen of Florence.

Last Saturday, I went with my wife to take tea at Miss Blagden's, who has a weekly reception on that evening. We found Mr. Powers there; and, by and by, Mr. Boot and Mr. Trollope came in.[80] Miss Shepard has lately been exercising her faculties as a spiritual-writing medium; and the conversation turning on that subject, Mr. Powers related some things that he had witnessed through the agency of Mr. Hume, who had held a session or two at his house....[81]

Powers seems to put full faith in the verity of spiritual communications, while acknowledging the difficulty of identifying spirits as being what they pretend. He is a Swedenborgian,[82] and so far prepared to put faith in many of these phenomena. As for Hume, Powers gives a decided opinion that he is a knave, but thinks him so organized, nevertheless, as to be a particularly good medium for spiritual communications. Spirits, I suppose, like earthly people, have to use such instruments as will answer their purposes; but rather than receive a message from a dead friend through the organism of a rogue and a charlatan, methinks I would choose to wait till we met. But what most astonishes me most is, the indifference with which I listen to these marvels. They throw old ghost stories quite into the shade; they bring the whole world of spirits down amongst us, visibly and audibly; they are absolutely proved to be sober facts by evidence that would satisfy us of any other alleged realities; and yet I cannot free my mind to interest itself in them. They are facts to my understanding (which, it might have been anticipated, would have been the last to acknowledge them,) but they seem not to be facts to my intuitions and deeper perceptions. My inner soul does not in the least admit them. So idle and empty do I feel these stories to be, that I hesitated long whether or no to give up a few pages of this not very important journal, to the record of them.

Villa Montauto Sept 25th, Saturday.

Una and I walked to town, yesterday morning, and went to the Ufizzi gallery. It is not a pleasant thought that we are so soon to give up this gallery, with little prospect (none, or hardly any, on my part) of ever seeing it again.... Perhaps it is the picturesque variety of the Ufizzi—the combination of painting, sculpture, gems, and bronzes—that makes the charm. The Tribune, too, is the richest room in all the world; a heart, that draws all hearts to it. The Dutch pictures, moreover, give a homely, human interest to the Ufizzi; and I really think that the frequency of Andrea del Sarto's productions, at the Pitti Palace—looking so very like master-pieces, yet lacking the soul of art and nature—have much to do with the weariness that comes from better acquaintance with the latter gallery.[83] The splendor of the gilded and frescoed saloons is perhaps another bore; but, after all, my memory will often tread them, as long as I live. What shall we do in America!

Villa Montauto, Sept 28th, Tuesday.

I went to the Pitti Palace, yesterday, and with Una and Julian to the Uffizzi gallery to-day, paying them probably my last visits, yet cherishing an unreasonable doubt whether I may not see them again. At all events, I have seen them enough for the present, even what is best of them; and at the same time with a sad reluctance to bid them farewell forever, I experience an utter weariness of Raphael's old canvass, and of the time-yellowed marble of the Venus de Medici. When their material embodiment presents itself outermost, and we perceive them only by the grosser sense, missing their ethereal spirit, there is nothing so heavily burthensome as masterpieces of painting and sculpture. I threw my farewell glance at the Venus de Medici, to-day, with strange insensibility.

Aquila Nera, October 11th, Monday.

Leaving the Cathedral, I took a walk out of the city, by I know not which gate, but I think it may have been the one called San Viene. A road turned immediately to the left, as I emerged from the city, and soon proved to be a rustic lane, leading past several villas and farm-houses, and running into another road that issued from the Porta Romana, as I suppose it to be. It was a very pleasant walk, with vineyards and olive-orchards on each side, and now-and-then glimpses of the towers, and sombre, heaped-up palaces of Siena, and now a rustic seclusion again; for the hills rise and fall, like the swell and subsidence of the sea after a gale; so that Siena may be quite hidden within a quarter of a mile of its wall, or may be visible, I doubt not, twenty miles away. It is a fine old town, with every promise of health and vigour in its atmosphere; and really, if I could take root anywhere, I know not but it could as well be here as in another place. It would only be a kind of despair, however, that would ever make me dream of finding a home in Italy; a sense that I had lost my country through absence or incongruity, and that earth, at any rate, is not an abiding-place. I wonder that we Americans love our country at all, it having no limits and no oneness; and when you try to make it a matter of the heart, everything falls away except one's native State;—neither can you seize hold of that, unless you tear it out of the Union, bleeding and quivering. Yet unquestionably we do stand by our national flag as stoutly as any people in the world; and I myself have felt the heart-throb at sight of it, as sensibly as other men.[84]

∾

Hawthorne returns to Rome in October 1858.

∾

68, Piazza Poli (Rome,) Octr. 17th, Sunday.

It really seemed like coming up out of the earth into the midst of the town, when we found ourselves so unexpectedly in the upper town of Bolsena....[85] Filth was everywhere; in the Piazza, in nooks and corners, strewing the streets (miserable lanes, rather) from side to side, defiling the platform before the Castle; the filth of every day and of accumulated ages. I wonder whether the ancient Romans were as dirty a people as we everywhere find those who have succeeded them; for there seems to be something in the places that have been inhabited by Romans, or made famous in their history, and in the monuments of every kind that they have raised, that puts people in mind of their earthly necessities, and incites them to defile therewith whatever temple, column, ruined palace, or triumphal arch may be nearest at hand. I think it must be an hereditary trait, probably weakened, and robbed of a little of its dirty horror, by the influence of milder ages; and I am much afraid that Caesar trod narrower and filthier ways, in his path to power than those of modern Rome, or even of this hideous town of Bolsena....

I did not mean to write such an ugly description as the above; but it is well, once for all, to have attempted conveying an idea of what disgusts the traveller, more or less, in all these Italian towns.... The whole town made me think how undesirable it is to build human habitations out of permanent materials, and with a view to their being occupied by future generations. All towns should be made capable of purification by fire, or of decay with half-a-century or so; else they become the hereditary haunt of vermin and noisomeness, and, besides, stand apart from the possibility of such improvement as is introduced into other of man's contrivances and accommodations. It is a very pretty thing, in some respects, to imagine our posterity living under the same floors as ourselves; but when people insist on building age-long habitations, they incur (or their posterity do) a misfortune analogous to that of the Sibyl who asked for immortality. They build immortal houses, but cannot keep them from growing old, musty, unwholesome, dreary, full of death-scents, ghosts, murder-stains; in short, houses such as one sees everywhere in Italy, be they hovels or palaces.[86]

68, Piazza Poli, Octr 21st, Thursday.

We have the snuggest little set of apartments in Rome, seven rooms, including an anti-chamber; and though the stairs are exceedingly narrow, there is really a carpet on them—a civilized comfort, of which the proudest palaces in the Eternal city cannot boast. The stairs are very steep, however; and I should not wonder if some of us broke our noses down them. Narrowness of space within doors strikes us all rather ludicrously, yet not unpleasantly, after being accustomed to the naked, brick-paved wastes and deserts of the Montauto Villa. It is well to be thus put in training for the over-snugness of our cottage in Concord. Our windows here look out on a small, and rather quiet piazza, with an immense palace on the left hand, and a smaller, yet statelier one, on the right; and just round a corner of the street leading out of our piazza is the Fountain of Trevi, of which I can hear the plash in the evening, when other sounds are hushed.

Piazza Poli, Novr 2nd, Tuesday.

The weather, lately, would have suited one's ideal of an English November, except that there have been no fogs; but of ugly, hopeless clouds, chill, shivery winds, drizzle, and now and then pouring rain—much more than enough. An English coal-fire, if we could see its honest glow within-doors, would compensate for all the unamiableness of the outside atmosphere; but we might ask for the sunshine of the New Jerusalem, with as much hope of getting it. It is extremely spirit-crushing, this remorseless grey, with its icy heart; and the more to depress the whole family, Una has taken what seems to be the Roman fever by sitting down to sketch in the Coliseum. It is not a severe attack, yet attended with fits of exceeding discomfort, occasional comatoseness, and even delirium to the extent of making the poor child talk in rhythmical measure like a tragic heroine—as if the fever lifted her feet off the earth. This fever is seldom dangerous, but is liable to recur on slight occasion hereafter.[87]

68, Piazza di Poli, March 7th, Monday.

Last week, we were in full Carnival; and, the weather being splendid, the merriment was far more free and riotous than as I remember it, the preceding year.[88] Going out in the morning, tokens of the festival were seen in baskets of flowers, for sale at the street-corners, or borne about on people's heads, while bushels upon bushels of confetti were displayed, looking just like veritable sugar-plums; so that a stranger might have thought that the whole commerce and business of stern old Rome lay in flowers and sweets.

I (as well as the rest of the family) have followed up the Carnival pretty faithfully, and enjoyed it as well, or rather better, than could have been expected; principally in the street, as a mere looker-on (which does not let one into the mystery of the fun) and twice from a balcony, whence I threw confetti, and partly understood why the young people like it so much. Certainly, there cannot well be a more picturesque spectacle in human life, than that stately, palatial avenue of the Corso (the more picturesque because so narrow) all hung with carpets, Gobelin tapestry, scarlet cloths with gilded fringes, flaunting from balconies and windows, and the whole palace-heights alive with faces; and all the capacity of the street thronged with the most fantastic figures that either the fancies of folks alive at this day are able to contrive, or that live traditionally from year to year, for centuries back. To be sure, looking critically at the scene, the spectator rather wonders that the masquing scene should not be more rich and various, when there has been so long a time (the immemorial existence of the Carnival) to prepare it, and crowd it with shapes of gaiety and humor. There are not many things worth remembering;—an infinite number of clowns and parti-colored harlequins; a host of white dominos; a multitude of masks, set to an eternal grin, or with monstrous noses, or made in the guise of monkies, bears, dogs, or whatever beast the wearer chooses to be akin to; a great many men in petticoats, and almost as many girls and women, no doubt, in breeches; figures, too, with huge, bulbous heads; and all manner of such easy monstrosities and exaggerations. It is strange how the whole humor of the thing, and the separate humor of each individual character, vanishes, the moment I try to grasp one and describe it; and yet there really was fun in the spectacle as it flitted by. For instance, in a large open carriage, a company of young men in flesh-colored tights and chemises, representing a party of girls surprised in the midst of dressing themselves, while an old nurse, in the midst of them, expressed ludicrous horror at their predicament; then the embarrassment of gentlemen, who, while quietly looking at the scene, are surrounded by groups of masques, grinning at them, squeaking in their ears, hugging them, dancing round them, till they snatch the opportunity to escape into some doorway; or, when a poor man in a black coat and cylinder hat is whitened all over with a half-bushel of confetti and lime dust, the mock sympathy with which his case is investigated by a company of masquers, who poke their stupid, pasteboard faces close to his, still with an unchangeable grin; or when a gigantic female figure singles out some shy, harmless personage, and makes appeals to his heart, presenting him with a boquet, avowing her passionate love in dumb-show; and a hundred other nonsensicalities, among which the rudest and simplest are not the least effective. A resounding thump on the back with a harlequin's sword, or a rattling blow with a bladder, half-full of dry peas or corn, answers a very good purpose. There was a good absurdity, one day, in a figure with a crinoline petticoat, riding on an ass, and almost filling the Corso with the circumference of Crinoline, from side to side. Some figures are dressed in old fashioned garbs, perhaps of the last century, or, even more ridiculous, of thirty years ago, or in the stately Elizabethan (as we should call them) trunk-hose, tunics, and cloaks of three centuries since.

Piazza di Poli, March 8th, Tuesday.

I went with Una to Mrs. Motley's balcony,[89] in the Corso, and saw the Carnival from it, yesterday afternoon; but the spectacle is strangely like a dream, in respect to the difficulty of retaining it in the mind and solidifying it into a description. I enjoyed it a good deal, and assisted in it so far as to pelt all the people in cylinder hats with handfuls of confetti. . . . There is no rudeness, except the authorized pelting with confetti, or blows of harlequin-swords, which, moreover, are within a law of their own; but nobody takes rough hold of another, or meddles with his masque, or does him any sort of unmannerly violence. At first sight, you would think that the whole world had gone mad; but, at the end, you wonder how people can let loose all their mirthful propensities without unchaining their mischievous ones. It could not be so in America, or in England; in either of those countries, the whole street would go mad in earnest, and come to blows and bloodshed, were the population to let themselves loose to the extent which we see here. All this restraint is self-imposed, and quite apart from that exercised by the presence of the soldiery, who stack their arms in the Piazza del Popolo, and in the Piazza Colonna, and at every other place of vantage in the vicinity of the Corso, and would rain bullets as plentifully as confetti, in case of an outbreak.

Piazza Poli, March 18th Friday.

Una and I went to the Sculpture-gallery of the Capitol, yesterday, and saw, among other things, the Venus in her secret cabinet. This was my second view of her; the other time, I greatly admired her; now, she made no very favorable impression. There are twenty Venuses whom I like as well, or better; and there is one view of the lower part of her back which seems to me exceedingly unbeautiful. On the whole, she is a heavy, clumsy, unintellectual, and common-place figure; at all events, not in good looks today. Marble beauties seem to suffer the same occasional eclipse that flesh and blood ones do.

We looked at the Faun, at the Dying Gladiator, and what other famous sculptures are to be seen there; but nothing had a glory round it, perhaps because a sirocco was blowing. These sculpture halls of the Capitol have always had a dreary and depressing effect on me, very different from those of the Vatican; I know not why, except that the rooms of the former have a dingy, shabby, and neglected look, and that the statues are dusty, and all the arrangements less magnificent than the Vatican's. The corroded and discolored surfaces of the statues take away from the impression of immortal youth, and turn Apollo himself into an old stone; unless at rare intervals, when he appears transfigured by a light gleaming from within. I used to admire the Dying Gladiator exceedingly; but, in my later views of him, I find myself getting weary and annoyed that he should be such a length of time leaning on his arm, in the very act of death. If he is so terribly hurt, why does he not sink down and die, without further ado? Flitting moments—imminent emergencies—imperceptible intervals between two breaths—ought not to be encrusted with the eternal repose of marble; there should be a moral stand-still in any sculptural subject, since there must needs be a physical one. It is like flinging a piece of marble up into the air, and, by some enchantment, or trick, making it stick there; you feel as if it ought to come down, and are dissatisfied that it does not obey the natural law. In painting, though it is equally motionless as sculpture, there does not appear to be this objection to representing brief snatches of time; perhaps because a story can be told more broadly in picture, and so the momentary circumstance can be buttressed about with other things that give it an epoch.

Piazza Poli, March 23rd, Wednesday.

I am wearing away listlessly these last precious days of my abode in Rome. Una's illness is disheartening; and by confining my wife, it takes away the energy and enterprise that were the spring of all our enterprises. I am weary of Rome, without having seen and known it as I ought; and I shall be glad to get away from it, though no doubt there will be many yearnings to return hereafter, and many regrets that I did not make better use of the opportunities within my grasp. Still, I have been in Rome long enough to be imbued with its atmosphere, and this is the essential condition of knowing a place; for such knowledge does not consist in having seen every particular object it contains. At any rate, in the state of mind in which I now stand towards Rome, there is very little advantage to be gained by staying here longer.

...I believe I go oftener to the Bank than anywhere else, and read Galignani and the American newspapers;[90] thence I stroll listlessly to the Pincian, or to the Medici Gardens. I see a good deal of General Pierce, and we talk over his presidential life, which, I now really think, he has no latent desire nor purpose to renew.[91] Yet he seems to have enjoyed it while it lasted; and certainly he was in his element, as an administrative man, not far-seeing, not possessed of vast stores of political wisdom in advance of his occasions, but endowed with a miraculous intuition of what ought to be done, just at the time for action.

Piazza Poli, April 14th, Thursday.

Yesterday afternoon, I drove with Mr. & Mrs. Story & Mr. Wilde to see a statue of Venus, which has just been discovered, outside of the Porta Portese, on the other side of the Tiber.[92] A little distance beyond the gate, we came to the entrance of a vineyard, with a wheel-track through the midst of it; and following this, we soon came to a hill side in which an excavation had been made, with the purpose of building a grotto for keeping and storing wine. They had dug down into what seemed to be an ancient bathroom, or some structure of that kind; the excavation being square and cellar-like, and built round with old subterranean walls of brick and stone. Within this hollow space the statue had been found, and it was now standing against one of the walls, covered with a coarse cloth or canvas bag. This being removed, there appeared a headless marble figure, earth-stained, of course, and with a slightly corroded surface, but wonderfully delicate and beautiful; the shape, size, and attitude, apparently, of the Venus de Medici, but, as we all thought, more beautiful than that. It is supposed to be the original from which the Venus de Medici was copied. Both arms were broken off (at the elbow, I think) but the greater part of both, and nearly the whole of one hand, had been found; and these being adjusted to the figure, they took the well known position before the bosom and the middle, as if the poor fragmentary woman retained her instinct of modesty to the last. There were the marks on the bosom and thigh, where the fingers had touched; whereas, in the Venus de Medici, if I remember rightly, the fingers are sculptured quite free of the person. The man who showed the statue now lifted from a corner a round block of marble, which had been lying there among other fragments; and this he placed upon the shattered neck of the Venus; and behold it was her head and face, perfect all but the nose! Even in spite of this mutilation, it seemed immediately to light up and vivify the entire figure; and whatever I may heretofore have written about the countenance of the Venus de Medici, I hereby record my belief that that head has been wrongfully foisted upon the statue; at all events, it is unspeakably inferior to this newly discovered one....

The proprietor of the vineyard stood by; a man with the most purple face and hugest and reddest nose that I ever beheld in my life. It must have taken innumerable hogsheads of his thin vintages to empurple his face in this manner. He chuckled much over the statue, and, I suppose, counts upon making his fortune by it. He is now awaiting a bid from the Papal government, which, I believe, has the right of pre-emption whenever any relics of ancient art are discovered. If the statue could but be smuggled out of Italy, it might command almost any price. There is not, I think, any name of a sculptor on the pedestal, as on that of the Venus de Medici. A dolphin, or some other fish, is sculptured on the pillar, or whatever it be, against which she leans. The statue is of Greek marble. She was first found about eight days ago, but has been open for inspection only a day or two; and already the visitors come in throngs, and the beggars gather about the entrance of the vineyard. A wine-shop, too, seems to have been opened on the premises for the accommodation of this great concourse; and we saw a row of German artists sitting at a long table, in the open air, each with his tumbler of thin wine and something to eat, before him; for the Germans refresh nature ten times to another person's once.

How the whole world might be peopled with antique beauty, if the Romans would but dig!

Piazza di Poli, April 19th, Tuesday.

Gen¹ Pierce leaves Rome this morning for Venice, by way of Ancona, and taking the steamer thence to Trieste. I had hoped to make the journey along with him; but Una's terrible illness has made it necessary for us to continue here another month, and we are thankful that this seems now to be the extent of our misfortune.[93] Never having had any trouble, before, that pierced into my very vitals, I did not know what comfort there might be in the manly sympathy of a friend; but Pierce has undergone so great a sorrow of his own, and has so large and kindly a heart, and is so tender and so strong, that he really did us good, and I shall always love him the better for the recollection of these dark days. Thank God, the thing we dreaded did not come to pass.

Pierce is wonderfully little changed; indeed, now that he has won and enjoyed (if there were any enjoyment in it) the highest success that public life could give him, he seems more like what he was in his early youth than at any subsequent period. He is evidently happier than I have ever known him since our college days; satisfied with what he has been, and with the position in the country that remains to him, after filling such an office. Amid all his former successes, (early as they came, and great as they were,) I always perceived that something gnawed within him, and kept him forever restless and miserable; nothing that he won was worth the winning, except as a step gained towards the summit. I cannot tell how early he began to look towards the Presidency; but I believe he would have died a miserable man without it. And yet, what infinite chances there seemed to be against his attaining it! When I look at it in one way, it strikes me as absolutely miraculous; in another, it came like an event that I had all along expected. It was due to his wonderful tact, which is of so subtle a character that he himself is but partially sensible of it.

Well; I have found in him, here in Rome, the whole of my early friend, and even better than I used to know him; a heart as true and affectionate; a mind much widened and deepened by his experience of life. We hold just the same relation to one another as of yore; and we have passed all the turning-off places, and may hope to go on together, still the same dear friends, as long as we live. I do not love him one whit the less for having been President, nor for having done me the greatest good in his power; a fact that speaks eloquently in his favour, and perhaps says a little for myself. If he had been merely a benefactor, perhaps I might not have borne it so well; but each did his best for the other, as friend for friend.[94]

Piazza di Poli, May 15th, 1859, Sunday.

Yesterday afternoon, my wife, Julian, & I, went to the Barberini picture-gallery, to take a farewell look at the Beatrice Cenci, which I have twice visited before. I attempted a description of it at my first visit, more than a year ago; but the picture is quite indescribable, inconceivable, and unaccountable in its effect; for if you attempt to analyze it, you can never succeed in getting at the secret of its fascination. Its peculiar expression eludes a straightforward glance, and can only be caught by side glimpses, or when the eye falls upon it casually, as it were, and without thinking to discover anything; as if the picture had a life and consciousness of its own, and were resolved not to betray its secret of grief or guilt, though it wears the full expression of it when it imagines itself unseen. I think no other such magical effect can ever have been wrought by pencil. I looked close into its eyes, with a determination to see all that there was in them, and could see nothing that might not have been in any young girl's eyes; and yet, a moment afterwards, there was the expression (seen aside, and vanishing in a moment) of a being un-humanized by some terrible fate, and gazing at me out of a remote and inaccessible region, where she was frightened to be alone, but where no sympathy could reach her. The mouth is beyond measure touching; the lips apart, looking as innocent as a baby's after it has been crying. The picture can never be copied.... I hated to leave the picture, and yet was glad when I had taken my last glimpse, because it so perplexed and troubled me not to able to get hold of its secret.

Thence we went to the church of the Capuchins, and saw Guido's Archangel.... The expression is of heavenly severity, and a degree of pain, trouble, or disgust, at being brought in contact with sin, even for the purpose of quelling and punishing it. There is something finical in the copy, what I do not find in the original; the sandaled feet are here those of an angel; in the mosaic, they are those of a celestial coxcomb, treading daintily, as if he were afraid they would be soiled by the touch of Lucifer.[95]

Hotel des Colonies (Marseilles) May 29th, Saturday.

Wednesday was the day fixed for our departure from Rome, and after breakfast, I walked to the Pincian, and saw the garden and the city, and the Borghese Grounds, and St Peter's, in an earlier sunlight than ever before. Methought they never looked so beautiful; nor the sky so bright and blue. I saw Soracte on the horizon,[96] and I looked at everything as if for the last time; nor do I wish ever to see any of these objects again, though no place ever took so strong a hold of my being, as Rome, nor ever seemed so close to me, and so strangely familiar. I seem to know it better than my birth place, and to have known it longer; and though I have been very miserable there, and languid with the effects of the atmosphere, and disgusted with a thousand things in daily life, still I cannot say I hate it—perhaps might fairly own a love for it. But (life being too short for such questionable and troublesome enjoyments) I desire never to set eyes on it again.

PART III: THE FRENCH AND ITALIAN NOTEBOOKS

Hotel d'Europe (Avignon) June 1ˢᵗ, Wednesday.

I remember nothing very special to put down about Marseilles; though it was really like passing from death into life, to find ourselves in busy, cheerful, effervescing France, after living so long between asleep and awake in sluggish Italy.

Hotel Wheeler, (Havre) June 22ᵈ, Wednesday.

We arrived at this Hotel, last evening, from Paris; and find ourselves on the border of the Petit Quay Notre Dame, with steamers and boats right under our window, and all sorts of dock business going on briskly. . . . But I flag terribly; scenes and things make but dim reflections in my inward mirror; and if ever I have a thought, the words do not come aptly to clothe it. I may as well give up all attempts at journalizing.

So I shall say nothing of our journey across France from Geneva; nor of our five days' stay in Paris; nor of our journey thence to Havre. We came thither principally to accompany Miss Shepard, whom I put on board the Steamer Vanderbilt for New York, last evening, and who sails this morning. Tonight, we ourselves shall take our departure in a steamer for Southampton, whence we shall go to London;—thence, in a week or two, to Liverpool;—thence to Boston and Concord, there to enjoy (if enjoyment it prove) a little rest, and sense that we are at home.

NOTES

Introduction

1. Joel Porte, Preface to *Emerson in His Journals*, ed. Porte (Cambridge, MA: Harvard University Press, 1982), vi.
2. Hyatt H. Waggoner, Introduction to *HLN*, 26.
3. Henry James, *Hawthorne* (1879; reprint, Ithaca, NY: Cornell University Press, 1956), 98.
4. Edwin Percy Whipple, unsigned review of *The House of the Seven Gables*, *Graham's Magazine* 38 (6 June 1851); reprinted in *The House of the Seven Gables*, ed. Robert S. Levine (New York: W. W. Norton, 2006), 325.
5. James, *Hawthorne*, 117.
6. Julian Hawthorne, "The Salem of Hawthorne," *Century Magazine* 28 (May 1885): 4.
7. James, *Hawthorne*, 51.
8. SH quoted in Brenda Wineapple, *Hawthorne: A Life* (New York: Random House, 2003), 156.
9. Herman Melville, "Hawthorne and His Mosses," in *The Piazza Tales and Other Prose Pieces, 1839–1860*, ed. Harrison Hayford, Hershel Parker, and G. Thomas Tanselle, vol. 9 of *The Writings of Herman Melville* (Evanston and Chicago: Northwestern University Press and the Newberry Library, 1987), 245.
10. Michael J. Colacurcio, *The Province of Piety: Moral History in Hawthorne's Early Tales* (Cambridge, MA: Harvard University Press, 1984), 39, 19.
11. Ibid., 20. Since NH's surviving notebooks begin in 1835 and several of the best historical tales date from the late 1820s and early 1830s, it is possible that they did reflect the kind of moral/historical interest Colacurcio ascribes to NH. Possible but unlikely: a writer's sensibility does not change so radically and quickly, and pertinent stories such as "The May-Pole of Merry Mount" and "The Minister's Black Veil"

appeared in the gift-book annual *The Token* for 1836 (published late in 1835), the time of the notebooks.

12. *Hawthorne and the Real: Bicentennial Essays,* ed. Millicent Bell (Columbus: The Ohio State University Press, 2005).

13. *HLN,* ms. leaf 25 (italics added).

14. Waggoner, Introduction, *HLN,* 25.

15. *HLN,* ms. leaf 8.

16. Waggoner, Introduction, *HLN,* 25.

17. In the early 1830s NH projected and partially completed a work called "The Story Teller," rooted in his travels through New England and upstate New York in the summer of 1832. The collection was a frame narrative that combined the adventures of a wandering storyteller with descriptions of scenes and persons, along with a number of tales themselves, some of them related to place and occasion. NH could not persuade a publisher to accept the collection, and its materials, including some of the travel sketches, appeared separately, most of them in *The New-England Magazine* of 1834–35. The introductory frame was published in the December 1834 issue of that periodical as "Passages from a Relinquished Work" and was reprinted in the second edition of *Mosses from an Old Manse* (1854). It is intriguing to speculate what direction NH's career might have taken if "The Story Teller," with its mixture of the real and the fanciful, had been published. The travel notebooks of 1837 and 1838 represent a further development of NH the realist, though ("Ethan Brand" excepted) almost entirely separate from his fiction.

18. James R. Mellow, *Nathaniel Hawthorne in His Times* (Boston: Houghton Mifflin, 1980), 48.

19. Henry Adams, *The Education of Henry Adams,* in *Novels, Mont Saint-Michel, and The Education,* ed. Ernest Samuels and Jayne N. Samuels (New York: Library of America, 1983), 727. For a discussion of the seasonal split in NH's character and writing, see Robert Milder, "Hawthorne's Winter Dreams," *Nineteenth-Century Literature* 54 (1999): 165–70 especially.

20. See Northrop Frye, *Anatomy of Criticism* (Princeton, NJ: Princeton University Press, 1957), 308–12.

21. Patricia Dunlavy Valenti, "Sophia Peabody Hawthorne's *American Notebooks,*" in *Studies in the American Renaissance,* ed. Joel Myerson (Charlottesville: University Press of Virginia, 1996), 116.

22. In this letter, Hawthorne complained about possible legislation to revise the salary provisions for the diplomatic corps. For more on Hawthorne's finances in Liverpool, see Mellow, *Nathaniel Hawthorne in His Times,* 453–56.

23. See especially the famous "moonlight" passage in "The Custom-House" Introduction, CE I: 35–36.

24. Qtd. in Ronald A. Bosco and Jillmarie Murphy, eds., *Hawthorne in His Own Time* (Iowa City: University of Iowa Press, 2007), 152.

25. Qtd. in CE XXI: 743.

26. Wineapple, *Hawthorne,* 228.

27. For a discussion of the context of Julian Hawthorne and Fuller, see Thomas R. Mitchell, *Hawthorne's Fuller Mystery* (Amherst: University of Massachusetts Press, 1998), 12–40.

28. Paul R. Baker, *The Fortunate Pilgrims: Americans in Italy, 1800–1860* (Cambridge, MA: Harvard University Press, 1964), 141.

29. For an account of Hawthorne's relationship with Louisa Lander, see T. Walter Herbert, *Dearest Beloved: The Hawthornes and the Making of Middle-Class Marriage* (Berkeley: University of California Press, 1993), 228–34.

30. Mellow, *Nathaniel Hawthorne in His Times*, 495.

Part I: The American Notebooks

1. In "Foot-prints on the Sea-shore" NH transferred the encounter to a September setting and amplified its dramatic details.

2. This paragraph suggests the monomania NH would develop in *BR* with the prison reformer Hollingsworth, who narrator Coverdale believes may be going mad. See also NH's treatment of reformers in "The Hall of Fantasy."

3. "and squalid," absent from SH's transcription and from the Centenary text, appears in the manuscript Lost Notebook (*HLN*, ms. leaf 25).

4. Morally, a rehearsal for the fate of Roger Chillingworth.

5. "fund of" appears in the Lost Notebook, not in the Centenary text (*HLN*, ms. leaf 35).

6. Horatio Bridge (1806–93), a Bowdoin College friend of NH, was living in Augusta, Maine, at the time of NH's visit. Bridge had encouraged NH in his burgeoning career as a writer and made possible the issuance of *TTT* by pledging $250 to guarantee the publisher against loss, but without letting NH know. Years after NH's death and not long before his own, Bridge published *Personal Recollections of Nathaniel Hawthorne* (New York: Harper's, 1893), which contains valuable information about NH's earlier life and assessments of his character.

7. Bridge did marry, in 1846.

8. Martin Van Buren, vice president under Andrew Jackson, had succeeded to the presidency on March 4, 1837.

9. Jonathan Cilley (1802–38) was a Bowdoin College graduate in the class of 1825. A member of the Maine legislature from 1832 to 1836 and Speaker of the House in 1835 and 1836, he was killed in a duel with W. J. Graves of Kentucky on February 24, 1838. NH's biographical sketch of Cilley may have helped him get an appointment as measurer in the Boston Custom House in 1839.

10. NH used details from this sentence in "Foot-prints on the Sea-shore." In *Clarel,* Melville would have the NH-based Vine throw stones at his shadow.

11. This idea figures centrally in the characterization of Dimmesdale, whose hypocrisy makes the world and his own being shadowy and unreal to himself, as NH indicates through his name.

12. The sentence also suggests the dividedness of Dimmesdale's character.

13. This entry and the one following it anticipate the galvanic power Chillingworth wields over Dimmesdale.

14. A version of this of old man, whose daughter has gone off with a circus, appears in "Ethan Brand."

15. NH's characterization of this maimed lawyer-turned-soap-boiler is the basis for Lawyer Giles in "Ethan Brand."

16. The surgeon-dentist is one of several picaresque figures (the essence-peddler NH meets is another) that entered into the conception of Holgrave in *HSG*. See chapter 12 (CE II: 76): "In an episodical way, he had studied and practiced dentistry,

and with very flattering success, especially in many of the factory-towns along our inland-streams."

17. A young boy named Joe figures in "Ethan Brand," but Hawthorne transforms him into a sensitive, fearful child and sets him against the coarse villagers who gather to hear Ethan Brand recount his search for the Unpardonable Sin.

18. In a rough sense, this passage might be said to encapsulate NH's attitude toward slavery and abolition. Though personally objecting to slavery, he had no confidence in political interventions to do away with it, a position in keeping with his general skepticism toward institutional reform. On the grand matters of human injustice—social, economic, sexual, and racial—NH tended to rely on the meliorism of history, or "Providence."

19. The Dutchman with his diorama and tail-chasing dog play symbolic roles in "Ethan Brand." The Dutchman is there associated with the Wandering Jew, condemned to roam the earth forever in consequence of hurling a gibe at Christ on his way to the cross; the dog suggests the morbid introversion and futility of Ethan Brand's quest for the Unpardonable Sin. The transformation of the Dutchman is typical of how NH recast naturalistic elements from the Berkshire notebook into fictive symbol.

20. The Tremont House was situated at the corner of Tremont and Beacon streets, Boston. This paragraph contains the kind of observed detail NH used in *BR*, chapters 27–28.

21. See NH's entry in the English Notebooks for July 4, 1855 (CE XXI: 226–29).

22. This looks ahead to Dimmesdale being watched by Chillingworth.

23. Cow Island is immediately adjacent to Brook Farm on the southeast.

24. See Coverdale's description of his arboreal "hermitage" in *BR*, chapter 12.

25. The allusion is to Matthew 7:16.

26. NH drew on this paragraph for his depiction of Priscilla in *BR*, chapters 5 and 9.

27. This idea is also the basis for the A on Dimmesdale's breast.

28. This also applies to Dimmesdale.

29. This apothegm was inscribed on the glass of one of the windows of NH's study in the Old Manse with the signature, "Sophia A Hawthorne 1843."

30. This idea never eventuated in a story of its own, but it applies both to Dr. Rappaccini's experiments with his daughter Beatrice and to Chillingworth's experimental probings and pricking with Dimmesdale. Years later, Harold Frederic used it in Dr. Ledsmar's experiments with his servant in Frederic's Hawthorne-influenced *The Damnation of Theron Ware* (1896).

31. In chapter 17 of *BR* ("The Hotel"), Coverdale peers out of his Boston hotel window at the backside of nearby residences. The entry is in keeping with the motif of voyeurism running through NH's fiction and most openly addressed in "Sights from a Steeple" and *BR*.

32. On the relation of this entry to the development of *The Ancestral Footstep*, see Edward H. Davidson, *Hawthorne's Last Phase* (New Haven, CT: Yale University Press, 1949), 13–29.

33. NH has no particular characterization in mind yet—his daughter Una, in some respects a model for Pearl in *The Scarlet Letter*, would not be born until 1844—but this entry shows Hawthorne at least drawn to the name Pearl as fictively picturesque.

34. An anticipation of Dimmesdale's mood in chapter 17 of *The Scarlet Letter* just before Hester rouses him with her plan of escape (CE I: 196).

35. Genesis 5:24.

36. George Prescott, a ten- or eleven-year-old son of Mrs. Timothy Prescott, lived nearby.

Ralph Waldo Emerson, the leading American thinker of NH's time, lived about a mile and a half from NH in Concord. It was Emerson who evidently helped arrange for NH to rent the parsonage (NH would call it the Old Manse) after the death of the incumbent minister, Emerson's step-grandfather Ezra Ripley (1751–1841). Emerson had recently extended his reputation with the 1841 publication of *Essays*. NH's relationship with Emerson—and Emerson's with him—was complex. Neither had much use for the other's writing, but Emerson personally liked NH a good deal and NH found Emerson a man of interest, if somewhat comically rarefied. NH publicly recorded some of his impressions of Emerson in "The Old Manse"; his private impressions were not different in kind, but they were often more bemusedly skeptical.

William Ellery Channing (1817–1901), an aspiring poet, protégé of Emerson's, and close friend of Thoreau's, married Margaret Fuller's sister Ellen in 1841 and settled at Concord in May 1843. Sophia had been a patient of Ellery's father, Dr. Walter Channing, about 1830 when her family was living in Boston, and she was, according to Elizabeth Peabody, "for some years the single influence that tamed" the young poet (*NHHW*, 1: 63–64).

"Mr. Thorow" is Henry David Thoreau (1817–62), a Concord native, a fledgling writer, and another protégé of Emerson's, who went to live in Emerson's home in April 1841. On July 4, 1845, Thoreau would take up residence at Walden Pond (on land owned by Emerson), where he remained until September 1847. Drafted in part at the pond, *Walden* would be published in 1854. In the late 1840s, when NH was again living in Salem and was secretary of the local lyceum, he arranged for both Emerson and Thoreau to lecture there.

Elizabeth Hoar (1814–78), a member of a prominent Concord family of lawyers and statesmen, helped prepare the Old Manse for occupancy by the Hawthornes. She had been engaged to marry Emerson's brother Charles, and after his death in 1836 she lived a retired life.

37. Rev. William Emerson (1743–76), Ralph Waldo's grandfather.

38. The reference is to *Henry IV*, act V, scene iii.

39. George Stillman Hillard (1808–79), lawyer and friend of NH. A conspicuous act of this friendship was Hillard's raising a considerable sum of money—the exact amount is not known—among NH's friends in January 1850 (*NHHW*, 1: 354–55) after his dismissal from the Salem Custom House and before publication of *SL*.

40. Emerson had described the sagacity of Edmund Hosmer (1798–1881) in "Agriculture in Massachusetts," *Dial* 3 (July 1842).

41. The Robert B. Storers of Boston. Mrs. Storer was Elizabeth Hoar's sister Sarah.

42. See "The Old Manse," CE X: 18–21.

43. Margaret Fuller (1810–50)—writer, critic, feminist—paid the Emersons an extended visit during the summer of 1842. SH had known Fuller and attended her "Conversations" for women before she married NH. Fuller's cordial relations with

the Hawthornes were strained somewhat by her suggestion that her sister Ellen and Ellery Channing be allowed to board at the Old Manse. NH declined courteously but firmly. Nonetheless, a friendliness continued, and in the summer of 1844 Fuller stayed for a time with the Hawthornes at the Old Manse as she worked on expanding her 1843 *Dial* essay, "The Great Lawsuit," into a book, *Woman in the Nineteenth Century* (1845). Fuller was then involved in a one-sided romantic relationship (perhaps with William Clarke, brother of her close friend James Freeman Clarke), and the "almost daily entries" in her journal, her editors remark, "show her struggle to reconcile" her hopes "with the wounding and disappointing reality of insufficient love" ["'The Impulses of Human Nature': Margaret Fuller's Journal from June through October 1844," ed. Martha L. Berg and Alice de V. Perry, *Proceedings of the Massachusetts Historical Society* 102 (Boston: Massachusetts Historical Society, 1990): 38]. As Fuller's host, NH was in a special position to appreciate the conflict in her between the proud, self-reliant feminist who in *Woman in the Nineteenth Century* would publicly champion celibacy as a condition for female autonomy and the romantically frustrated private woman—a conflict he would vividly dramatize with Zenobia in chapter 14 in *BR*. In his 1844 sketch "The Christmas Banquet," NH had described "a woman of unemployed energy," very likely modeled on Fuller, "who found herself in the world with nothing to achieve. Nothing to enjoy, and nothing even to suffer," and who "had, therefore, driven herself to the verge of madness by dark broodings over the wrongs of her sex, and its exclusion from a proper field of action." The dark heroines of NH's romances—Hester, Zenobia, and Miriam—are all variations upon this pattern. Indeed, NH's dark heroines, who have no prototype in his tales of the 1830s, may well have been inconceivable without the personal and intellectual influence of Fuller. In the mid-1840s Fuller moved to New York to write for Horace Greeley's *New York Tribune;* later she went to Europe, settling in Rome, where she actively involved herself in the struggle for Italian independence. Returning to America in 1850 with her husband, Angelo Ossoli, and their young child, Fuller and her family perished in a shipwreck off Fire Island, New York. Emerson dispatched Thoreau to Fire Island to hunt for Fuller's physical and literary remains—it was rumored she had written a history of the Italian revolution—but neither was ever found. NH's acerbic comment on Fuller in the the French and Italian notebooks should be understood in light of his entire relationship to her, of his deeply ambivalent feelings about feminism, and of his antipathy toward "public women" generally from Anne Hutchinson down. For NH's relationship with Fuller, see Robert Milder, "*The Scarlet Letter* and Its Discontents," *Nathaniel Hawthorne Review* 22 (Spring 1996): 9–25; and Thomas R. Mitchell, *Hawthorne's Fuller Mystery* (Amherst: University of Massachusetts Press, 1998).

44. Sarah Bradford Ripley (1793–1867) was the sister of George Bradford and the wife of Samuel Ripley; the Ripleys succeeded the Hawthornes in the Old Manse.

45. Rev. Barzillai Frost (d. 1858) was a minister in Concord and the unnamed target of Emerson's complaint about the coldness of formal Christianity in the Divinity School Address: "I once heard a preacher who sorely tempted me to say, I would go to church no more.... A snowstorm was falling around us. The snowstorm was real; the preacher merely spectral." It is to Emerson's everlasting credit that he refrained from making an open pun on Frost's name. Divinity School Address, in *Nature, Addresses, and Lectures*, Vol. 1 of *The Collected Works of Ralph Waldo Emerson*, ed. Robert E. Spiller and Alfred R. Ferguson (Cambridge, MA: Harvard University Press, 1979), 85.

46. NH's reference is to Thoreau's "Natural History of Massachusetts," *Dial* 3 (July 1842), 19–40, unsigned.

47. For at least two weeks in late summer NH's sister Maria Louisa (1808–52) was a guest in the Old Manse. Thoreau's boat, the *Musketaquid*, was built by himself and his brother, John, and was used by them in the memorable voyage of 1839 that Thoreau would describe in *A Week on the Concord and Merrimack Rivers* (1849). In renaming the boat the *Pond Lily*, NH was paying tribute both to a favorite local flower—rooting itself in the muck of the Concord River, the pond lily managed to rise pure, white, and fragrant, unlike the noisome yellow lily—and to his wife, whom he liked to compare to a pond lily, rooted in common human nature but remaining miraculously pure.

48. *The Boston Miscellany of Literature and Fashion* was a substantial but short-lived monthly (Jan. 1842–Feb. 1843) edited by Nathan Hale, Jr., and his successor, Henry T. Tuckerman.

49. Samuel Gray Ward (ca. 1817–1907) was a friend of Emerson, Ellery Channing, and Margaret Fuller.

50. In February 1843 SH had suffered a miscarriage.

51. After NH's marriage in July 1842, no publications of his appeared until the beginning of 1843. Then *Sargent's New Monthly Magazine* published "The Old Apple Dealer" (January) and "The Antique Ring" (February); the *Pioneer* printed "The Hall of Fantasy" (February) and "The Birth-mark" (March); and the *Democratic Review* took "The New Adam and Eve" (February), "Egotism; or The Bosom Serpent" (March), and "The Procession of Life" (April), as well as "The Celestial Railroad" (May), which had probably been written by the end of March.

52. Whatever NH's hopes may have been in March 1843, they were not to be realized until April 1846, when he was named surveyor at the Salem Custom House.

53. Mary Peabody (1806–87), the middle of the three Peabody sisters, married educator and sometime politician Horace Mann (1796–1859).

54. Amos Bronson Alcott (1799–1888), peddler, autodidact, experimental educator, transcendental philosopher, and father of author Louisa May Alcott, contributed "Orphic Sayings" to the *Dial* 1 (July 1840: 85–98, and Jan. 1841: 351–61).

55. "Pythagoras said, that it was either requisite to be silent, or to say something better than silence" (Iamblichus, *Life of Pythagoras* . . . , trans. Thomas Taylor [London, 1818], 264).

56. Channing's *Poems* (Boston, 1843), published at Ward's expense, drew one of Poe's most scathing reviews in *Graham's Magazine* 23 (Aug. 1843): 113–17, hardly offset by a brief notice in the *Dial* 4 (July 1843: 135), which described Channing's "genius" as "without a rival in this country."

57. NH's paragraph is a response to SH's rhapsody on the first anniversary of their marriage.

58. NH used this passage in "The Old Manse," CE X: 27–28.

59. The reference is anticipatory, since their first child, Una, was born on March 3, 1844.

60. Located on the edge of Concord, Sleepy Hollow became Sleepy Hollow Cemetery; many of the town notables, including NH, Emerson, Thoreau, and Alcott, are buried there.

61. Hawthorne adapted this entry in "The Old Manse" (CE X: 33).

62. The entry anticipates *The Scarlet Letter*, obviously, but NH had also used the

idea in his cameo description of a Salem woman in "Endicott and the Red Cross," published in *The Token* for 1838 and reprinted in the 1842 edition of *TTT*: "There was likewise a young woman, with no mean share of beauty, whose doom it was to wear the letter A on the breast of her gown, in the eyes of the world and her own children" (CE IX: 435).

63. NH drew heavily on this entry for chapter 27 of *BR* (CE III: 229–37), which describes the recovery of the body of the drowned Zenobia.

64. Probably General Joshua Buttrick, who owned a farm near the Concord River, just north of the town.

65. This Buttrick (b. 1801), of uncertain relationship to the general, also lived on a farm north of Concord.

66. With her husband Minot Pratt (d. 1878), Maria T. Pratt (d. 1891) owned five shares in the Brook Farm organization. In 1845 the Pratts left the association and settled in Concord.

67. An anticipation of the process of moral and physical deterioration that Roger Chillingworth will undergo in consequence of his decision to live for revenge.

68. NH reworked these three paragraphs for an important passage in "The Custom-House" (CE I: 35–36).

69. Priscilla M. Dike (1790–1873) was a sister of NH's mother and the second wife of John Dike.

70. The context suggests that NH may have been thinking of "dusty death," *Macbeth* act V, v. 23. The phrase is echoed in *MF*, chapter 21 (CE IV: 194). As might be expected, this is not a passage that SH included in her edition of the American notebooks.

71. Mrs. Elizabeth Manning Hawthorne died the following day, July 31, 1849.

72. This phrase is echoed in the opening chapter of *HSG* (CE II: 20) and is a central theme in the book.

73. James T. Fields (1817–81), a partner in the Boston publishing firm of Ticknor & Fields and editor of the *Atlantic* from 1861 to 1870, was one of the first great entrepreneurs in American publishing and an enthusiastic promoter of NH, beginning with his firm's publication of *The Scarlet Letter* in 1850. David Dudley Field (1804–94) was a noted New York attorney and an expert on law reform. Oliver Wendell Holmes (1809–94), doctor, author, and celebrated wit, had a summer house in Pittsfield. In the mid-1840s Evert A. Duyckinck (1816–78) was an editor at Wiley and Putnam's, which published *Mosses from an Old Manse* and Melville's *Typee* (1846). Duyckinck became a friend and sponsor of both writers and, as editor of the New York periodical *The Literary World* from 1847 to 1853, was an influential figure in New York literary circles. His reviews of NH's tales were laudatory and generally incisive, especially in describing (if genteelly trying to contain) the element of darkness in Hawthorne's writing. Cornelius Mathews (1817–89), an editor and minor writer, was a friend and colleague of Duyckinck's and a tireless proselytizer for American literary nationalism within the Duyckinck-led literary group known as "Young America." Henry Dwight Sedgwick (1824–1903), a pupil of Longfellow's, practiced law in New York City. Joel Tyler Headley (1813–97) was a popular historical writer.

The Monument Mountain expedition marked the first meeting of Melville and NH. It was unusual for NH to respond warmly to any new acquaintance, especially to other writers, but he took immediately to Melville, as Melville did to him. NH had reviewed Melville's *Typee,* approvingly, in 1846, but he did not yet know Melville's other work to date—*Omoo* (1847), *Mardi* (1849), *Redburn* (1849), and *White-Jacket* (1850). It is uncertain whether Melville had read NH's tales before meeting him; if not, he read *Mosses from an Old Manse* almost immediately and with astonishment. When Duyckinck returned to New York he carried with him a manuscript titled "Hawthorne and His Mosses" that would appear in *The Literary World* on August 17 and 24, 1850, under the byline "By a Virginian Spending July in Vermont." Neither a Virginian (he was born in New York City, where he lived until 1830 when the bankruptcy of his father, an importer of French goods, forced the family to remove to the Albany area) nor a vacationer in Vermont (he was visiting family in the Berkshires with the idea of settling in the area), Melville may have chosen the attribution both to distance himself from the ardor of the review and to further the nationalist case that NH was an *American* writer, not simply a regional one. "Hawthorne and His Mosses" is an extraordinary piece of writing—penetrating about NH yet most significant as the literary manifesto of a writer just coming into his powers and coalescing his vision. The identity of its author did not long remain a secret, and when the Hawthornes learned that it was Melville who had so glowingly praised NH, even likening him to Shakespeare, it solidified a friendship already in the making.

To Melville, on the verge of greatness but still unsure of himself, NH was a revelation, and over the next fifteen months, as Melville settled with his family on a farm in nearby Pittsfield, his relationship with NH would become (exclusive of his family) the most consuming in his life. The friendship cooled after NH left the Berkshires in November 1851—the cottage was too small for his family, now with a third child; he felt isolated in Lenox; he hated the Berkshire climate and missed the sea; he quarreled with his landlords—and NH, while retaining affection and literary and personal respect for Melville, went on to other things. On his side, it might be said, Melville never put NH behind him—as friend, colleague, confidant, father, brother, and (some have argued) would-be lover. The two men met for the final times when Melville stopped in Liverpool to and from his journey to the Mediterranean in 1856–57. In the late 1860s Melville began rereading NH's fiction, and he purchased the notebooks as they appeared in SH's edited volumes. Melville's brief elegy "Monody" is often taken as referring to his intimacy with, then estrangement from, NH, though whether this estrangement involved a dramatic break (unlikely in view of NH's Liverpool entries on Melville in the English notebooks) or a simple distancing is impossible to know. NH figures prominently as the character Vine in Melville's long philosophical poem *Clarel* (1876); as Walter E. Bezanson put it, Melville took the "opportunity [of his poem] to brood privately and at length over the man who had meant the most to him in his own life" ("Historical and Critical Note" to Herman Melville, *Clarel: A Poem and Pilgrimage in the Holy Land,* vol. 12 of *The Writings of Herman Melville,* ed. Harrison Hayford, Alma A. MacDougall, Hershel Parker, and G. Thomas Tanselle (Evanston and Chicago: Northwestern University Press and the Newberry Library, 1991), 596.

From NH's side, the fullest biographical discussions of the NH-Melville relationship are James R. Mellow's in *NH in His Times* and Edwin Haviland Miller's in *Salem Is My Dwelling Place* (Iowa City: University of Iowa Press, 1991). Miller has also treated the relationship in his biography *Melville* (New York: George Braziller, 1975). More complete, factual, and judicious on Melville is Hershel Parker's two-volume *Herman Melville: A Biography* (Baltimore: Johns Hopkins University Press,

1996, 2002). For a speculative literary/psychological reading of the relationship from Melville's side, see Robert Milder, "'The Ugly Socrates': Melville, Hawthorne, and the Varieties of Homoerotic Experience," in *Exiled Royalties: Melville and the Life We Imagine* (New York: Oxford University Press, 2006), 118–48. See also the volume of essays *Hawthorne and Melville: Writing a Relationship*, ed. Jana L. Argersinger and Leland S. Person (Athens, GA: University of Georgia Press, 2008).

74. Actually, the 8th of August. Allan Melville, Jr. (1823–72) was a New York lawyer four years younger than his brother Herman. Lewis William Mansfield (1816–99), a miscellaneous writer of Cohoes, New York, presented NH with a case of champagne upon his arrival at Lenox. Edwin Percy Whipple (1816–86), a Boston lecturer and critic, was one of the most perceptive contemporaneous commentators on NH.

75. William A. Tappan and his wife, Caroline Sturgis Tappan (a friend of Emerson's and formerly of Margaret Fuller's), owned the estate on which NH's red cottage was situated.

76. H. D. Parker's saloon-restaurant was located at 3 Court Street in Boston.

77. See NH's description of a saloon in chapter 21 of *BR*.

78. NH drew on this entry for many details in chapter 17 of *BR*.

79. Oak Hall was a large Boston establishment selling men's clothing at modest prices.

80. Palo Alto hats were wide-brimmed hats popularized during the 1849 gold rush and named for the battle of Palo Alto with which the Mexican War began on May 8, 1846.

81. E. P. P is Elizabeth Palmer Peabody (1804–94), the older sister of SH and Mary Mann, a teacher, author, editor, bookseller, and publisher, with whom, some biographers speculate, NH may have been (semi-)romantically involved before he met Sophia. See Mellow, *NH in His Times*, and Megan Marshall, *The Peabody Sisters* (Boston: Houghton Mifflin, 2005).

82. Mrs. Peters was a servant later described by Julian Hawthorne (*NHHW*, 1: 410) as "a stern and incorruptible African, and a housekeeper by the grace of God."

83. Founded in 1790, the Shaker establishment in Hancock lay between Pittsfield and the Massachusetts line and was one of the most important Shaker communities.

Part II: The English Notebooks

1. The Hawthornes had sailed from Boston on July 6 and arrived in Liverpool on July 17.

2. This description appears in "Consular Experiences" (CE V: 7–9).

3. Henry Arthur Bright (1830–84) had visited NH in Concord on September 23, 1852, having received a letter of introduction from Longfellow. In *OOH*, NH pays the following homage to his hospitality in England: "It would gratify my cherished remembrance of this dear friend, if I could manage, without offending him, or letting the public know it, to introduce his name upon my page. Bright was the illumination of my dusky little apartment, as often as he made his appearance there!" (CE V: 39).

4. Zachary Taylor (1784–1850), hero of the Mexican War and twelfth president of the United States. His election as a Whig in 1848 precipitated NH's removal from the Salem Custom House.

5. A residential community two miles south of the center of Liverpool, where the Hawthornes lived. Birkenhead, an industrial city of ten thousand, is immediately north of Rockferry.

6. At this time, the population of Liverpool was more than 375,000, far greater than that of any American city.

7. A coin smaller than the others likely to be contributed.

8. This description of the mayor of Liverpool's dinner appears in "Civic Banquets" (CE V: 317–30).

9. The periodic sessions of the judges of the superior courts in every county of England for the purpose of administering justice in the trial and determination of civil and criminal cases.

10. NH's aversion to public speaking is a consistent theme in his letters and throughout *EN*.

11. A city thirty miles north of Liverpool.

12. This entry, and the next two, contain material found throughout "Outside Glimpses of English Poverty" (CE V: 278–83).

13. Milton, *Paradise Lost*, XII, 644. Expelled from Eden, Adam and Eve look back at the Gate, which appears "With dreadful faces throng'd and fiery arms."

14. In the southern part of Rockferry. The description of NH's fireside at Rock Park appears in "A London Suburb" (CE V: 214).

15. The date of the residences mentioned here are Old Manse, 1842–45; Salem, 1845–46; Boston, 1846; Salem, 1846–50; Lenox, 1850–51; West Newton, 1851–52; Concord, 1852–53; England, 1853–57; Italy, 1858–59.

16. Matthew 5:35: "Swear not at all; neither by heaven; for it is God's throne: nor by the earth; for it is his footstool."

17. NH's lament over the "beefy" physique of English women, a recurrent theme throughout *EN*, appears in *OOH* as well (CE V: 48–50, 333–34). The question of national difference between American and English women is also an important theme in *The Ancestral Footstep*, NH's first version of his English romance, written in Rome in 1858 (CE XII: 24, 34, 71–72, 85, 87).

18. The Liverpool beggar without legs appears in "Outside Glimpses of English Poverty" (CE V: 290–92).

19. Allingham (1824–89), an Irish customs officer, published a book of poems in 1850.

20. Thomas Carlyle (1797–1881), Scottish essayist and historian, was enormously influential during the Victorian era in England and the United States. Alfred Lord Tennyson (1809–92), who succeeded William Wordsworth in 1850 as poet laureate of England, is widely regarded as England's preeminent Victorian poet. NH would see Tennyson at the Manchester Art Exhibition in 1857.

21. John Buck Lloyd (d. 1863) was mayor for 1853–54. John Naylor (1813–1889), a banker, lent works of art valued at £20,000 for exhibition at St. George's Hall, Liverpool, on September 18, 1854.

22. Leading members of the British School of modern painters, which NH would study at the Manchester Exhibition of 1857: Joseph Mallard William Turner (1775–1851), Sir David Wilkie (1785–1841), and Sir Edwin Henry Landseer (1802–73).

23. Genesis 2:23: "And Adam said, This is now bone of my bones, and flesh of my flesh; she shall be called woman, because she was taken out of man."

24. NH was in England throughout the Crimean War, fought between Russia on one side and an alliance of France, England, and the Ottoman Empire on the other. The war lasted from 1853 to 1856.

25. James Buchanan (1791–1868), secretary of state under James K. Polk, 1844–48; minister to Great Britain, 1853–56; and fifteenth president of the United States, 1857–61. His niece, Harriet Lane (1833–1903), an orphan brought up by her uncle, served as hostess for Buchanan, first at the American embassy and later in the White House.

26. Charles Anthon (whom NH followed in *WB/TT*) writes: "When [Meleager] was seven years old, the Moirae or Fates came to the dwelling of his parents, and declared that when the billet which was burning on the hearth should be consumed, the babe would die. Althaea, on hearing this, snatched the billet from the fire, and laid it carefully away in a coffer." When Meleager was grown, he killed Althaea's brothers in a quarrel, whereupon she "took from its place of concealment the billet, on which depended the existence of Meleager, and cast it on the flames. As it consumed, the vigor of Meleager wasted away; and when it was reduced to ashes, his life terminated" (*A Classical Dictionary* [New York: Harper, 1850], 815–16).

27. Sir Austen Henry Layard (1817–94) was M.P. from Aylesbury, 1852–57.

28. Henry John Temple, third viscount Palmerston (1784–1865), held many government positions and was prime minister from 1855 to 1865.

29. For NH's moralizing account of this episode, see "Consular Experiences" (CE V: 24–30).

30. Duncan Macauley, U.S. consul to Venice, 1854–55, would become consul to Manchester in 1859.

31. See Coleridge, "The Rime of the Ancient Mariner," line 370.

32. NH would use this comparison between English and American trees in "Recollections of a Gifted Woman" (CE V: 91–92).

33. Named for Robert Dudley, Earl of Leicester (?1532–88), Queen Elizabeth's favorite; the building was originally erected ca. 1383 and converted to a hospital by Dudley in 1571.

34. Built in the early sixteenth century as two separate buildings, half of Shakespeare's birthplace was used for business, the other half for living quarters. NH would use much of this description of Shakespeare's birth and burial places in "Recollections of a Gifted Woman" (CE V: 95–104).

35. Part of the tower of the Church of the Holy Trinity is ca. 1210, but most of it dates from the thirteenth to fourteenth centuries; the stone spire was added in 1763.

36. The old anathematizing stanza is as follows: "Good friend for Jesus sake forbeare / To dig ye dust enclosed here / Blese be ye man yt spares thes stones / And curst be he yt move my bones." Thomas Nash (1593–1647) married Elizabeth Hall, Shakespeare's last direct descendant, in 1626. Dr. John Hall (1575–1635) and Susanna Hall (1583–1649) acted as executors of Shakespeare's will. John Hall is said to have erected the bust as Shakespeare's executor.

37. Executed around 1623 by Gerald Johnson (or Garat Janssen), the bust is the earliest authentic statue of Shakespeare.

38. The statue is an early commissioned work by Richard Cockle Lucas (1800–83).

39. Illustrated are three episodes recorded in Boswell's *Life of Johnson*, ed. G. B. Hill and L. F. Powell, 6 vols. [Oxford: Clarendon, 1934–50]). The first relates his

rapt attention, at the age of three, to Henry Sacheverell (1674–1724), known for his eloquent sermons against dissenters (1: 38–39). The second notes that he was often "borne triumphant" to school by three admiring classmates (1: 47). In the third, Johnson tells how he once refused to attend the Uttoxeter fair when his father was ill, and, in later years, repenting for his disobedience, he "went to Uttoxeter in very bad weather, and stood for a considerable time bareheaded in the rain, on the spot where my father's stall used to stand" (1: 373). NH was fascinated by this episode in Johnson's life (see his entry for October 24, 1838, in the American notebooks); he recounts it in his description of his travels to Uttoxeter (CE V: 120–38).

40. The description of this "good-natured, fat-faced individual" appears in "Consular Experiences" (CE V: 15–18).

41. Ivan Stepanovich Mazepa (?1640–1709), a Ukrainian Cossack nationalist leader immortalized in Byron's poem of 1819 about his being bound naked to a horse's back after the discovery of his liaison with a Polish court lady.

42. Peter Ainsworth (1790–1870), M.P. for Bolton, 1837–47, was owner of Smithells Hall (NH misspells its name).

43. In March 1555 George Marsh was arrested for heresy and examined by Justice Robert Barton at Smithells Hall. Early records give no mention of the foot-stamping incident, and it is first mentioned in a tract dated August 22, 1787. But the legend attracted NH, who used it in his unfinished *American Claimant* romance.

44. In *The Acts and Monuments* (1641) of John Foxe, ed. Rev. George Townsens (1841–49; reprint, New York: AMS Press, 1965), Marsh's account of his examination of "Smirhill" [*sic*] is given (7: 40–41), but there is no mention of any oath or foot-stamping.

45. Located to the left of the south entrance, the monuments include those of Ben Jonson (1572–1637), Edmund Spenser (1552–99), Samuel Butler (1612–80), John Milton (1608–74), and Thomas Gray (1716–71). NH's visit to the Poets' Corner is recorded in "Up the Thames" (CE V: 259–64; 266–70).

46. As a young man, NH was infatuated with the poetry of Robert Southey (1774–1843). Thomas Campbell (1777–1844) was known for the "Pleasures of Hope" and for popular songs such as "The Wounded Hussar."

47. A political attack of 1860 commented, "Mr. B. has a shrill, almost female voice, and wholly beardless cheeks; and he is not by any means, in any aspect the sort of man likely to cut, or attempt to cut his throat for any Chloe or Phyllis in Pennsylvania" (quoted by John Updike from the privately printed biography of Philip Gerald Auchampaugh, in *Buchanan Dying: A Play* [New York: Knopf, 1974], 246).

48. In the election of 1848, when the Whig candidate Zachary Taylor defeated the Democrat Lewis Cass, he had the support of six southern states, including Georgia and Louisiana, which had voted Democratic in the previous election.

49. Francis Bennoch (1812–90) was a London merchant and sometime poet who opened his house to NH and his family. Although Bennoch struck some as pretentious in his cultivation of artists and writers, NH paid tribute to him when he wrote, "He and Henry Bright are the only two men in England whom I should be much grieved to say farewell" (CE XIV: 570), and he writes of Bennoch's garden in "A London Suburb" (CE V: 216–19). Sir David Salomons, first baronet (1797–1873), was a founder of the London and Westminster Bank. He was one of the first Jews to be elected to municipal office in London, becoming sheriff in 1835 and lord mayor in 1855.

50. Samuel Carter Hall (1800–1889), Irish-born editor and journalist, had founded one of Europe's leading journals of fine arts. His wife, Anna Maria Fielding Hall (1800–1881), a novelist, is mentioned in the next sentence. George Robert Gleig (1796–1888) was chaplain general of the army.

51. NH is referring to Emma Abigail Montefiore Salomons (1833–59), wife of the lord mayor's brother Philip; compare the description of Miriam in *MF* (CE IV: 48).

52. Philip Salomon (1796–1867), elder brother of the lord mayor.

53. George Arthur Hastings (1833–73), seventh earl of Grannard.

54. In *OOH*, NH chose to close his chapter on "Civic Banquets," and indeed the entire book, with the moment of his beginning to speak: "I got upon my legs to save both countries, or perish in the attempt. The tables roared and thundered at me, and suddenly were silent again. But, as I have never happened to stand in a position of greater dignity and peril, I deem it a stratagem of sage policy here to close these Sketches, leaving myself still erect in so heroic an attitude" (CE V: 345).

55. From an early age, NH adored the romances of Sir Walter Scott (1771–1832), including *Rob Roy* and *Ivanhoe*. Abbotsford is the farm in Scotland that Scott transformed into a quasi-baronial castle; the money he lavished on it ultimately contributed to his financial collapse.

56. NH had seen Horace Walpole's house in Surrey in 1856; like Scott, Walpole had created a "toy-castle" (CE XXI: 429).

57. NH had seen Battle Abbey, in Sussex, in 1856 (see CE XXI: 460–64).

58. *La Gazette Nationale, ou le Moniteur*, founded in 1789, was the semi-official newspaper of Napoleon's government.

59. Walter Scott (1801–47), the author's oldest son, became a major in the King's Hussars. Sir Walter Scott had married Charlotte Margaret Charpentier, the daughter of a French émigré.

60. John Graham of Claverhouse, first viscount of Dundee (?1649–89), was colonel of the Royal Life Guards of Scotland during the Restoration and a fierce protector of the Covenanters. James Graham, first marquis and fifth earl of Montrose (1612–50), was commander of the Royalist forces in the Highlands. They appear in Scott's *Old Mortality* and *A Legend of Montrose*, respectively.

61. William IV's (not George IV's) visit to Edinburgh in August 1822 was the first appearance of a Hanoverian king in Scotland. Scott organized an elaborate welcoming ceremony.

62. Richard Monckton Milnes (1809–85), later first Lord Houghton, politician, patron, critic, man of letters, and renowned host; NH first met him in September 1854. Annabel Hungerford Milnes (1814–74) had married Milnes in 1851.

63. Henry Petty-Fitzmaurice, third marquis of Landsdowne (1780–1863), was an influential moderate in the House of Lords as well as an active figure in London society.

64. Lord Landsdowne met the poet Thomas Moore (1779–1852) in 1817 and quickly became his patron and literary advisor. NH had read Moore's *Memoirs, Journal, and Correspondence* in 1853.

65. George Ticknor (1791–1871) was Longfellow's predecessor as Smith Professor of French and Spanish at Harvard. He was a cousin of NH's publisher, William D. Ticknor.

66. Elizabeth Barrett Browning (1806–61) and Robert Browning (1812–89) were widely acclaimed English poets, who married in 1846. During their marriage, E. B. Browning overshadowed her husband as a celebrated poet of love and social reform and, on the death of Wordsworth in 1850, was notably considered as a candidate for the poet laureateship, which Alfred Lord Tennyson received. By the end of the nineteenth century, however, literary circles recognized R. Browning as a master poet and a voice for the Victorian themes of progress, limitation, and confidence.

67. Frances Smith Nightingale (d. 1880) and Florence's elder sister, Frances Parthenope ("Parthe") Nightingale, later Lady Verney (1819–90).

68. Elizabeth Barrett Browning became interested in spiritualism in the summer of 1853 and took her husband to a memorable séance conducted by the American medium Daniel Dunglas Home on July 23, 1855. NH and the Brownings discussed spiritualism again in Florence in June 1858, Robert again playing the analytical infidel to his more credulous wife (CE XIV: 302).

69. Delia Salter Bacon (1811–59), an author of New England historical fiction, became obsessed with the idea that Shakespeare's plays were not the product of one genius but were written by a group of eminent Elizabethan philosophers and poets, including Francis Bacon (1561–1626), Edmund Spenser, and Sir Walter Raleigh (1552–1618). Encouraged by Emerson and Elizabeth Peabody, she settled in London in 1853 to work on her treatise. NH's involvement in her project—with much assistance from Francis Bennoch—which involved subsidizing publication of her book, *The Philosophy of the Plays of Shakespeare Unfolded* (1857) and, later, caring for her when she suffered a mental breakdown in 1857, is documented in *OOH*. See also the entry in this collection for July 29, 1856. NH's experiences with Delia Bacon would form the basis of "Recollections of a Gifted Woman" (CE V: 104–17).

70. For Margaret Fuller and William Wetmore Story, see n. 43 of "American Notebooks" and n. 16 of "French and Italian Notebooks," respectively.

71. Anne Isabella Milbank Noel Gordon, Lady Byron and Countess Wentworth (1792–1860), wife of the poet, took an interest in raising her two youngest grandchildren after her only daughter, Ada Augusta Byron Noel (1812–52), had died.

72. Thomas Babington Macauley (1800–1859), author of *Critical and Miscellaneous Essays*, which NH had read to SH in 1844.

73. John Gorham Palfrey (1796–1881) was Dexter Professor of Sacred Literature at Harvard, 1831–39, and editor of the *North American Review*, 1835–43.

74. For information about George Hillard, see n. 39 in "American Notebooks."

75. Thomas Chatterton (1752–70) produced in adolescence a large number of poems and miscellaneous essays, many alleged to be the work of a medieval monk, one Thomas Rowley. His suicide at the age of seventeen, after a vain attempt to live by his pen in London, created a romantic legend of him as a defeated genius.

76. Eliza Ware Farrar (1791–1870), widow of Professor John Farrar of Harvard, was author of a number of children's novels. She and SH had been friends since the early 1830s. Thomas Carlyle had expressed interest in Bacon's theory. Robert Blair Campbell (d. 1862), U.S. representative from South Carolina and general of South Carolina troops in 1833, was consul at London, 1854–61.

77. The Manchester Art Exhibition opened on May 5, 1857, and closed on October 7. NH and SH stayed near the exhibit to study the art, partly in preparation for their trip to Italy.

78. William Hogarth (1697–1764), English painter. The works NH refers to are *Sigismunda Weeping Over the Heart of Her Lover* (1759), *The March of the Guards to Finchley* (1750), and *Captain Thomas Coram* (1743).

79. Sir Thomas Lawrence (1769–1830) and Sir Joshua Reynolds (1723–92) were both British painters.

80. John Singleton Copley (1738–1815), born in Boston, had lived in London after 1775. Presumably NH's "slain man" refers to *The Death of Major Pierson, on the Invasion of Jersey by the French.*

81. Francis Danby (1793–1861) painted *The Evening Gun* in 1848.

82. Alexander Ireland (1810–94) was a native of Edinburgh but moved to Manchester in 1843. He was publisher and business manager of the *Manchester Examiner and Times*, a liberal paper, from 1846 to 1886. He was an organizer of the Manchester Free Library and a good friend of Emerson, Carlyle, and Leigh Hunt.

83. Thomas Woolner (1825–92), sculptor and poet, executed his bust of Tennyson in 1857.

84. A ground sloth of the Pliocene and Pleistocene ages, often of gigantic size. NH may be thinking of his recent visit to the Crystal Palace, where he saw large models of the iguanodon, the plesiosaurus, and the pterodactyl created by Sir Richard Owen of the British Museum.

Part III: The French and Italian Notebooks

1. Ann Adaline Shepard (1835–74) was governess of the Hawthorne children. Frances L. (Fanny) Macdaniel (b. 1815) had resided at Brook Farm and now taught English in Paris.

2. Annibale Carracci (1560–1609) was the principal artist of the Bolognese Academy of the late sixteenth century, known for its Baroque classicism. Claude Lorrain or Claude Gellée (?1604/5–1682), French draftsman, painter, and etcher, was renowned for his ideal landscape paintings. Raphael, or Raffaello Santi or Sanzio (1483–1520), was an Italian painter, draftsman, and architect whose art embodied the visual and psychological realism of the High Renaissance. Leonardo da Vinci (1452–1519) was an Italian painter, sculptor, architect, designer, theorist, engineer, and scientist of the High Renaissance. Michelangelo Buonarroti (1475–1564) was an Italian painter, draftsman, architect, sculptor, and poet of the High Renaissance. Peter Paul Rubens (1577–1640), whose capacity to transform profound themes into vivid and luxuriant images exemplifying his tradition, was a Flemish artist of the Baroque. Rembrandt van Rijn (1606–69), Dutch painter, draftsman, and etcher, was renowned for his attention to details and innovative approach to portraits and history paintings.

3. Benjamin Franklin (1706–90), the American printer, writer, scientist, inventor, and statesman. During the Revolutionary War, Franklin was sent to Paris and proved instrumental in winning French support for the colonies; he was also much in vogue in French society.

4. The church is Santissima Annunziata, at the end of the Via Balbi.

5. The Palazza Larazani on the Pincian Hill.

6. In *Plutarch's Lives,* Alexander the Great confronts Diogenes, who tarried lying in the sun rather than rushing to his side in an expedition against Persia. Upon asking Diogenes whether he wanted anything, Diogenes replied, "Yes ... stand a little out

of my sun." Impressed with the "haughtiness and grandeur" of Diogenes, Alexander declared, "But verily, if I were not Alexander, I would be Diogenes."

7. After the abortive Republican revolution of 1848, a French army restored Pope Pius IX to control of Rome and the Papal States; a garrison of thirty thousand remained during the 1850s.

8. The narrator of *MF* uses this description to capture the sense of Rome's former "magnificence" and present decay, but (like NH) he gradually develops a mysterious affection for "the Eternal City." See CE IV: 110–11.

9. St. Peter's marks the first of the five great basilicas in Rome. These lines were adapted for *MF* (CE IV: 348–49).

10. Constantine I, or Constantine the Great (?285–337 C.E.), ruled as emperor of Rome from 306 to 337.

11. Roman emperors returned from victories in Egypt with ancient obelisks as their monuments; popes, in turn, have used them to decorate the modern city. Augustan or Republican antiquities date from the time of Augustus (63 B.C.E.– 14 C.E., first emperor of Rome 27 B.C.E.– 14 C.E.) or the Roman Republic (ca. 509 B.C.E.–fifth century C.E.).

12. See CE XXI: 234–38 and XXII: 377–78 for NH's visits to Furness Abbey and Kenilworth, the ruins of the former inspiring NH to write, "they suggest a greater majesty and beauty than any human work can show—the crumbling traces of the half obliterated design producing somewhat of the effect of the first idea of anything admirable, when it dawns upon the mind of an artist or a poet—an idea which, do what he may, he is sure to fall short of" (CE XXI: 235). In the preface to *MF*, NH would note, "Romance and poetry, like ivy, lichens, and wall-flowers, need Ruin to make them grow" (CE IV: 3).

13. In *MF*, Hilda seeks sanctuary in a confessional and "reveal[s] the whole of her terrible secret" of Donatello and Miriam (CE IV: 354–62).

14. The Pantheon, a Greek temple dedicated, as its name suggests, to all the gods, was erected by Agrippa in 27 B.C.E. and rebuilt by the emperor Hadrian in the second century. It was converted to a Christian church in 609.

15. Maria Mitchell (1818–89) was the first American woman professor of astronomy (at Vassar College). The main purpose of her trip to Italy was to meet European astronomers and to demonstrate to them how photography was a tool for astronomy in America.

16. Built in 1640 and one of the largest palaces in Rome, the Barberini houses a small collection of paintings and a library. William Wetmore Story (1819–95), American sculptor, writer, musician, painter, and theatrical producer, was the unofficial leader of the American artists' community in Rome at the time of the Hawthornes' visit.

17. NH secured the renown of this idealized statue of Cleopatra by Story (1858) when he described it in *MF* (CE IV: 125–26), assigning it to his fictional Kenyon. He acknowledged his "robbery" of this "magnificent work" in his preface and generously credited Story (CE IV: 4).

18. Story turned thirty-nine years old on February 12.

19. *Marguerite*, a work of the 1850s, now in the Essex Institute, Salem.

20. Louisa Lander (1826–1923), of Salem, went to Rome in 1855 to study sculpture. She saw the Hawthornes frequently after their arrival, and by April had finished a bust of NH. Rumors about her sexual misbehavior, founded or not, soon prompted the Hawthornes to refuse to continue seeing her (see the Introduction to this volume).

Hawthorne used elements of his description of Louisa Lander in portraying Hilda (CE IV: 54–55).

21. The sculptor Antonio Canova (1757–1822) was the leading classicist of the early nineteenth century.

22. "Virginia Dare," a statue of the first English child born in America, completed in 1859.

23. The church, I Cappuccini, or S. Maria della Concezione, appears in *MF* as the church where Donatello, Kenyon, and Miriam witness a dead monk over whom his brothers sing a *de profundis* (a psalm of penitence) (CE IV: 181–82, 187–89).

24. Guido Reni (1575–1642) and Il Domenichino (or Domenico Zampieri) (1581–1641), Italian painters and students of Annibale Carracci.

25. The *Apollo Belvedere*, the *Laocoön*, and the *Torso Belvedere* (thought to represent Hercules) were considered by nineteenth-century tourists to be among the most inspiring examples of classical genius in sculpture. The *Apollo Belvedere* portrayed the Greek sun-god Apollo. In *MF*, Kenyon visits the Vatican sculpture gallery, but, missing the sympathetic intelligence of Hilda, he finds his enthusiasm for sculpture chill: "he suspected that it was a very cold art to which he had devoted himself ... and whether the Apollo Belvedere itself possesses any merit above its physical beauty, or is beyond criticism even in that generally acknowledged excellence. In flitting glances, heretofore, he had seemed to behold this statue as something ethereal and godlike, but not now" (CE IV: 391). The *Laocoön* is a marble statue group of a serpent assailing the Trojan priest Laocoön and his two sons outside the walls of Troy.

26. NH was astonished—and appalled—by what he felt was the uncleanness of contemporary Romans. SH's sense of propriety led her to omit from *Passages* "and along ... ancient wall," "or they will ... nastiness," and "in my opinion ... as other people." In *MF*, the narrator muses on "a kind of malignant spell ... an inherited and inalienable curse, impelling their successors to fling dirt and defilement upon whatever temple, column, ruined palace, or triumphal arch, may be nearest at hand, and on every monument that the old Romans built" (CE IV: 388).

27. A large fountain designed by Flamino Ponzio (1559–1613).

28. The *Pietà*, one of the great statues of the Italian Renaissance, was sculpted late in life by Michelangelo Buonarroti (1475–1564).

29. The picture of Christ was painted by Dürer in 1506, reportedly in five days.

30. The first of these is a portrait of a woman clothed only beneath the waist, traditionally identified as Raphael's mistress ("la fornarina" or baker's daughter). In fact, the artist is likely Raphael's student Giulio Romano (?1499–1546) and the subject, the Sienese lady Margherita di Francesco Luti. The *Beatrice Cenci* haunted NH's imagination during the composition of *MF*. Hilda copies the *Beatrice Cenci* to perfection, explaining to the astonished Miriam that she "had ... but to sit down before the picture, day after day, and let it sink into my heart. . . . She is a fallen angel, fallen, and yet sinless; and it is only this depth of sorrow, with its weight and darkness, that keeps her down upon the earth, and brings her within our view even while it sets her beyond our reach" (CE IV: 65, 66). In *MF*, Miriam suffers a similar "fallen, and yet sinless" fate. Recent scholars suspect the painting is neither Guido's nor of Beatrice Cenci, but perhaps Francesco Albani's (1578–1660) of a sibyl, an oracular or prophetic woman honored in ancient Greece and Rome.

31. Guido Reni's *St. Michael Trampling the Devils* is the most celebrated painting in St. Peter's. It, too, appears symbolically in *MF* (CE IV: 182–85).

32. The Capitol includes three buildings designed by Michelangelo: the Palace of the Senator in the center, the Palace of the Conservators on the right (or west side), and the Museum of the Capitol on the left (or east side).

33. Roman rulers took their title from Julius Caesar, the first of the Roman emperors (45–44 B.C.E.), and were honorarily called "Caesar." The words "Kaiser" and "Czar" derive from "Caesar."

34. A premier sculptural destination among nineteenth-century American tourists, the *Dying Gladiator* struck art critic John Bell as "a most tragical and touching representation, . . . [which] no one can meditate upon . . . without the most melancholy feelings." Despite his enthusiasm for the *Dying Gladiator* here, on a later visit in March 1859, NH suffered the vagaries of his artistic taste and lamented, "I used to admire the Dying Gladiator exceedingly; but, in my later views of him, I find myself getting wearied and annoyed that he should be such a length of time leaning on his arm, in the very act of death," a complaint he has Kenyon of *MF* share (CE XIV: 511; IV: 16–17).

35. A statue depicting Emperor Hadrian's beloved companion Antinous, whose mysterious drowning in the Nile inspired the legends of his apotheosis and assimilation into several deities, including Osiris, Silvanus, Apollo, and Dionysus. Despite the popularity of the *Antinous* among American tourists, NH failed to remark upon the statue until his fifth visit; the neighboring *Faun of Praxiteles* apparently captured the greater part of his attention. SH had a bust of Antinous in the Old Manse. Later in the century especially, Antinous became for some a symbol of homoerotic love.

36. The Palace of the Conservators on the west side of the square of the Capitol contains a number of frescoes, statues, and paintings, including a Gallery of Pictures.

37. The gallery of the Palazzo Borghese, a palace dating back to 1590.

38. In *MF*, NH translates his lassitude into an "icy Demon of Weariness," who scandalously suggests to Hilda the monotony of the Italian masters (CE IV: 336).

39. Unlike most American tourists, who preferred the paintings of the Italian High Renaissance masters, NH favored (abashedly so, at times) the Dutch and Flemish genre paintings of Rubens, Rembrandt, Anthony van Dyck (Flemish painter, 1599–1641), Paulus Potter (Dutch painter and etcher, 1625–54), and the David Teniers (Flemish painters, the Elder 1582–1649 and the Younger 1610–90). NH developed his taste for Dutch and Flemish genre paintings at the Manchester Exhibit of 1857 (see CE XXII: 356), but he had openly praised this style of art earlier in chapter 21 of *BR*.

40. The Gallery of Statues forms part of the larger palaces and museums of the Vatican.

41. When she edited this passage after NH's death, SH revised it for public consumption: out of which "Heaven alone can help them" (see CE XIV: 925). NH himself made a similar change in *MF* when he had the statue impress Kenyon as a representation of "the Fate of Interminable Ages"; Laocoön and his sons seem doomed to Kenyon "if no Divine help intervene" (CE IV: 391; see XIV: 925). The irony here is that it was a god, Poseidon, siding with the Greeks, who sent the serpents to strangle Laocoön to prevent him from warning the Trojans.

42. Joseph Mozier (1812–70), a successful New York businessman who retired to Florence in 1845 to study sculpture.

43. Horatio Greenough (1805–52), considered the "first American sculptor," traveled to Rome in 1825 to pursue his vocation, receiving commissions from James

Fenimore Cooper for *Chanting Cherubs* (1829–31), based on (at Cooper's suggestion) Raphael's *Madonna del Baldacchino,* and from the U.S. Congress for a monumental statue of George Washington (1832–41). In *MF,* Kenyon shares Mozier's disdain for Greenough's lack of original genius (CE IV: 124).

44. See n. 43 in "American Notebooks" for a discussion of NH's ambivalence toward Fuller; see also the discussion of Fuller in the Introduction.

45. Harriet Goodhue Hosmer (1830–1908), of Watertown, Massachusetts, resolved early to become a sculptor, studying anatomy in St. Louis in her youth, traveling to Rome with actress Charlotte Cushman in 1852, and studying there with the Welsh sculptor John Gibson as a beloved student and peer. Gibson (ca. 1790–1866) moved to Rome in 1820 and studied with Antonio Canova (1757–1822) and Bertel Thorvaldsen (1768 or 1770–1844); he represented the heart of the Anglo-Roman school and was one of the chief advocates of neoclassicism in the nineteenth century. His guiding principle was simple: "Whatever the Greeks did was right."

46. Gibson's *Tinted Venus* (ca. 1850) is the best known of his controversial colored statues. He used colored wax, in emulation of ancient Greek practice.

47. The Basilica of Julia had been recently uncovered in the Roman Forum in 1834.

48. In the preface to *MF,* NH putatively selects Italy as the setting of his "Romance," because "Romance and poetry, like ivy, lichens, and wall-flowers, need Ruin to make them grow" (CE IV: 3); yet in the *FIN* and in the text of *MF* (CE IV: 167), the Hawthornean voice marvels at the way in which stark Roman ruins diminish a sense of historicity and "Romance," while Gothic ruins intensify the same. Romance seems to need the softness of decay; Roman ruins are ageless petrifications, imposing but resistant to poeticizing, except perhaps by moonlight.

49. John Murray's guidebook *Handbook of Rome and Its Environs* (London: John Murray, 1858) describes the Villa Borghese as "one of the favorite resorts of the Roman people in summer, and the most convenient promenade for the upper classes and foreign residents of all seasons" (295).

50. Praxiteles (?ca. 400 B.C.E.–ca. 330 B.C.E.), the premier Attic sculptor of the Late Classical period, evidently created the original bronze statue from which nearly 150 copies derive, including those in the Vatican and the Villa Borghese, the last of which NH would visit on April 17. With this visit and subsequent ones on April 22 and April 30, the *Faun* would come to haunt NH's literary imagination, inspiring him to create the character Donatello and the romance *MF.*

51. George Loring Brown (1814–89), of Boston.

52. Edward Sheffield Bartholomew (1822–58), of Connecticut, came to Rome in 1850, where he did a number of portrait busts of Americans.

53. JH comments in *Hawthorne and His Circle* (New York: Harper Brothers, 1903), "Both in his notes and in his romance [CE IV: 8] he makes the same mistake as to the pose of the figure.... Of course, the left arm, the one referred to, is held akimbo on his left hip" (235).

54. In the fall of 1857, New York experienced a Great Awakening of sorts, a revival of ecumenical Christian spirit manifesting itself among the urban laity in daily interdenominational worship assemblies, which the secular press covered extensively. From the city it extended into New England cities, towns, and the countryside, reaching its peak from February to June 1858.

55. The cultivated landscape of Monte Pincio, one of the minor hills beyond Rome's famous seven and a favorite promenade.

56. The reference is to Byron's *Childe Harold's Pilgrimage,* canto IV, stanza 78, ll. 694–95: "Oh Rome! my country! city of the soul! / The orphans of the heart must turn to thee."

57. When Donatello and Kenyon travel through the Italian waysides in *MF,* they behold "wretched cottages" and "dreary farm-houses" that belie the pastoral bliss of the countryside; during their ride, the strangely melancholic Donatello kneels penitently at crosses and "the many shrines" like those described in the notebooks (CE IV: 295, 300, 297).

58. During the rambles of Donatello and Kenyon, "they would arrive at some immemorial city...built...[so] that they can never fall—never crumble away—never be less fit than now for human habitation." It "seems a sort of stony growth out of the hill-side, or a fossilized town" (CE IV: 301–2).

59. NH probably has in mind the painters of the late thirteenth and early fourteenth centuries, including Giotto, who developed sophisticated sacred designs and iconography that would fundamentally determine the course of Italian art. From the owl-tower of Donatello's castle, Kenyon and Donatello gaze upon "cities, some of them famous of old; for these had been the seats and nurseries of early Art, where the flower of Beauty sprang out of a rocky soil, and in a high, keen atmosphere, when the richest and most sheltered gardens failed to nourish it" (CE IV: 258).

60. According to Murray, Perugia was formerly "one of the most important cities of the Etruscan league, and is scarcely inferior in antiquity to Cortona." Murray also identifies Perugia as the center of the school of Umbria, characterized by "the transition from the classical style prevalent at Florence to the devotional, which attained its maturity and perfection under Raphael" (*Handbook for Travellers in Central Italy, Part 1,* 3rd edition (London: John Murray, 1853), 242, 244–45. An important scene in *MF*—Miriam and Donatello's reunion as arranged by Kenyon—is set in the marketplace in Perugia. See chapters 34–35.

61. The *Perugia Triptych: The Virgin and Child Enthroned with Angels between Saints Dominic, Nicholas of Bari, John the Baptist, and Catherine of Alexandria* (1437).

62. Paul de Kock (1794–1871), a popular French novelist of Parisian bourgeois life, whose books NH found entertaining during his stay in Concord in the 1840s, while SH considered them "abominable," at least on hearsay.

63. While recording a visit to a Gothic cathedral in Siena five months later, NH similarly imagined its Gothic architecture as "an antique volume written in black-letter of a small character, but conveying a high and solemn meaning" (CE XIV: 450). In *MF,* NH combines the passages in his description of a cathedral in Perugia (CE IV: 312–13).

64. The cathedral dedicated to San Lorenzo dates from the end of the fifteenth century. San Luigi does not correspond to any Perugian churches listed by Murray in *Handbook for Travellers.*

65. Most tourists were more impressed with the Fontana Maggiore (or Great Fountain, 1277–78) than with the statue of Pope Julius III. A Gothic fountain designed by Nicola Pisano, it portrays prophets, saints, the months, the arts, zodiacal signs, biblical stories, and the history of the founding of Rome. *Julius III* (1553–55), a vibrant, elaborately wrought bronze statue of the pope, becomes in *MF* a

"benignly awful representative of Divine and human authority," whose benediction "every man ... might hope to feel quietly descending upon the need, or the distress, that he had closest to his heart" (CE IV: 313–14).

66. Mountains of northwest Italy rising to 9,560 feet.

67. In John Bunyan's *Pilgrim's Progress,* an allegorical tale of temptation and salvation and a favorite book of the young NH, Christian and Hopeful "essayed to look, but the remembrance of ... [hell] made their hands shake, by means of which impediment they could not look steadily through the Glass; yet they thought they saw something like the Gate, and also some of the Glory" of Celestial City. John Bunyan, *Pilgrim's Progress,* ed. James Blanton Wharey, 2nd edition, rev. Roger Sharrock (Oxford: Clarendon Press, 1960), 122–23.

68. Hiram Powers (1805–73) was the most famous American artist of his time, at home and abroad.

69. *The Fisher Boy* (1846) and *Proserpine* (1839), the latter of which was the most popular of all neoclassical sculptures by American artists.

70. The Hawthornes' stay in Florence came during a period of neglect and deterioration for the Uffizi. In 1864, after Tuscany had become firmly allied with the new kingdom of Italy, the museum was reorganized and the collection presented in a more orderly, logical way. Hawthorne visited the gallery often and gradually came to have deep affection for it.

71. Paintings variously related to the Italian Renaissance, including the art of Giotto di Bondone (renowned Italian painter, ca. 1267/75–1337), Fra Angelico (or Fra Giovanni da Fiesole, Italian painter, ca. 1395/1400–1455), Botticelli, Cimabue (or Cenni di Pepo, Italian painter, ca. 1240–ca. 1302), and Fra Filippo Lippi (1406–69). Today art historians attribute the paintings NH viewed in the Uffizi not to those whom he mentions but to their students.

72. *Our Lord Burdened with the Weight of the Cross* by Italian painter Domenico Passignano, or Domenico Cresti (ca. 1559–1638).

73. Emperor of Rome (37–68 C.E.), infamous for cruelty and rumored to have set the Great Fire of Rome (64 C.E.). See the entry on June 16, 1858, where NH reflects on the relation of aesthetic taste and moral character (CE XIV: 321). In a passage of *The Ancestral Footstep* written on May 15, 1858, NH depicts the villain Eldredge in Neronian hues: "Taste seems to be a department of moral sense; and yet it is so little identical with it, and so little implies conscience, that some of the worst men in the world have been the most refined" (CE XII: 74). In *MF,* Hilda suffers from the perception of evil in the world and discovers newly the capacity for an "artificial character" to develop "a taste for pictorial art" (CE IV: 339). The relationship of the aesthetic to the moral fascinated Hawthorne, as it would Henry James.

74. The *Venus de' Medici,* a renowned antique statue created perhaps by a disciple of Praxiteles in the first century B.C.E. Probably a copy of a bronze Venus received from the *Venus of Knidos,* it represents a nude Venus with her head turned left and her hands demurely concealing her breasts and genitals.

75. NH alludes to paintings that Italian painter, draftsman, and printmaker Titian (Tiziano Vecellio, 1488–1576) produced during the second quarter of the sixteenth century, perhaps the Venus of Urbino (1538).

76. NH had first met poets Robert and Elizabeth Barrett Browning in England. See nn. 66 and 68 in "The English Notebooks."

77. Robert Wiedemann Barrett Browning (1849–1912), spoiled as a child, became a middling painter and sculptor in Italy. When the father Browning read NH's explanation for his child's nickname, he professed amusement and explained that it derived from young Robert's "first attempt at pronouncing his own second name of Wiedemann... by which it was first proposed that he should be called to the avoiding the ambiguous 'Robert.'"

78. Against the thrust of contemporary opinion, including his wife's, NH was defensive, or mock-defensive, about preferring the French, Dutch, and Flemish masters to "the general run of the Italians, who have tired me to death" (CE XIV: 297). The painters he refers to are Frans van Mieris the Elder (1635–81), a Dutch painter of exquisitely refined, delicately lit genre scenes, and Gerrit [Gerard] Dou (1613–75), a Dutch painter of precise and charming portraits and genre paintings.

79. Salvator Rosa (1615–73), a Neapolitan painter most known for dramatic scenes of uncultivated, beautiful wilds, which contrasted with the pastoral paintings of Claude.

80. Isabella Blagden (?1816–73), British poet and novelist celebrated not for her literature but for her hospitality as a hostess and friend to Anglo-American tourists and residents of Florence, in particular the Brownings. On the suggestion of Blagden, the Hawthornes settled in the Villa Montauto near her home for August and September. Francis Boott (1813–1904), amateur singer and composer, had taken his infant daughter Elizabeth (1846–88) from Boston to live in Florence after the death of his wife; Henry James based Gilbert and Pansy Osmond on the Bootts in *The Portrait of a Lady*. Thomas Adolphus Trollope (1810–92), older brother of the novelist Anthony, lived in Florence and wrote novels.

81. Daniel Dunglas Home (pronounced Hume, 1833–86), an American medium who discovered his talents during the initial delirium of the spiritualist movement. Spiritualism began in earnest in Rochester, New York, in June 1850, when the Fox sisters apparently communicated with a spirit, who knocked correct answers in response to their questions. Eventually they were exposed as frauds who cracked their toe knuckles to produce the anticipated "rappings," but others welcomed spiritualism as a stream of genuine religion, however muddy its origins. NH made frequent and serious literary use of spiritualism and mesmerism, the latter a tributary of spiritualism in its mystical manifestations, especially in *HSG* and *BR*. Hume conducted a séance at Hiram Power's house in the autumn of 1855.

82. Disciple of Emmanuel Swedenborg (1688–1772), who preached the correspondence between natural objects and spiritual truths, which one learns to perceive more clearly through instruction from the spirit world.

83. Andrea del Sarto (1486–1530), Italian painter and draftsman. His early sixteenth-century paintings embody aesthetic ideals of the classical High Renaissance, while later ones anticipated elements of Mannerism.

84. When Kenyon and Hilda return to the United States in *MF*, the narrator similarly moralizes, "between two countries, we have none at all, or only that little space of either, in which we finally lay down our discontent bones. It is wise, therefore, to come back betimes—or never" (CE IV: 461).

85. A small town on the site of the Roman city that supplanted the Etruscan city of Volsinium.

86. In *MF*, the narrator invokes the same sentiment when describing the buildings

"everywhere in Italy, be they hovels or palaces" (CE IV: 302). When the mythical figure Sibyl requested the gift of immortality, she forgot to ask also for the gift of eternal youth.

87. Over the next six months, Una suffered recurrent and ever worsening bouts of malaria. NH tried to remain composed, but occasionally he lost hope for her survival altogether. From November through late February, she seemed on the verge of recovery, and NH returned to writing, although not in his notebooks but in his romance, which provided a welcome distraction from his grim fears for Una's life. Una relapsed again in late March and seemed on the verge of death, but she recovered once more and appeared healthy in late May. Una survived the malarial bouts but afterwards endured poor health and nervous breakdowns. She would die at the age of thirty-three. T. Walter Herbert discusses Una's malaria in *Dearest Beloved* (248–55).

88. The preceding year, the Carnival failed to impress NH, especially given the persistently rainy weather. He found himself in better spirits this time with the apparent recovery of Una. In the climactic final scene of *MF,* Kenyon resembles the earlier NH with "his sad and contracted brow so ill accorded with the scene, that the revellers might be pardoned for thus using him as the butt of their idle mirth, since he evidently could not otherwise contribute to it" (CE IV: 445). Miriam, bearing an anguished countenance beneath the mask of a Contadina, paradoxically reflects, "There may be a sacred hour, even in Carnival-time!" (CE IV: 448).

89. Mary Elizabeth Benjamin Motley (1813–74), acquaintance of SH since the early 1830s in Boston. She lived in Europe during the 1850s with her husband John Lothrop Motley (1814–77), who composed *Rise of the Dutch Republic* (1856) and *History of the United Netherlands* (1860–68).

90. *Galignani's Messenger* was a daily newspaper for English-speaking persons on the Continent.

91. Franklin Pierce (1804–69), college companion and lifelong friend of NH, brigadier general in the Mexican War, and fourteenth president of the United States (1852–56), selected NH to write his 1852 campaign biography and, in return for his service, appointed NH to the Liverpool consulate in 1853. Hawthorne was deeply loyal to Pierce, whom contemporaries and history have alike judged severely.

92. Hamilton Gibbs Wilder (or Wild; 1827–84), American portrait, landscape, and genre painter. Late in *MF* Kenyon comes upon a newly unearthed Venus in the Roman countryside (see chapter 46).

93. The Hawthornes and Pierce had planned to travel together to Venice, Milan, Geneva, and Paris. On April 18, however, Dr. Franco strongly advised against Una's removal from Rome.

94. NH would make one final gesture of friendship in 1863 when he dedicated *Our Old Home* to Pierce, whose efforts to preserve the Union at all costs earned him opprobrium during wartime as a morally bankrupt president. Against the advice of his publishers, NH insisted on the dedication: "if I were to tear out the dedication," he wrote to his publisher, "I should never look at the volume again without remorse and shame." *OOH* succeeded admirably, even if numerous readers, including Emerson, tore out the dedication from their editions.

95. In February 1858, NH admired the mosaic copy of Guido's *Archangel Michael* as an illustration of "the immortal youth and loveliness of virtue, and its irresistible might against evil" (CE XIV: 100), although in April the same year, when he viewed

another copy in the Academy of St. Luke (which here he seems to remember as being in St. Peter's), he complained, "I . . . seem to see that there is something dainty in the foot which treads on Satan and that a warrior-angel ought not to be quite so delicate" (CE XIV: 170). In *MF,* NH conjures his memories of the copy in his characters' description of the original work. While Kenyon admires it as uniquely "beautiful," Miriam carps that the Archangel steps too "prettily" on the devil. "He should press his foot hard down upon the old Serpent, as if his very soul depended upon it. . . . And with all this fierceness, this grimness, this unutterable horrour, there should still be something high, tender, and holy in Michael's eyes, and around his mouth. But the battle never was such child's play as Guido's dapper Archangel seems to have found it!" (CE IV: 184).

96. A mountain near Rome.

SELECTED BIBLIOGRAPHY

Further reading about Hawthorne in his notebooks should begin with the excellent Historical Commentary to *The American Notebooks* by Claude M. Simpson (CE VIII: 677–98) and to *The English Notebooks* and *The French and Italian Notebooks* by Thomas Woodson (CE XXI: 709–48; XIV: 903–35). Other works pertinent to the notebooks and their biographical and cultural circumstances include the following.

Baker, Paul R. *The Fortunate Pilgrims: Americans in Italy, 1800–1860*. Cambridge, MA: Harvard University Press, 1964.
Baym, Nina. *The Shape of Hawthorne's Career*. Ithaca, NY: Cornell University Press, 1976.
Bell, Millicent, ed. *Hawthorne and the Real: Bicentennial Essays*. Columbus: The Ohio State University Press, 2005.
Berg, Martha L. and Alice de V. Perry, eds. "'The Impulses of Human Nature': Margaret Fuller's Journal from June through October 1844." *Proceedings of the Massachusetts Historical Society* 102 (1990): 38–126.
Bosco, Ronald A. and Jillmarie Murphy, eds. *Hawthorne in His Own Time*. Iowa City: University of Iowa Press, 2007.
Bunyan, John. *Pilgrim's Progress*, ed. James Blanton Wharey, 2nd ed.; rev. ed. Roger Sharrock (Oxford: Clarendon Press, 1960). 122–23.
Capper, Charles. *Margaret Fuller: An American Romantic Life*. New York: Oxford University Press, 1992.
Chevigny, Bell Gale. *Margaret Fuller: The Woman and the Myth*. Boston: Northeastern University Press, 1994.
Erlich, Gloria C. *Family Themes and Hawthorne's Fiction: The Tenacious Web*. New Brunswick, NJ: Rutgers University Press, 1984.
Franchot, Jenny. *Roads to Rome: The Antebellum Protestant Encounter with Catholicism*. Berkeley: University of California Press, 1994.
Hawthorne, Julian. *Nathaniel Hawthorne and His Wife: A Biography*. 2 vols. Boston: J. R. Osgood, 1884.

———. *Hawthorne and His Circle.* New York: Harper Brothers, 1903.
Hawthorne, Nathaniel. *Hawthorne's Lost Notebook, 1835–1841.* Transcript and Preface by Barbara S. Mouffe, Introduction by Hyatt H. Waggoner. University Park: Pennsylvania State University Press, 1978.
Hawthorne, Sophia. *Notes in England and Italy.* New York: Putnam and Sons, 1869.
Herbert, T. Walter. *Dearest Beloved: The Hawthornes and the Making of Middle-Class Marriage.* Berkeley: University of California Press, 1993.
Homer, Bryan. *An American Liaison: Leamington Spa and the Hawthornes, 1864–65.* Rutherford, NJ: Fairleigh Dickinson University Press, 1998.
Hull, Raymona E. *Nathaniel Hawthorne: The English Experience, 1853–1864.* Pittsburgh: University of Pittsburgh Press, 1980.
James, Henry. *Hawthorne.* 1879; reprint, Ithaca, NY: Cornell University Press, 1956.
Lawrence, Nicholas R. and Marta L. Werner, eds. *Ordinary Mysteries: The Common Journal of Nathaniel and Sophia Hawthorne, 1842–1843.* Philadelphia: American Philosophical Society, 2005.
Marshall, Megan. *The Peabody Sisters.* Boston: Houghton Mifflin, 2005.
Martin, Robert K. and Leland S. Person, eds. *Roman Holidays: American Writers and Artists in Nineteenth-Century Italy.* Iowa City: University of Iowa Press, 2002.
Mellow, James R. *Nathaniel Hawthorne in His Times.* Boston: Houghton Mifflin, 1980.
Milder, Robert. "'The Ugly Socrates': Melville, Hawthorne, and the Varieties of Homoerotic Experience." In *Exiled Royalties: Melville and the Life We Imagine.* New York: Oxford University Press, 2006. 118–48.
Miller, Edwin H. *Melville.* New York: George Braziller, 1975.
———. *Salem Is My Dwelling Place.* Iowa City: University of Iowa Press, 1991.
Mitchell, Thomas R. *Hawthorne's Fuller Mystery.* Amherst: University of Massachusetts Press, 1998.
Moore, Margaret B. *The Salem World of Nathaniel Hawthorne.* Columbia: University of Missouri Press, 1998.
Murray, John B. *Handbook for Travellers in Central Italy, Part 1,* 3rd edition. London: John Murray, 1853. 242, 244–45.
———. *Handbook of Rome and Its Environs 1858.* London: John Murray, 1858.
Newberry, Frederick. *Hawthorne's Divided Loyalties: England and America in His Works.* Rutherford, NJ: Fairleigh Dickinson University Press, 1987.
Parker, Hershel. *Herman Melville: A Biography.* 2 vols. Baltimore: Johns Hopkins University Press, 1996, 2002.
Reynolds, Larry J. "Hawthorne's Labors in Concord." In *The Cambridge Companion to Hawthorne,* ed. Richard H. Millington. Cambridge: Cambridge University Press, 2004. 10–34.
Valenti, Patricia Dunlavy. *Sophia Peabody Hawthorne: A Life.* Columbia: University of Missouri Press, 2004.
———. "Sophia Peabody Hawthorne's *American Notebooks.*" *Studies in the American Renaissance,* ed. Joel Myerson. Charlottesville: University Press of Virginia, 1996. 115–85.
Weber, Alfred, Beth L. Lueck, and Dennis Berthold, eds. *Hawthorne's American Travel Sketches.* Hanover, NH: University Press of New England, 1989.
Wineapple, Brenda. *Hawthorne: A Life.* New York: Random House, 2003.

INDEX

Adams, Henry, 9
Ainsworth, Peter, 152
Alexander the Great, 186
Allingham, William, 136
Angelico, Fra, 213, 217
Apollo Belvedere, 194–95, 201

Bacon, Delia, 14, 165, 167, 168–70
Bacon, Francis, 168, 169
Bartholomew, Edward Sheffield, 206
Bennoch, Francis, 155, 160, 174
Blagden, Isabella, 225
Boott, Francis, 225
Botticelli, 217
Bridge, Horatio, 32, 33, 34, 35
Bright, Henry Arthur, 125–26, 127, 171
Brown, George Loring, 206
Browning, Elizabeth Barrett, 164–65, 219–20
Browning, Robert, 165, 166, 219–20
Browning, Robert Wiedemann Barrett (Penny), 219–20
Buchanan, James, 138–39, 154–55, 169
Butler, Samuel, 153
Byron, George Gordon, Lord, 102, 166

Byron, Lady (Anne Isabella Milbank Noel Gordon), 166

Campbell, Thomas, 154
Canova, Antonio, 192
Carlyle, Thomas, 136, 169
Carracci, Annibale, 182
Channing, Ellery, 65, 85, 92–93
Cilley, Jonathan, 9, 37–38
Cimbue (Cenni di Pepo), 217
Colacurcio, Michael J., 6
Copley, John Singleton, 173–74

The Damnation of Theron Ware (Harold Frederic), 62
Danby, Francis, 174
De Kock, Paul, 213
Del Sarto, Andrea, 225
Diogenes, 186
Di [Da] Vinci, Leonardo, 182
Domenichino, Il, 193
Duow, Gerald, 223
Dürer, Albert, 197
Dying Gladiator, 199–200, 231

Emerson, Ralph Waldo, 1, 65, 76–77, 81, 82–83, 85, 87–88, 92–93

INDEX

Faun of Praxiteles, 205, 206, 207–8, 231
Fox, John, 153
Franklin, Benjamin, 182
Frost, Barzillai, 82–83
Frye, Northrup, 10
Fuller, Margaret, 24–25, 80–81, 92, 165, 202–4, 241–42n43

Gibson, John, 204, 218, 220
Giotto di Bondone, 217
Gray, Thomas, 153
Greenough, Horatio, 202

Hall, Anna Maria Fielding, 157, 160
Hall, Samuel Carter, 157, 159, 160
Hawthorne, Elizabeth Manning (mother), 111–13
Hawthorne, Julian, 2, 4, 12, 19, 107, 110, 112–13, 119–24, 142, 143, 151, 153, 176, 181, 182, 183, 191, 201, 204, 226, 234
Hawthorne, Nathaniel: at Brook Farm, 56–59; on Catholicism, 23; as consul in Liverpool, 13, 14; economic difficulties, 90; on England, 3, 140; on English churches, 148; on English poverty, 129–30, 135; on English women, 126, 133–34, 137–38; on France, 4, 19; on Italian churches, 184–85, 187; on Italy, 4, 18; at the Old Manse, 10–11, 64–105; on painting, 3–4, 13, 18, 21–23, 200–201, 223–24, 231; on race, slavery, and/or abolition, 49–50; on Rome, 4, 18–20; on reform, 28; on sculpture, 20–21, 22, 194–95, 201, 202, 231; on Sophia Peabody Hawthorne, 67, 81, 90, 94–95; on Stratford-upon-Avon, 142–46; on Walden Pond, 77–78, 97–98; on Westminster Abbey, 153–54
Hawthorne, Nathaniel, writings: *The American Claimant,* 15–16, 139; the American notebooks, 1–2, 7–12; *The Ancestral Footstep,* 63;

"The Artist of the Beautiful," 39, 55–56; "The Birth-Mark," 39, 55; *The Blithedale Romance,* 10, 114–15, 166; "Buds and Bird-Voices," 9; "The Christmas Banquet," 30; "The Custom-House," 106; "Earth's Holocaust," 63; "Egotism; or The Bosom Serpent," 62; the English notebooks, 2–3, 12–17; "Ethan Brand," 3, 8, 10, 41, 44–46, 48, 51–52, 53, 101–2; "Feathertop," 55; "Fire-Worship," 88; the French and Italian notebooks, 2–3, 4, 17–25; "The Great Stone Face," 55; *The House of the Seven Gables,* 113; "Lady Eleanore's Mantle," 59; the "Lost Notebook," 1, 8; "The Man of Adamant," 29; *The Marble Faun,* 17, 25, 224; "Monsieur du Miroir," 6–7, 29; "The New Adam and Eve," 31; "The Old Apple Dealer," 59–62; *Our Old Home,* 3, 13–14, 16; "The Procession of Life," 31; "Rappaccini's Daughter," 62; *The Scarlet Letter,* 10, 15, 31–32, 39, 55, 59, 63, 102; "A Select Party," 63
Hawthorne, Rose, 175, 181, 191, 204, 213, 221
Hawthorne, Sophia Peabody, 142, 153, 172, 175, 181, 182, 190, 191, 196, 199, 201, 204, 206, 210, 211, 214, 219, 221, 222, 224, 225, 234; as notebook editor, 5, 7, 8, 16, 19; at the Old Manse, 64
Hawthorne, Una, 2, 3, 12, 18, 107–9, 109–13, 142, 143, 176, 181, 182, 201, 211, 225, 226, 230, 231; illness of, 228, 231–32, 233–34
Hillard, George, 78, 166–67
Hogarth, William, 173
Home, Daniel Dunglas, 225
Hosmer, Edmund, 76–77
Hosmer, Harriet Goodhue, 204
Hunt [?], 102–5

Ireland, Alexander, 174

INDEX

James, Henry, 2, 4, 5
James, Henry, writings: *The Ambassadors*, 4
Johnson, Samuel, 3, 13, 55, 147–49
Jonson, Ben, 153

Lander, Louisa, 24, 192–93
Landseer, Edwin Henry, 137
Laocoön, 194, 201, 202
Lawrence, Thomas, 173
Layard, Austen Henry, 139–40
Leach [?], 53–54
Lippi, Fra Filippo, 217
Lord Mayor of London, 137, 156–60
Lorrain, Claude, 182

Macauley, Duncan, 141
Macauley, Thomas Babington, 166
Manchester Art Exhibition, 172–76
Marsh, George, 152–53
Mary, Queen of Scots, portrait of, 162–63
Mellow, James R., 9
Melville, Herman, 5, 12, 118, 120, 121, 170, 171–72, 244–46n73
Melville, Herman, writings: *The Confidence-Man*, 170
Michaelangelo, 182
Michaelangelo, works: *Pieta*, 196
Milnes, Annabel Hungerford, 164, 165
Milnes, Richard Monckton, 164, 166, 167, 220
Milton, John, 153
Mitford, Mary Russell, 15
Montaigne, Michel de, writings: "Journey to Italy," 168
Motley, Mary Elizabeth Benjamin, 230
Moore, Thomas, 164
Mouffe, Barbara S., 8
Mozier, Joseph, 202–4

Nash, Thomas, 146
Nelson, Horatio, 176
Nightingale, Florence, 165
Nightingale, Francis Smith, 165–66

Palfrey, John Gorham, 166
Palmerston, Lord (Henry John Temple), 140
Pearson, Norman Holmes, 19
Perugino, Pietro, 213
Petty-Fitzmaurice, Henry (Marquess of Lansdowne), 164, 167
Pierce, Franklin, 18, 139, 155, 171, 232, 232–34
Polk, James K., 138
Potter, Paul, 201
Powers, Hiram, 2, 215–16, 220, 221–22, 223, 225

Raphael, 22, 182, 190, 197, 201, 226
Raphael, works: *The Transfiguration*, 207, 223
Rembrandt van Rijn, 182, 201
Reni, Guido, 193
Reni, Guido, works: *Beatrice Cenci*, 197, 234–35, 254n30; *St. Michael Trampling the Devils*, 198–99, 235
Reynolds, Joshua, 173
Rosa, Salvator, 224
Rubens, Peter Paul, 182, 201, 224
Russel, Mary Ann, 35–36

Salomons, Emma Abigail Montefiore, 157–58
Salomons, Philip, 158
Scott, Sir Walter, 3, 145, 146, 160–64
Shakespeare, William, 3, 13, 144–46, 164, 165
Shepard, Anna Adaline (Ada), 179, 181, 191, 219, 225, 236
Simpson, Claude M., 7, 10
Sistine Chapel, 210
Sodoma, Giovanni, 22–23
Southey, Robert, 154
Spenser, Edmund, 153
Stewart, Randall, 7
Story, William Wetmore, 165, 191–92, 206, 232

Teniers, David, 201
Tennyson, Alfred Lord, 13, 136, 174–76

· 267 ·

Thoreau, Henry David, 1, 65, 83–84, 84–85, 91–92, 93
Ticknor, George, 164, 166
Titian, 21, 219, 224
Torso Belvedere, 194
transcendentalism, 2
Trollope, Anthony, 14
Trollope, Thomas Adolphus, 225
Turner, J. M. W., 3, 137, 174

Valenti, Patricia Dunlavy, 10–11
Van Dyck, Anthony, 201
Van Mieris, Frans, 223

Venus de'Medici, 218–19, 220–23, 226, 232–33

Waggonner, Hyatt H., 1, 8
Whipple, Edwin Percy, 2
Wilder, Hamilton Gibbs, 232
Wilkie, David, 137, 173
Williamstown, Massachusetts, 48–50
Wineapple, Brenda, 17–18
Woodson, Thomas, 4, 14, 18, 19
Woolf, Virginia, 6
Woolner, Thomas, 174, 175